CARLYLE AND HIS CONTEMPORARIES

CARLYLE AND HIS CONTEMPORARIES

Essays in honor of Charles Richard Sanders

Edited by JOHN CLUBBE

Duke University Press   *Durham, North Carolina*   *1976*

© 1976, Duke University Press

L.C.C. card number 74–31830

I.S.B.N. 0–8223–0340–x

Printed in the United States of
America by Heritage Printers, Inc.

Contents

vi *Contents*

List of Illustrations

Preface

The purpose of this volume is twofold: to cast light on significant aspects of Carlyle's work and to gauge his influence on major contemporaries. When writing to prospective contributors several years ago, I asked them to take up important subjects within the wide field of Carlyle studies. I looked forward to having a volume which would constitute a genuine reevaluation of Carlyle's position within nineteenth-century English culture. The essays published here amply vindicate, I think, my belief that such a volume was possible and indeed desirable.

Half the essays focus on Carlyle, the other half consider his impact on contemporaries. This division reflects the interests of the man in whose honor the volume was prepared. Even though the essays are broad-based and range widely over the nineteenth century, many of the contributors are specialists on the subjects they have chosen and in several instances have brought to bear on them unpublished or little-known materials. All the essays in *Carlyle and His Contemporaries* testify to the vitality of Carlyle as an intellectual force in nineteenth-century English society. Victorian England did not always like him or his ideas, but it could not ignore either. Both man and work tell us much about that troubled but endlessly interesting age and not a little about our own.

Many have helped in the making of this book, not least the contributors who have given generously of time and knowledge. They have my sincerest gratitude, as does Gordon N. Ray for allowing me to include the drawing of Carlyle by Samuel Laurence in his possession. I acknowledge with pleasure the generosity of Harold W. Lewis, Vice Provost and Dean of Faculty, and Frederic Cleaveland, Provost of Duke University, in helping to make possible this volume in honor of one of their faculty. Oliver W. Ferguson, former chairman of the English Department, also gave unstinting support to the project. Members of the Duke University Press, in particular its director Ashbel G. Brice and its associate editor John W. Dowling, afforded me advice and encouragement over the course of the book's progress from first inception to completed manuscript. It may seem surprising to thank the man whom this volume honors, but the contributors will at least acknowledge the justice of my doing so: Mr. Sanders read each essay with interest as it came in and commented incisively on them all. The completed book owes much to his care and example.

For aid of various kinds, generously given, I wish to thank Monika B. and Robert W. Brown, Peter H. Burian, Susan A. Clubbe, A. Leigh De Neef, and G. B. Tennyson. Dorothy Roberts, with her constant good cheer, lightened my labors on the index.

J.C.

Abbreviations and Short Titles

A. Carlyle, *CMSB* Carlyle, Alexander, ed. *Letters of Thomas Carlyle to John Stuart Mill, John Sterling, and Robert Browning.* London: T. Fisher Unwin, 1923.

CL Carlyle, Thomas, and Carlyle, Jane Welsh. *The Collected Letters of Thomas and Jane Welsh Carlyle. 1812–1828.* Duke-Edinburgh Edition. Edited by Charles Richard Sanders, Kenneth J. Fielding, Ian M. Campbell, John Clubbe, and Janetta Taylor. 4 vols. Durham, North Carolina: Duke University Press, 1970.

DNB *Dictionary of National Biography.*

Froude, *Carlyle* Froude, J. A. *Thomas Carlyle: A History of the First Forty Years of His Life, 1795–1835; A History of His Life in London, 1834–1881.* 4 vols. London: Longmans, Green, 1882; 1884.

Harrold, *Sartor* Harrold, Charles Frederick, ed. *Sartor Resartus.* New York: Odyssey Press, 1937.

NLS National Library of Scotland, Edinburgh.

PMLA *Publications of the Modern Language Association of America.*

Reminiscences Carlyle, Thomas. *Reminiscences.* Edited by C. E. Norton. 2 vols. London and New York: Macmillan, 1887.

TC Thomas Carlyle (1795–1881).

Wilson, *Carlyle* Wilson, David Alec. *Carlyle* [individual volumes have different titles]. 6 vols. London: Kegan Paul, Trench, Trubner and Co., Ltd; New York: E. P. Dutton and Co., 1923–1934.

Works Carlyle, Thomas. *Works.* Centenary Edition. Edited by H. D. Traill. 30 vols. London: Chapman and Hall, 1896–1899.

Charles Richard Sanders

JOHN CLUBBE

One of the finest hours in the academic career of Charles Richard Sanders occurred on the evening of 10 December 1970 at a formal dinner held at Duke University. The occasion commemorated a scholarly achievement of imposing magnitude—the publication of the first four volumes of *The Collected Letters of Thomas and Jane Welsh Carlyle*—but it also commemorated, as the guest speaker Gordon N. Ray reminded those present, the man responsible for the volumes coming into being. Nearly twenty years before, Richard Sanders had laid the cornerstone of this work; when completed, it will encompass approximately forty volumes and will include the letters from 1812, when Jane wrote her first, to 1879, when Carlyle dictated his last. No other correspondence illuminates so well the diversity and range of intellectual life in nineteenth-century England. Although the dinner brought together many of those who had contributed to the project over the years, the guest of honor that evening was, fittingly, Richard Sanders. It remains to his enduring credit that he not only saw the importance of the Carlyles' correspondence for understanding Victorian England but that he then had the courage to embark on this monumental task.

Richard Sanders was born in Murfreesboro, Tennessee, on 14 August 1904, the fifth of eight children of William Josiah and Fanny Adams Sanders. His father, after seven years as a country doctor, practiced dentistry for over fifty more. He did honor to the customary Sanders longevity by attaining the ripe age of ninety. Young Sanders was educated in Tennessee schools and then went to Emory University in Atlanta, where he received a B.A. in 1926 and an M.A. the next year. Instilled with a love of medieval metrical romances by James Hinton, Emory's fine medieval scholar, he wrote under Hinton's direction a master's thesis on Malory. For four years afterward he taught as an instructor at Emory Junior College in Valdosta, Georgia, and at the same time began during summers to work on a doctorate at the University of Chicago. Once at Chicago he pursued his medieval studies under J. M. Manly and did extensive work in the eighteenth century under George Sherburn and R. S. Crane, but came to realize that the nineteenth was to be his home. Working under the direction of Robert Morss Lovett, he was awarded a doctorate in 1934 with a dissertation on F. D. Maurice and Coleridge. Though other areas of literature were to exert their sway over him in the decades to come, the nineteenth century has remained his major field of intellectual endeavor.

Interest in Maurice led, in turn, to exploration of the larger implications of the Broad Church Movement in Victorian England. In 1942 Mr. Sanders published *Coleridge and the Broad Church Movement: Studies in S. T. Coleridge, Dr. Arnold of Rugby, J. C. Hare, Thomas Carlyle and F. D. Maurice.* Kathleen Coburn, in a recent evaluation of Coleridge scholarship, affirmed that Mr. Sanders' "essay on Coleridge as primarily an intellectual liberator was one that needed to be written; it was, moreover, one of the freshest of the near-centenary crop." The long introductory section focuses on Coleridge's seminal influence on nineteenth-century thought. A later chapter treats Carlyle's tangential, yet vital, relationship to the Broad Church group. In it we perceive Coleridge through Carlyle's eyes: as he meets him for the first time in 1824 when, fresh from Scotland, he makes the pilgrimage to Highgate with Edward Irving; in a series of brilliant pen portraits in letters written over a number of years; and finally in the masterly chapter on Coleridge in his *Life of Sterling* of 1851. Caustic as Carlyle could be toward the elderly sage whose conversation, in his view, shed light on all subjects but illumined few, Mr. Sanders shows that he submitted to Coleridge's influence more than he cared to admit. The relationship between the two thinkers continues to interest him, and in recent years he has offered a graduate seminar at Duke on their critical and philosophical ideas.

After receiving his doctorate, Mr. Sanders returned to the South in 1934 to take an assistant professorship at Emory in Valdosta. In 1937 he accepted a position of the same rank at Duke University, and at Duke he has remained, becoming an associate professor in 1943, professor in 1952. He has taught a wide range of courses, including the Romantic and Victorian surveys on the graduate and undergraduate levels, and he has guided dissertations in both areas—including those of two contributors to this volume. As his teaching prospered, so did his scholarship—and the recognition accorded it: a Rockefeller fellowship in 1947 and a Carnegie fellowship in 1947–1948, both to work on the Stracheys; and two Guggenheim fellowships, one in 1960 and the other in 1972–1973, to work on the Carlyle letters. He also taught a course in creative writing for many years, has written a delightful fairy tale, is an accomplished writer of sonnets and lyrics, and hopes to find time in his retirement to write a novel about the career of his great-great-grandfather, Ebenezer MacGowan, born in 1767. The movement of MacGowan's full, exciting life reflects the growth and expansion of the young republic: he grew up in London, emigrated to Virginia in the 1790's, and in 1816 crossed the Appalachians into Tennessee, where he lived on until mid-century.

Mr. Sanders' research, embodying his continual engagement with the imaginative life of the mind, has developed in what can be seen as a natural course. His first book had introduced him to Edward and Julia Strachey. Soon other members of the family attracted his interest. *The Strachey Family (1588–1932): Their Writings and Literary Associations*, appearing in 1953, recounted the history of this great English mandarin family as it evolved from Elizabethan times down to the twentieth century, contributing its share of public servants, educators, explorers, literary critics, patrons of literature and writers to the intellectual life of England. The last chapter, considering the career of the most famous Strachey as he "assimilated the cultural traditions of his family and found life in them," served as prelude to a full-length study published four years later as *Lytton Strachey: His Mind and Art*. Chapters discussing Strachey's work on French literature, Elizabethan drama, and the Victorians develop the basis for an evaluation of his career set against the wider background of the times in which he lived. Another chapter in this path-breaking study considers Strachey's conception of "detachment" in biography. Long interested in the history and evolution of literary biography, Mr. Sanders has offered a course at Duke in this subject, where Strachey's achievement finds its place in a survey of approaches to biography from Plutarch to our own time.

Well before the establishment of the Carlyle letters project in the early fifties, Mr. Sanders had recognized that Carlyle was the pivotal influence on the Victorian scene. But he also saw that, as he wrote in a 1955 article "Carlyle's Letters," "both the perspective and adequate means for observing the age through Carlyle's eyes have been lacking. The passing of time has gradually solved the problem of perspective, but the privilege of seeing Carlyle's world fully through his own eyes will become a possibility only when the complete texts of all his letters have been gathered and put in order." That formidable task he began with the aid of his wife in 1952. It staggers the imagination to conceive the years of toil put in by Mr. Sanders and his assistants not only in bringing the letters together and organizing them but also in preparing the various files and indices needed for—Carlyle's own phrase is apt—"cosmos" to emerge from "chaos." In 1955 he decided to include as well all the correspondence of Jane Welsh Carlyle. No more than a checklist of letters was contemplated at first, and not until 1960 did he reach the decision to publish a complete edition of the letters of both Carlyles. About that time Mr. Sanders also saw the desirability of working with the University of Edinburgh, and the "Duke-Edinburgh Edition" testifies to his sustaining belief in the worth of this cooperative venture. The edition will not only be a notable contribution to literary and social history but will also illuminate various other disciplines as they flourished in the nineteenth century.

Mr. Sanders has written a number of important articles on aspects of Carlyle's literary genius and on his relationships with other Victorians. These include the already cited "Carlyle's Letters"; the publication, with commentary, of Carlyle's correspondences with Ruskin and Leigh Hunt; several articles on the Carlyle-Browning relationship, now being brought together in a major study; "Carlyle and Tennyson" for *PMLA*; "The Byron Closed in *Sartor Resartus*," a study of the counterpointing movement from Byron to Goethe in Carlyle's mind; an article on "Carlyle as Editor and Critic of Literary Letters," another on "Retracing Carlyle's Journey of 1849 through Ireland"; and, most recently, "The Carlyles and Thackeray." He has also compiled the Carlyle entry for the *New CBEL*. His substantial introduction to the first four volumes of the *Collected Letters* vibrantly affirms their literary merit and their unequaled importance within the wider context of Victorian studies. Still other essays—of Carlyle's pen portraits of Victoria and Albert and of his relationships with Jeffrey and Sterling—await forthcoming publication. Mr. Sanders wears his scholarship lightly, is tolerant of the views of others, and always tries to be fair to writer or work. His style is firm rather than opulent, thoughtful rather than scintillating. On occasion he will enliven his analysis with arresting metaphors drawn from the world of nature or underscore his points with a dry humor. It is no accident that he sees humor as a guiding element in fathoming Carlyle's intent in his writings.

Carlyle's vivid accounts of his contemporaries first drew Mr. Sanders to him, and several of his articles have served as preliminary studies for a long-planned work, which he hopes to complete in his retirement, on "Carlyle's Pen Portraits of His Contemporaries." Although he values Carlyle's achievement as a historian, he believes that—even more than as an interpreter of past epochs—Carlyle will be remembered as a historian of his *own* times. Only when all his letters have seen print will the extent of this achievement as a chronicler of his contemporaries be recognized. "Certainly no instinct in [Carlyle] was stronger than that which led him to observe with burning interest and intensified powers of observation men and women in the world around him," he wrote in 1955. "No talent in him was more marked than that through which he skillfully delineated their features. Whatever value the world may attach to his moral and political ideas . . . the portraits which he drew of his contemporaries will always be too important and too fascinating to be ignored by students of the period." Mr. Sanders' study of Carlyle's psychological and pictorial artistry will constitute, when completed, a fascinating panorama of Victorian life.

Besides his love of books, of scholarship, and of the life of the mind, Mr. Sanders has sought breadth and balance in his life. His respect for tradition has led him to maintain a strong interest in local history in his native Tennessee, in South Carolina where he had family, and in the Durham area where he has resided since 1937. Two of his interests—in local history and in the history of families—combined in a recently published monograph, *The Cameron Plantation in Central North Carolina and its Founder, Richard Bennehan.* Richard Bennehan founded Stagville and Fairntosh Plantations, north of Durham, which by the time of the Civil War had become, with over 30,000 acres and 1900 slaves, the largest in the South east of the Mississippi. With a fine awareness of Southern tradition, Mr. Sanders traces the history of the plantations and the interconnections between their owners and the growth of an area. Having as a child heard his Confederate grandfather relate many stories reflecting the horrors of the Civil War and having lived through two World Wars as well as the other wars of this century, he has had throughout life an intense abhorrence of war, a belief that no war is necessary, and a conviction that war can always be prevented through the proper and vigorous functioning of government, diplomacy, and public opinion.

Nor are his interests exclusively literary or historical. All his life he has retained a deep love of the soil. An active conservationist, he has campaigned effectively for the preservation of wilderness areas and maintains a tree farm of his own. Each year he also plants a varied crop of vegetables in a plot of ground near his Durham home. He has said many times that as a gardener, teacher, and scholar his chief delight is in seeing things grow. Vigorous health has buttressed this love for the outdoors. I remember vividly an outing we took several years ago near his tree farm along the Haw River. It was midsummer, and the Haw was at low water. We decided to explore an island in the middle of the river. It would take some intrepid leaping from rock to rock to get over: Dick made it, I landed in the river. But the day's adventures had more to them than an episode out of Tom Sawyer: the outing with Richard Sanders was a lesson in the ways of the natural world, as he identified the songs of birds, commented on the trees and their growth patterns, and spoke knowledgeably of the island's history. In all fields of activity, in nature as much as in scholarship, he displays a craggy independence of spirit. His sense of personal integrity, of principle, is unswerving: in everything he does he will be very much his own man.

In 1932 Mr. Sanders married the former Virginia Hightower, a native of Georgia whom he had met while teaching in Valdosta. Those who know Virginia Sanders are impressed by her dignity and poise, which never conceal the warmth of her greeting nor dim her radiant smile. Many years a teacher in the Durham schools, she was there a favorite of several generations of students. Now as then she takes great pleasure in working with her husband in the superb wild-flower garden they have made behind their Durham home. Portraits of figures in the Bloomsbury group look down in their living room upon beautifully arranged displays of these rare flowers. The Sanders seem happiest amid close friends and with their three children—Charles, Nancy (now Mrs. Craufurd Goodwin) and Martha (now Mrs. George Gilmore).

The years to come will allow Richard Sanders to work on the scholarly projects he has under way, to devote more time to his garden and tree farm, to camp and to travel. Since his retirement from Duke, which occurred in 1973, his enthusiasm for scholarship has remained unabated and he continues to work on the Carlyle letters, bringing to bear on successive volumes his vast store of knowledge about the Carlyles and their circle. The contributors to this book of essays honor his achievement by writing on subjects that reflect the range of his interests in Carlyle. Several discuss aspects of Carlyle's thought and work, others consider his influence upon major Victorian authors, all freely acknowledge a debt to the man who has done more than anyone else in our time to further the study of Carlyle.

The Publications of Charles Richard Sanders

BOOKS

Editor (with Charles E. Ward). Sir Thomas Malory, *The Morte Darthur: An Abridgment with an Introduction.* New York: F. S. Crofts, 1940.

Coleridge and the Broad Church Movement: Studies in S. T. Coleridge, Dr. Arnold of Rugby, J. C. Hare, Thomas Carlyle, and F. D. Maurice. Durham, North Carolina: Duke University Press, 1942. Reprinted, New York: Octagon Books, 1972.

The Strachey Family (1588–1932): Their Writings and Literary Associations. Durham, North Carolina: Duke University Press, 1953. Reprinted, New York: Greenwood Press, 1968.

Lytton Strachey: His Mind and Art. New Haven: Yale University Press, 1957; London: Oxford University Press, 1957. Reprinted, Port Washington, New York: Kennikat Press, 1973.

General Editor. *The Collected Letters of Thomas and Jane Welsh Carlyle. 1812–1828.* Durham, North Carolina: Duke University Press, 1970. Volumes 1–4.

The Cameron Plantation in Central North Carolina and Its Founder, Richard Bennehan. Durham, North Carolina: Privately printed by Charles Richard Sanders, 103 Pinecrest Road, Durham, N.C. 27705, August 1974. Limited to 600 copies.

ARTICLES

Was Frederick Denison Maurice a Broad-Churchman? *Church History,* 3 (September 1934), 222–231.

Coleridge as a Champion of Liberty. *Studies in Philology,* 32 (October 1935), 618–631.

Coleridge, F. D. Maurice, and the Distinction between the Reason and the Understanding. *PMLA,* 51 (June 1936), 459–475.

Maurice as a Commentator on Coleridge. *PMLA,* 53 (March 1938), 230–243.

Sir Leslie Stephen, Coleridge, and Two Coleridgeans. *PMLA,* 54 (September 1940), 795–801.

Coleridge, Maurice, and the Church Universal. *Journal of Religion,* 21 (January 1941), 31–45.

The *South Atlantic Quarterly*: The First Forty Years. *South Atlantic Bulletin*, 8 (December 1942), 1, 12–13.

Freshman English for War and Peace. *South Atlantic Bulletin*, 9 (February 1944), 1, 6–7.

Lytton Strachey's Revisions in *Books and Characters. Modern Language Notes*, 60 (April 1945), 226–234.

Inflowing and Outflowing Poetry. *Emory University Quarterly*, 1 (December 1945), 238–245.

Lytton Strachey Improves His Style. *College English*, 7 (January 1946), 215–219.

A Chronological Check List of Lytton Strachey's Writings. *Modern Philology*, 44 (February 1947), 189–192.

Portrait of a Strachey. *Emory University Quarterly*, 3 (December 1947), 238–247.

William Strachey, the Virginia Colony, and Shakespeare. *Virginia Magazine of History and Biography*, 57 (April 1949), 115–132.

Lytton Strachey as a Critic of Elizabethan Drama. *Philological Quarterly*, 30 (January 1951), 1–21.

Lytton Strachey's Conception of Biography. *PMLA*, 66 (June 1951), 295–315.

The Strachey Family, Sutton Court, and John Locke. *Virginia Magazine of History and Biography*, 59 (July 1951), 275–296.

Lytton Strachey's Miniature Portraits. *Emory University Quarterly*, 8 (December 1952), 196–207.

Lytton Strachey's "Point of View." *PMLA*, 68 (March 1953), 75 94.

Lytton Strachey and French Literature. *South Atlantic Quarterly*, 53 (April 1954), 238–259.

Lytton Strachey and the Victorians. *Modern Language Quarterly*, 15 (December 1954), 326–342.

Carlyle's Letters. *Bulletin of the John Rylands Library*, 38 (September 1955), 199–224.

The Victorian Rembrandt. *Bulletin of the John Rylands Library*, 39 (March 1957), 521–557.

Tennyson and the Human Hand. *Victorian Newsletter*, No. 11 (Spring 1957), 5–13.

Carlyle's Letters to Ruskin: A Finding List with Some Unpublished Letters and Comments. *Bulletin of the John Rylands Library*, 41 (September 1958), 208–238.

Carlyle, Browning, and the Nature of a Poet. *Emory University Quarterly*, 16 (Winter 1960), 197–209.

Carlyle and Tennyson. *PMLA*, 76 (March 1961), 82–97.

Retracing Carlyle's Journey of 1849 through Ireland. *Studies: An Irish Quarterly Review*, 50 (Spring 1961), 38–50.

Carlyle, Poetry, and the Music of Humanity. *Western Humanities Review*, 16 (Winter 1962), 53–66.

Lytton Strachey. In *Collier's Encyclopedia*. New York: P. F. Collier & Sons, 1962. Volume XXI, p. 551.

The Correspondence and Friendship of Thomas Carlyle and Leigh Hunt. *Bulletin of the John Rylands Library*, 45 (March 1963), 439–485; 46 (September 1963), 179–216. Reprinted, Manchester: The John Rylands Library, 1963, [pp. 1–85].

Some Lost and Unpublished Carlyle-Browning Correspondence. *Journal of English and German Philology*, 62 (April 1963), 323–335.

The Byron Closed in *Sartor Resartus*. *Studies in Romanticism*, 3 (Winter 1964), 77–108.

Carlyle as Editor and Critic of Literary Letters. *Emory University Quarterly*, 20 (Summer 1964), 108–120.

Editing the Carlyle Letters. In *Editing Nineteenth Century Texts*, edited by John M. Robson. Toronto: University of Toronto Press, 1967. Pp. 77–95.

Thomas Carlyle. In *New Cambridge Bibliography of English Literature*, edited by George Watson. Cambridge: Cambridge University Press, 1969. Volume III (1800–1900), pp. 1248–1270.

Introduction. *The Collected Letters of Thomas and Jane Welsh Carlyle 1812–1828*. Edited by Charles Richard Sanders, Kenneth J. Fielding, Ian M. Campbell, John Clubbe, and Janetta Taylor. Durham, North Carolina: Duke University Press, 1970. Volume I, pp. ix–xliv.

The Ancient Mariner and Coleridge's Theory of Poetic Art. In *Romantic and Victorian: Studies in Memory of William H. Marshall*, edited by W. Paul Elledge and Richard L. Hoffman. Rutherford, New Jersey: Fairleigh Dickinson University Press, 1971. Pp. 110–128.

The Background of Carlyle's Portrait of Coleridge in *The Life of John Sterling*. *Bulletin of the John Rylands Library*, 55 (Spring 1973), 434–458.

The Carlyles and Thackeray. In *Nineteenth-Century Literary Perspectives*, edited by Clyde de L. Ryals, with the assistance of John Clubbe, and Benjamin Franklin Fisher IV. Durham, North Carolina: Duke University Press, 1974. Pp. 161–200.

The Carlyle-Browning Correspondence and Relationship. *Bulletin of the John Rylands University Library of Manchester*, 57 (Autumn 1974), 213–246; 57 (Spring 1975), 430–462.

"Richard Bennehan," "Bennehan Cameron," "Duncan Cameron," "Paul Carrington Cameron." In *Dictionary of North Carolina Biography*, edited by William Powell. Chapel Hill: University of North Carolina Press, 1976. Volume I.

Blumine; Chartism; Craigenputtock; *Cromwell's Letters and Speeches*; Diogenes Teufelsdröckh; Ecclefechan; *Frederick the Great*; *The French Revolution*; Jane Welsh Carlyle; *Latter-Day Pamphlets*; *Life of John Sterling*; *Past and Present*; *Reminiscences*; *Sartor Resartus*; Thomas Carlyle. In *Reader's Encyclopedia to English Literature*, edited by Edgar Johnson. New York: Thomas Y. Crowell Company. In press.

"Carlyle's Pen Portraits of Queen Victoria and Prince Albert." In *Carlyle Past and Present: A Collection of New Essays*, edited by K. J. Fielding and Rodger L. Tarr. London: Vision Press, 1976.

CARLYLE AND HIS CONTEMPORARIES

Carlyle's Religion: The Scottish Background

IAN CAMPBELL, *University of Edinburgh*

Writing from Craigenputtoch on 16 October 1832, Thomas Carlyle already had thoughts of living in London, and these thoughts were communicated most openly to John Stuart Mill:

In London alone of all places in this country have I found some men (belonging to this century and not to a past one) who believed that Truth was Truth: of such men, how obstructed otherwise soever, all may be hoped, for they have attained the source of all. Considered as European Thinkers, our poor Utilitarians make the mournfullest figure: yet in this one fact, that they were the re-originators of *any* Belief among us, they stand far above all other Sects. Young minds too will not *end* where they began; under this point of view, you and certain of yours are of great interest for me; indeed, I may say, form the chief *visible* encouragement I have to proceed in this rather hazardous course of mine.[1]

Carlyle was by this time almost thirty-seven and had undergone the spiritual agonies of doubt and rebirth which were to appear, fantastically transformed, in *Sartor Resartus.* Phoenix-like, a new faith had emerged, retailored to Carlyle's own circumstances. Above all, he had a faith. To Mill, whom he had met in London the previous winter and whom he regarded as a "partial disciple,"[2] he made the point with all the emphasis he could that belief was vital in the times they lived in and that in the rebirth of belief alone was there hope.

The times he lived in were, of course, a familiar subject to Carlyle, times he had described in "Cruthers and Jonson" as "times so stupid and prosaic as these; times of monotony and safety, and matter of fact, when affections are measured by the tale of guineas, where people's fortunes are exalted, and their purposes achieved by the force, not of the arm or of the heart; but of the spinning-jenny and the steam-engine."[3] The theme runs through Carlyle's seminal essay

---

1. TC to John Stuart Mill, 16 Oct. 1832, in A. Carlyle, *CMSB*, p. 17.
2. TC to his mother, Margaret Aitken Carlyle, 22 Jan. 1832, MS: NLS, 519.76.
3. "Cruthers and Jonson" is a semi-autobiographical fragment which was published in *Fraser's Magazine* in Jan. 1831 and is here quoted from *Works*, XXX, 169.

"Signs of the Times," singled out by Raymond Williams as a vital document in the relationship between culture and society in the nineteenth century:[4] we will return to "Signs of the Times" later in this study, but we will approach it by way of Carlyle's earlier career and the experiences which led up to his own fire-baptism.

I have argued elsewhere that the Burgher Seceder Church of Ecclefechan was to play a part of paramount importance in the shaping of Carlyle's religious thought.[5] Brought up in a close community, intensely admiring both his parents and the "old hoary Heads"[6] who were the ministers and elders of his childhood church, Carlyle never shook off the influence of the teaching of that church, nor his respect for the personalities who were the most important visible operating forces in it. Yet his respect coexisted in his mind with the realization that the world of the Secession Church in Ecclefechan was part of the irrecoverable past:

It began to alter just about that period, on the death of those old hoary Heads; and has gone on with increasing velocity ever since. Irving and I were probably among the last products it delivered before gliding off, and then rushing off, into self-consciousness, arrogancy, insincerity, jangle and vulgarity, which I fear are now very much the definition of it.[7]

Like Edward Irving, Carlyle recommended to the world the observance of an ideal which belonged to the past. A conclusion could be drawn that Carlyle's "religious teaching to the nineteenth century might be in part defined as recommending the ideal, and seeking to bridge the gulf"[8] between the reality of nineteenth-century life and the memory of the pious Seceder community of eighteenth-century Ecclefechan.

Yet is this all Carlyle's religious message? Must we agree with David Daiches, in referring to the "inadequate intellectual foundations of his faith,"[9] or can Carlyle's religious thought be seen more cogently in the light of his experience after leaving home, at the University in Edinburgh and in his largely unhappy days of indepen-

4. Raymond Williams, *Culture and Society 1780–1950* (London, 1961), pp. 85–98.
5. See my "Carlyle and the Secession," *Records of the Scottish Church History Society*, 18 (1972), 48–64; also my "Irving, Carlyle and the Stage," *Studies in Scottish Literature*, 8 (Jan. 1971), 166–173.
6. *Reminiscences*, II, 13.   7. Ibid.
8. Campbell, "Carlyle and the Secession," p. 64.
9. David Daiches, *Carlyle and the Victorian Dilemma* (Edinburgh, 1963), p. 17.

dent writing and tutoring, spent mostly in the same city? One key to this problem seems to lie in Professor Daiches' choice of words, for in Carlyle's own terms the "intellectual" choice is remote from that of "faith." Carlyle quotes with approval in his *Reminiscences* the story of the Annandale farmer who sacrificed his harvest to a sudden whirlwind rather than interrupt family worship in order to save it.[10] In terms of rational intellect this is indefensible, for the worship might have been resumed, and the family fed from the harvest which was saved. The idea does not detain Carlyle for a moment: his praise for the deed is unqualified, and again it takes the form of a comparison with the present: "There is a kind of citizen which Britain used to have; very different from the millionaire Hebrews, Rothschild money-changers, Demosthenic Disraelis, and inspired young Göschens, and their 'unexampled prosperity.' Weep, Britain, if these latter are among the honourable you now have!"[11]

Already, then, we see emerging a thread in the understanding of Carlyle's early religious thought, a position which could allow him to commend to Mill "*any* Belief"—of whatever kind—without rational enquiry into that belief, as better than no belief at all. For the intellectual enquiry and the belief belonged to different worlds.

It is vitally important to make a distinction here between unquestioning belief, consciously (and self-approvingly) irrational, and the position which Carlyle thought he was recommending to the world. In the *Reminiscences* Carlyle stresses again and again the "natural endowment" of his father, his incisive intellect and power of words, his commanding personality and crushingly dismissive arguments. "He was Religious with the consent of his whole faculties: without Reason he would have been nothing; indeed his habit of intellect was thoroughly free and even incredulous, and strongly enough did the daily example of this work afterwards on me." James Carlyle, in brief, required belief as a fundamental part of his daily life, yet he retained his rational powers of enquiry simultaneously with this deep emotional loyalty to his faith. "But he was in Annandale, and it was above fifty years ago; and a Gospel was still preached there to the heart of a man, in the tones of a man. Religion was the Pole-star for

10. *Reminiscences*, II, 10–11.
11. Ibid. The passage was written in 1866 when Carlyle's prejudice against Jews was strongly formed.

my Father. . . ."[12] The extent to which Carlyle was affected by his father's example needs no underlining.

To the author of the *Reminiscences*, there is virtue in a man who retains a strong and unquestioning religious belief of a strongly authoritarian nature, yet simultaneously a questioning turn of mind which takes nothing for granted. To the author of "Cruthers and Jonson" the nature of the world which confronts such a man is clearly hostile to belief: the present time is prosaic, it is mechanical, and its disease is one which Carlyle spent much of his formative years in studying.

Carlyle's early and extensive knowledge of French literature, for instance, fostered in him an admiration for the literary genius of certain brilliant individual authors from the eighteenth century in France, yet it left an overall impression of profound disgust at the sceptical tone of the Age of Enlightenment. Ironically his doubts were to some extent solved by a French writer, Madame de Staël. Yet her compatriots had been responsible for much of Carlyle's early unhappiness: "She did not make it clear what she thought was so important in Germany, but she made me feel that there had been something which would solve all the questions with which I had been tormented."[13] Perhaps the clue lay in her remark, early in the first volume of *De l'Allemagne*: "Sans la morale, tout est hasard et ténèbres":[14] perhaps she merely showed him there was an alternative to Paris, "the Vanity-fair of our modern world!"[15] as he early dubbed it. The French books emerge from a study of Carlyle's references to them as too much dependent on intellect, too little on accepted faith. "French books," said Carlyle to Richard Monckton Milnes, "have most dancing-dog thought about them; ours are like the quite intelligent meditation of an elephant or a horse."[16] Although a French book "exhilarates us and fills us with glorying for a season," it is the "comfort of the Indian who warmed himself at the flames of his—bed."[17] Not only in abstract matters, but in personal ones, the contagion of

12. Ibid., pp. 14–15.
13. Arthur A. Adrian, "Dean Stanley's Report of Conversations with Carlyle," *Victorian Studies*, 1 (Sept. 1957), 73.
14. Mme de Staël, *De l'Allemagne* (Paris, 1813), I, 18.
15. *Two Note Books of Thomas Carlyle*, ed. C. E. Norton (New York, 1898), p. 64.
16. T. Wemyss Reid, *The Life, Letters, and Friendships of Richard Monckton Milnes, First Lord Houghton* (London, 1890), II, 478.
17. *Two Note Books*, p. 85.

the French is visible to Carlyle: in 1851 he reported himself disgusted by "their wretched mockeries upon marriage, their canine libertinage and soulless grinning over all that is beautiful and pious in human relations."[18] The overall ruin of a way of life based on this premise is inevitable, and at the beginning of *The French Revolution* Carlyle clearly points to it—"Faith is gone out; Scepticism is come in. Evil abounds and accumulates."[19] Scepticism, he writes in *Heroes*, "means not intellectual Doubt alone, but moral Doubt; all sorts of infidelity, insincerity, spiritual paralysis."[20]

Against this background of bankrupt scepticism, individual characters may emerge strongly. Voltaire is "the man of his century," even if he lives in what "is among the most barren of recorded ages,"[21] for although he is infected by the Spirit of the Age, "he can talk blasphemy, and build Churches, according to the signs of the times."[22] Diderot, too, is "a Polemic of decided character, in the Mechanical Age,"[23] and he too can read the signs of the times. Strong individuals offer a kind of hope to Carlyle, faced by this barrenness of the times. It is not just that they are there as God-given guides to a stricken age, as is argued at the beginning of *Heroes and Hero-Worship*: they can, in addition, use their rational powers to come to grips with the times, and with their own characters. Carlyle believed deeply that the individual human character could not rest content with mechanism and unbelief. "Referring to the mechanical spirit of the age, he remarked, 'Human beings with souls in their bodies cannot rest satisfied in that belief; they will have to come out of that!' "[24] The Mechanical system of thought, "in its essence, Atheistic,"[25] will not satisfy the soul: the men of the eighteenth century failed to see that "the only use to which they put the intellect was not to look outwardly upon nature, and love or hate as circumstances required, but to inquire why the thing was there at all, and to account for it and argue about it."[26] The same fault explains Carlyle's curiously ambivalent attitude to Edward Gibbon, whom he enormously admired when

18. Carlyle, "Excursion (Futile Enough) to Paris, Autumn, 1851," in *The Last Words of Thomas Carlyle* (London, 1892), p. 164.

19. *Works*, II, 14.   20. Ibid., V, 170.
21. Ibid., XXVI, 401, 465.   22. Ibid., XXVI, 410.
23. Ibid., XXVIII, 231.
24. E. W. Marrs, Jr., "Reminiscences of a Visit with Carlyle," *Thoth*, 8 (1967), 82.
25. *Works*, XXVIII, 234.
26. *Lectures on the History of Literature*, ed. J. Reay Greene (London, 1892), p. 162.

first reading him in Kirkcaldy in 1818, and whom he described to Emerson in 1833 as "the splendid bridge from the old world to the new."[27] In the *Lectures on the History of Literature*, Gibbon is much more harshly treated: "With all his swagger and bombast, no man ever gave a more futile account of human things than he has done of the decline and fall of the Roman Empire; assigning no profound cause for these phenomena, nothing but diseased nerves, and all sorts of miserable motives, to the actors in them."[28] "Profound causes" were accessible not to mechanical—or atheistic—analysis, but to a true use of reason in a world apprehended in a believing spirit. Profound causes were something Carlyle always tried to apprehend: great as his affection was for his father, he saw that between James Carlyle and himself there was a wide gulf. "*He* was never visited with Doubt; the old Theorem of the Universe was sufficient for him, and he worked well in it, and in all senses *successfully* and wisely as few now can do."[29] No more than Gibbon could Carlyle accept the old Theorem of the Universe.

By this transition we reach the second major thread of enquiry in this essay on Carlyle's religious beliefs, in their earlier phase. The study of old theorems of the Universe, or of Leslie's System of Geometry, was an overwhelming interest in Carlyle's early youth, when he found in the study of mathematics and natural philosophy a substitute for the certainties of life he had known in Ecclefechan and which were temporarily displaced in his mind by the doubts and questions of his adolescence.

As Carl Becker noted with rich irony in *The Heavenly City of the Eighteenth-Century Philosophers*, the enlightened minds of the eighteenth century inherited from Locke's philosophy the belief "that since man and the mind of man were shaped by that nature which God had created, it was possible for men, 'barely by the use of their natural faculties,' to bring their ideas and their conduct, and hence the institutions by which they lived, into harmony with the

27. Emerson, *English Traits* (London, 1883), p. 18.
28. *Lectures on the History of Literature*, pp. 176–177. About 1877 Carlyle reread Gibbon and was surprised by the change which had taken place in him since his youthful admiration. Now he seemed "a man of endless reading and research, but of a most disagreeable style, and a great want of the highest faculties (which indeed are very rare) and of what we would call a classical historian, compared with Herodotus, for instance, and his perfect clearness and simplicity in every part." Froude, *Carlyle*, IV, 461–462.
29. *Reminiscences*, I, 6.

universal natural order."[30] As Becker pointed out, the corollary to the Lockean argument is that man himself is a product of God, as much as of nature (which is the product of God), and so all his acts, present and past, must be in accord with God's laws and wishes. The arguments which followed were manifold: Carlyle stumbled across them unwittingly when his divinity studies were found to include an essay requirement, namely, a paper on the subject "Num detur religio naturalis?" (1816). The paper, unfortunately, is lost. Indirectly, we can guess its progress, by the fact that Carlyle's Divinity Library borrowings become more and more concerned with English literature, and less and less connected with divinity.[31] His references in his letters to the preparation of the paper are halfhearted, his letter after the event not even seeing fit to mention how it was received. His ambition to enter the ministry of the Church of Scotland (or the Burgher Seceder Church) was fast disappearing, maybe already nonexistent. In this mood, he encountered the Lockean questions and the literature which surrounded them—for however halfhearted, Carlyle was a powerful reader and would certainly have made some progress in pursuing the literature on the question he was considering. The results may best be guessed at from a remark in his 1828 essay on Burns which characterizes Scottish thought in the eighteenth century as "a flat, continuous thrashing-floor for Logic, whereon all questions, from the 'Doctrine of Rent' to the 'Natural History of Religion,' are thrashed and sifted with the same mechanical impartiality!"[32] Admittedly, there is an implied judgment that doctrines of rent are of a lower order of concern than questions of religion, but the overall point of the satire is to throw ridicule on the "Natural History of Religion" as a wrong approach to the subject of religion. The mechanical approach to a subject which cannot be treated mechanically offends against religion as it does the general Spirit of the Age; in Edinburgh Carlyle experienced a system which seemed, in retrospect, to be wholly mechanical and wholly dangerous.

Carlyle spent the years 1809–1814 at Edinburgh University; he

30. *The Heavenly City of the Eighteenth-Century Philosophers* (New Haven and London, 1932), p. 65. Becker's quotation is from Locke's *An Essay Concerning Human Understanding*, I, 2.

31. D. Masson, *Edinburgh Sketches & Memories* (London and Edinburgh, 1892), p. 254, and Ian Campbell, "Carlyle's Borrowings from the Theological Library of Edinburgh University," *The Bibliotheck*, 5 (1969), 165–168.

32. *Works*, XXVI, 289.

studied the foundation course in arts, and spent one year at Divinity Hall before leaving to earn his living as a schoolteacher. He could, theoretically, have qualified as a minister in due course by continuing to prepare sermons (such as "Num detur religio naturalis?") and deliver them at the University annually, but his final withdrawal from divinity studies took place in 1817 or 1818. Successive attempts to study law, natural history, and advanced mathematics after this time were rapidly abandoned, and Carlyle had no more to do with his alma mater. Increasingly, his memory of it coalesced with his overall impression of the temper of mind of Edinburgh at the beginning of the nineteenth century. The picture which he paints in *Sartor* is no flattering one, of professors who "lived with ease, with safety, by a mere Reputation, constructed in past times, and then too with no great effort, by quite another class of persons,"[33] and of rational, dangerous ideas:

Besides all this, we boasted ourselves a Rational University; in the highest degree hostile to Mysticism; thus was the young vacant mind furnished with much talk about Progress of the Species, Dark Ages, Prejudice, and the like; so that all were quickly enough blown out into a state of windy argumentativeness; whereby the better sort had soon to end in sick, impotent Scepticism; the worser sort explode . . . in finished Self-conceit, and to all spiritual intents become dead.[34]

No proof can be found today of exactly what it was that so repelled Carlyle from the arts professors in his time at Edinburgh University. Perhaps the easygoing John Leslie infected Carlyle with easygoing ideas on all subjects, including the hitherto sacrosanct one of religion; perhaps the gentlemanly professors, who were very often moderate ministers of city churches, repelled Carlyle after the austere example of the clergy of the Seceder Church. Certainly Carlyle took from his years of university education a habit of mind which was to a considerable extent, and in a wide meaning, "rational." He had been trained by philosophers, logicians and scientists: he had shown his greatest aptitude in the exact science of "natural philosophy" and in the study of advanced mathematics. He had trained himself by enormous reading in the University Library, and despite an unfortunate

33. Harrold, *Sartor*, p. 111.   34. Ibid., p. 112.

and arrogant manner he had impressed at least two of his professors.
It is a fair assumption that he *was* rational in the sense that he had
trained his mind to look incisively into a question and to try to probe
to the heart of it. His blundering attempts to investigate religion in
this way—"Did God Almighty come down and make wheelbarrows
in a shop?"—were met in his family by his mother's tears, and he
wisely learned not to pursue this line of enquiry at home.[35]

The "rational" turn of mind which Carlyle learned at the university, and which to some extent alienated him from the simple piety
of his home, was no mere "freethinking"—Carlyle himself mocks
freethinkers in his early letters.[36] What he did take part in was a last
generation of education on the old Scottish system, described by
George Elder Davie in *The Democratic Intellect* (1961). The university system evolved in eighteenth-century Scotland, and persisting in
the first two decades of the nineteenth century, was one which cen-
tered its attention on the mind. The training of the mind by philosophy was the *summum bonum* of this system, and frequent courses in
mental and moral philosophy, logic, metaphysics and other disciplines
were allied to a later, specialized vocational training after the basic
"philosophical" courses were mastered. Thus the student studied,
not physics as we know it, but "natural philosophy": the approach to
"natural philosophy" was through mathematics, and John Leslie (who
taught both subjects at different periods) complained of the students'
poor ability to master "natural philosophy" with their slender mathematical competence. "Natural philosophy" and mathematics in this
tradition were (as Davie illustrates at length in *The Democratic Intellect*) very different from the modern disciplines which are taught
under the titles of physics and mathematics. Strongly influenced by
Newton and by Greek mathematical ideas, they treated the nature of
reality and the nature of the universe. Their boundaries extended far
beyond a mere specialized subject, and their teachers (like Sir William Hamilton) had a great effect on their students by drawing connections between the disciplines and by showing how the various
branches of learning in this "philosophical" school were integrated.
Carlyle was taught in this way: his Latin lectures were delivered by

35. *William Allingham: A Diary*, ed. H. Allingham and D. Radford (London,
1907), p. 253.
36. E.g., TC to Robert Mitchell, 14 June 1815, in *CL*, I, 51.

Professor Christison, "a very diligent and delighted student of the higher mathematics,"[37] who lectured on classical texts, "calling in to his aid the writings of the most celebrated critics, poets and philosophers, ancient and modern. He made frequent allusions to the sciences and even to the arts, all of which he occasionally laid under contribution, and ingeniously pointed out to the students what reference they bore to the passage to which their attention might happen to be directed."[38]

At its best, this system gave the student a wonderfully interconnected view of what knowledge he had accumulated: under inspiring teaching (such as John Wilson's after his appointment to the moral philosophy chair in 1820) the students might perform prodigies of self-education, reading widely after the model of their teachers. To a certain extent, this was the effect the system had on Carlyle, for despite his scathing attacks on the university and its effect on him, he did read enormously and widely, and did do considerable outside study and reading for two of his professors, Leslie and Playfair, in mathematics and natural philosophy respectively. Insofar as he was to enjoy this part of his university education, he was fortunate in his choice of instructors, and there is no doubt that he felt the fever of knowledge as they would have wished. Geometry, he was later to recall, for several years after 1813 "shone before me as undoubtedly the *noblest* of all sciences," and remained so until "far more pregnant enquiries were rising in me, and gradually *engrossing* me, *heart* as well as head."[39] In mathematics he had won the class prize, in natural philosophy the professor asked him to translate articles for him. "Mathematics and the kindred sciences, at once occupying and satisfying his logical faculty, took much deeper hold of him; nay, by degrees, as he felt his own independent progress, almost alienated him for a long season from all other studies."[40]

The weakness of the system was that while in a minority of cases it could lead to magnificent interdisciplinary lecturing and self-

37. [J. G. Lockhart], *Peter's Letters to His Kinsfolk* (Edinburgh, London and Glasgow, 1819), I, 167–168.

38. A. Bower, *The History of the University of Edinburgh* (Edinburgh, 1830), III, 300.

39. *Two Reminiscences of Thomas Carlyle*, ed. John Clubbe (Durham, N.C., 1974), p. 36.

40. From the autobiographical *Wotton Reinfred*, quoted in *The Last Words of Thomas Carlyle*, p. 22.

educating inspired students, it could all too often in lesser hands degenerate to a mechanical search for connections, for systems, for explanations—the sort of nadir to which Teufelsdröckh's semi-fictitious university has sunk in *Sartor*. It could also lead to a habit of mind which Carlyle was himself to satirize in a canceled passage of *Wotton Reinfred*:

At home, what have we? Hunger and Logic! Theories without end and no Practice; Political dissension with nothing to divide; twenty Critics for one Poet: Essays innumerable on civil government and no Public Spirit; full accounts of the Formation of the Earth and land that maintains a sheep and a half per acre! Confess with me, it [is] a poor and barren country, and altogether very pleasant to—quit.[41]

It was exactly such a weakness that was to lead to Carlyle's impatience with the Scottish university system, and lead him into the new ground of German literature and thought which was to open a "new heaven and new earth" to him.

Writing to Matthew Allen in 1820, Carlyle confessed:

I am nearly tired of what is called natural science, mathematics, and the ordinary systems of philosophy; yet this had not prevented me from coasting all summer on the borders of German or Italian literature. . . .[42]
I am not surprised that you have quitted science. The thing designated by that name nowadays in Britain is little else than a dry bead-roll of facts, good enough for metallurgists and artisans; but tasteless to the [so]ul. . . .
I have even nearly lost all relish for Mathematics, which some years ago I reckoned the loftiest pursuit of the human intellect.[43]

Carlyle may have lost his taste for it, yet it sustained him through a difficult period when his grasp of Ecclefechan Christianity was wavering, and his restless mind needed the stimulus of some challenging subject. The Scottish schools of mathematics and natural philosophy provided this: more, they allowed him to earn a living tutoring in these fields till his tutorship in the Buller family from 1822 onwards and later his German studies brought him some adequate income.

The reaction, when it came, was bound to be severe. Goethe, Kant,

41. Cited in my "Carlyle and Sir Gideon Dunn," *English Language Notes*, 9 (March 1972), 185–191. The canceled passage was found in the manuscript of *Wotton Reinfred* (in the Pierpont Morgan Library, New York) by Professor K. J. Fielding.
42. 15 Sept. 1820, in *CL*, I, 272–273.
43. 19 May 1820, in *CL*, I, 252.

Fichte, Novalis, and the other German minds he encountered, read eagerly, and understood with varying success, seemed far more exciting than the "bead-roll of facts" which had sustained him up till then. The university receded into darkness, and with it the system it offered him.

The darkness was not just Carlyle's indifference; the "Scottish School" which has been briefly described here was even more rapidly eroded as the nineteenth century progressed by a new approach to mathematics, more analytical and less philosophical, and a similar approach to "physics" as distinct from "natural philosophy": the innovations were largely from Cambridge, and the appointment of Cambridge-trained professors to key chairs in the Scottish universities was rapidly to replace old ideas with new ones quite alien. Irving and Carlyle may have been among the last products of the Seceder Church before it glided off into the past, and so were they of the Scottish universities.

Yet the difference between Carlyle's attitude to the two circumstances is crucial. While the Ecclefechan Church was bound up with his earliest memories, with his family (to whom he remained intensely loyal all his life) and his strong affection for Scotland, Edinburgh had none of these advantages. It was something alien, foreign, socially uncomfortable to a poor student; above all, in mature years it was something which Carlyle came to see as not Scottish, but paradoxically *French*. Referring to enlightened Edinburgh, Carlyle wrote, in "Burns":

And yet in this brilliant resuscitation of our "fervid genius," there was nothing truly Scottish, nothing indigenous; except, perhaps, the natural impetuosity of intellect, which we sometimes claim, and are sometimes upbraided with, as a characteristic of our nation. It is curious to remark that Scotland, so full of writers, had no Scottish culture, nor indeed any English; our culture was almost exclusively French. It was by studying Racine and Voltaire, Batteux and Boileau, that Kames had trained himself to be a critic and philosopher; it was the light of Montesquieu and Mably that guided Robertson in his political speculations; Quesnay's lamp that kindled the lamp of Adam Smith. Hume was too rich a man to borrow; and perhaps he reacted on the French more than he was acted on by them: but neither had he aught to do with Scotland; Edinburgh, equally with La Flèche, was but the lodging and laboratory, in which he not so much morally *lived*, as metaphysically *investigated*. Never, perhaps, was there a class of writers so clear and well-ordered, yet so totally destitute, to all appearance, of any patriotic affection, nay of any human affection whatever.[44]

Enough has been said to indicate his disenchantment with Edinburgh as a moral influence to be admired: and so the Edinburgh Enlightenment figures, and the university system they created, were alike dismissed.

Where, then, did this leave Carlyle, facing manhood and searching for a religious faith? Clearly, he could not accept his childhood creed uncritically, for Edinburgh had taken it from him irrevocably, and his reading of philosophers and historical writers like Gibbon had widened the breach. Equally clearly, he could not long remain in the mainstream of the Scottish university schools of mathematics and natural philosophy. Not only was he temperamentally unsuited to staying there for long, but his discovery of German literature and thought destroyed any chance of his remaining in such a constrained philosophical system.

A common theme running through both discarded creeds is that of the individual; the Scottish university's schema bases itself on the cultivation of the individual mind and places a heavy responsibility on the individual to examine his perceptions, to analyze his thoughts, to enlarge his knowledge. Similarly the creed of Ecclefechan shares the Calvinist awareness of an Immanent God, ruling the universe He created, yet expecting clearly defined rules of duty and behavior from each individual who lived on the earth—an individual responsible not to some intermediary church, not to a priest, but to God Himself. The position in each case is a lonely one: the responsibility is severe, whether it is self-culture to an extent worthy of the God-given mind, or whether it is living the good life as interpreted by a preaching church. The former lies heavy on the conscience of Teufelsdröckh, the latter is a potent influence (if not the major one) in the picture of James Carlyle in the *Reminiscences*. Neither of these is Carlyle himself, although each embodies traits which Carlyle would clearly like to live up to. Teufelsdröckh is partly "symbolical *myth*,"[45] James Carlyle a figure from an age gone by. Inevitably, Carlyle tried to be both, and to be more—so he compromised. At times, he believed seriously, and with his heart. At times, he was assailed by doubt, and also by guilt:

44. *Works*, XXVI, 288–289.   45. *Two Reminiscences*, p. 49.

Wonderful, and alas! most pitiful alternations of belief and unbelief in me. On the whole *no* encouragement to be met with here in Edinburgh; "all men," says John Gordon naively, "are quite taken up with making a livelihood." It is taken for granted, I find, that of me nothing can be made —that I am, economically speaking, but a lost man. No great error there, perhaps; but if it is added by my friends themselves that therefore I am spiritually lost? One's ears are bewildered by the inane chatter of the people; one's heart is for hours and days overcast by the sad feeling: "There is none then, not one, that will believe in me!" Great in this life is the communion of man with man. Meanwhile continue to believe in *thyself*. Let the clattering of innumerable gigmen pass by thee as what it is. Wait thou on the bounties of thy unseen Taskmaster, on the hests of thy inward *Daemon*. Sow the seed field of Time. What if thou see no fruit of it? Another will. Be not weak.

Neither fear thou that this thy great message of the Natural *being* the Supernatural will wholly perish unuttered. One way or another it will and shall be uttered—write it down on paper any way; speak it from thee— so shall thy painful, destitute existence not have been in vain. Oh, in vain? Hadst thou, even thou, a message from the Eternal, and thou grudgest the travail of thy embassy? O thou of little faith![46]

The individual, the lonely individual that Carlyle increasingly became, is notable in this passage from his private journal. The comment is from 1833, yet its relevance grows throughout the London years. The reader of Carlyle's Journal and letters in the Craigenputtoch years will sense the continuation of a familiar theme, a desperate and dogged determination to carry out his "task" despite its seeming variance with commercial needs. If the commercial journals do not want his effusions, argues Carlyle in this period (and he could find no publisher for *Sartor*), then the journals are at fault, not he. Familiar, too, is the lack of companionship, "communion of man with man." Irving's death in 1834 was a blow, but the spiritual communion between Carlyle and Irving had ceased by 1830. In London, in the winter of 1831 and again in the summer of 1834, Carlyle tried to reason his friend out of his increasing preocupation with the "gift of tongues," which was to ruin his career in the ministry: Irving would not listen, and so the two saw each other less and less. Jeffrey, Carlyle's other friend, had political cares (intensified when the success of the Whigs in the first Reformed Government took him to

46. The passage, dated 31 March 1833, is quoted from Carlyle's Journal in Froude, *Carlyle*, II, 345.

London, and the office of Lord Advocate) and the two drew apart.

The separation from his earlier friends intensified the other movements we have seen in this paper: the passage quoted from the Journal emphasizes beyond doubt the eventual position which Carlyle took on the question of his own personal religion. He had been thrown upon his own resources by the disillusion with Edinburgh and its values, and the break with Ecclefechan: he *had* to believe in himself and the validity of his "message." The spiritual agonies of Teufelsdröckh are an assertion of just this message, the removal of overwhelming doubt in the "Everlasting No" leading not to peace, but to "Spiritual New-birth, or Baphometic Fire-baptism; perhaps I directly thereupon began to be a Man."[47] Manliness is something repeatedly stressed in the pen portrait of James Carlyle: manliness is the ability to stand aloof from the storm of doubt and worldliness and be serenely convinced of the validity of one's own religious stance. Teufelsdröckh to some extent is in this position: he stands aloof in the "Centre of Indifference," and even in the "Everlasting Yea"; in his "skyey tent,"[48] looking over mankind below him, he keeps his distance from them. He looks at them with love, but also with *pity*: the adjective "poor" is perhaps the one he most frequently ascribes to other people. His pity implies a separateness, an awareness that he is separate, and judging the party who is pitied. Certainly the self-awareness which sweeps over Teufelsdröckh in the "Everlasting Yea" is one which implies a self-centered separateness from the rest of the world, not self-pitying ("What Act of Legislature was there that *thou* shouldst be Happy?")[49] but self-responsible: "Love not Pleasure, love God."[50]

The tone is unmistakably a return to that of Ecclefechan, to the "reminiscence" of James Carlyle, who believed that "man was created to work, not to speculate, or feel, or dream. Accordingly, he set his whole heart thitherwards: he did work wisely and unweariedly (*ohne Hast aber ohne Rast*), and perhaps *performed* more (with the tools he had) than any man I now know."[51] With the tools Carlyle had, very different tools, he set himself to work likewise: the great message "One way or another . . . will and shall be uttered—write it down on paper any way; speak it from thee—so shall thy painful, destitute

47. Harrold, *Sartor*, p. 168.
48. Ibid., p. 187.
49. Ibid., p. 191.
50. Ibid., p. 192.
51. *Reminiscences*, I, 7.

existence not have been in vain."[52] This Journal entry echoes the semi-private *Reminiscences*, and crystallizes most clearly the nature of his "mission," as he recognized it in his mature years.

And so, to return to "Signs of the Times," we see Carlyle bringing together the threads of his essay in his castigation of the times. Their mechanical nature, we have noticed, is particularly condemned. Poetry, religion, society, the social contract, are all sick owing to an excessively mechanical nature. "Again, with respect to our Moral condition: here also he who runs may read that the same physical, mechanical influences are everywhere busy. . . . Of any belief in invisible, divine things, we find as few traces in our Morality as elsewhere. It is by tangible, material considerations that we are guided, not by inward and spiritual." That morality should be mechanically considered is hateful to a man brought up in a community where morality is the unquestioned basis of life, as shown when a man sacrifices his harvest in the interests of family worship. "Self-denial, the parent of all virtue, in any true sense of that word, has perhaps seldom been rarer." While self-interest (one of the sins of Edinburgh) rules, true morality must languish: no man loves truth, "Nay, properly speaking, he does not believe and know it, but only *'thinks'* it, and that 'there is every probability'!" And in conclusion "Truly may we say, with the Philosopher, 'the deep meaning of the Laws of Mechanism lies heavy on us': and in the closet, in the marketplace, in the temple, by the social hearth, encumbers the whole movements of our mind, and over our noblest faculties is spreading a nightmare sleep."[53]

To conclude where we began, we return to Carlyle writing to Mill from Craigenputtoch, praising the Utilitarians "that they were the re-originators of *any* Belief among us." As it stands, the sentiment seems meaningless, for Utilitarianism is precisely the sort of logic-chopping (to use Carlyle's term) which he spent a lifetime inveighing against, nowhere more than in "Signs of the Times." Yet we do not now look for logic in Carlyle: as John Nichol wryly but perceptively remarks, "It is impossible, were it desirable, accurately to define his religious, social or political creed. . . . No printed labels will stick to him: when we seek to corner him by argument he thunders and lightens."[54] The point of this apparently illogical praise of the Utilitarians lies in their advocacy of a belief in a system—Carlyle held any

52. See 46, above.   53. *Works*, XXVII, 78–80.
54. *Thomas Carlyle* (London, 1892), p. 7.

belief preferable to the wholly unbelieving, mechanical concepts of his age.

What this essay has tried to show is the reasoning behind this craving for a belief in an age of unbelief: "What," as he wrote in his Journal, "if thou see no fruit of it? another will." The message of his religious belief is the reestablishment of an epoch of belief, or trust and faith in a doubting age. Yet it is not mere retreat into a past age, which would have been easy. To copy James Carlyle in all things would have presumably produced a life style which Carlyle could have accepted as truly Christian. Yet he was too honest to do this: he realized that his father belonged to a past age, which did not apply to a more complicated present; he realized that his own education had put him apart from his father's strong-minded, yet relatively simple-minded belief.

No more could Carlyle accept the way out which Edinburgh offered, a consistent logical system which gave its exponent insight into the universe, and the satisfaction of penetrating the secrets of the stars. Partly because he was temperamentally unsuited to the rigorous logical exercise, partly because of the inherited religious faith (in the general sense) which he retained from Ecclefechan, and which was enormously stimulated by the Germans (particularly *Wilhelm Meisters Wanderjahre*), Carlyle could not accept this either. *Wotton Reinfred* records the anguish Carlyle felt as a result.

In addition, we have seen how each system, after offering Carlyle an inadequate answer to his own personal problem, receded to an unattainable distance. The Seceder Church receded as its hoary old men died, and the Edinburgh philosophers fell out of fashion in the 1820's.

The sum total of these experiences was to throw Carlyle back on his own devices, to reinforce an inherited tendency to regard the place of the individual as of paramount importance. As Ecclefechan had taught him to see his position as an individual accountable to God, and as Edinburgh had trained him to cultivate his powers as a gifted individual, so loneliness threw him back on his powers of reading and reasoning (and, fortunately, of letter-writing). Goethe refined these interests in the *Bildungsroman Wilhelm Meister* which Carlyle studied, in close detail, while translating it for British readers. Alone Carlyle might always feel, and his letters certainly echo the refrain, yet his mature life was spent in improving his God-given powers and preaching what he took to be his message. The message at the end of the "Everlasting Yea," "Work while it is called Today, for the night cometh, wherein no man can work"[55] is dangerously misleading, in that it is a Biblical quotation, and might seem to be a ready-made slogan, the Biblical "côterie-Sprache" of the family's letters to each other. In the light of the investigations of this essay it is seen as more than an inherited moral injunction, but an articulation of the only possible way open to Carlyle, morbidly conscious of his individual abilities and his wish to communicate them, yet cut off increasingly from moral positions with which he might identify. Eventually he was thrown back on himself, and his responsibility to himself as a man: his religious beliefs in the earlier period of his life led him to this essentially lonely position, and for the rest of his life he remained in proud isolation, while growing in power as a religious force throughout the world.

55. Harrold, *Sartor*, p. 197.

Carlyle and Goethe as Scientist

CARLISLE MOORE, *University of Oregon*

The apparently unpromising subject of Carlyle's concern with science yields promise when we remember that by his twenties he was expert in mathematics, spent a good portion of five years (1817–1822) studying physics, astronomy, geology, and mineralogy, and as late as 1827 was seriously considering a scientific career.[1] True, by this time a literary career attracted him far more, but it appeared far less likely to support him financially than would a professorship of mathematics at Sandhurst (1822) or of moral philosophy, which included teaching mathematics, at the Universities of London and St. Andrews (1827), or the directorship of the Edinburgh Astronomical Observatory (1834).[2] He was understandably reluctant to commit himself to literature. Not only were the times inhospitable to aspiring men of letters, but his own repeated attempts to find himself and to establish himself as a writer, translating *Wilhelm Meister*, writing *Schiller* and the periodical essays and his aborted histories of the Commonwealth and of German literature, had at best met with uncertain success. Moreover, despite his distinct preference for literature and the loss of his early enthusiasm for mathematics, he retained in a somewhat curious way a deep respect for science as a primary branch of knowledge, a respect that never left him. How this lasting respect for science survived his disenchantment with logical analysis and mechanistic physics is to be explained, I believe, by the very source of his early enchantment with literature—the works of Goethe.

It is not surprising that his contemporaries regarded him as an enemy of science. In 1829 he had designated science as one of the ominous "signs of the times," as one more victim of that machinery,

1. A full study of science in Carlyle's work and thought—a subject too large to be more than touched on here—is in course of completion by the present writer.

2. Carlyle was offered, or was a candidate for, these positions. For that at Sandhurst see *CL*, II, 194, and passim; for the professorships at London and St. Andrews see ibid., IV, 225, and passim. Carlyle made serious and prolonged efforts to obtain these two university posts. For the Edinburgh Observatory directorship see Froude, *Carlyle*, II, 390.

that "great art of adapting means to ends," which was affecting and infecting not only the traditional sciences but philosophy, art, and literature also.[3] All were being made mechanical, artificial, unnatural: "No Newton, by silent meditation, now discovers the system of the world from the falling of an apple; but some quite other than Newton stands in his Museum, his Scientific Institution, and behind whole batteries of retorts, digesters, and galvanic piles imperatively 'interrogates Nature'—who, however, shows no haste to answer."[4] In observing that scientific inquiry no longer depends on intuitive and reflective genius, Carlyle is deploring the descent of the scientist to the level of the machine. At the same time he is expressing both a faith and a fear: faith that inductive, mechanical approaches will ultimately prove powerless in discovering the secrets of Nature, and fear that nevertheless there exists an awful danger in the Machine, in its power both literally and symbolically to dominate and take over all inquiry and to displace with its mechanical action all individual initiative and moral values.[5]

Thirty years later Darwinian evolution presented another danger, although Carlyle's true opinion of it is not to be inferred from his celebrated fulminations against the hypothesis of man's descent from the ape. Yet here too he reveals a fear that science is debasing man by undermining the concept of human dignity, denying the mystery and divinity of man's soul. With the basic idea of evolution he was familiar enough and had no quarrel, nor much sympathy either, except as it could be accommodated to his spiritual concept of man's development. After Lyell's *Geology* and Chambers' *Vestiges*, science meant evolution, and after Huxley and Spencer evolution meant the "survival of the fittest." Considering the number of highly reputed scientists who initially rejected Darwin's hypothesis—Owen, Agassiz, Tyndall, even Huxley—one wonders that Carlyle displayed as much sympathy for it as he did. But his opinion was mixed, and at different times found different expression. In animated conversation he could and often did attack it with such eloquent scorn that many of his hearers were offended, and in the *Reminiscences*, written in the

3. *Works*, XXVII, 59.   4. Ibid., pp. 61–62.
5. Carlyle was well aware how from the eighteenth century science had accelerated the growth of industrialism, which he also viewed with mixed enthusiasm and alarm. For a discussion of his views see Herbert L. Sussman, *Victorians and the Machine: The Literary Response to Technology* (Cambridge, Mass., 1968), pp. 13–40. Carlyle's ambivalent attitude seems to have an analog in our attitude toward the computer today.

sorrow and bitterness that followed Jane's death, he declared that he "never could *read* a page of it [the *Origin of Species*], or waste the least thought upon it";[6] while in soberer mood, to friends like Allingham, Conway, and Tyndall, he avowed familiarity and sympathy with both the work and its author. Allingham reports that Carlyle liked and respected Darwin and on occasion joshed him about the prospect of man returning to the ape, both men laughing good-naturedly.[7] On his side, Darwin admired Carlyle as a moral teacher and vivid historian, but regretted that Carlyle "despised . . . all branches of science."[8] Such amenities do not conceal the fact that, at the same time, Darwin resented Carlyle's prejudice against experimental science and that Carlyle deplored Darwin's hypothesis, with all its implications, as irrelevant to much more important truths.

Yet Carlyle did not despise all branches of science, or even science generally. There is ample testimony of his active, though specially biased, interest in science throughout his life. Conway observed that he seemed to prefer older scientists like Newton, Franklin ("America's greatest man"), and the Erasmus Darwin of *Zoönomia*,[9] but he nevertheless knew well the work of his contemporaries Richard Owen, Michael Faraday, Charles Lyell, and John Tyndall and was sensible, with his own reservations, of the advances they were making. Tyndall especially affirmed the probity of Carlyle's scientific knowledge, and as if to correct Darwin's remark that "I never met a man with a mind so ill adapted to scientific research,"[10] denied that Carlyle's mind was unscientific or that he was either incurious or hostile with respect to science: "In physical subjects I never encountered a mind of stronger grasp and deeper penetration than his. . . . During my expositions, when these were clear, he was always in advance of me, anticipating and enunciating what I was about to say."[11] It is clear that what Tyndall admires, and is defending, is Carlyle's intuitive understanding rather than logical or analytical processes of thought, which Carlyle

6. *Reminiscences*, I, 173.

7. *William Allingham: A Diary*, ed H. Allingham and D. Radford (London, 1907), p. 239. See John Tyndall, *New Fragments* (New York, 1896), p. 388, and *New Letters of Thomas Carlyle*, ed. Alexander Carlyle (London, 1904), II, 314, for evidence of his later affection for Darwin.

8. *The Autobiography of Charles Darwin*, ed. Nora Barlow (New York, 1958), p. 113.

9. Moncure D. Conway, *Thomas Carlyle* (London, 1881), pp. 84–85.

10. *Autobiography*, p. 114.

11. *Times* (London), 4 May 1881, p. 13.

frankly denounced. Darwin was right. But though scientific research did not appeal to Carlyle, he appealed to scientists and philosophers (whose logical reasoning powers he either lacked or scorned) by virtue of his extraordinary power of insight, "the divine foundation" which they lacked, and by his ability to enter into the particulars of a scientific question and often by a flash of intelligence trace them to their most profound and vital cause.[12] With all their commitment to empiricism, they admired the author of *Sartor Resartus*, and a number of eminent scientists besides Tyndall, Owen, and Huxley became his close personal friends at various times—men such as Faraday, Lyell, and Charles Babbage. Even those who had felt the lash of his tongue, like Darwin and Spencer, though they had their strong reservations, welcomed his company. After about 1823 nothing of Carlyle's dealt directly with mathematics or science, but as Tyndall notes, the final proof of his lively and accurate scientific interests is to be found throughout his writings:

The scientific reader of his works must have noticed the surprising accuracy of the metaphors he derived from Science. Without sound knowledge such uniform exactitude would not have been possible. He laid the whole body of the sciences under contribution—Astronomy, from the nebular hypothesis onwards; mathematics, physics, chemistry, geology, natural history—drawing illustrations from all of them, grinding the appropriate parts of each of them into paint for his marvellous pictures. Quite as clearly as the professed physicist he grasped the principle of Continuity, and saw the interdependence of "parts" in the "stupendous Whole."[13]

We have thus two anomalies: Carlyle's continued contacts with science and scientists after he had repudiated science and turned to literature, and the special nature of his attitude toward science and scientific methods. Both are to be explained, in large part, by Goethe's scientific writings. My purpose is to suggest that at a critical stage of his life, when he was growing under the influence of Goethe as a poet and novelist, as the author of *Faust* and *Wilhelm Meister*, he was also strengthened and confirmed by the example of Goethe as the author of

12. A. Francison, *National Lessons from the Life and Works of Thomas Carlyle* (London, 1881), p. 11. See also the anonymous "Herbert Spencer: A Portrait," *Blackwood's Edinburgh Magazine*, 175 (March 1904), 110–116, in which Spencer, who met Carlyle in the 1840's and soon disliked him, is shown to have felt and acknowledged his influence.

13. John Tyndall, *New Fragments*, p. 385.

the *Farbenlehre* and the *Metamorphose der Pflanzen* in a particular conception of science and scientific thinking which not only rescued it from mechanism and industry but restored it to its older high eminence among the liberal arts. Without Goethe, Carlyle's repudiation of science might have been total.

One of the happy incidents during his early years was his discovery of German poetry.[14] On his first looking into *Faust* new planets swam into his ken. Further exploration of Goethe and of the German Romantics, during the 1820's, produced in Carlyle an aesthetic and philosophic awakening of tremendous consequence; and yet it occurred at a time when he was still under the strong influence of science and mathematics. After completing his studies at Edinburgh in 1814 and while struggling painfully to find a profession, he had spent much of his time in learning, teaching, and writing mathematics. At first there was no conflict. Like Coleridge before him, he saw no discrepancy between science and the religious studies which he had walked his hundred miles to the University to take up in preparation for the ministry. Ample precedent for this accommodation was to be found in the careers of such fellow Scots as his close friend Edward Irving and Thomas Chalmers, both of whom were ministers with active mathematical inclinations. For them and for the young Carlyle mathematics provided a much-needed support for truth. The great Newton had geometrized space and explained the phenomena of the heavens and earth by a single mathematical law which reestablished the idea of design; he had rebutted eighteenth-century skepticism and triumphantly proved the existence of a divine cosmic order. "God said, Let Newton be! and all was light." Carlyle, reading the *Principia* in 1817, exulted that Newtonian science enabled man to see past, present, and future in a single view and to arrive at permanent truth.

14. This was in 1819 when things German were almost wholly unknown to the English public. Before 1800 Henry Mackenzie, William Taylor of Norwich, Scott, and Coleridge were almost the only writers interested in Germany at all. Scott's contacts were not with the German Romantics, while Coleridge, when he traveled in Germany with Wordsworth in 1798, visited only Klopstock. Coleridge's German interests, it may be noted, were scientific as well as literary: at about the same time that he was working Schiller's *Die Räuber* into his play *Osorio* (1797) and translating *Wallenstein* (1800) he was completing his education at Göttingen, studying physiology and attending the famous Blumenbach's lectures on natural history, as if he saw no disparity between the sciences and poetry. See F. W. Stokoe, *German Influence in the English Romantic Period, 1788–1818* (Cambridge, Mass., 1926); Hill Shine, *Carlyle's Unfinished History of German Literature* (Lexington, Ky., 1951), pp. ix–xxi; and René Wellek, *Confrontations* (Princeton, 1965), pp. 6–12.

"Assuredly," he wrote his friend Robert Mitchell, "the human species never performed a more honourable atchievement."[15]

Behind Newton was Euclid with his *Geometry*, an even stronger symbol of imperishable truth. Although non-Euclidean geometry was then evolving in Germany with Gauss and in Russia with Lobachevski it was hardly known in England, where geometry remained Euclidean, resting firmly on demonstrable proof derived from self-evident assumptions.[16] Euclid was still alone in looking on beauty bare. The appeal of geometry, or of mathematics generally, lay in its power to extract new truths from old. "Where shall we find her [truth] in her native purity," Carlyle wrote Mitchell, "if not in the science of quantity and number?"[17] Especially in Scotland mathematical thought was still dominated by synthetic geometry at the expense of the analytic algebra which flourished on the continent. While Euler, Laplace, and Lagrange were employing the more modern methods of algebraic analysis, Scottish mathematicians like John Playfair and John Leslie, although they were not unfamiliar with these methods and on occasion admitted their superiority over the ancient geometry, continued to teach "to the almost total exclusion of modern analysis."[18] Philosophers of the Common Sense School like Thomas Reid and Dugald Stewart insisted that mathematics must not lose sight of its basis in sensory data. They objected to the use of "imaginary" or "impossible" numbers like the square root of minus one, since these could not be related to external objects. Leslie also deplored the algebraist's concepts of "quantities less than nothing," or negative numbers, as well as complex numbers. The scope of mathematical inquiry had thus to be deliberately limited in order to protect its epistemological claim to truth. In addition, analysis was regarded as mechanical, "little better than a *mechanical knack*, in which we proceed without ideas of any kind, and obtain a result without meaning and *without being conscious of any process of reasoning*."[19] Synthetic geometry, on the other hand, was recommended both as a means of training the mind to think clearly and as a necessary part of a liberal education.

Carlyle's mathematical proficiency developed early, and by 1824

15. *CL*, I, 103, 5 July 1817.
16. See Richard Olson, "Scottish Philosophy and Mathematics, 1750–1830," *Journal of the History of Ideas*, 32 (Jan.–March 1971), 35–37, and passim for an analysis of mathematical thought and teaching in the Scotland of Carlyle's time.
17. *CL*, I, 120, 16 Feb. 1818.   18. Olson, p. 29, n. 1.
19. Ibid., pp. 40–42.

he had attained a more than modest distinction in Scotland as a solver of difficult geometrical problems. He was highly esteemed by his teacher John Leslie, was praised long afterwards by the eminent Cambridge mathematician Augustus De Morgan, and even today is mentioned in such histories of mathematics as that by Howard Eves.[20] Among his accomplishments was the working out of an ingenious solution of the real roots of any quadratic equation by purely geometrical means, for which he is still given credit as innovator. Besides teaching mathematics in schools at Annan and Kirkcaldy (1814–1818), he contributed with characteristic vigor to a mathematical correspondence in the *Dumfries and Galloway Courier*; he made plans to write on Johannes Hevelius, the seventeenth-century German astronomer and founder of lunar typography; he translated German works on mineralogy by Mohs and on magnetism by Hansteen, both of these calling on his mathematical acumen; and in 1821–22 he translated the famous *Elements of Geometry* by Legendre, which was to become a standard text in England and the United States and go through many editions. In addition to translating this work Carlyle wrote for it an introductory chapter of his own, an "Essay on Proportion," which according to De Morgan proved that Carlyle "would have been a distinguished teacher and thinker in first principles."[21]

Carlyle was also interested in the other sciences, chiefly astronomy and geology. We do not forget that he nourished strong literary interests at the same time, interests in poetry, fiction, and history, which would ultimately prove the stronger. But literature would offer no sure promise of a career for another dozen years. In 1819, with no prospects before him, he could only hope he might find a career among the natural sciences. His old mathematics teacher Professor Leslie told him that "upon the whole . . . the best plan for *you* seems to be to learn the engineer business, and go to America."[22] Carlyle

20. *An Introduction to the History of Mathematics*, 3d ed. (New York 1969), pp. 73, 374, 410. The subject of Carlyle's mathematical concerns has nevertheless received scant attention. Peter A. Wursthorn's account in "The Position of Thomas Carlyle in the History of Mathematics," *Mathematical Teacher*, 59 (1966), 755–770, provides helpful details about Carlyle's early mathematical thinking and teaching. Jacques Cabau, in his *Thomas Carlyle, ou le Prométhée enchaîné* (Paris, 1968), explores some of the mathematical imagery. My forthcoming "Carlyle: Mathematics and 'Mathesis'" is part of an attempt to determine the importance of all the sciences in his work and thought.

21. Augustus De Morgan, *A Budget of Paradoxes* (London, 1872), p. 499.

22. *CL*, I, 158.

had no intention of going to America, but he did attend classes in mineralogy and geology taught by Professor Jameson and commenced reading works by German and French geologists. As he later told Goethe, "it was the desire to read *Werner's* Mineralogical Doctrines in the original, that first set me on studying German" that same year.[23] Though he may have had other reasons too for learning German there is evidence enough in his letters and from his translations of Mohs and Hansteen that he was reading much geology in German and that in the process he discovered Goethe.

What happened now, of course, was that the German language, which he had mastered, largely by his own efforts, in order to gain first-hand knowledge of the German sciences, led him away from science, back to literature, and on into the whole new world of German Romanticism. He was not the first who ever burst into that stormy sea, but there is little reason to believe that his explorations were inspired by any of his predecessors. It is barely possible that he had heard of the pioneer lecture on German drama which in 1788 Henry Mackenzie, author of *The Man of Feeling*, gave before the Royal Society of Edinburgh; and his unflattering opinion of the many articles on German literature by William Taylor of Norwich is clear from his 1831 essay. More likely incentives may be found in Mme de Staël's *De l'Allemagne*, which appeared in England in 1813 and was known to Carlyle at least as early as 1817, and Henry Crabb Robinson, whom F. W. Stokoe calls "the first Englishman to realize clearly the literary importance of Goethe and to understand him aesthetically."[24] Carlyle's own understanding of Goethe came slowly and imperfectly; nevertheless his numerous essays on Goethe and his works, published between 1822 and 1832, helped to correct much British misunderstanding and ignorance. His translations, *Wilhelm Meister's Apprenticeship* (1824) and *Travels* (1827), are still standard. In 1827 he even attempted to write a Wertherean novel *Wotton Reinfred*, which he was unable to finish and had to abandon at the eighth chapter.

To Carlyle, Goethe was not a scientist but a poet, prophet, and moralist. Nevertheless, C. F. Harrold, René Wellek, and others have

23. *Correspondence between Goethe and Carlyle*, ed. C. E. Norton (London, 1887), pp. 156–157. See Rodger L. Tarr and Ian M. Campbell, "Carlyle's Early Study of German, 1819–1821," *Illinois Quarterly*, 34 (Dec. 1971), 19–27, for an interesting demurrer.

24. Stokoe, p. 57.

demonstrated the cogency of Carlyle's moral reading of Goethe. Rather than blame him for the bias, we may observe that he read creatively and transformed what he found to suit his own needs and regarded Goethe's work as he regarded all that he read, as a quarry of adoptable and adaptable truth. What he found there was what he had been looking for in mathematics and the natural sciences, a *Weltbild*, a philosophic-poetic picture of the world which compelled his belief. Such a picture seemed to exclude the sciences, for these were, in Carlyle's terms, "descendental" and belonged to the realm of the Understanding only, not to that of Reason. After 1822 his devotion to mathematics began to decline; by 1829 in his essay on Novalis he adduced Leslie's old reprehension of analytic algebra in his own reprehension of "the higher mathematics," which he called mechanical because "assisted with visible symbols, with safe *implements* for thinking." In "Signs of the Times" he said too: "The science of the age, in short, is physical, chemical, physiological; in all shapes mechanical. Our favourite Mathematics, the highly prized exponent of all these other sciences, has also become more and more mechanical."[25]

Yet he could not fail to perceive that Goethe was a lover and practitioner of the sciences and considered them useful, even necessary branches of knowledge. Novalis and Schelling were also men of letters *and* science. Goethe sometimes said that he took less pride in his poetry than in his theory of colors, his discovery of the intermaxillary bone in the human skull, and his pioneering in botany. He wrote Carlyle: "The happiest time of my life was when I was eagerly at work on the works of Nature." Even if there is some exaggeration here, we are impressed, as Carlyle must have been impressed, to hear such an assertion from the master poet. Moreover, Goethe took pains to acquaint Carlyle with this aspect of his life work, offering in July 1829 to send him a copy of the *Farbenlehre*: "Besides what relates to Natural Philosophy, there is so much of general and human interest in it that it cannot fail to please you." Carlyle gratefully accepted, and the two volumes were sent in April 1830, with careful instructions how he should read them for full understanding: the second or historical part first, then the didactic and polemic parts together with the plates illustrating Goethe's elaborate experiments. "The Work," Goethe wrote a month later, "is indeed too much flesh of my flesh and bone of my bone not to create in you a friendly interest. Say something

25. *Works*, XXVII, 51, 63.

to me about it." In June 1831 he sent Carlyle a copy of the *Metamorphose der Pflanzen* and again expressed the hope that "it may be of some importance to you." Whether Carlyle read these two works carefully, or would have fulfilled his promise to send his comments on them, there is no evidence.[26] Goethe died not long after, and perhaps Carlyle's early admiration for Newton's *Optics*, with which Goethe's theory was so much at odds, helps to explain the silence. On the other hand, there seems no reason to doubt his admiration for Goethe's scientific work or, more importantly, for Goethe's mode of scientific inquiry. He praised the *Farbenlehre* in the essays, defended it against attack in the presence of Darwin, and discussed it sympathetically with Tyndall. To Goethe he said that he knew enough "of your method in such inquiries [to] give me hope of great satisfaction in studying it."[27]

What *was* this method? Goethe's approach to science was intuitive, unitive. Just when Carlyle was ready to dismiss all science as mechanical, he found Goethe, and Novalis too, affirming that science, literature, philosophy, and religion were all complementary, all interrelated parts of a whole. In the *Geschichte der Farbenlehre* Goethe spoke of the arts as something that man continually produces without conscious volition (*ohne zu wollen*), spontaneously, like plants growing and flowers blooming. Goethe was not a methodical scientist. He went no further than the rudiments of mathematics and geometry, believing them to be precise and useful, but empty of life.[28] This approach recalls Carlyle's old complaint that mathematics had no content and, applied to the natural sciences, only produced numerical results.

26. We may assume that, with his interest in everything of Goethe's, he did look into the *Farbenlehre* but was unable to make much of it. That his interest did not die is attested by his several talks with Tyndall about its meaning and value as a scientific work, and by Carlyle's asking Tyndall in 1878 to write on it, a request which elicited Tyndall's essay "Goethe's 'Farbenlehre,'" *New Fragments*, pp. 47–77.

27. *Goethe-Carlyle Correspondence*, pp. 150, 157, 275. Goethe's attachment to science and his scientific ideas and activities are discussed in many works: G. H. Lewes, *Life of Goethe* (London, 1855); Rudolf Magnus, *Goethe as a Scientist*, trans. Heinz Norden (New York, 1949); Asa C. Chandler, "Goethe and Science," *Rice Institute Pamphlet*, 18–19 (1931–1932), 120–147; Willy Hartner, "Goethe and the Natural Sciences," *Goethe and the Modern Age*, ed. Arnold Bergstraesser (Chicago, 1950), pp. 75–94, rpt. in *Goethe: A Collection of Critical Essays*, ed. Victor Lange (Englewood Cliffs, N.J., 1968), pp. 145–160; Heinrich Henel, "Type and Proto-Phenomenon in Goethe's Science," *PMLA*, 71 (Sept. 1956), 651–668; Walther Gerlach, "Goethe as a Scientist," *Times Literary Supplement*, 3 Aug. 1973, pp. 907–908.

28. Chandler, pp. 131–132; Magnus, p. 233.

Goethe's approach was deductive, based on his own powers of insight rather than on analysis. "In science," he said, "all depends on what is called *aperçu*, on growing aware of what lies at the bottom of the phenomena."[29] Hence in his botanical studies his constant search for the *Urpflanze*, the archetype. Ultimately, his approach to the natural sciences was the same as his approach to poetry, intuitive and unitive, an exercise of his creative imagination. First hitting upon a theory, he then attempted to unify and coordinate natural phenomena, proceeding like a geometrist from theorem to proof. Most Goetheans agree that he was not really a scientist, but a poet of genius with an all-absorbing interest in Nature. Lacking the patience to accumulate facts systematically, he contemplated phenomena in search of the *Urphänomene*.

That Carlyle was already familiar with this "method" without yet being converted to it seems clear from an appendix to his *Life of Schiller*, in which he quotes Goethe's reply to Schiller in the course of their famous altercation over scientific method, to this point: "that there surely was another way of representing Nature, not separated and disunited, but active and alive, and expanding from the whole into parts."[30] The *Metamorphose der Pflanzen*, which Goethe then showed to Schiller for proof, but in vain, is described by Carlyle in the footnote as a "curious physiologico-botanical theory by Goethe, which appears to be entirely unknown to this country."

Looking around him in 1829, Carlyle saw that England was in all things mechanical. Science was advancing by "laborious analysis" and mere gathering of facts. Mathematics, limited more and more to the elaborate manipulation of visibles and measurables, was losing its usefulness to the moral philosopher. Yet with the example and teaching of Goethe before him, he stopped short of repudiating mathematics and the sciences altogether, if only because Goethe confirmed his own non-analytic tendencies, and because Goethe argued for an ideal science in which intellection remained intuitive and imaginative. For this ideal Carlyle resorted to the old term "mathesis," meaning the action of learning mathematical science in distinction to exhibiting it. "Mathesis" connotes mental discipline, silent meditation, and pure intuition at work on the mystery of Nature. To Goethe he

29. Magnus, p. 228.
30. *Works*, XXV, 316. Erich Heller discusses this altercation and its importance in *The Disinherited Mind* (New York, 1959 [1952]), pp. 6–7.

wrote in 1829 that his early "love of Natural Science still subsists, or might easily be resuscitated."[31] If it were to be resuscitated, it would be after Goethe's example. W. H. D. Rouse has speculated that with only slightly different circumstances during his early years Carlyle might indeed have become a scientist.[32]

Carlyle did not become a scientist, but the ideal of science stayed with him all his life. There is space only for a few instances of this. As Tyndall noted, all his work is rich in scientific metaphor. *Sartor Resartus* is infused with science in its imagery and concepts. In the first chapter, current scientific works, real and fictitious, are parodied unmercifully to prepare the way for the ideal science which is the Clothes Philosophy itself, the new science from Germany: "here, as in so many other cases, Germany, learned, indefatigable, deep-thinking Germany comes to our aid" with its "pure moral Science."[33] Rising to oppose the new science of Mechanics is the newer science of Dynamics. Industrial images everywhere signify unhappiness and death—the Motive Millwrights, the Utilitarian "Armament of Mechanisers," the "Mill of Death," the "one huge, dead, immeasurable Steam-engine, rolling on, in its dead indifference, to grind me limb from limb."[34] But in the realm of Dynamics, the problem of happiness is put in the form of a proportion: the Fraction of Life may be increased in value by decreasing the denominator rather than by increasing the numerator.

Some twenty years later Carlyle's old interest in optics was "resuscitated" in an unfinished essay which, left untitled, Froude calls "Spiritual Optics."[35] It promised to be an extended analogy drawn from optics and astronomy, but Carlyle could not work it through to a conclusion and seems never to have returned to it after about 1852. The fragment is apparently Carlyle's last attempt with the help of science to explain or figure forth the truth as he saw it. Following

31. *Goethe-Carlyle Correspondence*, p. 157. Even after the move to London in 1834 and for the next several years, Carlyle fared so poorly with his writing that he had constantly to look for possible employment in other professions. See Froude, *Carlyle*, I, 22 ff. For the concept of "mathesis" see Carlyle's "Novalis" and "Signs of the Times," *Works*, XXVII, 51 f. and 64.

32. *Towards the Twentieth Century* (Cambridge, Eng., 1937), p. 116.

33. Harrold, *Sartor*, pp. 6–7, 191.　　　34. *Ibid.*, pp. 220, 234.

35. Froude, *Carlyle*, II, 8–19, and IV, 77. A new and more complete version has been published, with commentary and textual notes, by Murray Baumgarten, in *Victorian Studies*, 11 (June 1968), 503–522.

Galileo, Newton had described the laws of the new, Copernican, heliocentric universe, and thus exposed the falsity of the old geocentric one, in which man thought himself at the center, with the stars and the planets (and God too) moving about him for his pleasure. Carlyle notes that there are still Ptolemaists living in the mid-nineteenth century who, optically deceived, judge by appearances and fancy themselves still at the center, sufficient unto themselves. If there were but a modern Galileo to correct their sight! Carlyle thus employs a scientific analogy to argue for our perceiving that it is God who is at the center and not ourselves, who are moving at His divine behest, in obedience to His laws, in His divine universe. The essay shows Carlyle's enduring hope that the language of science may yet be adduced in the expression of moral and religious truth, and it demonstrates again how strong an influence Goethe's conception of science had on Carlyle's thought. Science was always a valid means of reaching for truth, as long as it remained intuitive and non-analytic and proceeded upon the knowledge that Nature would never reveal all of God's mystery. Yet man must continue the search. "There is after all," Goethe wrote him in 1831, "a feeling of exaltation in once again throwing light on any part of the Impenetrable."[36]

The development of science in nineteenth-century England followed the Continent and grew more analytical, empirical, inductive. Like Goethe, Carlyle went the other way, and though mostly silent on the subject, sought in his work to unite art and science. It must be admitted that Germany's science can claim small influence in Romantic England. Perhaps it is even true, as Erich Heller has asserted in *The Disinherited Mind*, that Goethe's science has contributed nothing substantial to scientific progress from his time to ours. But Heller adds that by its opposition to empirical science it did "lay bare in his time, with remarkable precision, the very roots of that crisis and revolution in scientific method in which the Twentieth-Century scientist finds himself involved"; it exposed "the potential *hubris*" inherent in the modern reliance on purely experimental methods conducted in accordance with a mechanistic philosophy of nature. By separating work and symbol, experience and idea, the whole and its parts, this procedure threatened to "abolish in the world all creative interest in

36. *Goethe-Carlyle Correspondence*, p. 275.

what this, that or the other *are* and *mean.*"[37] Carlyle, in his effort to unite science, poetry, and religion in a total perception, was in spirit and in fact following Goethe's example. His attempt constitutes one more bond between Germany and England, and reaffirms the vitality of Goethe's influence, as poet and scientist.

37. Heller, pp. 8, 16, 259–266.

Carlyle and the Saint-Simonians (1830–1832): New Considerations

K. J. FIELDING, *University of Edinburgh*

Every Carlyean knows about the Saint-Simonians, and a full examination of their relations here would be not only undesirable but impossible. Rather, in the light of some new information, I mean to suggest that new consideration is needed, and that for a time they meant more to him than often supposed.

They appear most noticeably in his writings at the end of *Sartor Resartus*, when the Hofrath reports that Teufelsdröckh has disappeared from Weissnichtwo. No one knows why, though there is a "shadow of a suspicion" that it is to do with events in Paris:

For example, when the *Saint-Simonian Society* transmitted its Propositions hither, and the whole *Gans* was one vast cackle of laughter, lamentation and astonishment, our Sage sat mute; and at the end of the third evening said merely: "Here also are men who have discovered, not without amazement, that Man is still Man; of which high, long-forgotten Truth, you already see them make a false application." Since then, as has been ascertained by examination of the Post-Director, there passed at least one Letter with its Answer between the Messieurs Bazard-Enfantin and our Professor himself; of what tenor can now only be conjectured. On the fifth night following, he was seen for the last time.[1]

It is a teasing allusion to the disciples of Saint Simon. Already the Editor has noted that, among the Professor's papers, he had found

quoted without censure that strange aphorism of Saint-Simon's, concerning which and whom so much were to be said: "*L'âge d'or, qu'une aveugle tradition a placé jusqu'ici dans le passé, est devant nous*; The golden age, which a blind tradition has hitherto placed in the Past, is Before us."[2]

Yet, slight as these references are, the final one in *Sartor* appears particularly significant coming at a climax to the work when the

1. Harrold, *Sartor*, pp. 296–297. Saint-Amand Bazard (1791–1832), and Barthélemy Prosper Enfantin (1796–1864) were the two leaders or "fathers" of the Saint-Simonians.
2. Harrold, *Sartor*, p. 236.

Professor leaves the *Wahngasse* [Dream Lane] and is thought to have set out for two of the greatest centers of potential uprising—Paris and London. It may well seem part of the whole development of *Sartor,* from self-concern to speculation, social concern and then action.

A few other direct references to the Saint-Simonians have been noticed in Carlyle's works, which by no means exhaust the evidence of their influence. In his "Boswell's Life of Johnson," Carlyle recalls the Saint-Simonian phrase, "*à chacun selon sa capacité, à chaque capacité selon ses œuvres*"—how happy for Johnson had their golden age arrived![3] His other specific comments all deplore their folly in trying to establish a new religion.[4] Various writers on Carlyle and the Saint-Simonians have argued more or less convincingly that their influence on him went well beyond what this suggests; but their effect on his social philosophy is extremely difficult, if not impossible, to determine in spite of efforts that have been made. Without pursuing the matter further it is sobering to read the corrections of Ella M. Murphy on D. B. Cofer and then of Hill Shine on Miss Murphy. The most central work on the subject, as is well known, is Shine's *Carlyle and the Saint-Simonians: The Concept of Historical Periodicity* (Baltimore, 1941); and I might not have ventured to add these fairly tentative comments but for the fact that Shine's promise of a "later study" about what Carlyle learned from the Saint-Simonians' social philosophy (p. 143, n. 68) has not been fulfilled. As a result, what we have is so excellent a study of "historical periodicity" that it has left unbalanced the general question of the relations of Carlyle and the Saint-Simonians, which has a place in both his biography and interpretation.[5] Even though the balance has since been partly redressed

3. *Works,* XXVIII, 92.

4. See "The Parliamentary History of the French Revolution" (1837), *Works,* XXIX, 7; *Chartism* (1839), in *Works,* XXIX, 61; and *The Life of John Sterling* (1851), in *Works,* XI, 47.

5. Hill Shine and R. K. P. Pankhurst, as cited in the text, are indispensable; also useful is Emery Neff, *Carlyle and Mill: An Introduction to Victorian Thought* (New York, 1926); some other works may be referred to but should be used with caution, such as D. B. Cofer, *Saint-Simonism in the Radicalism of Thomas Carlyle* (Austin, Texas, 1931), a 68-page pamphlet, and Ella M. Murphy, "Carlyle and the Saint-Simonians," *Studies in Philology,* 33 (Jan. 1936), 93–118. Only after finishing the present essay have I been able to see the doctoral thesis by Dwight L. Lindley, "The Saint-Simonians, Carlyle, and Mill, A Study in the History of Ideas" (Columbia University, 1958), which, making good use of published sources, offers a well-balanced and reliable study. It is particularly interesting in considering the relationship between

by R. K. P. Pankhurst's *The Saint Simonians, Mill and Carlyle* (London, [1957]), further attempts need to be made. Carlyle was no doubt wrong when he wrote in his Journal in 1830, "I have now almost done with the Germans";[6] but it is certainly right for us to look more closely at the direction he was taking at the time.

The remark was made when Carlyle was at Craigenputtoch, struggling to write his unfinished *History of German Literature,* and when (not for the first time or the last) he had been gloomily debating his prospects in the Journal: "Doubtful it is in the highest degree, whether ever I shall make men hear my voice to any purpose or not. Certain only that I shall be a *failure* if I do not" (p. 152). It was just about this point that the Saint-Simonians opened communication with him, when, although he was as far from the centers of thought and action as if at Weissnichtwo, they sent him a flattering letter and a selection of their publications. So far the story is a familiar one in Carlyle's biography, and so is the way in which their contact with him arose. They had been impressed by his anonymous essay "Signs of the Times" in the *Edinburgh Review* of June 1829. By November it had been reprinted in translation in Paris, in the *Revue Britannique,* and the Saint-Simonians had then discussed it in a two-part article in their own journal, *L'Organisateur* (21 March and 18 April 1830). It is then that they dispatched their letter. It is curious in view of what has been written before that it has not been noticed that both the letter and most of the Saint-Simonian publications have long been in the National Library of Scotland.[7]

Sartor Resartus and the Saint-Simonians and in its survey of comments in the contemporary press. For some other works, see further notes. The spelling and accentuation of titles and quotations in French have been followed as exactly as possible.

6. *Two Note Books of Thomas Carlyle,* ed. C. E. Norton (New York, 1898), p. 150.

7. NLS, MS, L.C. 2275, acquired 1926. The publications are as listed in the text, (ii) to (vi). They are bound with further publications, sent later: (vii) *Doctrine de Saint-Simon: exposition: première année. 1829* (Paris, 1830); (viii) *Exposition de la doctrine de Saint-Simon: deuxième année* (Paris, 1830), only 16 pp.; (ix) *Religion Saint-Simonienne. Appel, par Benjamin-Olinde Rodrigues* (Paris, 1831); (x) *Religion Saint-Simonienne. Lettre du Père Enfantin à Charles Duveyrier. Lettre du Père Enfantin à François et Peiffer, Chefs de L'Eglise de Lyon* (including "Le Prêtre—L'Homme et La Femme") (Paris, 1831); (xi) *Religion Saint-Simonienne. Réunion générale de la famille . . . Note sur le mariage et le divorce; . . . par le Père Rodrigues* (Paris, 1831); (xii) *Religion Saint-Simonienne: réunion générale de la famille . . . Enseignements faits par le Père Suprême* (Paris, 1832). On the cover of (v) Carlyle wrote, "Thomas Carlyle.–1830.–"; on the front flyleaf of the bound volume, he wrote, "Saint-Simonisme. Piéces Diverses./ 1818–1831"; on the back flyleaf he wrote, "The foregoing Works, with

The packet of publications they sent is interesting because they help to establish what Carlyle was able to read. The letter itself is, perhaps, less important and has long been available in a copy kept by the author Gustave d'Eichthal and published by his son.[8] Gustave and his brother Adolphe were members of a Jewish banking family who were, strangely enough, known to the Carlyles, since Dr. John Carlyle had stayed with their uncle Baron d'Eichthal in Munich in 1827–1828. "A good kindhearted man," wrote John, "as I ever knew."[9] Gustave knew England quite well. He had visited it in 1827–1828, when he had written an account of a tour of the manufacturing towns and struck up a friendship with the twenty-two-year-old John Stuart Mill.[10] To Carlyle he was to be the best known and most respected of the Saint-Simonians.

D'Eichthal explained in his letter that he addressed the anonymous author of "Signs of the Times" at the request of his Fathers, the leaders of the Saint-Simonians. After telling how they had been attracted by "Signs of the Times," he begged that careful attention should be paid to a number of publications which he was sending with the letter, especially to *Nouveau Christianisme* by Saint Simon himself and to an explanatory article about it in number 36 of *L'Organisateur*. He then went on to address him in the fervent tones of a missionary wishing to convert someone to his faith, which was exactly how he saw himself:

. . . Si vous n'êtes point allé au delà de ces *Desirs vagues* et de ces *Espèrances incertaines*, Ils ne vous l'ont point reproché. Car ils savent, qu'aux

many other of less moment, were sent to me at Craigenputtoch, in 1830 and subsequently. The Saint-Simonian Sect, after attracting considerable notice for a space of two years, began to split in pieces, underwent a Sentence of Law (apparently on false charges) in 1832, and soon dissolved and disappeared. The little Truth that lay among their crudities has not disappeared, or even properly *appeared*, but yet waits its time. As a constituted Sect these men are not without significance; not undeserving some slight remembrance./ T.C./*6th* May, 1834–." The pamphlets are clean and otherwise unmarked.

8. 29 April 1830, MS: NLS, 1765.170–171; and Eugène d'Eichthal, "Carlyle et le Saint-Simonisme: lettres à Gustave d'Eichthal," *Revue Historique*, 88 (1903), 292–306. But see also "Letters from Thomas Carlyle to the Socialists of 1830," *New Quarterly*, 2 (1909), 279–283.

9. 12 Feb. 1831, MS: NLS, 1775A.136. Many of the Saint-Simonian disciples were Jewish, partly because after the Restoration careers had once more been closed to them in the public service and universities (for which Carlyle may have sympathized with them). See Frank E. Manuel, *The New World of Henri Saint-Simon* (Cambridge, Mass., 1956), pp. 344 ff.

10. Ed. Eugène d'Eichthal, "Condition de la Classe Ouvrière en Angleterre (1828)," *Revue Historique*, 79 (1902), 63–64.

hommes seulement, qui ont été eclairés de la lumière nouvelle que Dieu a donnée au monde par St. Simon, appartient de voir l'avenir *sous une forme précise*, et pour ainsi dire, *Face à Face.*[11] Mais aujourd'hui, ils viennent à vous; ils vous demandent d'ouvrir les yeux a cette lumière qui a lui sur eux; car plus que tout autre vous leur semblez préparé à la recevoir.

From d'Eichthal's comments in the letter, from a note on the cover, and from items which survive, it can be seen that the enclosed publications were as follows: (i) seven numbers of the weekly periodical *L'Organisateur* (Paris, August 1829 to August 1831) including two numbers to which Carlyle's attention was drawn—numbers 32 and 36, containing P. M. Laurent's comments on "Signs of the Times," and the article mentioned already; (ii) Saint Simon's *Nouveau Christianisme* (Paris, 1825); (iii) the same author's *L'Industrie, ou Discussions politiques, morales et philosophiques* (Paris, 1818), tome quatrième, premier cahier; (iv) *Le Producteur, journal philosophique de l'industrie, des sciences et des beaux-arts* (Paris, October, 1826), tome cinquième, premier cahier, containing articles to which d'Eichthal drew Carlyle's attention; (v) Eugène Rodrigues, translation of G. E. Lessing, *L'Education du genre humain* (Paris, 1830); (vi) Emile Barrault, *Aux Artistes, Du Passé et de L'avenir des beaux-arts* (*Doctrine de Saint Simon*) (Paris, 1830). These works were to introduce their reader to the *Nouveau Christianisme* and to current views of the brotherhood. The "Note explicative" in *L'Organisateur* 36 would explain how and why Saint Simon had only come to be inspired by religious faith, long remaining a mere philosopher, or, in the words of one of d'Eichthal's "brothers": "Notre Maitre a commencé ses Travaux comme Socrate; et les a terminés comme Jésus." The letter ends with a salutation of "fraternité Chretienne," hoping that its recipient will one day return that of "la fraternité St. Simonienne." Further works were to be sent later. Even so, future study of the influence of the Saint-Simonians on Carlyle's social views will have to take into account that, as far as we can see, it looks as if his reading in their

---

11. *Face à Face*: cf. 1 Cor. 13:12, 2 John 12, 3 John 14, etc.; the stylistic trick is used in much the same manner as Carlyle uses it. Gustave d'Eichthal had been converted from the Jewish faith at the age of fourteen, when he became an ardent Roman Catholic; at age nineteen he became a Saint-Simonian as taught by his tutor Comte, but "ce n'était certes pas une foi religieuse"; only a further conversion by Enfantin had brought him to "la foi religieuse nouvelle." S. Charléty, *Histoire du Saint-Simonisme, 1825–1864* (Paris, 1931), p. 73, from *Œuvres de Saint Simon et d'Enfantin* (Paris, 1865–1878), XVI, 43.

works may have been rather overestimated by Hill Shine. Yet, for the purposes of the present essay, I wish to confine myself to Carlyle's direct relations with the movement and to Saint Simon's last work, *Nouveau Christianisme*, which both had a special value for his followers and was to attract Carlyle's attention.

His response to the parcel and the accompanying letter was clearly one of delight at the way in which work of his had not only reached Paris but made such a marked impression. He tells his mother, "in my present solitude, I am very glad of these small encouragements."[12] Yet in the *Two Note Books* he cautiously speaks of d'Eichthal's letter as "strange," adding:

These people have strange notions, not without a large spicing of truth, and are themselves among the *Signs*. I shall feel curious to know what becomes of them. *La classe la plus pauvre* is evidently in the way of rising from its present deepest abasement; in time, it is likely, the world will be better divided, and he that has the toil of ploughing will have the first cut at the reaping. —I answered these *St. Ss.* and partly expect to hear from them (p. 158).

But his entries in the *Two Note Books* show signs that he was deeply interested by what he read, and it was unduly reserved to speak of only "partly" expecting a reply when the letter he sent warmly encourages one.

Yet it is at this point that we sometimes come on the accustomed biographical snippet about Carlyle and the Saint-Simonians—the true account of how he wrote to Goethe to ask him what he thought of them, and how Goethe replied (30 Oct. 1830), "from the St. Simonian Society pray hold yourself aloof," ". . . bitte Sich fern zu halten."[13] In fact the usual view (if it is fair to call it that) is one given by the soundest authorities. C. F. Harrold, for example, in his edition of *Sartor* confines an account of their relationship entirely to his two footnotes:

The Saint-Simonians were attracted to Carlyle . . . and for a short period Carlyle viewed their doctrines with considerable enthusiasm. Goethe, however, urged him to hold himself aloof from their movement, and he delicately declined their invitation to join them (pp. 236 and 297).

12. MS: NLS, 519.62. [Aug.] 1830.
13. *Correspondence between Goethe and Carlyle*, ed. C. E. Norton, (London, 1887), pp. 226, 225.

G. B. Tennyson has said much the same:

When Carlyle wrote to Goethe during the brief period around 1830 when he flirted with the Saint-Simonians, Goethe, as is well known, admonished him. . . . Goethe was right, but Carlyle on his own soon discontinued his association.[14]

Froude remarks:

Carlyle too had been attracted to the Saint-Simonians. He had in a letter to Goethe expressed some interest and hope in them; and the wise old man had warned him off the dangerous illusion.[15]

The interesting thing is that when the wise old man warned him off, he kept straight on. It is as if some of those who best understand Carlyle's debt to the Germans have been reluctant to see how his views were changing. For while it would be wrong to exaggerate the attraction of the Saint-Simonians, it was clearly strong enough to overcome even his idolatry of Goethe. As long as the movement remained in being, Carlyle was extremely interested in it, although not uncritical; and it is, perhaps, of some significance that Carlyle, a man who was never to vote in an election, who despised political movements in Britain, and who was notably contemptuous of the great cry for Reform, no sooner received a "strange letter" from some Parisians with "strange notions" than he was immediately drawn towards them. Or so it appears from his reply. This, too, has already been published, and the original letter has long been available in the Bibliothèque de l'Arsenal in Paris.[16] Since it will soon be reprinted in the *Collected Letters* of the Duke-Edinburgh edition, I only summarize and excerpt.

Carlyle writes on 9 August 1830 expressing "friendly acknowledgments" and "true satisfaction," saying that "mechanical" as the age may be, he is pleased that it means "the thoughts of a solitary man, which he casts forth silently into the stream of things, can travel onwards over seas to distant Capitals." He then says explicitly:

In these Books of your Society, which for the most part were new to me, I find little or nothing to dissent from: the spirit at least meets my entire

14. *Sartor Called Resartus* (Princeton, 1965), p. 320.
15. Froude, *Carlyle*, II, 137. Froude indexes only one reference to the Saint-Simonians, "failure of, ii, 178," at which page nothing will be found, although there are several other comments in the text, as in Jane's letter (Dec. 1831), II, 224, which speaks of them as "the most interesting acquaintances we have made."
16. Both letters used by R. K. P. Pankhurst. I am most grateful to the authorities for providing me with microfilm copies.

sympathy—the opinions also are often such as I, in my own dialect, have been accustomed to cherish, and more or less clearly to enunciate. That the last century was a period of Denial, of Irreligion and Destruction; to which a new period of Affirmation, of Religion, must succeed, if Society is to be reconstituted, or even to continue in existence: this with its thousand corollaries is a proposition for which the thinking minds of all nations are prepared. No less true is it that as Religion is the only bond and life of societies, so the only real Government were a Hierarchy. . . . These prospects and interests of society I find set forth in your Works, in logical sequence and coherence, with precision, clear illustration, and the emphasis of a noble zeal.

He does make one strongly implicit criticism, through his questioning: what do they mean by coupling Saint Simon and Christ? How can they say that Saint Simon was sent by God, other than as any inspired teacher is sent? But, though he is clear that further than this he cannot go, he is extremely tactful:

In what sense, not of exaggerated metaphor, men of cultivated talent, strong power of thought, and far above all superstition and deception, use these extraordinary words: *Dieu est revenu à la France en Saint-Simon, et la France annoncera au monde le Dieu nouveau.* . . . For, let not loving Disciples take it amiss of a stranger to their Doctrine and their Master, in these writings of Saint-Simon himself, even in the *Nouveau Christianisme*, I find indeed an ardent, all-hoping temper, a keen, far-glancing, yet often, as seems to me, hasty and flighty, vision; surely nothing of a Divine character; no Inspiration, save what every man of genius, who has once seen Truth . . . may be equally said to feel; none, indeed, but what several of his Disciples manifest. . . . Doubt not, therefore, but the Book wherein you are to unfold your Religious principles, will be specially welcome here: the whole history and actual constitution of your Society, its aspects internal and external, its numbers, its political and economical relations, its whole manner of being and acting, are questions of unusual interest for me.

There is more about "the true element of Religion," and his own belief that "indeed the Communion of Saints, spoken of in the Creed, is no delusion, but the highest fact of our destiny." Then the letter concludes:

That you are in the right direction I know; for you are animated by that high, martyr, apostolic spirit which was never altogether wrong: that you are on the right path I shall rejoice to find, and shall still hope till the contrary has been made plain to me. And so, heartily wishing you good speed, nay in my own place and way, striving to work together with you, I remain,

My Dear Sir,
Your and Your Society's friend and Servant
Thomas Carlyle.

It should not be necessary to underscore that Carlyle himself was obviously wise enough to question the most extreme pretensions of the movement, doubting if they are on "the right path" though convinced that they were "in the right direction." It is equally clear that he was not so much "influenced" by them as ready to accept that they were correct in believing that they and he were in agreement. Their "spirit" is one with which he is in "entire sympathy," and he finds "little or nothing to dissent from." This goes much further than a "flirtation" or coolly expressing "some interest"; and even Louis Cazamian underestimates Carlyle's enthusiasm when he speaks of the "general but intangible influence" of Saint Simon. Yet he also makes exactly the right point: "It is wrong to forget, as so many of his readers do, that beside the dark raging spirit of the older Carlyle must be put the noble and perhaps more perspicacious enthusiasm of his glowing youth."[17] He implies, and we may accept, that the chapter on "Organic Filaments" (*Sartor*, Book III, ch. vii) and perhaps much else, was not written without the movement's being in mind.

Carlyle did not need the French to teach him simple radicalism, but he was obviously moved to these direct comments by both economic hardship and the peculiar appeal of the Saint-Simonians. The rents the Carlyles paid for their farms were high, tenancies were scarce, and though they were not exactly among "the poor" themselves, Carlyle himself knew poverty and felt keenly for it.[18] This, with the "new" Christian beliefs, the Saint-Simonians' teaching on economics, and their doctrine (already expressed by Carlyle) that society must find a new faith in order to be regenerated, was a powerful combination. It was exactly at this period that he was writing *Sartor*.

17. Louis Cazamian, trans. E. K. Brown, *Carlyle* (New York, 1966 [1932]; French original, Paris, 1913), pp. 127–128.

18. His radicalism arises less from personal grievance than a deep concern for "the poor"; nor is this shown only in *Chartism, Past and Present* and in *Sartor* (as in III, x, "The Dandiacal Body," or Teufelsdröckh's toast "Die Sache der Armen"— "The Cause of the Poor"), but in some of his best verbal sketches and letters about neighbors or men and women casually met, e.g., Froude, *Carlyle* III, 253 and 321, 269, 318, 325–326. They may be contradicted but are not annulled by later aberrations.

Froude's comments about Carlyle's radicalism at this time are a little vague, since made mainly in connection with his correspondence with Jeffrey. But Jeffrey's daughter refused to allow Froude to see Carlyle's letters and (because of his mis-editing of the *Reminiscences*) she would not let him quote from the letters her father had written to Carlyle.[19] The consequence is that from Froude we have mere inferences, indirect summaries, and the bland anecdote about "the wise old man." Clearly, whatever he wrote, Carlyle did not believe in a violent uprising any more than the Saint-Simonians, who were totally non-violent; and it may have been reasonable enough for Froude to write, "It is likely, too, that he had come to some hasty conclusions on the intractable problems of social life, and believed changes to be possible and useful which a fuller knowledge of mankind showed him to be dreams."[20] Yet at thirty-five Carlyle was no young firebrand; he had passed his first youth well before he observed the radical troubles of 1819–1820; and though he may have gone on to relapse into thinking that some social problems were "intractable," it is not in the least necessary for us still to look at him as he was in the 1830's through the eyes of his elderly biographer of the '80's.

Carlyle had written to Goethe about the Saint-Simonians on 31 August 1830; Goethe's reply to "hold aloof" was in October; and Carlyle's immediate response was to tell his brother John about it, adding "Nevertheless send me their Books by the very first chance"[21] —and this was his second request for them. In London, John was seeing Charles Buller (Thomas's former pupil), who had been over to Paris in August, had met the Saint-Simonians there, and had seen Carlyle's letter in their hands. Even John says that Buller spoke of them as blind to what he called the "hidden satire" in Carlyle's reply;[22] but, as we have seen, there is nothing satirical in it to miss.

Meanwhile Carlyle's enthusiasm was warm enough for him to have done something for his new friends in return. As he explained in the next letter to John:

I have translated Saint-Simon's *Nouveau Christianisme*, a heterodox Pamphlet (about 40 Review pages), which I mean soon to send *you*. I have pre-

19. Froude, *Carlyle* II, 32 and 132–139. I expect to publish soon an essay on Froude's misadventures in editing.
20. Ibid., II, 136.
21. 12 Nov. 1830, MS: NLS, 522.89
22. John Carlyle–TC, 17 Feb. 1831, MS: NLS, 1775A.138.

fixed a very short introduction; and you may try whether any pamphlet-printing Bookseller (some Socinian, or Anti-Church, or quite indifferent character) will give you the matter of five pounds for the copyright thereof. . . . It contains several strange ideas, not without a large spice of truth; is ill-written, but easily read, and deserves a reading.[23]

For the time being he withheld it. Yet, as we shall see, though he wished to remain anonymous, he meant to publish it.

Saint Simon's *Nouveau Christianisme*, though a compact work, can be summed up fairly briefly; and its chief emphasis, as Carlyle saw, was to demand help for *la classe la plus pauvre*, although it does also include something about historical change coming in cycles. The phrase about "the poor" recurs again and again. For its main message was simple: Christianity meant loving one's neighbor and, now that society had developed, this could no longer be seen merely as a personal duty but required a change in society itself. The *Two Note Books* show clearly how this was the aspect of Saint Simon's work which Carlyle most immediately responded to. He notes, in an observation of his own:

A man with £200,000 a year eats the *whole* fruit of 6,666 men's labour thro' a year: for you can get a stout spademan to work and maintain himself for that sum of £30. . . . What do those highly beneficed individuals *do* to society for their wages? *Kill Partridges.* CAN this last. No, by the soul that is in man, it cannot and will not and shall not!—[pp. 159–60].

His radicalism has been underrated. Having read Sir Walter Scott's *History of Scotland* he speaks of the Scottish nobility as

A selfish, ferocious, famishing, unprincipled set of hyaenas, from whom at no time and in no way has the country derived any benefit. The day is coming when these our modern hyaenas (tho' *toothless*, still mischievous and greedy beyond limit) will quickly I hope, *be paid off.* "Canaille fainéante, que faites-vous là? Down with your double-barrels; take spades . . . and work or die!" [p. 169]. . . .

September   Rain! Rain! Rain! The crops all lying tattered, scat-
(about the 28th).   tered and unripe; the winter's bread still under the soaking clouds! God pity the poor! [p. 173] . . .

The Whigs in office, and Baron Brougham Lord Chancellor! Haystacks and corn-stacks burning all over the South and Middle of England! Where will it end? Revolution on the back of Revolution for a century yet? *Re-*

23. 19 Dec. 1830, MS: NLS, 522.90.

ligion, the cement of *Society* is not here. . . . Were the Landlords all hanged, and their estates given to the poor, we should be (economically) much happier perhaps for the space of thirty years. . . . Alas! that there is no Church . . . [pp. 178–179].[24]

There is much else than this, and there are such letters as one of 21 August 1830 to John, about their brother Alick, who had said he

could not keep this Farm any longer than Whitsunday; finding it a ruinous concern. . . . I often calculate that the land is all let some thirty per cent too high, and that before it can be reduced . . . the whole agricultural tools (which are Capital) broken in pieces and burnt in the Landlords' fire— to warm his pointers with. *Ach Gott!* the time is sick and out of joint: . . . Since the time of Nero and Jesus Christ there is no record of such embarrassments, and crying.[25]

What struck fire from Carlyle was not the theoretical ideas about history uttered by Saint Simon, but something like his native radicalism. His doubts of political reform arose not from indifference but because he thought it a sham; at this time, he recalls Edward Irving "found *Democracy* a thing forbidden," whereas to himself it was "a thing inevitable."[26] He could hardly be in Jeffrey's company without being provoked to outrage him, so that at last his friend refused to support him in any application to a university since it would be a waste of time with such "doctrines" and such a "tone."[27] For his part, Carlyle was clear that he enjoyed offending. When a dinner party is arranged for him, he exults, "I . . . astonished them, I fear, with my exposition of Belief and Radicalism"; and, at other times, "I appear like

24. This must have been written soon after Wellington's resignation (he was succeeded by Lord Grey) on 16 November 1830. The burning haystacks came from the great laborers' revolt, in the name of "Captain Swing," already ablaze and reported in the press. This also might be suggestive of much, as for example the wider British context of Carlyle's radicalism; the way in which this was, to an uncertain extent, related to French radicalism and revolution; the manner in which, as Carlyle is aware, the laborers' destruction of threshing machines is the practical issue of his general sense that the age had become merely a mechanical one; and the expression of much of this, almost immediately, in his essay "Characteristics," *Edinburgh Review* 54 (Dec. 1831) e.g., 367. See also E. J. Hobsbawm and George Rudé, *Captain Swing* (Harmondsworth, Middlesex, 1973), esp. pp. 62–66, 183–184.

25. MS: NLS, 522.86.

26. *Reminiscences,* II, 197.

27. Letter of Jan. 1834, in Wilson, *Carlyle,* II, 353. Much earlier Jeffrey made his stand even clearer by telling Carlyle not to despise his "fellow-scribblers" who were "as much above" his Dumfriesshire "hedgers and ditchers, as *they* are above their collies" (p. 131).

a wild monstrous Orson," or "my utterances fall like red-hot aëro-lithes."[28] He despised any Radicals he met, for "Radicalism enough I can utter for myself . . . enough and to spare."[29]

It would need more than an essay to discuss fully even the first moves in Carlyle's association with the Saint-Simonians from 1830 to 1832, especially since one of the next developments was his meeting with John Stuart Mill. Mill himself, as already mentioned, was known to Gustave d'Eichthal and had recently been approached in hope of his conversion. His own connection with the new movement can best be sought in the first two volumes of his *Letters* (including those to Carlyle) and his later opinion in his *Autobiography*. Less easily available is the selection edited by Eugène d'Eichthal, *John Stuart Mill: correspondance inédite avec Gustave d'Eichthal, (1828–1842)–(1864–1871)* (Paris, 1898). At this early period, however, Carlyle's opinion was caught by Mill's anonymous writings in the *Examiner*, which he saw at once were indebted to the new movement, though they did not directly mention it. A letter to John of 21 January 1830 says that the *Examiner* "spoke lately of the Saint-Simonians (whom I love and pity and dissent from)"; the reference is to the first of Mill's series on "The Spirit of the Age."[30] The direct result was to be that, on coming up to London, Carlyle hunted out the author—as Mill told Sterling (20–22 October 1831), adding that "his acquaintance is the only substantial good" he had got from them.[31]

Meanwhile John Carlyle had sent on a further packet of the movement's publications from London—as Carlyle confessed to Goethe;[32] and though it is not clear what was in them it certainly included the *Doctrine de Saint Simon: Exposition Première Année 1829* (Paris,

28. To Dr. John Carlyle, 10 Feb. 1833, MS: NLS, 523.11; and to J. S. Mill, 22 Feb. 1833, MS: NLS, 618.15.

29. To Mill, 19 Nov. 1832, MS: NLS, 618.11.

30. Mill's series appeared between 23 January and 29 May. It is interesting that Carlyle saw the Saint-Simonian influence in the first essay before he was told about it or knew anything of the authorship. See also F. von Hayek, *The Spirit of the Age: John Stuart Mill* (Chicago, 1940).

31. *The Earlier Letters of John Stuart Mill, 1812–1848*, ed. F. E. Mineka, (Toronto and London, 1963), I, 85–86.

32. Letter of 22 Jan. 1831, in *Correspondence between Goethe and Carlyle*, pp 252–60, in which Carlyle added, "They seem to me to be earnest, zealous and nowise ignorant men, but wandering in strange paths," and "I have every disposition to follow your advice" though he looked on them "as a true and remarkable Sign of these Times."

1830), and some numbers at least of *Le Globe*. Gustave then wrote
(on 27 April 1831)[33] an enthusiastic reply to Carlyle's letter of 9
August 1830. He explained that, being too busy to write sooner, he
had at least sent publications expounding the Doctrine, "L'Exposition, les lettres sur la religion et la politique, les Collections du Globe
et de L'Organisateur." He recalls the changes since his last letter, the
July Revolution and the fall of Charles X, on whom Carlyle had also
remarked at the end of his last letter: "Your foolish old King has
come to England." The Saint-Simonians had, in fact, stood apart from
the revolution (which had come on them unexpectedly) and were
soon disappointed by its results except in its destruction of part of the
old order and new opportunities it gave for making themselves
known, so that d'Eichthal's letter gives too rosy a picture of their
progress. It is true that they had had a remarkable success in gaining
thousands of temporary followers, and of ensuring that there was
hardly an educated person in Europe who had not heard of their
ideas. But their achievements all lay in the spoken and printed word,
which had little immediate effect, though a remote and lasting influence. The mission to Belgium, for example, which he mentions,
was mainly ill-received. Nevertheless d'Eichthal writes:

Notre temps etait venu. Disciples, de celui qui a donné aux hommes l'evangile nouveau, l'evangile du classement selon la capacité et de la rétribution
suivant les œuvres, nous devions paraître hardiment sur la scène du monde,
pour reconcilier les opprimés et les oppresseurs, changer les ennemis en
frères, et les camps opposés en une famille tendrement unie. En depit des
Sarcasmes, des menaces, des contrariétés et des difficultés de tout genre,
nous l'avons fait. Aujourd'hui une feuille quotidienne, distribue . . . notre
parole régenérative. . . . Depuis quelques semaines nos missions se croisent
sur le sol de la France; partout notre parole est desirée. . . . En même temps
la *famille nouvelle* s'accroît et se fortifie sans cesse. Les noms sacrés de
Pere de *mère* de *frère* de *sœur*, de *Fils* de *Fille*, échangés entre nous, sont
l'expression de plus en plus vraie des sentiments qui animent cette *communion d'élus*, bien plus supérieure encore au monde qui l'environne, que
la famille Chrétienne ne l'était au monde Romain. . . .

Cependant notre *Apostolat*, avant coureur du *Sacerdoce vraiment Catho-
lique*, ne doit pas rester circonscrit entre les frontières de la France. Partout
où les masses populaires, impatients du joug, commencent à se révolter
contre la *féodalité Bourgeoise*, le temps est venu pour nous de nous pré-

33. MS: NLS, 1765.200–201.

senter comme des Messagers de Paix. . . . C'est ainsi que les troubles de la
Belgique ont été le signal de notre apparition dans ce pays. . . .

Ce grand événement politique que vient de s'accomplir en Angleterre,
nous prouve que là aussi le temps est venu pour nous nous montrer. . . .

D'Eichthal goes on to mention that the disciples already have contacts
among Owenites, Unitarians, and even young political economists, as
he might see from a series of articles on "The Spirit of the Age"; but
there was no one he would rather meet in London than Carlyle if it
were possible. He hoped, too, that Carlyle would let him have his
opinion of the Saint-Simonian Doctrine, ask for any necessary explanations, and tell him what he thought might be useful about the
present state of Britain.

In the present connection it is Carlyle's reply which is interesting,
since once again there is not the least hidden satire about it but the
warmest interest and good will. Invited to ask for explanations, he
does not hide that he still finds the greatest difficulty in the religious
question. D'Eichthal was perhaps as deeply concerned about the new
religion as any of his "brothers," and the fervor of the Saint-Simonians
(as Carlyle might have seen from reports in the *Globe*) had gone far
beyond that of their founder. Yet Carlyle expresses delight at being
on friendly terms:

To see a little Brotherhood of such men, strong in Faith, uniting itself as
a forlorn hope in the Good fight, and heroically, with such weapons and
tactics as it has, making front against the boundless armaments of Evil,—
this is a spectacle full of significance, perhaps of pathetic beauty, for all
good men. . . .

I may say, with great sincerity, that my respect for your Brethren and
Chiefs, personally considered, has not diminished but increased, on closer
survey; that I discern in you men of clear intellectual insight, of decisive
character, animated with a noble zeal which enlightens as well as inflames.
. . . Farther, I may say that your speculative opinions, political, moral,
philosophical, for the most part carry their own evidence, and find hearty
assent with me: often, indeed, I discern therein only a more decisive systematic exposition of what I had already gathered elsewhere. Especially
important I reckon your delineations of our actual No-Society, of the Critical and the Organic alternation in man's history; your strongly emphatic
precept of our duty towards the Poor; which, properly speaking, is but the
old duty of Love, of Mercy towards the weak, whether weak by want of

pecuniary or other means; and has been and must be the basis of all social Morality. Neither can it be doubted that your motto and maxim, *To each according to his capacity, to each capacity according to its works*, is the aim of all true social arrangements.[34]

We may notice that though an interest in the theoretical ideas of the movement about historical development is mentioned, Carlyle is more concerned with what it has to say about Man's duty not only to "the poor" but to "the weak." As a "Scientific Doctrine," he could "subscribe to it" with "few reservations," but the difficulty still lies in their religion. He cannot accept it unless it means no more than that the Universe is a symbol of God, and "our Gospel" and the history of Man. But, if this is so, it is no more than "the Religion of all Thinkers . . . for the last half century: of Goethe . . . of Schiller, of Lessing, Jacobi, Herder." Even so, they would be wrong to "impute these strictures to wilful blindness, to unfriendly indifference, to anything but honest doubt." There then follows a tribute to the movement in the same phrases as the final reference to it in *Sartor*: "I have said to myself, and still repeat: Here too are men that know and feel thro' their whole soul the grand and almost forgotten truth, *Man is still Man*, and glory in it as they ought; with such I am heartily, if not Brother in Saint Simon . . . yet Brother in God." He regrets that he cannot meet them in London, but invites them to Craigenputtoch; and finally, he concludes by speaking of the agitation for Reform: "Democracy has arisen, and will never lie down again. . . ." Of the three "Sects busy among us," he characterizes the Christians as "even worthy," the Whigs as "Unbelievers whose principle is *Dilettantism*," and the Radical or Utilitarian Unbelievers, "for whom *Soul* is synonymous with *Stomach*; an *honest* class, of whom there is hope."

Clearly this is the language of *Sartor*,[35] just as one might expect; which is not to say that because Carlyle uses the same phrases in letters and in other current writing, any easy relationships are necessarily significant. Yet, at least, we should be aware of them so that they can if necessary be taken into account as much as other echoes so carefully recorded, for example, in the apparatus of C. F. Harrold's edition. For *Sartor* was still in progress. "I calculate on finishing early

34. 17 May 1831, MS: Bibliothèque de l'Arsenal.
35. For example, as well as "Man is still Man," Harrold, *Sartor*, p. 296, there are "Soul is not synonymous with Stomach," p. 159 (cf. p. 117), and frequent references to "Dilettantism."

next month," writes Carlyle to John (6 June 1831);[36] and in the same letter he says once again that he is "very anxious" to see more Saint-Simonian publications and that they would be "a great delight here." They are the only publications he asks for. It is true that, as in writing to John Bowring of the *Westminster Review*, he can be rather supercilious about "our wondrous . . . Friends" (11 July 1831),[37] but we can count on his comments to his brother John as entirely unaffected. The new friends seem to be always in his mind, and once he goes up to London, with the manuscript of *Sartor*, there are numerous references to them in his letters and Journal.

As everyone knows, Carlyle had no luck in disposing of *Sartor*— nor with the placing of his translation of *Nouveau Christianisme*. Perhaps because no one responded it was lent to Bowring, who had first met the Saint-Simonians in Paris in July 1830, when (as he said) he "looked at them closely" and "frequently discussed matters with their chiefs."[38] So, when Carlyle wrote to d'Eichthal (3 October, 1831), to say that he was in London, and that it would give him the "greatest pleasure" to see him there, he added:

. . . I had resolved on sending you an English version of the *Nouveau Christianisme*, which I executed many months ago in Scotland: but the Manuscript which is in Dr Bowring's hands cannot be procured at this moment, and must wait another opportunity. If on any other occasion it could be of service to you, it is heartily at your disposal.[39]

Within a week he was actually to meet d'Eichthal, as he had hoped, and they must have discussed the work then. But it was not until 15 February 1832 that it was actually sent to d'Eichthal with a letter from Carlyle:

L'éditeur du "Magazine" se décidant à ne pas publier cette traduction, je la mets, selon ma promesse, à votre entière disposition. Je vous autorise pleinement à l'imprimer ou à la brûler, ou à en faire ce que vous voudrez, à la seule condition que *mon nom ne soit pas mentionné*.

La "Notice du traducteur" sera sans doute inutile à présent, je vous l'envoie cependant aussi; j'y exprime sincèrement mon impression sur l'influence possible de Saint-Simon et de son écrit sur notre public anglais,

---

36. MS: NLS, 522.100.   37. Forthcoming in *CL*, V, 300.
38. 4 March 1831, MS: NLS, 1765.196, in which Bowring had also told Carlyle that he would be including an essay on the Saint-Simonians in the *Westminster Review*: "you should have done the deed."
39. MS: Bibliothèque de l'Arsenal.

et cela dans des termes plutôt en dessous qu'au dessus de l'opinion que je me suis faite de ce dernier écrit (ce à quoi j'étais naturellement forcé). Ma tâche, en ci qui concerne ce sujet, est, je le crois, maintenant accomplie.

J'espère vous voir bientôt et avoir de bonnes nouvelles de Paris, et je suis, cher Monsieur, votre tout dévoué.

T. CARLYLE.[40]

The loss of the manuscript has raised a great deal of curiosity and some special problems. The odd thing is that there has been more wish to imagine what happened to it than to read what Saint Simon wrote that so aroused Carlyle. For the introduction and translation are unlikely to be found now, while the sense of Carlyle's translation is obviously there in the original. Yet it is the unattainable that has drawn almost all the attention.

We even find Hill Shine, for example, turning away from Saint-Simon's work to follow Miriam Thrall in saying (frankly enough) that "it would be pleasant to think that Carlyle's hand could be found" in an article in *Fraser's* entitled "Letter on the Doctrine of Saint-Simon" (5 [July 1832], 666–669).[41] Yet Miriam Thrall gives no evidence, and she had a decidedly offhand way of appropriating for Carlyle articles she also thought it pleasant to think his but which it is a relief to find the new *Wellesley Index* attributing to others.[42] Hill Shine's article on the subject, in *Notes and Queries* (171[1936], 291–293), is just as inconclusive, although much more thorough; for, in the end, it claims no more than that it is an interesting possibility that Carlyle may have shown his translation and preface to someone connected with *Fraser's*, who remembered some of it when he wrote the "Letter." Why not? It is a negative conclusion presented as a positive one; and what is interesting is that it reveals the limitations of this type of "evidence," since even when the passages from the "Letter" are shown to be like some in other writings by Carlyle, they suggest no more than that their writer may have read and remembered some of Carlyle's other writings. But the argument is spoken of as "evi-

---

40. Eugène d'Eichthal, "Carlyle et le Saint-Simonisme," pp. 304–305, translated from Carlyle's original letter, which is now untraced.

41. Miriam Thrall, *Rebellious Fraser's* (New York, 1934), pp. 268–272. As well as the "Letter," she refers to an article, "Fashionable Novels" (April 1830), 318–335, and another on Bulwer's novels, (June 1830), 509–532.

42. *The Wellesley Index*, II (London, etc., 1972), attributes the "Letter" to J. A. Heraud, "Fashionable Novels" to William Maginn, perhaps with J. A. Heraud, and the article on Bulwer to Maginn, perhaps with Heraud.

dence" and with interlocking repetition is twice cited within a few pages in *Carlyle and the Saint-Simonians* (pp. 92 n., 96 n.).

For even if Hill Shine were correct, it would be impossible to disentangle the lost preface from the vapidities of Heraud and Maginn.[43] Yet we know, in fact, that Carlyle thought *Nouveau Christianisme* partly "strange," partly truthful, and that it deserved reading; and, if we are to believe him, he may even have found it for a time a work in which there was "little or nothing to dissent from," logical, clear, precise, and containing "the basis of all social Morality." It only remains to turn to it.

Because *Nouveau Christianisme* is so comprehensive though short, in discussing it here I single out only a few of its most remarkable features if we think of it in connection with Carlyle—leaving a great deal on one side, including almost all its remarks about historical development.[44]

At first, part of its doctrine may well seem something of an anticlimax, since Saint Simon's Christianity was "new" partly because it seemed new to him as a self-made convert. Thus its basic message is: "Tu aimeras ton prochain comme toi-même" . . . (titlepage); "Dieu a dit: *Les hommes doivent se conduire en frères à l'égard les uns des autres*; ce principe sublime renferme tout ce qu'il y a de divin dans la religion chrétienne" (p. 2); "La nouvelle organisation chrétienne déduira les institutions temporelles, ainsi que les institutions spirituelles, du principe que *tous les hommes doivent se conduire à l'égard les uns des autres comme des frères*. Elle dirigera toutes les institutions, de quelque nature qu'elles soient, vers l'accroissement du bien-être de la classe la plus pauvre" . . . (p. 8); . . . "*La religion doit diriger la société vers le grand but de l'amélioration la plus rapide possible du sort de la classe la plus pauvre*" . . . (p. 12); "Jésus-Christ a promis la vie éternelle à ceux qui auraient le plus contribué à l'amélioration de l'existence de la classe la plus pauvre sous le rapport moral et sous le rapport physique. . ." (p. 15), etc.

43. It would not be at all pleasant to think it was by Carlyle, whom we would have had to suppose capable of writing a letter to Fraser signed "Your obedient Servant, FAIR-PLAY." It is a typical "dog's meat" contribution of thrown-out scraps.

44. I have followed the text of the copy sent to Carlyle, number (ii) above in the first parcel, sent to him with d'Eichthal's letter of 29 April 1830. There is a modern translation by Felix Markham in his *Henri de Saint-Simon: Social Organization and the Science of Man and Other Writings* (New York, 1964); an earlier version is *New Christianity; by Henri de St. Simon*, translated from the original French by Rev. J. E. Smith, A.M. (London, 1834).

Saint Simon then accuses the Roman Catholic Church of being chiefly concerned with perpetuating its own power, of lacking the knowledge to guide its followers, and of showing its unfitness to govern by its actions in its own papal states. On the other hand he regards Protestants as, in certain ways, even less ready to admit a connection between their religion and the constitution of society; and he declares that the effect of Luther was beneficial only because he was so effectually critical of Rome: "Luther a rendu un service capital à la civilisation; sans lui, le papisme eût complètement asservi l'esprit humain aux idées superstitieuses" (p. 37). He did little constructive:

La partie de ses travaux relative a la réorganisation du christianisme a été bien inférieure à ce qu'elle aurait dû être: au lieu de prendre les mesures nécessaires pour accroître l'importance sociale de la religion Chrétienne, il a fait rétrograder cette religion jusqu'à son point de depart; il l'a replacée en dehors de l'organisation sociale . . . [p. 55].

Luther also erred in directing men's attention too exclusively to the Bible, which not only made it difficult for his followers to change their ideas as society developed but actually encouraged political ends contrary to public welfare. For the Bible led to an impracticable belief in Man's equality, thus preventing Protestants from working for a social system of the kind Saint Simon believed in, which would entrust only the ablest men with the direction of science, art and industry.

The New Christianity, on the other hand, recognized that Christ gave his followers the task of organizing mankind in order to aid the poor, at the same time using no methods but gentleness, persuasion and example (p. 39). The Pope is enjoined, therefore, to take action to create a social organization, and to use the resources of science, art and industry to improve the lot of the poor far more than he might by any amount of charity. He should recognize, too, that he ought to do everything in his power to prevent war, for "L'esprit du christianisme est la douceur, la bonté, la charité, et, par dessus tout, la loyauté; ses armes sont la persuasion et la démonstration" (p. 25); "il avait remplacé la loi du plus fort; le droit de conquête n'était plus considéré comme le plus légitime de tous les droits" (p. 43).

Saint Simon's *Nouveau Christianisme* is the expression of his doctrine in its simplest and most fundamental form, and such a partial summary as this drastically reduces its arguments to something still more basic. But this was the work which Carlyle was persuaded to give special attention to, and in 1831–1832 it is the one he chose to translate. What is really a matter for regret is not that his manuscript and its preface have been lost, but that he never carried out his plan of writing a separate article about the movement. There are many other important points: for example, its demand that the inheritance of property (or, at least, of the means of production) should cease, which is neither a point that Carlyle can have missed nor one he questions. There is his basic agreement with them, as he says himself, that "with regard to Morals strictly so called, it is in Society . . . that Morality begins; here at least it takes an altogether new form."[45] There is the manner in which the Saint-Simonians write with the greatest respect of the period of the Middle Ages, which obviously chimed in with Carlyle's beliefs, although theirs was not the only influence of this kind he may have felt. Saint Simon even most markedly insists that the "new" religion must make full use of the arts, which might be thought repugnant to Carlyle, although I am not clear that there is good evidence for this. The church of his parents was one of drastic simplicity of style, yet it had failed to hold him. For anyone wishing to trace general influences, there is still much to be said about the possible effect of the Saint-Simonians on Carlyle.

For the present I suggest that the association gives us some clues to understanding Carlyle at this time; they forcibly remind us how sharply his opinions were to change; they should dissuade us from generalizing about him without specifying the period; and they might incline us to look on the Carlyle of the thirties as a radical writer. Lastly, it might encourage us to question some accepted comments and return us to the position of Emery Neff, of being willing to see *Sartor* as, in content, "a synthesis of the ideas of the German philosophers and the Saint-Simonians."[46]

For example, although Neff's work preceded Harrold's edition of *Sartor*, we must surely question the latter's comments on "The Social Doctrines in *Sartor*":

In spite of Teufeldröckh's "radicalism"—which reflects Carlyle's indignation at the economic injustice he saw in Annandale—there is at the heart of *Sartor* a profound conservatism. Its social doctrine is *étatiste*; its collec-

45. "Characteristics," *Works*, XXVIII, 11; cf. "Signs of the Times," *Works*, XXVII, 78–79.
46. Emery Neff, *Carlyle and Mill* (New York, 1924), p. 172.

tivistic implications point towards the super-state. Though it may at times suggest socialism, it expresses only the socialism of responsibility hierarchically administered which Carlyle inherited from Calvin.[47]

This curious remark illustrates two weaknesses of some Carlylean comment: the tendency to explain Carlyle himself mainly by systematic cross-reference, and then to justify conclusions by appealing to one's own previous pronouncements. For Harrold's footnote here refers first to pp. xxxiii–xxxv, which say nothing about Calvinism that is not equally applicable to almost any form of Christian belief; then pp. 236–237 are marked, as it happens, chiefly by the first reference to Saint Simon and *l'âge d'or*, but their relevance is elusive; and pp. 244 ff. are the chapter "Organic Filaments" (III, vii). In addition, the remark about Carlyle's being *étatiste* is borrowed (without acknowledgment) from Cazamian's *Carlyle*, "His social doctrine was *étatiste*, it never was and never could be socialist."[48] It is really all nonsense, which is not helped by some confusion about the meaning of *étatisme*.

Cazamian appears to distinguish between state ownership of the means of production (or state control) and "socialism" itself, which presumably implies ownership and perhaps democratic control by the people. Historically *Etatisme* is said to have been a movement started (by Bismarck among others) as a counter to socialism.[49] But while it may have been comprehensible to use the term in this rather special sense when Cazamian wrote in 1913, it is dubious now, and it is impossible to make "profound conservatism" lie down with "collectivist implications" and "the super-state." It is confusing a moral and a political outlook, and it is no doubt missing the point to talk about collectivism and socialism in connection with *Sartor*. The Saint-Simonians wanted to put their moral beliefs into political effect, though rather unsure where they were leading them. Carlyle is even more uncertain; but it hardly makes a conservative of him. Finally, to put everything down to "Calvinism" (even with the cross-references) is another bad habit.

Of course, it is an extremely interesting question how far Carlyle's views about society were affected by Calvinism *as he knew it* both

47. Pp. xlix–l. Harrold's footnote simply reads: "see pp. xxxiii–xxxv, 236–37, and 244 ff."
48. P. 126.
49. *Nouveau Larousse Illustré* (Paris, 1897–1907), IV, 326, under "Etatisme."

by upbringing and by later experience; and it is certainly arguable that, in the long term, its influence was stronger than Saint-Simonianism. But there were differences too deep for it to be right to speak as if Carlyle could reconcile his parents' religion with that of Saint Simon: Calvinism teaches that even good works outside the Christian faith are sinful, whereas Carlyle's new friends insisted that their religion was based on good works and strongly denounced any more complicated theology. The Saint-Simonian missionaries found, in fact, that Scotland was much less favorable to their propaganda than England.[50] The idea that the two faiths are reconcilable may lie in a general tendency to ascribe what are really national or personal characteristics to something vaguely called "Calvinism." Yet what Carlyle may certainly have derived from the Burgher church to which his family belonged was an independence of commitment to the existing social order which allowed him to question it as freely as French Jews did.

The further the association between Carlyle and the Saint-Simonians is pursued, the less simple it is, and what their ultimate influence on him was it is hard to say. Even the story of their friendship is not over, though their correspondence was at an end. For the present it must be broken off, but when the next few volumes in the *Collected Letters* are published, it will be easy to trace that story for a year or two more. After that, as Carlyle said, it disappears as a movement; and, unlike Mill, Carlyle did not later in his life renew his friendship with individuals who belonged to it, though they were by no means forgotten.

Yet about the nature of their influence on Carlyle a few points can be made. One is that the writings of the Saint-Simonians were so voluminous that they have been made to assume various forms, which is one reason why the present study has kept as closely as possible to *Nouveau Christianisme*. Even in their own day their doctrines meant (and were intended to mean) different things to different men. Yet nothing is so clear as that the following they gained in Britain was a radical one, including such men as Mill and his friends, Albany Fonblanque, Bowring, and W. J. Fox, and that they provoked to exasperated comment men such as Robert Southey in the *Quarterly Re-*

50. D'Eichthal was hopeful, but was strongly advised by William Burns about "prejudices and obstacles" to be met with in Scotland (Pankhurst, pp. 43 and 69), where the movement appears to have made less headway than elsewhere.

view,[51] Tennyson and Hallam in private letters, and reporters for the *Times*.[52] A related question about the influence of the Saint-Simonians is how far they can be said to have been "authoritarian," or even "totalitarian," terms used by Georg C. Iggers in *The Cult of Authority* (The Hague, 1958). It is sometimes said, or implied, that this was an element in their appeal to Carlyle. But this is, once again, all part of the endeavor to read his earlier life in order to *make* it correspond to what we know of his later career. Of course they were not democratic, but they were curiously naïve about politics. They believed in having leaders, but somehow supposed they would arise from among their fellows, chosen or selected by popular acclaim. It was a dangerous view, but it arose chiefly from naïveté as Carlyle may have suspected from the first and soon came to see clearly. By using the expression "totalitarian," Iggers generally means that they had a view of society and how it should be governed which saw it as a whole, and which laid down that science, industry, the arts, politics, and everything in the state were interconnected and must be controlled. (So far this is certainly "authoritarian," a word with different implications.) Yet Iggers, in his more recent introduction to his English translation, *The Doctrine of Saint-Simon: An Exposition* (New York, 1972), has remarked that he would now place the emphasis differently, noting that the more strongly authoritarian note is "for the most part absent in the writings" of Saint Simon himself;[53] and the work itself could not leave us in doubt of the Saint-Simonians' selflessness, their wish to appeal to all classes, the moral basis of their doctrine, their aim to serve "the poor," and their concern to open government to all men of ability. As for their being authoritarian, some recent implicit objections already read oddly: most of their proposals to regulate and coordinate society have long been accepted by the mildest British liberal; and that they are at all remarkable is chiefly in the way in which Saint Simon, and no doubt Carlyle,

51. *Quarterly Review*, 45 (July 1831), 407–450, describing the new movement as "blasphemous and dangerous," inspired by "an adventurer—half profligate, half madman," who was aiming at "a new distribution of property": Carlyle justly called it "trivial, purblind and on the whole erroneous and worthless" (to Macvey Napier, 6 Feb. 1832, British Museum Add. Mss. 34615) and "altogether miserable; written in the spirit of a Parish Precentor: he knows what they are *not* . . . but nothing of what they *are*." To Dr. John Carlyle, 14 Sept. 1831, MS: NLS, 610.17.

52. To Tennyson, the movement's existence was "a proof of the immense mass of evil . . . extant in the nineteenth century"; the *Times* recommended ducking its leaders in a horse pond (R. K. P. Pankhurst, p. 47).

53. P. v.

transcended limitations of thought which restricted most of their contemporaries.

How Carlyle grew away from the Saint-Simonians is another question. By November 1831 he had first-hand reports on the movement from his brother, Dr. John Carlyle, in Paris who told him: "they must fail, I still think, very rapidly if no second revolution come to further them"; and, even then, Carlyle replied: "I was much instructed by your sketches of Saint Simonism; concerning which I do not differ far from you in opinion or prediction. It is an upholstery aggregation, not a Promethean creation; therefore cannot live long: yet the very attempt to build the old dilapidated Temple, were it only with deals and canvas is significant."[54]

When he came to write *The French Revolution* what he told Froude appears to be true: it made him a changed man. He begins to judge by practicalities and the whole work leads up to the "whiff of grape-shot" which disperses its disorders. Even after this, Carlyle should still be judged by what he writes, and not by generalities derived from his complete *Works*; but, as he reviews a "Parliamentary History of the French Revolution," written by two old Saint-Simonians, it is the divorce between their doctrines and what they actually approve that strikes him. They, too, have become conventional and jingle "with formulas"; and their "strangest doctrine" is "that the French Revolution was at bottom an attempt to realise Christianity, and fairly put it in action, in our world." It is a view which he already countered in his own history: it is not only outrageous, but not "profitable."[55] Even so, this is written in a tone of regret. So are all Carlyle's allusions, once the Saint-Simonians had certainly failed. They tried once more "for the salvation of the world," and "the men are to be honoured and loved in this, that they have dared to be men."[56]

54. 29 Oct. 1831, MS: NLS, 1775A.159; 13 Nov. 1831, MS: NLS, 522.105.
55. *Works*, XXIX, 21.
56. To John Stuart Mill, 16 June 1832, MS: NLS, 618.5.

Carlyle and the Logic-Choppers: J. S. Mill and Diderot

EDWARD SPIVEY

John Stuart Mill's companion essays on Bentham (1838) and Coleridge (1840) were intended to clarify two modes of perception and thought which had come to dominate the intellectual life of England in the early nineteenth century. While each of the essays is informative in itself, each gains considerably when read in the light of the other. Mill makes a number of specific comparisons between the two thinkers but leaves most of the synthesis to the reader. Less attention has been given to a similar pair of essays by Thomas Carlyle which attempt to set forth two of the leading figures of the preceding century. Written in 1832, some six years before Mill's essays, Carlyle's review of Boswell's *Life of Samuel Johnson* is one of his best-known efforts. The companion essay on Denis Diderot,[1] however, is seldom considered along with it. Like Mill's two essays, those of Carlyle illuminate each other, and they do much to clarify our conceptions of Carlyle's thought in 1832.

My object in the present study is to examine the two essays in the light of Mill's greatly differing responses to them. "Diderot" will be emphasized because it brought forth Mill's first open acknowledgment of dissent from Carlyle's views. Having formerly allowed Carlyle to think of him as a disciple, upon reading "Diderot" he decided to declare his intellectual independence. Henceforth the nature of his relationship with Carlyle changed in important ways, although Carlyle for a time refused to recognize those changes. Mill's letters began to reveal more reliance upon his own judgment and less willingness to acquiesce in Carlyle's opinions or to let them pass unchallenged. By investigating the essays in conjunction with Mill's reactions to them, I hope to elucidate two closely related matters: the negative aspects

1. *Works*, XXVIII, 177–248; subsequent references are included in the text. Carlyle's letters are quoted from A. Carlyle, *CMSB*; Mill's letters are quoted from *The Earlier Letters of John Stuart Mill 1812–1848*, ed. Francis E. Mineka (Toronto, 1963), vols. XII and XIII of *The Collected Works of John Stuart Mill*. As all of the letters referred to may be found in chronological order in these editions, I shall refer to them in the text by date of composition.

of Carlyle's early conception of the Hero, and the initial stage in the gradual estrangement of Carlyle and Mill.

If one may judge by the frequency of its appearance in anthologies, "Boswell's Life of Johnson" has long been one of Carlyle's most popular writings. In *Sartor Resartus*, as B. H. Lehman has said,[2] Carlyle had wrestled with his shapeless and sometimes self-contradictory concept of the Hero and had brought it to some semblance of consistency. The opinions expressed soon afterwards in "Johnson" are at the heart of his early conception. More personal and engaging than "Signs of the Times" or "Characteristics," and as a whole more so even than *Sartor*, "Johnson" repeats in graphic form much of their essential import, along with renewed emphasis upon the life of man as the only perennially interesting and meaningful history. The interpretations of Johnson and Boswell are striking and immediate. They do not at all seem to falsify, or to be falsified by, Carlyle's theories. In Samuel Johnson, as portrayed by Boswell, Carlyle had found as nearly perfect a vehicle for the positive aspects of his concept as he was ever to find. The resulting integration of idea and historical reality culminated in an essay notable for its unity, clarity, warm humanity, and felicity of expression. In the 1840 lecture series Carlyle was to modify some of the claims he made in "Johnson" and in "Biography," which was initially part of the same essay. With Johnson as their leading exemplar, however, the theories seemed unobjectionable in 1832 to Carlyle and to his recent acquaintance John Mill.

It is significant that this essay, concerned as it was with a strong personality, religiously oriented and striving creatively against great odds, gave rise to few negative aspects of Carlyle's beliefs about great men. The other side of the picture, exemplified by the antireligious man of comparable endowments who finds creativity possible only after removing the detritus of tradition, was presented immediately afterwards. "Diderot," although less interesting to most readers than "Johnson," deserves more attention than it has received. Lehman, for example, does not mention it at all. Although it appeared in a different journal and its publication was delayed for several months, it was consciously designed as a companion piece to "Johnson." Carlyle had contracted for it at the time he was writing "Johnson," and it is obvious that the historical proximity of Diderot and Johnson suggested many matters for comparison to Carlyle, who used antithesis as one

2. *Carlyle's Theory of the Hero* (Durham, N.C., 1929), pp. 75–88.

of his most characteristic devices. As Mill was later to do, Carlyle made brief but specific comparisons in each of the two essays, but left much to the reader. Further, the homologous structure of the pieces leads the reader to think of Johnson and Diderot in terms of more extensive but less explicit comparisons.

"Your parting gift, the paper on Biography and on Johnson, has been more precious to me than I well know how to state," Mill wrote on 29 May 1832. "I have read it over and over till I could almost repeat it by heart; and have derived from it more edification and more comfort, than from all else that I have read for years past." Less than a year later (18 May 1833), after the belated publication of "Diderot," Mill wrote:

Of the man, and of his works and of his co[n]temporaries, so far as I think at all, I think very much as you do: yet I have found more to differ from in that article of yours than in anything of *your* writing I commonly do. The subject seems to have carried you . . . over a range of topics on which there has always been a considerable extent of undiscussed and unsifted divergence of opinion . . . between us two; on some of which too I sometimes think that the distance has rather widened than narrowed of late.

It is unfortunate for us, the readers of the twentieth century, that Mill did not elaborate upon the divergences of opinion. Because he was planning to visit Carlyle at Craigenputtoch later that summer, he postponed the matter until it could be dealt with in the greater intimacy of conversation. But the visit was later canceled, and Mill's subsequent letters do not mention the essay specifically. They do, however, take issue upon a number of the points it raises, and I shall attempt at least a partial reconstruction. It should be kept in mind that throughout this period Mill was becoming more and more closely attached to Harriet Taylor, whose effect upon his opinions was extensive. Although he did not write of her to Carlyle, his letters to William Johnson Fox clearly indicate her increasing influence.

In Carlyle's presentations both Diderot and Johnson are shown to have been underprivileged "peasants" who achieved the pinnacles of literary importance through force of mind and force of will. Born within the space of four years (Johnson in 1709, Diderot in 1713), they died within five months of each other in 1784. Historical coincidence aside, the two had much in common. Both were, as Carlyle admits, men of genius. Both endured hardship as the necessary precursor to fame, both gained much from their schooling in adversity, and both achieved success through their own merits in unpropitious circumstances. Both, incidentally, received the tributes of royalty without at all compromising their individual beliefs. Both insisted upon freedom of inquiry as the necessary basis for the advancement of knowledge; and although Carlyle might not consider this freedom as absolutely desirable per se, he at least recognized its worth within a moribund intellectual orthodoxy and its signal value as an indication of courage. Both Diderot and Johnson founded clubs or associations of the most brilliant men of their time in order to stimulate their own minds and to provide opportunities for the exchange of worthwhile opinion. Working under conditions of privation, one prepared a dictionary of a language while the other compiled an encyclopedia—and neither made much effort to eliminate from his work evidence of his intense convictions.

Approximately three-fourths of "Diderot" is narrative: a biography of the man and a cursory treatment of other individual *philosophes*, taking for granted the reader's familiarity with the nature, purposes, causes, and achievements of the school. The last quarter is an appraisal of Diderot's work. The two sections seem like separate essays. Differences in style between narrative and evaluation are inevitable, of course, but much more striking is a dichotomy in Carlyle's attitude. Throughout the narrative section he manifests sympathy with the persecuted encyclopedist—tenuous sympathy at times, but sympathy nonetheless. Here Diderot seems a congenial character and possibly even a great man, although Carlyle registers a bemused disapproval of numerous actions and beliefs. Diderot is one who "struggled toughly," an admirable iconoclast who triumphed over many personal difficulties. By great insight and force of character he dealt a death blow to crumbling and outmoded beliefs, codes, and institutions. In this respect Diderot closely resembles the Hero and, like Johnson, becomes a deserving object of Carlyle's esteem. The portrayal is vivid and detailed, with such circumstances as Diderot's chronic indigestion increasing Carlyle's sympathy.

The final section of the essay brings a sudden about-face. Without warning, the reader is carried directly from a qualified approval to a virtually unmitigated denunciation. Here we see more clearly than in any of Carlyle's other essays the elements of the "great man" in an irreconcilable form. Goethe, Burns, Johnson, the semi-fictional Teu-

felsdröckh—all these and later protagonists such as the Abbot Samp-
son and Cromwell were well chosen in that they generally reinforce
Carlyle's theories as those theories are set forth in *Heroes and Hero-
Worship.* Diderot does not, and Diderot thus points up some difficulties which Carlyle chose to ignore in almost all his writings. In other
words, Carlyle's real Heroes are, to a man, fusions of spiritual man
and active man. The two roles reinforce each other in presenting the
superior man as the natural leader of mankind. In Diderot the
two roles are irreconcilable by Carlyle's standards. Carlyle becomes
trapped in a paradox of his own making: general approval of a man's
work but general disapproval of the man's character. Rather than
grappling with the conflicting elements of his belief, Carlyle leaves
the issue unresolved and brings his essay to a lame conclusion. Mill
reflected upon this important and characteristic disjuncture in Carlyle's thought some twenty-two years later:

> Is it true, as Carlyle says, that nobody ever did a good thing by reason of
> his bad qualities, but always and necessarily in spite of them? Surely this
> can only be made true by an arbitrary limitation of the term "good" to
> *morally* good, which reduces the brilliantly sounding assertion to a mere
> identical proposition. Useful and even permanently valuable things are
> continually done from vanity, or a selfish desire of riches or power; some-
> times even from envy or jealousy, and the desire to lower others. What is
> true is, that such good things would almost always have been *better* done,
> and would have produced greatly more good, if they had been done from
> a more virtuous motive.[3]

In the evaluative section of the essay it becomes clear that Carlyle
had two objections to Diderot. These were, in brief, Diderot's conception of the man-to-God and the man-to-man relationships. Here
Carlyle's own social and spiritual doctrines clashed. On the one hand,
he believed as fully as did Diderot that mankind's inherited institutions were outworn and should be razed and replaced by more suitable ones. On the other hand, all institutions were to Carlyle merely
material manifestations of an underlying spiritual reality, as he had
vociferously proclaimed in the yet unpublished *Sartor Resartus.* Diderot, an atheist, put his faith in the institutions themselves and would
set them up as self-justifying by reason of their social benefits.

Carlyle's two objections to Diderot become Mill's two objections

3. Diary entry for 20 Jan. 1854; published in *The Letters of John Stuart Mill,* ed.
Hugh S. R. Elliot, 2 vols. (London, 1910), II, 361.

to Carlyle's discussion. Both stem from Carlyle's fundamental assumption that intuition is a necessary element of the Hero's character. Lacking that, a man must somehow recognize the validity and essentiality of intuition in others, accept their guidance, and aspire to the second rank of leadership; or he must become either a hindrance or an unwitting ally of the true Hero. That intuition is desirable and perhaps even essential to human progress is in accord with Mill's belief at this time. His well-known discussion of the roles of the artist and the logician was a direct outgrowth of his dissatisfaction with "Diderot" and occurs in his next letter to Carlyle (5 July 1833). Despite its familiarity and its length, it must be included because it is integral to an understanding of his dissent:

This brings to my mind that I have never explained what I meant when writing once before in this strain I called you a Poet and Artist. I conceive that most of the highest truths, are, to persons endowed by nature in certain ways which I think I could state, intuitive; that is, they need neither explanation nor proof, but if not known before, are assented to as soon as stated. Now it appears to me that the poet or artist is conversant chiefly with *such* truths and that his office in respect to truth is to declare *them*, and to make them *impressive*. This, however, supposes that the reader, hearer, or spectator is a person of the kind to whom truths *are* intuitive. Such will of course receive them at once, and will lay them to heart in proportion to the impressiveness with which the artist delivers and embodies them. But the other and more numerous kind of people will consider them as nothing but dreaming or madness: and the more so, certainly, the more powerful the artist, *as* an artist: because the means which are good for rendering the truth impressive to those who know it, are not the same and are often absolutely incompatible with those which render it intelligible to those who know it not. Now this last I think is the proper office of the logician or I might say the metaphysician, in truth he must be both. The same person may be poet and logician, but he cannot be both in the same composition: and as heroes have been frustrated of glory *"carent quia vate sacro,"* so I think the *vates* himself has often been misunderstood and successfully cried down for want of a Logician in Ordinary, to supply a logical commentary on his intuitive truths. The artist's is the highest part, for by him alone is real *knowledge* of such truths conveyed: but it is possible to convince him who never could *know* the intuitive truths, that they are not inconsistent with anything he *does* know; that they are even very *probable*, and that he may have faith in them when higher natures than his own affirm that they are truths. He may then build on them and act on them, or at least act nothing contradictory to them. Now this humbler part is, I think, that which is most suitable to my faculties, as a man of speculation. I am not in the least a poet, in any sense; but I can do homage to poetry. I can to a very considerable extent feel it and understand it, and can make others who are my inferiors understand it in proportion to the measure of their capacity. I believe that such a person is more wanted than even the poet himself; that there are more persons living who approximate to the latter character than to the former. I do not think myself at all fit for the one; I do for the other; your walk I conceive to be the higher. Now one thing not useless to do would be to exemplify this difference by enlarging in my logical fashion upon the difference itself: to make those who are not poets, understand that poetry is higher than Logic, and that the union of the two is Philosophy—I shall write out my thoughts more at length somewhere, and some*when*, probably soon.

As one can easily infer from these remarks, Mill was not simply discussing the subject disinterestedly. His self-esteem was dependent upon establishing for himself a role which allowed for the possibility of greatness—a role which seemed to be denied him by Carlyle's insistence upon the necessity of intuition in great men. The importance of the question is evident in much of his writing, notably in the *Autobiography* and the *Examination of Sir William Hamilton's Philosophy*, both written decades after the end of his close association with Carlyle. Obviously he saw in many of Carlyle's explicit denunciations of Diderot implicit criticisms of himself. Carlyle's frequent disparagement of "Logic-choppers" in his letters to Mill and in "Diderot" doubtless increased Mill's identification with the *philosophe*.

It is virtually certain that Mill's adverse reactions to the essay were prompted primarily by the attitude of negation which pervades it. Whereas the essay on Johnson tends to lift the spirits of the reader by focusing upon earnestness and solid achievements, "Diderot" is dominated by Carlyle's disapproval. It was, in essence, Diderot's atheism which damned him in Carlyle's eyes. That the encyclopedist should have been an atheist was, Carlyle admitted, inevitable because of the temper of the times in France. Nevertheless, Diderot's atheism limited him to "a half-world, distorted into looking like a whole; it is properly, a poor, fractional, insignificant world; partial, inaccurate, perverted from end to end" (p. 228). Even his atheism, however, was partially a saving grace. He had at least taken a stand. Those who posited "a probable God" were much worse than the convinced denier.

Diderot, despite this sop thrown to him, was still an atheist, and "whosoever, in one way or another, recognizes that 'Divine Idea of the World, which lies at the bottom of Appearances,' can rightly interpret no Appearance; and whatsoever spiritual thing he does, must do it partially, do it falsely" (pp. 234–235). Carlyle, even if only by stating his own preconceptions, had established a basis for dismissing any of Diderot's beliefs or statements. Thenceforth he was free to belabor the *philosophe* on all sides. Many judgments and expressions were borrowed from his essay on Voltaire (1829), but the sureness of purpose Carlyle had since gained in wrestling with the concept of the Hero is reflected in the increased severity with which he treated Diderot's lack of spiritual vision.

Although it is possible with the help of hindsight to deduce the negative aspects of the Hero from Carlyle's earlier writings, "Diderot" revealed to Mill the strongest expression of them he had yet encountered. His desire to garner truth from every source had, he admitted, led him to discount negation whenever possible.[4] It was not possible to do so with "Diderot," however, as its main thrust is denunciatory. Even Carlyle was unhappy with it. While composing it he had written to Mill (16 October 1832), "It is a wearisome straggling affair and to you will not communicate much; tho' readers enough may learn from it, if they will please to look." That Mill learned much from it can be seen in the letters following his reading of it, in which matters pertinent to the essay (and occasionally reflecting its phrasing) appear at odd intervals. One of the most readily apparent of these passages occurs in the letter of 12 January 1834, in which he speaks of the "differences" between himself and Carlyle. Its recollection of the "probable God" from the essay makes the passage important not only for its expressed meaning, but also for its further indication of Mill's identification with Diderot:

The first and principal of these differences is, that I have only, what appears to you much the same thing as, or even worse than, no God at all; namely, a merely probable God. By *probable* I do not mean as you sometimes do, in the sense of the Jesuits, "that which has weighty authorities in its favour." I mean that the existence of a Creator is not to me a matter of faith, or of intuition; & as a proposition to be proved by evidence, it is but a hypo-

4. See, e.g., his letter to Carlyle of 18 May 1833.

thesis, the proofs of which as you I know agree with me, do not amount to absolute certainty. As this is my condition in spite of the strongest wish to believe, I fear it is hopeless; the unspeakable good it would be to me to have a *faith* like yours, I mean as firm as yours, on that, to you, fundamental point, I *am* as strongly conscious of when life is a happiness to me, as when it is, what it *has* been for long periods now past by, a burthen. But I know that neither you nor any one else can be of any use to me in this, & I content myself with doing no ill, by never propagating my uncertainties. The reason why I think I shall never alter on this matter is, that none of the ordinary *difficulties* as they are called, as the origin of evil, & such like, are any serious obstacles to me; it is not that the logical understanding, invading the province of another faculty, will not *let* that other higher faculty do its office; there is wanting something positive in me, which exists in others; whether that something be, as sceptics say, an acquired association, or as you say, a natural faculty.

Mill's identification with Diderot comes about through no fault of Carlyle's. Even the detailed account of Diderot's life does not permit a dispassionate reader to identify with him. Such praise as Carlyle grudgingly bestows upon him is overshadowed by adverse judgments or expostulations following immediately upon the praise. Wherever direct qualifications would seem forced, Carlyle resorts to sarcasm or to a vocabulary designed to diminish Diderot. Frequent repetitions of metaphorical descriptions give the metaphors a life of their own, allowing Carlyle to diminish Diderot's character and accomplishments simply by tricks of style. Among the characterizations which are repeatedly applied to Diderot are "King Denis," "the beagle," "the Encyclopedical Head," and "female." Others, occurring singly, include "spiritual swashbuckler," "patient milkcow," "smoky tar-link," and "gilded tongue." The device of referring to him condescendingly as "Denis" is applied throughout the essay. One senses a shrillness, perhaps even a trace of fear, in the very persistence of Carlyle's attempts to denigrate Diderot by stylistic devices. No doubt he felt the essay to be "straggling" and "wearisome" because he was compelled to denounce and had little scope for his usual exuberance, expansion, and exhortation. "The earnest soul, wayfaring and warfaring in the complexities of a World like to overwhelm him, yet wherein he by Heaven's grace will keep faithfully warfaring, prevailing or not, can drive small solacement from this light, fluctuating, not to say flimsy existence of Diderot" (p. 246). Mill, likewise, could derive small solacement from this presentation of Diderot.

The question of spiritual belief is at the heart of Carlyle's disparaging attitude, and to him belief was the key to character.[5] Samuel Johnson, needing stability in a changing world, had clung to orthodoxy in spite of his doubts. Diderot denied because his confidence in himself made religion unnecessary. Carlyle had excused Johnson's devotion to antiquated forms by showing that his dependency was firmly based upon spiritual beliefs. The problem had occupied much of Carlyle's attention; how much is not apparent at first glance, as it probably was not to Mill. The brief comparison of Johnson with David Hume brings it out somewhat, but it is only by comparison with Diderot in the latter essay that Carlyle's conflict becomes clear.

Carlyle found some elements of his own original creed in both Diderot and Johnson. So far as Diderot the man was concerned, within the human context, he received much the same approbation as Johnson. But in matters spiritual Diderot was at a disadvantage. This, apparently, was sufficient justification for Carlyle to make opposite judgments upon their respective departures from rationality. By a very partisan consideration of human experience, dominated by his own predilections, Diderot found the universe to be not only without a God but also positively opposed to the very concept of divinity. By an equally partisan method Johnson found the opposite. Perhaps more inclusive than Diderot, he found much room for doubt, but succeeded in subordinating that doubt to a compulsive adherence to Christianity. Religion, of course, was one of his many compulsions, and thus his insistence upon observing all of the Church's formalities was part of a large and consistent pattern of behavior. Diderot, on the other hand, seemed equally insistent upon contravening both the formalities and the moral codes of Christianity. For Carlyle the affirmation of things spiritual—even the glossolalia of the Irvingites—was preferable to any denial, no matter how logical. Johnson's foun-

5. Note, for example, Lehman's discussion of sincerity (pp. 42–56). Cf. also the following extract ("Diderot," pp. 240–241): "Vivacity, far-darting brilliancy, keenness of theoretic vision, paradoxical ingenuity, gayety, even touches of humour; all this must have been here: whosoever had preferred sincerity, earnestness, depth of practical rather than theoretic insight, with not less of impetuosity, of clearness and sureness, with humour, emphasis, or such other melody or rhythm as that utterance demanded,—must have come over to London; and, with forbearant submissiveness, listened to our Johnson."

dation of theism, therefore, outweighed his devotion to establishments. Diderot's atheism outweighed his opposition to obsolete institutions. For Carlyle the balance was not hard to strike.

Carlyle's other major objection to Diderot was, as I have noted, in the realm of human relationships. Given Carlyle's firm conviction that character grows from spiritual awareness, his initial bias against Diderot's phenomenalism easily became extended into questions of morality and ethics. Carlyle's own exclusion of marriage from his general beliefs about institutions combined here with his antipathy toward Diderot's spiritual failings. "Omitting his whole unparalleled Cosmogonies and Physiologies; coming to his much milder Tables of the Moral Law, we shall glance here but at one minor external item, the relation between man and man; and at only one branch of this, and with all slightness, the relation of covenants; for example, the most important of these, Marriage" (p. 235). Carlyle made much of this topic. Marriage, according to Diderot, is a pledge of emotion. Man can pledge his actions and be bound to his pledge; but he cannot pledge his beliefs or, least of all, his emotions. In marriage

"thou makest a vow," says he, twice or thrice, as if the argument were a clencher, "thou makest a vow of eternal constancy under a rock, which is even then crumbling away." True, O Denis! the rock crumbles away: all things are changing; man changes faster than most of them. That, in the meanwhile, an Unchangeable lies under all this, and looks forth, solemn and benign through the whole destiny and workings of man, is another truth; which no Mechanical Philosophe, in the dust of his logic-mill, can be expected to grind out for himself. . . . O Denis, what things thou babblest in thy sleep! How, in this world of perpetual flux, shall man secure himself the smallest foundation, except hereby alone: that he take preassurance of his Fate; that in this and the other high act of his life, his Will, with all solemnity, *abdicate* its right to change; voluntarily become involuntary, and say once for all, Be there then no further dubitation on it! [p. 236].

Carlyle then attacked Diderot's personal life on the basis of his liaison with Mme Volland and his consequent unfaithfulness to his children and to the youthfully married wife whose companionship he had outgrown. In this context Carlyle felt no compunction about employing the *argumentum ad hominem*. He carried his reflections upon Diderot's marital life over into the realms of thought. The negation of the marriage contract was sufficient evidence for Carlyle to assume Diderot's disbelief in the validity of all contracts. Thus the *philosophe*, already condemned in questions concerning a relationship with God, was now denied credence in questions of relationships among men.

This synopsis, sketchy as it is, suggests several reasons for Mill's dislike of the essay. His thoughts on the "sanctity of marriage" had already been fully written out for Mrs. Taylor.[6] That document incorporates the sentiments Carlyle ascribed to Diderot as well as many objections to the current legal situation, which deprived married women of their property and made the wives themselves literally the property of their husbands. We cannot determine from available evidence whether any such questions had ever arisen in Mill's conversations with Carlyle. Certainly Carlyle did not know anything of Mill's relationship with Harriet Taylor at this time and therefore could not know how close to Mill he was striking.

As Mill's friendship with Mrs. Taylor was rapidly drawing toward an outright confrontation with her husband, we may assume that Mill was acutely attuned to matters of especial interest to her. In view of his obviously high regard for Carlyle and his subsequent attempts to develop friendship between Mrs. Taylor and the Carlyles, we may also assume that in the summer of 1833 he was hoping to find ways to pacify the antagonism which Carlyle's "Diderot" would certainly have aroused in her. Some five months after Mill read "Diderot," a casual remark in one of Carlyle's letters led him to declare his belief about the woman question in rather cautious terms (5 October 1833):

There was one thing in what you said of Madame Roland which I did not quite like—it was, that she was almost rather a man than a woman: I believe that I quite agree in all that you really meant, but *is* there really any distinction between the highest masculine & the highest feminine character? I do not mean the mechanical *acquirements*; those, of course, will very commonly be different. But the women, of all I have known, who possessed the highest measure of what are considered feminine qualities, have combined with them more of the highest *masculine* qualities than I have ever seen in any but one or two men, & those one or two men were also in many respects almost women. I suspect it is the second-rate people of the two sexes that are unlike—the first-rate are alike in both—except—no, I do not think I can except anything—but then, in this respect, my position

6. Published in F. A. Hayek, *John Stuart Mill and Harriet Taylor* (Chicago, 1951), pp. 58–75.

has been and is, what you say every human being's is in many respects "a peculiar one."

Carlyle's reply, while professing agreement with Mill, leaves one suspecting that there was little real agreement between them after all, that he was following Mill's lead in subordinating the strength of his feelings to the requisites of personal friendship (28 October 1833):

That request of Madame's [Madame Roland] on the way to the guillotine, "for pen and paper that she might write the strange thoughts she had"— kindles me for her, helps her with me very greatly. For her grand fault was being too *conscious*; too much of a reasoner, too little of a prophetess (one must put up with these words); but on the verge of Time, she too looks into the Eternal, one can fancy her too inspired. This was my "woman man"; in which, for the rest, I agree with your correction.

The question of women's rights seems inextricably associated with that of whether they possess peculiar characteristics and abilities. The strong-minded Harriet Taylor was as unbending an egalitarian in sexual matters as are many advocates of comparable causes today. Suggestions of inherent or acquired differences in temperament or cultural conditioning carried connotations of irremediable inferiority. Like other crusaders, she tended to suspect value judgments even where none had been consciously implied. In "Diderot" the implications of inferiority are obvious even to an impartial reader, as Carlyle found repeated opportunities to mention sexual differences of temperament. Doubtless he had seen emancipated women, but the importance of women seemed to him an unusually exaggerated characteristic of the *Encyclopédie* circle and had given it a markedly undesirable tone. Not uncommon in the essay are statements like the following, which describes Diderot's reaction to governmental hindrances: "At every new concussion from the Powers, he roars; say rather shrieks, for there is a female shrillness in it; proclaiming, Murder! Robbery! Rape! invoking men and angels; meanwhile proceeds unweariedly with the printing" (p. 217). Although the emphasis of this remark is upon perseverance, it is of a piece with Carlyle's frequent derogatory characterizations of Diderot as "female." As another example we might note a portion of his characterization of the movement as a whole:

Nor is heaven's last gift to man wanting here; the natural sovereignty of women. Your Châtelets, Epinays, Espinasses, Geoffrins, Deffands, will play their part too: there shall, in all senses, be not only Philosophers, but Philosophesses. Strange enough is the figure these women make: good souls, it was a strange world of nature, fashion of dress-caps, vanity, curiosity, jealousy, atheism, rheumatism, *traités*, *bouts-rimés*, noble-sentiments, and rouge-pots,—the vehement female intellect sees itself sailing on a chaos, where a wiser might have wavered, if not foundered. For the rest, (as an accurate observer has remarked,) they become a sort of Lady-Presidents in that society; attain great influence; and, imparting as well as receiving, communicate to all that is done or said somewhat of their own peculiar tone [pp. 211–212].

Mill, because of his own predilections and the strong convictions of Mrs. Taylor, was finding the feminist cause more and more a preoccupation. Such passages would be offensive to him for two reasons. The more immediate was the feminist cause itself, but the more comprehensive was Carlyle's denial of moral character to those who protested the sanctity of marriage. The matter was to remain a stone of stumbling for the duration of their association, and it rankled in their memories for decades after that.[7]

In brief, Carlyle's essay on Johnson had served to enlarge Mill's vision of human possibility. It had deluded him into an assumption of extensive identities of belief with Carlyle, and it had fostered his human affection for him. The essay on Diderot, as a consequence, came as a greater shock than it would have come otherwise. Finding it repugnant on an intellectual level, he also found that its assumptions and declarations struck at large and integral components of his character. His cautious protests in the subsequent letters were undertaken with determination but also with the assumption that Carlyle would reject him. A study of their later relationship leaves no doubt that, despite Carlyle's attempts toward friendship, Mill's fears were justified.

7. Carlyle's insistence upon the sancitity of marriage was also criticized extensively by Leigh Hunt after reading "Diderot." In a letter on 28 May 1833 he told Carlyle that the institution of marriage and the corollary insistence upon female chastity had been upheld only by the "sacrifice, in the metropolis, of a sixth part of the poor female sex for the convenience of prudential young gentlemen." Carlyle replied on 18 July 1833 that marriage had its flaws but that the institution must be preserved; he pointed to self-denial and the improvement of the individual as remedies. Both letters are published in Charles Richard Sanders, *The Correspondence and Friendship of Thomas Carlyle and Leigh Hunt* (Manchester, 1963), pp. 15–20.

The Hero as Revolutionary: Godefroy Cavaignac

FREDERICK W. HILLES, *Yale University*

Judging Cavaignac from a preface he had written, Carlyle remarked that there was a "gloomy Satanic Strength" in him, that he was "*possessed* with 'Revolution,'" "a kind of frightful man" (20 January 1834). After meeting him he added: "A courageous energetic man, with much free Nature and *bonhomie* in his composition, really a Son of Nature" (2 May 1836). Jane Carlyle's early comments (11 September 1836) are, not surprisingly, a good deal more specific: "We have another foreigner, that beats all the rest to sticks, a french republican of the right thro'-going sort, an *accusé d'Avril* who has had the glory of meriting to be imprisoned, and nearly losing his head, a man with that sort of half-savage beauty with which one would paint a fallen angel, who fears neither Heaven nor Earth for aught one can see; who fights and *writes* with the same passionate intrepidity, who is ready to dare or to suffer, to love or to die, without disturbing himself much about the matter, who *defies* all men and *honours* all women— and whose name is—Cavaignac!"[1]

If any of the many notables who frequented the house in Cheyne Row exemplified Carlyle's idea of the hero, Jacques-Eléonore-Louis-Godefroy Cavaignac was the man. Tall and erect, with a thin face (*maigre* according to one, to another *émaciée*), he had dark hair, brilliant eyes, a nose like an eagle's beak, and lips shaded by a bushy moustache which, with the great frock coat that he normally wore, gave him the appearance of an army officer;[2] perhaps an officer cam-

---

1. Except for what is said concerning him in letters of the Carlyles, information about Cavaignac in this article is chiefly based on M. Prevost's brief but excellent article in Balteau's *Dictionnaire de biographie française*, Joachim Ambert's far more detailed sketch in *Portraits républicains* (Paris, 1870), and G. Weill's *Histoire du parti républicain en France de 1814 à 1870* (Paris, 1900), esp. pp. 50–53. References to letters by the Carlyles are given by date parenthetically within the text. Unless noted, they are from standard published sources. Mill's letter of 25 Nov. 1833 is cited from *The Earlier Letters of John Stuart Mill, 1812–1848*, ed. Francis E. Mineka (Toronto, 1963), vol. XII of *The Collected Works of John Stuart Mill*.

2. This may explain how an error crept into the illustrated catalogue of *Carlyle's House, Chelsea* (London, 1966), p. 24, item 161. What is there described as "Plaster Plaque of General [Louis Eugène] Cavaignac" should be listed as a bas-relief

paigning, for his coat was ill-fitting and unpressed, the knot of his cravat "plus souvent par derrière que par devant!" Cigar—or at times a pipe—in mouth, enveloped in a cloud of smoke, he spoke rapidly and *au débit saccadé*, with an abrupt delivery. "Something of the lion in his face," wrote A. F. Rio after meeting him at the Carlyles (1 April 1839), ". . . noble and serene when not excited, but awful when he is aroused." Proud of being the son of a *conventionnel* who had voted for the guillotining of Louis XVI and who had spent the last twelve years of his life in exile, this "genuine wild man" from beginning to end of his short life seems to have impressed all whom he met as one not in the roll of common men.

His remarkable mother[3] tells us what he was like as a child: gentle and obliging enough but not at all pliant or docile, never breaking the yoke but constantly slipping it, differing from most children of promise in his lack of perseverance. Yet, carefree and noisy as he was, he could sit motionless for hours at a time, thinking who knows what thoughts, then overwhelming you with questions far beyond his age and size. Uninhibited to the point of rudeness, he nevertheless gave promise of becoming generous, high-spirited, independent, a leader of men. Normally obedient at school, according to a schoolmate, his combative and fiery nature was revealed in his passionate opposition to injustice. In 1815 when Napoleon was entering Paris after having left Elba, Cavaignac, aged fourteen, was the acknowledged leader of the Bonapartists in school, vigorously opposing his Royalist classmates. A year later he organized a student riot, characteristically taking upon himself all the blame. What especially distinguished him at this time was the control he naturally exercised over his fellow students and the sympathy he could inspire not only in them but in his teachers as well.

For several years after leaving school he was in Brussels, where his

---

of the general's brother Godefroy (see below, n. 13). The artist, David d'Angers, inscribed it "G. Cavaignac" and signed it "David 1834." See illustration. It gives a much better idea of what he must have looked like when the Carlyles first met him than the photographs used by Huxley (facing p. 48 in his *Jane Welsh Carlyle: Letters to Her Family, 1839–1863*, [London, 1924]) or by Lawrence and Elisabeth Hanson in *Necessary Evil* (London, 1952), facing p. 283. The quotations from Rio below in this paragraph are from Wilson, *Carlyle*, III, 60.

3. Balteau's *Dictionnaire de biographie française* contains articles not only on Mme Cavaignac's husband and both her sons but on herself as well. Her autobiography, published anonymously long after her death (*Mémoires d'une inconnue*, 1894), unfortunately recounts her life to 1815 only.

father lived with other regicides—Levasseur, Vadier, Cambon, David. The young man is said never to have tired listening to them talk about the revolution, particularly about the National Convention. Then for some ten years he took an active part in *la Charbonnerie*, emerging in July 1830 as the leader of the young republicans. It was at that time that he demonstrated his qualifications as a military leader: a captain of artillery, he helped to plant the tricolor on the Tuileries. He was one of those to whom Louis Philippe talked just before making himself Citizen King. Often quoted is Cavaignac's cool remark to him at that time, that he would end his life as had his father Philippe Egalité—that is, be guillotined.

Cavaignac had inherited a comfortable income on *his* father's death, and lived on the outskirts of Paris with his mother and sister. His sturdy and speedy pony took him to and from the city each day. Sometimes he would ride slowly in the Bois de Vincennes, thinking out the solution of a social problem; more often, in the words of an old friend and neighbor, he *dévorait l'espace*, ate up space, reaching Paris early in the morning before the workshops were open, surprising the laborers from whom he learned what progress was being made in underground organizations, giving them advice and instructions, and gaining their love and confidence. The day he would spend presiding at some political meeting, taking part in the deliberations of a committee, attending to his voluminous correspondence, drafting articles for the newspapers. On Sundays his home was the gathering place of friends who happily damned Louis Philippe, talked about France's future, planned to overthrow the government. An admirer noted that Cavaignac always led the conversation to what was the true passion of his life. He would speak of France, of the people; would search avidly for what could make the one free, the other happy. His tireless mind thus worked—even, it was said, when he was resting.

John Stuart Mill met him at about this time and in an important letter to Carlyle (25 November 1833) described him as

a man whose name is energy, who cannot ask you the commonest question but in so decided a manner that he makes you start; a man who impresses you with a sense of irresistible power and indomitable will. You might fancy him an incarnation of Satan if he were your enemy and the enemy of your party, and if you had not associated with him, and seen how full of sweetness and amiableness and gentleness he is. Intense in everything, he is the intensest of atheists, and says, "Je n'aime pas ceux qui croient en Dieu," because "it is generally a reason for doing nothing for man"; but his notion of duty is that of a Stoic—he conceives it as something quite infinite, and having nothing whatever to do with happiness, something immeasurably above it. . . . He is a much more accomplished man than most of the political men I saw [in Paris]; has a wider range of ideas, converses on art and most subjects of general interest, always throwing all he has to say into a few brief, energetic sentences, as if it was contrary to his nature to expend one superfluous word.

Cavaignac's place in history, however, is not that of an original thinker. Very much the man of action, he played a leading role in the early 1830's as spokesman for the opposition. His fiery speeches have been preserved. They are confident reaffirmations of what motivated those idealists who in 1793 had sat in the National Convention. First and foremost he was an optimist. "As for us, I repeat, we can wait. In so rapid a movement that catches up (*entraîne*) society, men and systems succeed one another to lead it to the goal. The last relay is the one that arrives."

Repeatedly he was acquitted after being jailed, but he was far too involved in the uprising of April 1834. For this he ("an *accusé d'Avril*") was imprisoned in Sainte-Pélagie and some time later condemned to death. In prison he and his close friend Armand Marrast reigned over a little court, amused themselves, received visits, sang songs against the king. The complicated story of their escape from the prison (13 July 1835) sounds like one of those that later inspired Tom Sawyer.[4] Eventually the two men made their way to England, where Cavaignac quickly won the friendship of leading citizens, including, as Ambert surprisingly phrases it, "les deux éminents historiens sir William Mackintosh et sir Thomas Carlyle."

His first meeting with Carlyle took place early in 1836. By mid-June he was a frequent visitor at Cheyne Row and had won the hearts of host and hostess by his passionate opposition to the Establishment and his boundless sympathy for the downtrodden. An old Italian woman, unable to speak English and lacking money, friends, or plans for the future, had somehow reached London. "Ah cieux!" said Cavaignac, "si cette femme là fût votre mère, par exemple!" If your Mother were left like that woman! (TC to his brother John, 25 June 1836).

4. See Ambert, pp. 134–138.

Cavaignac's own mother and sister soon came to England, "good French people; ugly, but true to their fashion" (TC to John, 14 July 1836). While Jane was in Scotland Carlyle on 6 August reported to her on them: "The old Madame really seems to me a most cheery, shifty [i.e., resourceful], indomitable little body;—as like *you* as I to Hercules. The Démoiselle fills me with pity. I think she must have had some hurt to her *mind*. Palpitations, palpitations; a *sœur toujours souffrante*! She has a great deal of intelligence, of spirit, vehemence, affection: in speaking, her rude face with its large blue eyes gets almost beautiful, her voice is clear musical; and she coughs (toux nerveuse), and cannot sleep, and cannot &c.; and looks as if she could not live." Her looks were not deceiving. "They returned to Paris," Carlyle wrote to his mother at the end of November, "the Sister still very unwell. The Doctors all along wrote that there was no danger; the poor Mother had bid them do it; thinking her Son would come back at all risks, and be clapt hold of. And now all at once comes the news that the poor Sister is dead.[5] We hear, the fiery Cavaignac is almost out of his wits; his poor Mother, to avoid his flying to *her*, is coming over hither: she has now nothing else left, other Son only, who is far from her, an officer with the Army in Algiers."

Carlyle was busily writing the third and last volume of his *French Revolution* and seems to have made considerable use of Cavaignac's special knowledge of the thoughts and feelings of members of the Convention.[6] The Carlyles were now also seeing a good deal of Harriet Martineau, "very intelligent-looking," wrote Carlyle to his mother (20 November 1836): "full of talk, tho' unhappily deaf almost as a post, so that you have to speak to her through an ear-trumpet." Late in May 1837 when Jane was recovering from one of her many attacks of influenza, *The French Revolution* was finally published. A few weeks later Carlyle, thoroughly exhausted, went to Scotland for a long vacation. According to Jane (17 July) Cavaignac was annoyed that he had not been told of this trip—"is to give me a letter for you next

---

5. According to the simple inscription on her tomb, Cavaignac's sister died at the age of twenty-five on 17 September. She is buried in the family vault in Montmartre.

6. "We had many dialogues while *French Revolution* struggled through its last two volumes; Cavaignac . . . elucidating many little points to me" (*Reminiscences*, I, 111). Cavaignac's father appears for a vivid moment in Book V, chap. vi, of the last volume (*Works*, IV, 237).

week." Cavaignac has not written," was the reply on the 22d, "nor, I think, will write."

Carlyle was wrong. The letter, which I acquired some forty years ago, is a very long one and is extremely difficult to decipher.[7] Cavaignac must have written it at great speed; and his use of accents is highly unconventional. (In the French text, reprinted at the end of this chapter, accents and to a lesser extent punctuation and capitalization have been normalized.)

London, 24 July 1837

My dear Sir,

With men of your worth I keep no account of indebtedness. That being the case, even though you show no signs of writing to me I shall address you without further ceremony.

Mrs. Carlyle has told me that you are thoroughly enjoying yourself in Scotland. From this I assume that it's not too hot; that you are having pleasant outings on foot and horseback; that Miss Martineau's ear-trumpet, in spite of its extraordinary range, doesn't reach *that* far and is not forcing you to strain your lungs while you toss pregnant words into it; perhaps (to bring this to an end) that making the most of the custom of the country you, a man who dreads discomfort and who has written the history of the sans-culottes, are escaping the confinement of that tyrannical bit of clothing which you mustn't mention in England and which you don't have to wear in Scotland; finally, then, that where you are you have succeeded in stripping your mind of that no less binding habit in which you have written your beautiul, your excellent revolutionary trilogy.

In short you are free—that is to say, the only master you now have is the harshest of them all, the *self*—to say nothing of all the other physical and moral powers that surround us, so customary that we don't notice them and believe we carry nothing when all that we carry is the weight of that enormous column of air which bears down upon us for ever and ever. Enjoy yourself, then, to your heart's content. Take walks. When you have had a good dinner, go out and worship nature, burning for incense, in this temple of your god, tobacco in pipe or cigar, and saying as your prayer:

7. Only one other letter from Cavaignac to Carlyle seems to have survived. It is a brief note, asking Carlyle to borrow for him a book from Leigh Hunt (NLS, 1773. 210). A number of people have kindly offered help in deciphering and translating the long letter on which this article is based, but my indebtedness is almost entirely to Henri Peyre. Any mistakes in transcription or translation that remain are mine; there would have been many more had it not been for Professor Peyre's thoughtful and careful reading. Cavaignac's occasional three ellipsis periods (. . .) have been silently deleted.

"Oh God, deliver me from this devil that you have placed in each of us, as if hell were not large enough or as if we must serve as a corridor for those wandering demons who run about the earth and end by settling down with us."

After this jocose opening with its echo of Teufelsdröckh's "Custom doth make dotards of us all," Cavaignac talks of himself, quickly moving from what he had been doing to what he believed about this mysterious universe. Carlyle had, as we should have assumed, talked with him about religion, finding him "not so barren there" (25 June 1836):

As for me, I have broken with beautiful nature—I mean that unsullied nature that you admire so—and in a little excursion that I made three weeks ago along the Channel coast I noticed that I wasn't paying much attention to sky and earth. What I was admiring was not the sea over which we were sailing without its being aware of it, but that active and intelligent machine (*chef d'œuvre* of human theory and practice) the steamboat, which made the wave carry us, mastered it without calling the wind to its aid, even imposed its laws on the wind.[8]

Between works of God and those of man I am naturally prejudiced in favor of those of our colleague, who though not all-powerful does the best he can. His achievement, in spite of its imperfections, testifies more to his strength than to his weakness, proves his genius and his good will. Indeed, as you look at natural objects, where do you find proof of an all-powerful Being whose intentions are good? All the world could prove is that God may have made all that exists. Yes, but what about the rest? about what ought to be? I like to say what will be? for I refuse to believe that we may have reached the *ultimatum*, the *ne plus ultra* of the universe. How could this "best," which we can at least imagine, not enter into the thought and power of the Great All? Without doubt our imagination is the instinct of truth carried to the sublime. It is the future that will realize our dreams. And our desires are, I hope, a prophecy for the times that are coming. That there was a golden age in the past is an absurd and cruel fiction. Neither less cruel nor less absurd, in my opinion, is it to think that paradise is somewhere in the present and hell only where we are. I imagine that the world is not a finished work but a work in progress, that our life is only an accident in an immense creative undertaking that has been going on continuously during these aeons (short moments of eternity); and *that* recon-

8. At this point in the MS there is a line that seems to be a quotation (Cavaignac has underlined it). The last word is illegible, and my attempts to supply what he must have intended are unacceptable to my French friends. I have therefore omitted the line in this translation.

ciles me with the idea of a better future existence, which will be that of the universe, as well as with the idea of a providence against which present evil ceases to be a proof, because, the work being unfinished, we can infer nothing against its author.

We know that Cavaignac was reading *Sartor Resartus* at the time (JWC-TC, 17 July 1837). Perhaps his allusion here to the golden age is an echo of Teufelsdröckh's allusion to "that strange aphorism of Saint-Simon's . . . : *'L'âge d'or, qu'une aveugle tradition a placé jusqu'ici dans le passé, est devant nous*; the golden age, which a blind tradition has hitherto placed in the Past, is Before us.' "[9] But what Cavaignac here says is what he had been saying long before he met Carlyle. As Mill had reported to Carlyle in the letter of 25 November 1833 that has already been quoted, "according to him man's life consists of one perennial and intense struggle against the principle of evil, which but for that struggle would wholly overwhelm him: generation after generation carries on this battle, with little success as yet: he believes in perfectibility and progressiveness, but thinks that hitherto progress has consisted only in removing some of the impediments to good, not in realising the good itself." Cavaignac's letter continues:

When I once more turn my attention toward these mysteries, and try, for my own satisfaction, to account for those great beings who live in the heavens, I imagine they are like the citizens of an immense and magnificent society that we call the universe. They are giving themselves up to a long and weighty cooperative task of conservation and amelioration that ought in time to produce a superior order. Revolutions that have left their mark on our world are in this universal society as in human communities—the effect, proof, means of this beneficial work. Indeed, can we admit that these superb machineries, heavenly bodies, stars, suns, may be senseless stupid bodies? Can we believe that intelligence has bypassed those immense beings, those giants both in size and speed, to come and imprison itself exclusively in tiny human skulls? If thought animates these powerful and magnificent organisms, ought it not in them as in us tend to better the world? All that, if it is a small part of the truth, does not make the present whole, physical and moral, any better.

In the meantime I have neither faith nor worship nor gratitude. I have little use for the critical faculty. When, however, it makes so bold as to judge the works of providence, when it protests through the idea of justice

9. Harrold, *Sartor*, p. 236.

and goodness that is in us, it is then an act of boldness, of courage, which our littleness only serves to render more meritorious. I don't like men who would have us grovel before those incomprehensible tyrannies that we call divine. Above that spectacle (a good man wrestling against fortune) which has been thought beautiful enough for God I put that grand and congenial aspect of all mankind wrestling against God himself and performing miracles to improve the sad lot that was his in the creation.

Cavaignac then turns to Carlyle's newly published book. The parcel he refers to is one that he had arranged to have taken to Carlyle's brother John, who was in France at this time. And he speaks of a number of his political associates. Auguste Dornès (1799–1848) was the advocate whom Carlyle had mentioned in his letter of 24 July 1836. Barthélemy Hauréau (1812–1896), whose revolutionary ardor was already beginning to cool, was destined to become an outstanding historian of the Middle Ages. Ulysse Trélat (1795–1879), saintly doctor and revolutionary pamphleteer, had just been appointed—it was announced 26 July—co-editor of the *National*. Most famous of them all was Hugues-Félicité Robert de Lamennais (1782–1854), a former priest who had been forced out of the church and had become an influential political writer:

Apropos of criticism and heavenly bodies, I would say of your book (that comet which you have launched into the midst of the shooting stars of the contemporary literary world) not only that your parcel has gone (on the second of June) but that on the fifteenth of June I sent my own copy by Dornès to a young Parisian writer, Mr. Hauréau, who is better qualified to appreciate your way of writing and your ideas than anyone else, asking him to write articles on it for the *National*, with which he is on good terms, something I have not been lately, which explains why I have not done it myself. Moreover, control of the *National* is passing into the hands of Mr. Trélat, who will put it back on the right path, so that I can write for it again. Mr. de Lamennais too is about to found a new paper that I shall contribute to, so if Mr. Hauréau doesn't censure you, don't worry! I shall have the opportunity to take issue with you bluntly.

Ah, Mr. Carlyle, you are *impartial*! Good. I shall make you smart for this. You judge our revolution as if it were an ordinary lawsuit, and in spite of all your vigorous aptitude and honesty you evince no passionate preference for the good or the bad people. A fig for passionate preferences, say you? When one writes history he must etc. etc. I think I can hear you from here. But there are situations where, as Molière puts it, justice is quite unjust.[10] Seriously, my grudge against you is that such an eminent and conscientious man refuses to take sides. The genius that there is in your book only makes me harder to please. In my opinion you are particularly at fault with regard to Robespierre. We must respect the memory of those unusual men who have borne the burdens of public necessities. They are the victims that modern times sacrifice to fate. Today when peoples, endowed with an inexhaustible vitality, can no longer perish, this law of destruction (without which nothing gets done in this world), and the thunderbolts of political tempests, fall on a very few heads. But nations change and calm down, the upheavals leave them with a soil that is improved, and a fresh fertility springs from these very lacerations. A few solitary tombs remain, arid and desolate; no one brings regrets or wreaths there. But history, the fairest history, ought in honor of these dedicated victims to engrave some words of eulogy, solemn and grave as had been their mission, their genius, their destiny.

No words of eulogy, it might be noted in passing, are inscribed on the admirably simple tomb of Cavaignac himself. François Rude's recumbent statue in bronze, situated near the entrance of the Cemetery of the North (Montmartre), assumes that words for him are unnecessary.

The defense of Robespierre here could have been predicted. Cavaignac had been president of the Societé des Droits de l'Homme, an organization that accepted as its basic belief Robespierre's declaration of the rights of man.

After a reference to Mrs. Carlyle's health, the long letter ends with mention of the death on 20 June of William the Sailor King, the accession of Victoria, and the general elections that followed:

I have had the honour since you left of seeing Mrs. Carlyle. Her health does not look good to me, and I don't believe in the sincerity of that laugh which she often mixes with her talk. We can counterfeit everything except gaiety, doubtless because it is something so rare that we rarely have the chance of studying it and copying it.

Aside from that, there is nothing new here in spite of a king's death, a queen's accession, and the elections. I have, as you can believe, seen none of the ceremonies of the day. I shall see the elections; they have a false appearance of democracy that pleases me, for want of something better. Poor England, you are certainly the country of *seeming*. Your institutions move along here precisely like old people taking their constitutionals

10. Alceste in *Le Misanthrope*, v, i, says: "J'ai pour moi la justice, et je perds mon procès!"

to keep healthy, but that doesn't restore their youth. I share Nero's wish: would to God that these people had but one head—not to be cut off, but to hold one thought only, the rest to be brushed away at a single sweep.[11]

Good bye, my dear sir. This is a long letter. You'll read it, if not *two times*, at least *at two sittings*. Enjoy yourself. As for me, my life with my mother continues to be a sad one. A year ago my sister was here. Where is she now? Good bye.

Your most devoted

G. Cavaignac

Here just now is Marrast who wants to do an article on your book for the *National*. I am going to write to your lady, asking her to send him a copy.

Jane's letter of 3 August[12] reminds us that postage was in those days paid by the recipient. Her mother was about to return to Scotland. Cavaignac sent this "imme[n]se long letter" to her so that, carried by Mrs. Welsh, "it might *couter* you *rien*." At the same time Cavaignac sent Jane a note

requesting, or rather, *kurt und gut, requiring* that I should *order* your bookseller to send a copy of your book to Mar[r]ast in such a street of such a square who "proposed reviewing it in *the National*." Now as I was quite at a loss to know whether you would consider *a Review in the National (still only proposed)* worth TWO copies of the book, one as I understand having been sent by Fraser already for that purpose—I rather thought not—but as you were not there to tell me, I did what seemed best to myself. I made Mr. Darwin drive me up to Fraser's where I stated the case in all plainness to *the versifier of Teufelsdreck*, desiring simply that Mr. Fraser would use his own discretion in the matter, as he could judge better than I "whether it was or was not compromising the dignity of the book to give away another copy of it for the sake of even a *clever* notice in the National." *Our* Poet Laureat seemed tickled with this putting of the question. What they decided on I have had no opportunity of hearing.

A reasonably careful search of the *National* uncovers no mention of *The French Revolution* this year or the next.

Carlyle wrote to his brother John (12 August): "Cavgc is angry

---

11. Failing to discover where Nero's famous remark was recorded, I asked Cora Lutz in the Beinecke Library at Yale. "Unfortunately," she replied, "there were several Roman emperors hateful enough to voice the quotation you were seeking. It was not Nero. It was Caligula, and the words are quoted in Suetonius 30"; but before looking this up she had said, quite rightly, "Not *head*, but *neck*."

12. Quoted with permission from the original in the Pierpont Morgan Library.

with me for my treatment of the Seagreen Man [Robespierre] and my *impartialité* generally: I take no side in the matter; how very singular! . . . Cavaignac has renounced *his* review (I think) in favour of somebody or other, or even some*bodies*, in *National* and elsewhere; about whom he wrote me largely. His own mind is struck with perplexing variety of emotions about it; not to be uttered as yet except by a snort thro' the moustachios." To Jane (18 August) his comment is "I think his Letter very sprightly and unsound; but I do value the man as among the manfullest I know."

The amnesty of 1837 had excepted such militant republicans as Cavaignac. This exception disappeared with the amnesty of 27 April 1840, so he went to Africa, where he stayed for a short time with his brother, at that time a colonel in the army.[13] He returned to Paris. But the world had changed. His republican friends had grown soft, were subdued. Marrast was preaching moderation. Discouraged, Cavaignac made various visits to his brother. Although he was obviously a very sick man, suffering from tuberculosis, his talk was still as fiery, his anecdotes as colorful, as ever. One who knew him only at that time pictures him as an exalted demagogue, an angry conspirator, an enthusiast for all great and noble causes, a convinced admirer of all fine sentiments.[14] In Paris he became editor of the *Journal du Peuple* and was founding editor of *La Réforme*, which violently attacked the once revolutionary *National*. But his health rapidly deteriorated, and he died on 5 May 1845, surrounded by friends, not many weeks before his forty-fourth birthday.

There seems to be no record of how the Carlyles learned the sad news.[15] Jane's feelings are best revealed in the account she gave some years later (5 February 1849) on learning that Louis Blanc was coming to tea. "I am sure you will like him," said John Robertson; "he was talking to me to-day many things that would have interested

13. Louis Eugène Cavaignac (1802–57) is far better known than his more interesting brother Godefroy (see above, n. 2). Although a republican, he was an officer in the army, finally becoming a divisional general in 1848 after the overthrow of Louis Philippe. Elected to the National Assembly, he was made dictator during the June uprisings. Only the success of Louis Napoleon kept him from becoming first President of the Second Republic. See Frederick A. deLuna, *The French Republic Under Cavaignac* (Princeton, 1969).

14. Germain Bapst, *Le Maréchal Canrobert* (Paris, 1899), I, 414.

15. Lawrence and Elisabeth Hanson (*Necessary Evil* [New York, 1952], p. 320) imply without giving evidence that news of the death did not reach the Carlyles until July. This is hard to believe; there were two references to Cavaignac's funeral in the *Times* for 9 May.

even *you*. It was in *his* arms, he tells me, that Godefroi Cavaignac died!"

I started as if he had shot me— the thing took me so by surprise—and I could not answer one word— this man was coming on Friday night! I felt as if he would transmit to me even thus late Godefroi Cavaignac's last breath! And Robertson was watching the effect of his words! I cared not— why should I? I had my boa gloves reticule &c. in my lap, I flung them all violently on the floor— why, I don't know— I could not help it! Robertson went on to say that he, Louis Blanc, talked of Godefroi as of a Divinity. . . . I believe Robertson said that about Godefroi, in the devilish intention of watching its effect on me— I *know* he has been heard to speculate on my intimacy with him. Well! let him draw his inferences— it is no disgrace to *any* woman to be accused of having loved Godefroi Cavaignac, the only reproach to be made me is that I did not love him as well as he deserved. But now he is dead I will not *deny him* before all the Robertsons alive!

The many references to Cavaignac by his countrymen in letters, orations, memoirs, historical writings, fail to comment on the impact he made upon his friends in England. His winning the admiration and love of the Carlyles ought to be considered testimony equal to the most glowing tributes of others. If there had been in him a touch of pomposity, of insincerity, of cheapness, it would certainly have called forth what Carlyle called his "atrabilious censures," nor could it have escaped the keen eyes of Jane. She enjoyed his stamping on the floor and snorting "Bah." She was delighted with his anecdotes, with his sense of humor, even with his abrupt way of scolding her. "One evening that I was talking to him rather *wittily* (as I thought) he said to me *brusquely*—'Spare me your *cleverness, Madame*. Je ne le veux pas—*moi*! it is not *my pleasure* to rank among those for whom you have to *make minced meat* of yourself!' regal words, truly! as all his words were!—if that man be not an absolute monarch yet before he die, Nature will have missed her intention with him!" (7 January 1843).

Looking back on those first ten years of his life in London, Carlyle in old age neatly summed up the relations between Cavaignac and the two Carlyles.[16] Speaking of the many revolutionaries that were to be found in the London of that decade, he wrote: "Except with Cavaignac I never had any intimacy, any pleasant or useful conversation,

16. *Letters and Memorials of Jane Welsh Carlyle*, ed. J. A. Froude (London, 1883), I, 248.

among these people—except for Mazzini and him any real respect. ...She, too...had always an affection for Mazzini, and for the chivalrous and grandly humorous Cavaignac (and for the memory of him afterwards) still more."

Cavaignac to Carlyle, 24 July 1837: The French Text

Londres, 24 juillet 1837

Mon cher monsieur,

Je ne compte pas avec des hommes de votre valeur, et quoique vous n'ayez pas l'air de songer à m'écrire, je me mets à le faire sans autre cérémonie. Madame Carlyle m'a dit que vous vous plaisiez fort en Ecosse. J'en conclus qu'il n'y fait pas trop chaud, que vous y avez de belles promenades à pied et à cheval, que le cornet de Miss Martineau ne va pas jusque là, malgré sa redoutable étendue, et ne vous force pas d'y injecter à grand effort de poumons des mots qui lui donnent des idées—peut-être, enfin, que, profitant de la mode nationale, en homme qui craint la gêne et qui a écrit l'histoire des sans-culottes, vous échappez à l'étreinte de ce vêtement tyrannique, qu'il n'est pas permis de nommer en Angleterre et qu'en Ecosse il est permis de ne pas porter—j'en conclus encore que là où vous êtes vous avez achevé de dépouiller votre esprit de cet habit non moins gênant où vous l'avez internée durant deux années, de cet habit de papier où vous avez écrit votre belle et bonne trilogie révolutionnaire. Bref, vous êtes libre, c. à d. que vous n'avez plus de maître que le plus rude de tous, le *moi*, sans parler de toutes ces autres dominations physiques et morales qui nous entourent, si habituelles que nous finissons par ne plus les sentir, et que nous nous croyons libres quand elles sont notre seule servitude, comme nous croyons ne rien porter quand nous portons seulement le fardeau de l'énorme colonne d'air qui pèse sans cesse sur nous. Prenez donc du bon temps, promenez-vous—quand vous aurez bien dîné, allez admirer la nature, brûlant pour encens dans ce temple de votre dieu tabac de pipe ou de cigare, et pour prière disant: mon dieu, délivrez-moi de ce diable que vous avez mis en chacun de nous, comme si l'enfer n'était pas assez grand, ou que nous dussions servir de lieu de passage à ces démons touristes qui courent le monde et se viennent loger chez nous.

Quant à moi, j'ai rompu avec la belle nature—je parle de cette nature brute que vous admirez tant; et dans une petite excursion que j'ai faite, il y a trois semaines, le long des côtes du détroit, j'ai pu[?] voir que je regardais fort peu le ciel et la terre. Ce que j'admirais, ce n'était pas la mer qui nous portait bêtement, mais cette active et intelligente machine, ce chef d'œuvre de la théorie et de la pratique humaine, le bateau à vapeur qui forçait le flot à nous porter, le maîtrisait sans appeler le vent à son aide, faisait au vent aussi la loi—

et le charbon de terre est devenu [word indecipherable]

Entre les ouvrages de Dieu et ceux de l'homme, ma partialité, naturellement, est acquise aux ouvrages de notre collègue, qui n'est pas tout-puissant et qui fait de son mieux. Sa besogne, malgré ses imperfections, atteste plus sa force que sa faiblesse, elle prouve son génie et sa bonne volonté. Aussi bien, où trouver dans le spectacle des choses naturelles la preuve d'une toute puissance bien intentionnée? Le monde prouverait seulement que Dieu a pu faire tout ce qui est—oui, mais le reste? ce qui devrait être? j'aime à dire: ce qui sera; car je me refuse à croire que nous en soyons à l'*ultimatum*, au *nec plus ultra* de l'univers. Comment ce *mieux* que nous pouvons imaginer du moins n'entrerait-il pas dans la pensée et dans la puissance du Grand Tout? Notre imagination, c'est sans doute l'instinct de la vérité porté au sublime; c'est l'avenir qui réalisera nos rêves, et nos désirs sont, j'espère, une prophétie pour les temps qui viendront. L'âge d'or dans le passé est une fiction absurde et cruelle; il n'est ni moins cruel ni moins absurde, à mon sens, de penser que dans le présent le paradis est quelque part, et l'enfer seulement où nous sommes. J'imagine que le monde n'est pas une œuvre achevée, mais une œuvre qui se continue, que notre vie n'est qu'un accident dans une immense entreprise de création qui se poursuit encore durant ces âges, courts momens de l'éternité; et cela me réconcilie avec l'idée d'une existence future meilleure qui sera celle de l'univers, comme avec l'idée d'une providence contre laquelle le mal présent cesserait d'être une preuve, parceque l'ouvrage n'étant pas terminé on ne peut rien conclure contre son auteur.

Quand il m'arrive encore de me tourner vers tous ces mystères, de chercher à me rendre raison de ces grands êtres qui vivent dans les cieux, je me figure qu'ils sont comme les citoyens d'une immense et magnifique société que nous nommons l'univers, et qu'ils se livrent de concert à un long et puissant travail de conservation et d'amélioration qui doit dans la durée des temps produire un ordre supérieur; les révolutions dont notre monde porte la trace sont dans cette société universelle comme dans les communautés humaines l'effort, la preuve, le moyen de ce travail bienfesant. Peut-on admettre, en effet, que ces superbes appareils, astres, étoiles, soleils, soient des corps bruts, stupides? Peut-on croire que l'intelligence a passé à côté de ces êtres immenses, de ces colosses d'étendue et de mouvement, pour venir se circonscrire exclusivement dans le très petit crâne humain, et si la pensée anime ces organisations puissantes et magnifiques, ne doit-elle pas en elles comme en nous tendre éternellement à améliorer l'ensemble des choses? Tout cela, fût-ce un bout de la vérité, ne rend pas l'ensemble actuel, physique et moral, meilleur. Provisoirement je n'ai ni foi, ni adoration, ni reconnaissance. J'estime peu la faculté critique; mais quand elle s'enhardit jusqu'à juger les œuvres de la providence, quand elle proteste par l'idée de justice et de bien qui est en nous, c'est là un acte d'audace, de vertu, qui notre petitesse ne fait que rendre plus méritoire. Je n'aime pas ceux qui veulent que nous nous prosternions devant ces incompréhensibles tyrannies qu'on nomme divines, et au dessus de ce spectacle qu'on a dit être assez beau pour dieu, celui d'un homme de bien luttant contre la fortune, je mets ce grand et sympathique aspect de l'humanité toute entière luttant contre Dieu lui-même et fesant des miracles pour améliorer la triste part qu'il lui a faite dans la création.

A propos de critique et d'astres, je vous dirai pour votre livre, cette comète lancée par vous au milieu des étoiles filantes du monde littéraire actuel, que non seulement votre paquet est parti (le 2 juin), mais que le 15 juin j'ai envoyé mon propre exemplaire, par Dornès, à un jeune écrivain de Paris, Mr. Hauréau, qui est plus propre que tout autre à goûter votre manière et vos idées, en le priant de faire des articles pour le *National* avec lequel il est bien et avec lequel je suis mal depuis quelques mois. C'est ce qui m'a empêché de m'en charger. Du reste, le *National* va passer dans les mains de Mr. Trélat qui le remettra en assez bonne voie pour que je puisse y mettre de ma besogne; Mr. de Lamennais va aussi fonder un nouveau journal où j'aurais part, et si Mr. Hauréau ne dit pas de mal de vous, soyez tranquille, j'aurais moyen de vous dire votre fait. Ah, Monsieur Carlyle, vous êtes *impartial*! Bon, vous me le paierez. Vous jugez notre révolution comme un procès ordinaire et avec toute cette force de talent et d'honnêteté qui est en vous, vous ne montrez point de passion entre les bons et mauvais. Fi de la passion, n'est-ce pas? Il faut quand on écrit l'histoire etc. Je vous entends d'ici. Mais, il y a des cas où, comme dit Molière, la justice est bien injuste. Sérieusement, j'en veux à un homme aussi éminent et aussi consciencieux que vous de n'avoir pas plus de parti pris et ce qu'il y a de génie dans votre livre ne me rend que plus exigeant. Vous êtes surtout en faute, à mon sens, envers Robespierre. Il faut respecter la mémoire de ces hommes rares qui ont porté le poids des nécessités publiques, ce sont les victimes que les temps modernes immolent à la fatalité aujourdhuy que doués d'une vitalité inépuisable, les peoples ne peuvent plus périr, c'est sur quelques têtes que retombent cette loi de destruction sans laquelle rien ne s'accomplit en ce monde, et les coups de foudre des tempêtes politiques. Cependant, les nations se refont et se rasseoient, les commotions leur laissent un sol meilleur, et une fertilité toute jeune part de ces déchiremens mêmes. Quelques tombes, seules, restent arides et désolées, nul n'y apporte des regrets, des couronnes. Mais l'histoire, l'histoire plus juste, doit y graver, en l'honneur de ces victimes dévoués, quelques mots d'un éloge austère et grave, comme le furent leur mission, leur génie, leur destinée.

J'ai eu l'honneur, depuis votre départ, de voir Madame Carlyle. Sa santé ne me parait pas bonne, et je ne crois pas à la sincérité de ce rire qu'elle mêle souvent à ses paroles. On contrefait tout hors la gaîté, sans doute parceque c'est chose si rare que nous avons rarement l'occasion de l'étudier, et d'en prendre copie.

Du reste, rien de nouveau ici, malgré la mort d'un roi, l'avènement d'une reine, et les élections. Je n'ai vu, comme vous pouvez croire, aucune des cérémonies du jour. Je verrai les élections; elles ont un faux air de peuple qui me plaît, faute de mieux. Pauvre Angleterre, tu es bien le pays des *semblant*. Vos institutions marchent ici, justement comme les vieillards, pour se mieux tenir en santé; mais cela ne les rajeunit point. Je fais le vœu de Néron: plût à Dieu que ce peuple n'eut qu'une tête—non pour la couper, mais pour lui voir une seule pensée, et tout balayer d'un seul coup.

Adieu, mon cher monsieur, voici une longue lettre. Vous la lirez, si non *deux fois*, du moins *à deux fois*. Divertissez-vous. Moi, j'ai toujours une triste vie avec ma mère. Il y a un an, ma sœur était ici. Où est-elle maintenant? Adieu. Votre bien dévoué

G Cavaignac

Voici justement Marrast qui veut faire un article sur votre livre pour le *National*. Je vais écrire à Madame pour qu'elle lui fasse envoyer un exemplaire.

Carlyle and the Fictions of Belief:
Sartor Resartus *to* Past and Present

JANET RAY EDWARDS

Many of the characters, settings and events in Carlyle's works are factual, but the dominant mode is fiction. His success in making the Minerva Press novel one of his symbols for sham tends to obscure his critical recognition that fiction has important, if limited, uses in works of history and social criticism[1] and his extensive use of fictional methods in practice. Fictional devices determine the texture and structure of Carlyle's major works from *Sartor Resartus* to *Past and Present*, from about 1830 to 1843. Like the novelist, he attempts to seize and embody the totality of life in all its fullness, to make every aspect of experience cohere as part of a single organism, sharing a common moral existence.[2] He shares the novelist's interest in fictional disguises, in problems of point of view, in character as the best means for expressing and testing the validity of ideas; and his conviction that the facts of ordinary life must not be distorted by invention.[3]

His most significant fictional methods are not those of the novelist, however. Carlyle as artist required fictional devices which would illuminate rather than obstruct his perceptions of reality. Two of these devices—which seem to conflict with nineteenth-century realistic fiction, but may in fact have suggested new possibilities for it—have been called antifictional. Carlyle is said to lack the novelist's feeling for fictional "facts," to be unwilling to invent the multitude of

---

1. Carlisle Moore, "Thomas Carlyle and Fiction: 1822–1834," in *Nineteenth Century Studies*, ed. Herbert Davis, William C. DeVane, R. C. Bald (Ithaca, N.Y., 1940), pp. 152–153.

2. Morton Dauwen Zabel, ed., "Introduction," *Bleak House*, by Charles Dickens (Boston, 1956), p. viii.

3. George Levine, *The Boundaries of Fiction: Carlyle, Macaulay, Newman* (Princeton, N.J., 1968), pp. 51–78. See also G. B. Tennyson, *Sartor Called Resartus: The Genesis, Structure and Style of Thomas Carlyle's First Major Work* (Princeton, 1965), pp. 173–185, for a comprehensive and generally persuasive discussion of *Sartor* as novel. However, Tennyson's definition of the novel as "a continuous story involving human relationships in a sustained illusion of a world," because of his use of the concept of story, inevitably returns him to the categories of nineteenth-century realistic fiction into which, as he realizes, *Sartor* cannot be forced.

details that make for verisimilitude.[4] He is also described as anti-narrative: he has little interest in plot and cultivates the appearance of disorder.[5] In place of verisimilitude and narrative plot, he developed other fictional devices which establish the texture of reality and provide structural unity. For verisimilitude, he substituted the concreteness of facts; for narrative, or undermining its "outward method,"[6] he substituted the development of character, setting, and event into symbols.

Carlyle rejected verisimilitude less out of some curious inability to invent realistic detail, which his brilliant powers of observation supply wherever he deems it needed,[7] than from his reluctance to deal in illusion. Novelists in a positivist age sought means of demonstrating that their fictions were not "invented" but were based on real-life experiences, but even realistic novel-fiction makes no pretense of being true in a provable, factual sense; it seeks from the reader a momentary "suspension of disbelief."[8] Carlyle's intention, unlike the novelist's, was to find a way of expressing truth that would have nothing in it that could possibly be thought false.[9] Thus he stresses the "wonder of reality" in Sartor, or the infinite superiority of "the poorest historical Fact" to any fiction whatsoever.[10] In Sartor, it is true, he used invented fictions, but not to convey ultimate truth. The fictions deliberately foster a hoax, a joke for those who grasped them. In The Diamond Necklace, a conscious experiment with fictional technique, he prides himself on "the strictest fidelity" to fact.[11] In The French Revolution and Past and Present, he uses historical

4. Moore, p. 148, and Levine, p. 39.

5. Levine, pp. 61–64. Levine mentions Carlyle's deliberate mystification of his basically simple ideas in Sartor Resartus.

6. Harrold, Sartor, p. 34. Further references cited in the text as SR. References to the Centenary Works are also cited parenthetically.

7. See Charles Richard Sanders, "The Victorian Rembrandt: Carlyle's Portraits of His Contemporaries," Bulletin of the John Rylands Library, 39 (March 1957), 524–531.

8. Robert A. Colby, Fiction with a Purpose: Major and Minor Nineteenth-Century Novels (Bloomington, Ind., 1968), pp. 11–13, and Frank Kermode, The Sense of an Ending: Studies in the Theory of Fiction (New York, 1967), pp. 38–40. In Kermode's terms, Carlyle uses fictional devices to create myths. The danger of myths is that their claim to truth carries with it the demand that you "rearrange the world to suit them."

9. Walter E. Houghton, The Victorian Frame of Mind, 1830–1870 (New Haven, 1957), pp. 131–132.

10. Past and Present, in Works, X, 46.

11. Froude, Carlyle, II, 386, TC–John Aitken Carlyle, 24 Dec. 1833.

materials, principally memoirs, with scrupulous care and minimal distortion.[12]

It is important to note that Carlyle does not grant equal credence to all facts. By exerting a rhetorical control over the meaning of *fact* (as he exerts control over many meanings by verbal, not logical, processes)[13] he shows that two classes of facts lack solidity, density, and stability: the abstractions of quantitative science, philosophy, or history, which separate fact from value; and the disparate, often transient facts making up "the incongruous ever-fluctuating chaos of the Actual" (*Works*, II, 10), which fit into no humanly ordered constellation of meaning. Often he makes skillful use of catalogs of concrete facts to recreate the "chaos of the Actual" or the emptiness of abstractions. George Fox the Quaker works "on tanned hides, amid pincers, paste-horns, rosin, swine-bristles, and a nameless flood of rubbish" (*SR*, 209). Like Teufelsdröckh in his disorderly study, he is oblivious of his surroundings, ever hearing "amid the boring and hammering . . . tones from that far country" (*SR*, 209). But, significantly, in the rubbish surrounding him Fox finds the materials for a "perennial suit of Leather" (*SR*, 210), thereby giving a shape to his material world and freeing himself from chaos. The rapid flow of events in the Revolution "is all phenomenal, what they call spectral; and never rests at any moment" (*Works*, III, 159). Chaos presses on industrial England in the guise of "Five-point Charter, Free-trade, Church-extension, Sliding-scale" (*Works*, X, 29)—abstractions, mistaken for ultimate fact.

But to other kinds of physical facts, Carlyle attributes fundamental truth. The cyclical changes of the seasons, the heat of the sun, the solid mass of the earth, the green and gold of its fields are part of the mighty web of life. They have their counterpart in human patterns of birth, growth, work, and death—the shared, repeated destiny of man. The rhythms of earth and sun and seasons and human life, interwoven through space and time, establish a sense of a pulsing, ongoing physical existence which, while it is not verisimilitude, functions like it to thicken the texture of reality. Such facts evoke the

12. Charles Frederick Harrold, "Carlyle's General Method in *The French Revolution*," *PMLA*, 43 (Dec. 1928), 1150–1169; and Grace Calder, *The Writing of Past and Present* (New Haven, Conn., 1949), p. 45.

13. John Holloway, *The Victorian Sage: Studies in Argument* (New York, 1965 [1953]), pp. 41–57.

continuum linking past and present: "this England of the year 1200 was no chimerical vacuity or dreamland, peopled with mere vaporous Fantasms, Rymer's Fœdera,[14] and Doctrines of the Constitution; but a green solid place, that grew corn and several other things. The Sun shone on it; the vicissitude of seasons and human fortunes. Cloth was woven and worn; ditches were dug, furrow-fields ploughed, and houses built" (*Works*, X, 44). The plurals work in opposite directions: the first set lists a multiplicity of meaningless abstractions; the second describes solid, tangible events which are not singular and transient but universal, part of a process recognizable in its concreteness then as now.

Frequently, Carlyle goes on to associate these concrete details of setting with the supernatural world, with mystery, miracle, and wonder. Descriptions of places are first anchored in the concrete and then suffused with a transcendental light or transcendental darkness which carries them beyond the limits of the material. Thus the description of "this England of the year 1200" concludes, "In wondrous Dualism, then as now, lived nations of breathing men; alternating, in all ways, . . . between rest and toil,—between hope, hope reaching high as Heaven, and fear deep as very Hell" (*Works*, X, 44).

Particular facts are also "real" when they reveal the inner qualities of persons. That Robespierre had a "sea-green" bilious complexion, that Teufelsdröckh once laughed till the tears ran down, that Jeanne de Valois had a face "with a certain piquancy," that Abbot Samson tucked his robes into his belt to walk with longer strides—such details bring characters in their flesh-and-blood humanity before the reader, and in their concreteness offer clues to the unseen inner life as well. Marat's "bleared soul looks forth, through [his] bleared, dull-acrid, wo-stricken face"; through Mirabeau's "shaggy beetle-brows, and rough-hewn, seamed carbuncled face, there look natural ugliness, small-pox, incontinence, bankruptcy,—and burning fire of genius" (*Works*, II, 136–137). Carlyle images the "prose Fact" of Edmund's life, glimpsed through Jocelin's chronicle: "This landlord Edmund did go about in leather shoes, with *femoralia* and bodycoat of some sort on him; and daily had his breakfast to procure" (*Works*, X, 52). The fictional quality of these details is especially striking when Car-

14. Thomas Rymer, an early-eighteenth-century rationalist critic and historiographer, collected England's state papers from the Middle Ages down to 1654 in twenty volumes, which he entitled *Foedera* (1704–1735).

lyle uses them in place of more conventional identifications of historical figures. For instance, in the one sentence he devotes to the ancient Merovingian kings of France in *The French Revolution,* he mentions neither dates nor wars nor political alignments, but pictures them "slowly wending on their bullock-carts through the streets of Paris, with their long hair flowing" (*Works,* II, 7).

Carlyle's desire to discover and communicate the concrete humanity of his characters grows out of his early critical ideas of tolerance and humor. In reading *Wilhelm Meister* as a young man, he had been greatly moved by Goethe's willingness to withhold judgment from his characters:[15] "For all lives freely within him: Philina and Clärchen, Mephistopheles and Mignon, are alike indifferent, or alike dear to him; he is of no sect or caste: he seems not this man, or that man, but a man" (*Works,* XXVI, 245). Carlyle's own tolerance was a self-imposed discipline; the habit of judgment was strong with him, never long set aside. Yet the ideal of tolerance leads him to make a conscious effort, if not to refrain from judging entirely, at least to view a life relatively, from within the perspectives of its own time. Croker's edition of Boswell's *Johnson,* he complained, presents facts about Johnson, but they are abstractions, "Tombstone-information," not helpful for gaining an understanding of the man himself. The wide question is, "What and how was *English Life* in Johnson's time: . . . What things have we to forget, what to fancy and remember, before we, from such distance, can put ourselves in Johnson's *place*; and so, in the full sense of the term, *understand* him, his sayings and his doings?" (*Works,* XXVIII, 64). In the four essays on eighteenth-century French figures which preceded *The French Revolution,* he attempted to enter imaginatively and sympathetically into the consciousness of the *philosophe* and the quack, with whom he disagreed both philosophically and morally: "As to this Diderot, had we once got so far that we could, in the faintest degree, personate him; take upon ourselves his character and his environment of circumstances, and act his Life over again, in that small Private-Theatre of ours (under our own Hat), with moderate illusiveness and histrionic effect,—*that* were what, in conformity with common speech, we should name *understanding* him, and could be abundantly content with" (*Works,* XXVIII, 181). The technique is a fictional one, requiring like the dramatic monologue "an act of imaginative projection

15. Tennyson, p. 72.

into the external object . . . so that the living consciousness perceived in the object is [his] own."[16] Carlyle frequently uses physical vision as a metaphor for this projection. In Jocelin's chronicle, for all its irritating vagueness, "our earnest loving glance" discloses "here and there, some real human figure . . . whom we could hail if he would answer;—and we look into a pair of eyes deep as our own, *imaging* our own, but all unconscious of us" (*Works*, X, 49, 50).

Humor, like tolerance, affirms the humanity of the other, accepting with laughter but without contempt his human limitations. Carlyle defined it as an "inverse sublimity; exalting, as it were, into our affections what is below us" (*Works*, XXVI, 17). Humor prevents love from being corrupted into sentimentality; love, in turn, prevents humor from becoming the "mere logical pleasantry" of wit (*Works*, XXVI, 451), a form of intellectual repartee in which *philosophes* and nineteenth-century dandies alike excelled. Carlyle appreciated Voltaire's fine wit—"the inexhaustible readiness, the quick force, the polished acuteness" but he thought it of a lower species than humor. "Wit of this sort cannot maintain a demure sedateness; a grave yet infinitely kind aspect, warming the inmost soul with true loving mirth; it has not even the force to laugh outright, but can only sniff and titter" (*Works*, XXVI, 450–451).

Humor as Carlyle understands it need not be bland; it may well have a satirical bite. In two of Diderot's works, he writes approvingly, "wearisomely crackling wit gets silent; a grim, taciturn, dare-devil, almost Hogarthian humor rises in the back-ground" (*Works*, XXVIII, 245). Such a grim humor informs Carlyle's essay on Cagliostro. As an adept at mystification himself, he recognizes and yields grudging admiration to Cagliostro's abilities in the "element your Quack specially works in: the element of Wonder" (*Works*, XXVIII, 296). His tone is mock-heroic, for the truth of a Quack's existence lies partly in his ability to deceive himself with belief in his own greatness: "No Quack can persuade like him who has himself some persuasion. Nay, so wondrous is the act of Believing, Deception and Self-Deception must, rigorously speaking, co-exist in all Quacks" (*Works*, XXVIII, 295).

Carlyle presents individual characters with a sure instinct for the

16. Robert Langbaum, *The Poetry of Experience: The Dramatic Monologue in Modern Literary Tradition* (New York, 1963 [1957]), p. 24.

detail of appearance or incident which vivifies them for the reader, working from the concrete facts toward a sympathetic understanding of their consciousness. The characters in *The French Revolution* are caught up, Holloway asserts, in an historical process which tends to negate their individuality and to magnify instead what they represent.[17] Yet it is also true that Carlyle's fictional method of presenting characters conveys a sense of the humanity of those who find themselves so caught up. Only heroic men may actually alter the course of history, and neither Danton nor Mirabeau ultimately deflects the course of the Terror; yet the response of every individual is of infinite importance. In an imaginatively realized vignette, Carlyle portrays the pathetic, neglected existence of Louis XIV's three daughters, "*Graille, Chiffe, Coche* (Rag, Snip, Pig, as he was wont to name them)." They alone wait on the old king, dying of smallpox; for this "good and loving" act they will be remembered (*Works*, II, 16–17).

Carlyle often makes effective use of quotations taken from historical sources to present character. By speaking for themselves in their own voices, characters authenticate their human existence. The Editor organizes, summarizes, comments, even enters into dialogue with them, but he does not invent. Quotations also provide the vividness of specific detail essential to Carlyle's fictional method. These details sound like fiction, because they center on the speaker's self-consciousness or they appeal to the senses like the verisimilar details of novel-fiction. But Carlyle can quite legitimately point to them as "fact" since he has not made them up. Louis XV, goaded by Du Barry to dismiss his minister Choiseul, "finally mustered heart to see [him]; and with that 'quivering in the chin (*tremblement du menton*)' natural in such case, faltered out a dismissal" (*Works*, II, 3). Both the footnote to "in such case," citing volume and page of Besenval's *Mémoires*, and the French phrase quoted after its translation, emphasize the authenticity of the description. At the same time, the image of the trembling chin provides the kind of telling detail revelatory of an inward state of mind for which the writer of prose fiction searches. Philippe d'Orléans goes to the guillotine, dressed like a dandy. "On the scaffold, Samson was for drawing off his boots: 'Tush,' said Philippe, 'they will come better off *after*; let us have done, *dépêchons-nous!*' " (*Works*, IV, 209). In *Past and Present*, Carlyle

17. Holloway, pp. 72–74.

captures the vigorous colloquial tone of Abbot Samson's rebuke to an old monk: "I am obliged to thee as if thou hadst cut off both my feet! By God's face, *per os Dei*, I will not eat bread till that fabric be torn in pieces" (*Works*, X, 113).

Carlyle's use of disconnected quotations or fragments in *Sartor Resartus* has been identified as a typical Romantic mode which goes far to account for the "rhapsodic, oracular, and lyric tone," a tone well suited to the "mystic, mantic Teufelsdröckh." In its open-endedness and brevity it permits the expression of ecstatic utterance which could not well be sustained in longer passages.[18] But the fragmentary quotations in *Past and Present* and *The French Revolution* create a different effect; those who are quoted are not mystics but a wide variety of different personalities. The "oracular" voice in these books is that of the Editor; it is he who perceives the symbolic and transcendental meanings. He gazes from the present into a past which in some very real sense still exists, and addresses the reader directly as one who looks and listens with him to its voices. The Editor's vision of the dying Mirabeau combines with voices from the past to enable us to "take upon ourselves his character and his environment of circumstances": "In January last, *you might see him* as President of the Assembly, 'his neck wrapt in linen cloths, at the evening session': . . . 'At parting he embraced me,' says Dumont, 'with an emotion I had never seen in him: "I am dying, my friend; dying as by slow fire; we shall perhaps not meet again" ' "(*Works*, III, 140; my italics). There are certain limitations to the Editor's vision. His inability to see more than his sources disclose to him actually intensifies our sense of being *in* the past, as does the recurrent use of the present tense. He is no more able than the French citizens to discern the truth of rumors: "Much is invisible; the very Jacobins have their reticences. Insurrection is to be: but when? This only we can discern . . ." (*Works*, III, 279). The direct communication with the reader, the moralizing commentary which goes on simultaneously with the effort to recreate the consciousness of the characters, the occasional retreat from omniscience are techniques Thackeray will use with equal daring in *Vanity Fair*. In the handling of detail, however, Carlyle's art differs wholly from Thackeray's, for where Thackeray multiplies invented details to establish verisimili-

18. Tennyson, pp. 223–231.

tude, Carlyle seeks to compel belief through grounding character, event and setting in the "concreteness of fact."

Through the Editor's complaints about the style of Teufelsdröckh, Carlyle jabs lightly at his own way of writing. "Considered as an Author," the Editor declares, "Herr Teufelsdröckh has one scarcely pardonable fault, doubtless his worst: an almost total want of arrangement. In this remarkable Volume, it is true, his adherence to the mere course of Time produces, through the Narrative portions, a certain show of outward method; but of true logical method and sequence there is too little" (*SR*, 34). Carlyle deliberately avoids chronological narrative at times, or when he uses it, undercuts it by various means. In *The French Revolution* the energy of the narrative drive is undermined not only by intermittent philosophizing, but also by vast numbers of characters, appearing sometimes only once or twice, who challenge both the reader's memory and his sense of logical connection. In the non-chronological sections of *Past and Present* starving Irish children, the Sphinx, King Midas, and Chactaw Indians somehow become part of the England of Bobus Higgins and Sir Jabesh Windbag. Jocelin's narrative like Teufelsdröckh's autobiography suffers frequent editorial interruptions, and narrated events often fall into anecdotal units instead of advancing plot relationships.

Carlyle does not believe in the logic of cause and effect, but in the whole, "a broad, deep Immensity," in which each atom is " 'chained' and completed with all." [19] History written under the rubric of cause-and-effect sequences fails to represent the complexity, the unity, and the interrelatedness of human experience. [20] To develop fictions which will represent experience more adequately without depending on conventional plotting (although they may well function within a loose narrative framework), Carlyle takes off from the idea, rather generally absorbed by him from Hegel, that the concepts of time and space put illusory limits on human experience. He possesses a "modern" consciousness of inner time: "for Time, like Space, is *infinitely* divisible; and an hour with its events, with its sensations and emotions, might be diffused to such expansion as should cover the whole field of memory, and push all else over the limits" (*Works*, XXVIII, 172). As

19. *Works*, XXVII, 88–89, quoted by Levine, p. 41.
20. Levine, pp. 40–42.

Teufelsdröckh enters the labyrinths of his own inner space in a crisis
of personality, his inner time expands, negating strict chronology.
The French Revolution is like a novel in its general shape—its rapid
moving to a climax in the Terror, and the quieter closing chapters,[21]
but it attains this shape less by attention to plot than by the exploration of the inner time of the period. The death of Louis XVI drags
over four slow chapters, like the slow, reluctant end of the age; the
rhythmic "systole-diastole" of the guillotine sets the quickening tem-
po of the Terror. "Philosophical-speculative" editorial comments over-
lap, indent, and indeed run quite through the historical events,
further fragmenting linear time, for Carlyle sees life as a "mystic
loom" on which linear time, the warp, is shot through by the woof of
the mysterious and unknown.

Carlyle develops character, setting, and event, then, not through
the logical sequences of plot, but through other devices—primarily
through leitmotif and symbol. Leitmotifs draw on the concrete details, metaphors, or mythological allusions which have been associated with particular characters. These identifying phrases echo
through the work like musical themes. In various permutations and
combinations, they elaborate and emphasize character. The inter-
twined leitmotifs of many different characters unify the work as a
whole, much as leitmotifs structure Wagnerian opera at the same
time that they enrich and complicate it. Carlyle intended in *The
Diamond Necklace* to combine factual concreteness with a sort of
musical development, as he wrote to his brother John: "The story of
The Diamond Necklace is all told in that paper with the strictest
fidelity, yet in a kind of *musical* way."[22] Carlyle uses leitmotifs most
effectively in the works in which he interweaves numbers of characters, showing how they are complexly interrelated in a musical, not
a logical, unity.

Prince Louis de Rohan, soon to become a cardinal, appears to be
held together by his clothing; beneath the "plush cloaks and wrap-
pages" that swathe his plump figure, he lies stagnant and fermenting,
"overlaid with such floods of fat material: . . . a true image of the
shamefulest Mud-volcano, gurgling and sluttishly simmering . . .
with occasional terrifico-absurd mud-explosions" (*Works*, XXVIII,
342). Somnolence and violence are observed in the Cardinal's every

21. Holloway, p. 61.
22. Froude, *Carlyle*, II, 386, 24 Dec. 1833.

action: "if Monseigneur grew choleric; wrapped himself up in reserve, spoke roughly to his domestics and dependants,—were not the terrifico-absurd mud-explosions becoming more frequent?" (*Works*, XXVIII, 347). Rohan's leitmotif is interwoven with that of the Countess de Lamotte, with her "face of a certain piquancy" and a sharp "spark of Life;" with the jeweller Boehmer's "bland, blond face," with half a dozen other characters, including the Arch-quack Cagliostro—each of whom has his or her distinguishing characteristics.

In *The French Revolution* scores of such leitmotifs interweave with one another, revealing a complex yet firmly controlled pattern of relationships. For the more important characters, the "theme" is introduced in some detail. Carlyle describes Robespierre as he marches in the procession of the States-General: an "anxious, slight, ineffectual-looking man, under thirty, in spectacles; his eyes (were the glasses off) troubled, careful; with upturned face, snuffing dimly the uncertain future time; complexion of a multiplex atrabiliar colour, the final shade of which may be the pale sea-green. . . a strict-minded, strait laced man" (*Works*, II, 141–142). As the "sea-green Robespierre," "Robespierre the Incorruptible," he stalks through the book; stalks at the end, "this poor Robespierre, like a seagreen ghost, through the blooming July" (*Works*, IV, 275).

So too in *Past and Present* characters are tagged, identified by some specific physical detail or perhaps by an action. The indomitable Plugson, Chactaws and Chevaliers, Gurth born thrall of Cedric, Quaker Friend Prudence, Apes and Nomads, the Irish widow who dies of typhus fever to prove her relationship to her neighbors, the rugged, inarticulate John Bull—all are interwoven through the book and come together in a final, symphonic unity in the last chapters. As a leitmotif is repeated, its significance increases; frequently, the burden of meaning associated with it becomes so great that the leitmotif itself may properly be called a symbol, embodying a meaning far beyond the literal.

The relationship between Carlyle's prophetic vision, which is expressed through symbols, and the novel has not been fully explored, although Holloway finds *The French Revolution* "midway between the novel and the prophetic essay,"[23] and Kathleen Tillotson is suggestive about ways in which Carlyle awakened the novel of the 1840's to its "poetic, prophetic, and visionary possibilities." In his works he

23. Holloway, p. 60.

adds to the interest in human conduct and in the whole range of social life—"the novelist's true sphere"—another dimension, involving not only a widened sense of time and space, but a claim for the infinite value of any particular moment and location.[24] Through juxtapositions of the everyday real and the transcendent, as well as through rhythmical repetitions of character, event, and setting, and through variations in point of view—all devices closely linked with the novel—Carlyle transforms facts into symbols. E. M. Forster has named, and E. K. Brown has explored, the "prophetic" novel, the novel which through its story, characters, and setting attempts to communicate a belief in an unnamable mystery and in an order belonging to that mystery which lies behind them. The reader, Brown observes, is moved to believe in such a mystery when something in the foreground of the novel becomes a symbol.[25] It is this power of the symbol to compel belief which led Carlyle to structure his works by symbols rather than by narrative plot.

Like other Romantics, Carlyle was reluctant to analyze the process by which he created symbols, beyond maintaining that they enter literature from the writer's fruitful encounters with the unconscious, in which he discerned the source of virtuous action (SR, 219).[26] Yet he recognizes their origin in the everyday real. The two kinds of symbols which Carlyle identifies, the intrinsic and the extrinsic, are analogous to E. K. Brown's fixed and expanding symbols. Fixed or extrinsic symbols acquire a limited number of meanings, which are often associated with them almost accidentally; they are more than literal, but less than ineffable. More important are intrinsic or expanding symbols, which accrete multiple meanings. "All works of art," "Death," and religious symbols are intrinsic symbols, and above all, for Carlyle, the life of the heroic man (SR, 223–224). He recognizes that symbols into which personality enters are capable of an almost indefinite widening and deepening of significance.[27]

Symbols come into being in the novel, Brown further suggests, through combinations of repetition and variation. Fixed symbols are

24. Kathleen Tillotson, *Novels of the Eighteen Forties*, rev. ed. (Oxford, 1956), pp. 154, 134.

25. E. K. Brown, *Rhythm in the Novel* (Toronto, 1950), pp. 58–59.

26. See Eugene Goodheart, "Goethe, Carlyle and *The Sorrows of Werther*," *The Cult of the Ego* (Chicago, 1968), pp. 81–84. Goodheart points out the anti-Romantic quality of Carlyle's assumption that "the demon—that is, the unconscious,—of the community was wise, healthy, and moral."

27. Cf. Brown, pp. 35–57.

established when words, phrases, or character traits are repeated
without variation in meaning. But when the symbol means different
things or appeals in varied ways to different persons in the novel,
that is, when it is repeated with variation, it effectively suggests to
the reader that it has a "surplus of meaning" which perhaps even
the narrator has not been able to plumb. In the symbol with a
"residue of mystery,"[28] the expanding or intrinsic symbol, "there is
ever, more or less distinctly and directly, some embodiment and
revelation of the Infinite" (*SR*, 220). As they are repeated, both fixed
and expanding symbols interweave and interact to express larger
themes. Like the "prophetic" novelist, Carlyle works through events,
persons, and settings in the foreground to create symbols; his works
derive their unity from a similar interweaving in both the narrative
and non-narrative sections.

In the chaotic swirl of the Revolution, these repetitions establish
an ordered structure. The processions form a major sequence of repeated events, varied sufficiently to measure change and disclose its
ironic or transcendent meaning. As the States General marches
through the streets of Paris on 4 May 1789, led by the king, the end
of feudalism may be seen converging with the birth of democracy. In
each successive procession, the king's position is less exalted; at the
last he rides in a cart to the guillotine, ironically self-martyred by his
own weakness. From being a symbol of powerful and purposive leadership, he has become the symbol of the end of an age.

Repetition with variation also establishes the symbolic value of individual lives. Lafayette's white charger, for example, suggests the
chivalric element in his character, the courtesy, generosity and valor
of the feudal past. But the rider of the white horse is also the admired
"Hero of Two Worlds," supporter of the American Revolution, advocate of liberty, equality, and fraternity, trusted by the hungry poor of
Paris. Unfortunately chivalry, like the white charger which symbol-
izes it, cannot cope with the rapidity and totality of change. In the Insurrection of Women, Lafayette is as irrelevant as his steed, although
neither knows it: "All hearts [are] set, with a moody fixedness, on one
object. Moody, fixed are all hearts: tranquil is no heart,—if it be not
that of the white charger, who paws there, with arched neck, com-
posedly champing his bit; as if no World, with its Dynasties and Eras,
were now rushing down" (*Works*, II, 259). Increasingly, Lafayette is

28. Ibid., p. 51.

caught between violent extremes. When he returns to Paris from the front, seeking to rally popular support against the Jacobins, only a hundred answer his first call; thirty, the second. "Colossal Hero of two Worlds, having weighed himself in the balance, finds that he is become a gossamer Colossus" (*Works*, III, 266). The weight, the "colossal" stature of the man, made meaningful through repetition, gains ironic depth by the sudden denial of "weight" where it had come to be expected—"a gossamer Colossus."

Variation in point of view is another device by which repeated facts become symbols in Carlyle's literary universe. To characters gifted with insight, the most ordinary object or event may body forth transcendent mystery. To the literal, mechanist, or materialist mind, these perceptions are likely to seem mad or impractical. When the visionary confronts an opposing insistence on literal meaning, a symbol comes into being which may express ironic depths or transcendental heights. If the variations in angle of vision ascend from the literal to the spiritual, the symbol will suggest a beneficent mystery. But if the variations are modulated downwards through different points of view, from the infinite towards the more limited, the residual meanings will be ironic, suggesting something of the "waste wild-weltering chaos" which boils beneath the "thin Earth-rind" of habit (*Works*, II, 38). Carlyle works his symbols in both directions; the opposition of movements creates a tension which is not completely resolved by the final victory of the up-beat, ascendant point of view in the major works of this period.

Often these varied viewpoints are brought together within a single paragraph, making it possible thereafter, to evoke the symbolic meaning by repetition alone. The report in *Past and Present* of the children murdered by their desperate parents for a few pence in burial insurance drives from the literal to the symbolic in a dozen successive sentences. Courts of law present the "fact" in impersonal, unemotional language; but the "idle reader of Newspapers" perceives the indicted parents as "brutal savages, degraded Irish." The parents themselves give voice to a terrible isolation: "A human Mother and Father had said to themselves, What shall we do to escape starvation? We are deep sunk here, in our dark cellar; and help is far" (*Works*, X, 4). The narrator's wider vision links their suffering to that in Dante's Inferno: society has locked them in a "Ugolino Hunger-tower." The surplus of meaning in this symbol is not transcendental mystery but ironic terror. Through the contrasting viewpoints, the crisis for the suffering family is revealed as a crisis of ultimate import for the community.

A last device by which Carlyle creates symbols is through contrasts in scale. Repeatedly, and with a "magical" touch,[29] he sets his concrete facts—persons, events, settings—into the widest possible contexts. In cinematic terms, he uses a "zoom" technique: the focus shifts with startling rapidity from close-up to panoramic view, from the minnow in the creek to the vast ocean, from the moment in which Lafayette's white charger abstractedly paws the ground to the whole of past and future. Transformed imaginatively through this device, the most ordinary and commonplace scenes take on something of the supernatural world of which they are suddenly seen to be a part. In "On History" (1830) Carlyle placed the farmer in such a setting: "The simple husbandman can till his field, and by knowledge he has gained of its soil, sow it with the fit grain, though the deep rocks and central fires are unknown to him: his little crop hangs under and over the firmament of stars, and sails through whole untracked celestial spaces, between Aries and Libra" (*Works*, XXVII, 90). To Teufelsdröckh, gifted with insight, no place is ordinary; all are filled with wonder: "'a whole immensity of Brussels carpets, and pier-glasses, and or-molu . . . cannot hide from me that such Drawing-room is simply a section of Infinite Space, where so many God-created Souls do for the time meet together'" (*SR*, 29). Sometimes the wider context discloses the frantic bustle of men absorbed in the temporal, spectral world. When news of Louis XVI's flight to Varennes reaches Nantes, in one of the "dull leathern Diligences" of the mail office, patriots rush into the streets in their nightshirts. "Here and there a faint farthing rushlight, hastily kindled; and so many swart-featured haggard faces with nightcaps pushed back. . . . And overhead, as always, the Great Bear is turning so quiet round Boötes; steady, indifferent as the leathern Diligence itself" (*Works*, III, 166, 167).

Contrasts in scale may reveal human concerns as petty or magnify their importance as expressions of the cosmic spiritual life. In *Sartor Resartus* the dominant, if always ambiguous, emphasis falls on man's ability to transcend, to look "fixedly on Existence, till, one after the other, its earthly hulls and garnitures have all melted away . . ." (*SR*, 255). In *Past and Present*, the emphasis falls on his ability to trans-

29. Sanders, "The Victorian Rembrandt," p. 553.

form chaos into order, into "a green flowery World," a kind of Heaven (*Works*, X, 298). Such a transformation of setting will come about through work, which has become for Carlyle the only miracle. In *The French Revolution*, however, the transitory nature of human existence, its brevity and closeness to death, is the overpowering theme. Death, inescapable irony and ultimate mystery, provides the context for every action, from the long-drawn-out, quickly forgotten death of Louis "the Well-Beloved," to the pitiable, terror-filled death of Robespierre. Death, the wider context, discloses a measure of humanity even in the meanest or weakest, and in a few, an heroic nobility.

The future to which the Revolution finally looks is a distant one—the end of time itself. Metaphors of madness and disorder, or fire and darkness, suggest the coming apocalypse and magnify the particular event to an ultimate significance. At the fall of the Bastille "Straw is burnt; three cartloads of it, hauled thither, go up in white smoke, almost to the choking of Patriotism itself; so that Elie had, with singed brows, to drag back one cart; and Réole the 'gigantic haberdasher' another" (*Works*, II, 192). Carlyle seizes on the concrete details—the exact number of cartloads, the singed brows, the description taken, as the quotation marks declare, from an historical source. But he also sets the event in the wider context, generalizing by allusion and with rhythmic effect: "Smoke as of Tophet; confusion as of Babel; noise as of the Crack of Doom!" (*Works*, I, 192).

If the past and the future do not in some way exist in the present moment, Carlyle writes in *Sartor Resartus*, then we live in a "spectral Necropolis, or rather City both of the Dead and of the Unborn" (*SR*, 249). In *Past and Present* he pictures contemporary England as existing in such a Necropolis, cut off temporally from its own past and future, cut off spatially, every man from every other. The Editor-narrator expands the present, juxtaposing it with the successful community of the medieval past and the potential community of the industrial future. The wider temporal context diminishes the present, revealing its narrowness and isolation. In contrast, Abbot Samson, who perceives himself as a spiritual being, lives "in an element of miracle" between Heaven's splendor and Hell's darkness. His work links him with the infinite: only workmen become immortal, "they alone surviving; peopling, they alone, the unmeasured solitudes of Time" (*Works*, X, 116, 202).

In the non-chronological sections of *Past and Present* Carlyle has moved away from the conscious fictions of *Sartor* and from the large narrative framework of *The French Revolution*. Yet *Past and Present* bears comparison with *Sartor* both in its organization—a central, chronological narrative from the past is buttressed on both sides by long, non-chronological sections set in the present—and in its use of fictional techniques; and with *The French Revolution* in its handling of the Editor as persona. Jocelin's chronicle, like Teufelsdröckh's autobiography, maintains "a certain show of outward method"; the organizing fictions of the non-chronological sections are less immediately obvious. Yet in these sections Carlyle does set up two fictions, complexly interwoven (which extend by way of the persona of the Editor into the narrative section), through which he brings together his understanding of the diminished nature of contemporary England and his vision of its heroic future.

An ongoing fictional dialogue is one source of unity in *Past and Present*. Like Teufelsdröckh, the Editor of this work possesses a sage's wisdom and a prophetic voice. He dominates the narrative more completely than Teufelsdröckh, whose views are subject to the Sartorean Editor's misapprehensions. Like the Editor of *The French Revolution*, he speaks frequently in tones of ominscience, at the cost of the openness and duality of vision which characterize *Sartor*.[30] The role of the Sartorean Editor, whose slow progress from a literal misinterpretation to a profound understanding of the Clothes philosophy provides much of the comedy of *Sartor*, is taken in *Past and Present* by a dozen or more personae, voices from all segments of English society. Their objections to the narrator's wisdom seem often ridiculous or obtuse. Nevertheless, it is the dialogue between the Editor and these personae which goes far to create a particular and vivid picture of English society.

The Editor speaks with the voice of the returned hero, filled with insight which he wishes to share with his interlocutors. Their voices— sneering, querulous, or despairing—raise questions. They are the wrong questions, which reveal their preoccupations with money, laissez-faire economics, "doing what one likes with one's own," and respectability:

"My starving workers?" answers the rich mill-owner: "Did not I hire them fairly in the market?" [*Works*, X, 146].

30. Levine, pp. 29–35.

"Fair day's-wages for fair day's-work!" exclaims a sarcastic man [X, 19].

"Men cease to regard money?" cries Bobus of Houndsditch: "What else do all men strive for? The very Bishop informs me that Christianity cannot get on without a minimum of Four thousand five hundred in its pocket. Cease to regard money? That will be at Doomsday in the afternoon! [X, 295].

Occasionally the Editor, interrupting the questioner, will characterize him in his response—not infrequently, it is true, with a blunt contempt: " 'Man of Genius?' Thou has small notion, meseems, O Maecenas Twiddledee, of what a Man of Genius is. Read in thy New Testament and elsewhere. . . . Thou fool, with *thy* empty Godhoods, Apotheoses *edgegilt*; the Crown of Thorns made into a poor jewel-room crown, fit for the head of blockheads; the bearing of the Cross changed to a riding in the Long-Acre Gig!" (*Works*, X, 292). These voices clash with the Editor's, their perceptions of the world as material with his insight into its spiritual nature. Their way of the ballot box diverges from his path of hero worship; their "cash-nexus" devalues his concept of mutual loyalty between employer and employee. The movement of the book proceeds through these polar oppositions, swinging from the misapprehensions of a disturbed and despairing public to the insights of the Editor. It is the thinnest of disguises but nonetheless something of an aesthetic mask for Carlyle himself. In the end, predictably, his voice dominates, refutes, silences, and—one can only suppose—convinces all the others. The effect is jarring to modern sensibilities, the disguise altogether too thin. Yet the other voices do exist, and through their exaggerated names and in the energy of their blunt, dense statements, they emerge with amazing vitality. And it is the existence of these voices, vestigial though they are at times, which maintains a tenuous balance, keeping the non-narrative sections in the realm of imaginative fiction and preventing them from sliding wholly into the hortatory discourse of sermon or harangue.

The Editor's voice unites the heroic narrative with the diminished present, thus enlarging the context for the present. His attitudes towards the inhabitants of the past and those of the present differ strikingly. While he does not romanticize Samson, he treats him with an affectionate dignity, emphasizing his concrete humanity. Bobus, Maecenas Twiddledee, Dog-draught, the Hon. Alcides Dolittle are diminished by their opposition to Samson. The Editor sees into the mystery and wonder of human life in the past, but he sees *through* the pretense and hypocrisy of the present. Thus his use of caricature, a form closer to satire than to comedy but including elements of both, is appropriate for the personae of the present. Here is Bobus, whose very name sounds slow and dull, close to "booby," and who is "rounder than one of [his] own sausages" (*Works*, X, 31). The humor is Hogarthian, coruscating; nevertheless, it is not contemptuous. The Editor sees in Bobus what Bobus fails to recognize in himself—a soul of infinite worth. Plugson of Undershot, though he is a vulgar fellow with false ideas who prides himself on his double-entry bookkeeping, is also recognized by the Editor as a man of tremendous energies. From wrestling with the "dim brute Powers of Fact" he has acquired "Patience, Courage, Perseverance, Openness to light, readiness to own [him]self mistaken" (*Works*, X, 198). The Editor calls upon him to become a Captain of Industry, to undertake the heroic journey beyond the material world into the depths of his own soul:

Thou must descend to the *Mothers*, to the *Manes*, and Hercules-like long suffer and labour there, wouldst thou emerge with victory into the sunlight. . . . The world and its wages . . . shall be as a waste ocean-flood; the chaos through which thou art to swim and sail. . . . thy star alone . . . shalt thou strive to follow. . . . O, it is a business, as I fancy, that of weltering your way through Chaos and the murk of Hell. . . . You look fixedly into Madness, and *her* undiscovered, boundless, bottomless Night-empire; that you may extort new Wisdom out of it, as an Eurydice from Tartarus [*Works*, X, 205–206]

But by itself the fiction of a dialogue between voices is too slight to give body to the England which Carlyle perceived. His vision of the Condition of England was a vision not only of its people, but of its lands and cities, its factories and fields. To bring into being a coherent, inhabited universe, without recourse to sequential narrative, he employed a stunningly diverse potpourri of fictions and facts. The personae with their outlandish names are interwoven with descriptions of rural and urban scenes; characters and events taken literally from daily newspapers or Parliamentary reports are set beside characters and events from myth, literature, or Scots anecdote. England at harvest time, Manchester with its sooty furnaces, Sir Jabesh Windbag, Dr. Alison's report of the death of a poor Irish widow from typhus, the Sphinx and King Midas, Dante's Inferno and a rusty Scottish meat-jack—all become part of the same world. Fact and fiction are melded together through Carlyle's handling of all as leitmotifs and ultimately as symbols which disclose the reality of nineteenth-century England.

Or rather, *two* Englands. For he sees at one and the same time an England "waving with yellow harvests; thick-studded with work-shops" (*Works*, X, 1) in which "the rugged Brindley," silent, Hercu-lean laborer, should be happily at work. Superimposed upon that England, blocking its fruition, is an "Atheist world, [extending] from its utmost summits of Heaven and Westminster-Hall, downwards through poor seven-feet Hats and 'Unveracities fallen hungry,' down to the lowest cellars and neglected hunger-dens of it" (*Works*, X, 148). Carlyle's imagination is especially drawn to Manchester as an emblem of the Atheist world. The Manchester insurrection symbol-izes its human alienation. He describes the scene just before the massacre in spare words: "A million of hungry operative men . . . came all out into the streets, and—stood there." They stood there until, in panic, the armed soldiery shot thirteen of them, men and women. Manchester itself is a dirty, overcrowded industrial city. It can never return to its pre-industrial past, when its rivers ran clean and no coal was mined to fill its skies with smoke; its future lies in its potential for heroic accomplishment through its machines.[31] But if its present inhabitants recover their awareness of their own souls, they will be able to perceive the transcendental reality of the city: "Sooty Manchester,—it too is built on the infinite Abysses; over-spanned by the skyey Firmaments; and there is birth in it, and death in it;—and it is every whit as wonderful, as fearful, unimaginable, as the oldest Salem or Prophetic City" (*Works*, X, 228). Insight coupled with energy can make this vision a concrete fact. Carlyle calls for "Manufacturing Towns" which "let-in the blessed sunlight, the blue of Heaven, and become clear and clean"; where the mills offer the workers "baths, free air, a wholesome temperature, ceilings twenty feet high," and within walking distance "a hundred acres or so of free greenfield, with trees on it, conquered, for its little children to disport in; for its all-conquering workers to take a breath of twi-light air in" (*Works*, X, 265). Plugson, as Captain of Industry, will

31. See Herbert L. Sussman, "Transcendentalism and the Machine: Thomas Carlyle," *Victorians and the Machine: The Literary Response to Technology* (Cam-bridge, Mass., 1968), pp. 14–15. The "million hungry men" is quoted from *Works*, X, 15.

bind his workers to him by love, which "cannot be bought by cash-payment" (*Works*, X, 272). The repeated fictions create two coherent and inhabited worlds, linked by the prophetic vision which perceives the transformation of the one into the other. "Sooty Hell of mutiny and savagery and despair can, by man's energy, be made a kind of Heaven; cleared of its soot, of its mutiny, of its need to mutiny; the everlasting arch of Heaven's azure overspanning *it* too, and its cunning mechanisms and tall chimney-steeples, as a birth of Heaven . . ." (*Works*, X, 298).

Past and Present: *Topicality as Technique*

RICHARD D. ALTICK, *The Ohio State University*

> *For indeed it is well said, "in every object there is inexhaustible meaning; the eye sees in it what the eye brings means of seeing."*
> *The French Revolution* (*Works*, II, 5)

In the summer of 1842 the "condition of England question" which had worried Carlyle for a number of years came to a crisis. He was, of course, not alone in his anxiety, nor did he exaggerate the desperate state of affairs. As more than one modern historian has observed, the year was the most ominous, the most critical, of the whole century. And so Carlyle, after beholding the idle able-bodied men who had been pauperized into the St. Ives workhouse and reading news accounts of the August riots in the cotton towns and elsewhere, put aside his research for the *Cromwell* and in October or early November began to write what he intended to be a tract for the times: a tract, indeed, for the very moment.

Although the rhetorical texture of *Past and Present* is dense with allusions to the Bible, to classical and Scandinavian mythology, to ancient Rome, and to the Middle Ages, this "matter of the past," as it may be called, was balanced by the "matter of the present," a system of topicalities and allusions to more or less recent history designed to underscore the urgency of the condition of England question. From one angle Carlyle looked at the crisis of English society *sub specie aeternitatis*; but from another, the one that concerns us here, he regarded it as the most pressing business before the men who read the *Times* and the newly founded *Illustrated London News* in the autumn and winter of 1842–1843. In *Past and Present* the prophetic voice merges with the voice of the polemic journalist. These, Carlyle's topical references imply, are the things that affect us *today*, and must be attended to *today*.

The manifold topicalities of the book were put to numerous uses: illustration, symbolism, irony, analogy, contrast, invective. They served not only to particularize but, in Carlyle's characteristic fashion, to provide material for frequent repetition and variation. But how successful were these techniques of stimulating a sense of "present-ness" in his first readers? To reconstruct with any semblance of scientific precision the impact which the topical allusions had upon the book-buyers of April 1843 would be a hopeless ambition. We do not have sufficient data, and in any case what psychologists would term the recognition- and affection-factors attached to each individual allusion inevitably varied from person to person. Despite the daunting number of imponderables, however, the mere attempt to estimate the effectiveness of Carlyle's topicalities may cast some light upon the nature of his artistry and the shrewdness of his insight into the contemporary public mind and its allusive equipment.

The term "topicality," it must be said at once, is necessarily an elastic one. As some of our most striking instances will suggest, it embraces, in addition to yesterday's headlines, allusions to events removed from the present by one or two years, or by a dozen. Unfortunately, in the psychology of literary response we possess no such neat formulation as do nuclear physicists with their concept of an isotope's half-life. It is impossible to determine how long a given topicality retained its original power, or how long it retained any at all. Some of the allusions that reached back as much as a decade had undoubtedly diminished in strength by 1843; others retained a persistent resonance, a steady and even expanding connotative aura. Which faded, and which survived with unimpaired vitality, depended to some extent on the nature of each: on the depth to which it had initially rooted itself in the contemporary communal mind, on its recurrent applicability, and on what might be termed its magnetic strength, its self-renewing power of attracting kindred associations to it.

One index of an allusion's lasting vitality is the number of writers who employ it, and over how long a period. Here external evidence comes to our aid. A notable example of perennial topicality is St. John Long, the practitioner of drastic medicine whose administration of his accurately named "corrosive mixture" landed him in the dock at least twice, charged with manslaughter, some dozen years before he turned up in *Past and Present*: "This is sad news to a disconsolate discerning Public, hoping to have got off by some Morrison's Pill, some Saint-John's corrosive mixture and perhaps a little blistery friction on the back!"[1] Long's misadventures had received wide publicity at the time, not only in the newspaper press but in *Fraser's Magazine* for May and October 1830 and January 1831— articles written by Carlyle's physician brother, John Aitken Carlyle— and in the *Lancet*, whose editor, the combative Thomas Wakley, waged against Long an editorial campaign as corrosive as his salve. This fashionable quack and his trusting patients were so well known to the public as to be satirized in prints and in a Covent Garden pantomime, *Harlequin Pat and Harlequin Bat*. The scandal of the trials was reflected in such diverse places as Greville's diary (12 December 1830) and the first of John Stuart Mill's essays on "The Spirit of the Age" (*Examiner*, 6 January 1831). Repeated allusions kept Long's memory green over the next decade; in December 1842, even as *Past and Present* was being written, an article in the *Quarterly Review* (p. 91) recalled his notoriety. Nobody needed to be reminded who St. John Long was, even though Carlyle by oversight used only his given name.

A retrospective measure of the degree to which Long was embedded in the public consciousness is afforded by his subsequent career in literature. Thackeray referred to him in *The Book of Snobs* (*Punch*, 1846), and as late as the seventies he appeared in *Middlemarch* (chapter 45) and *Far from the Madding Crowd* (chapter 22: "an anticlimax somewhat resembling that of St. John Long's death by consumption in the midst of his proofs that it was not a fatal disease"). While mention of Long in *Middlemarch* may have been due in part to George Eliot's research in the files of the *Times* and the *Lancet*, both she and Hardy obviously relied upon their readers' ready recognition of a forty-year-old allusion. Probably Long's prominence in several editions of the *Newgate Calendar* had something to do with his enduring celebrity.

Another case in point is the almost legendary George Stulz (or Stultz), the fashionable tailor who appeared first in the *Post Office Directory* in 1815. (In 1842 his firm was styled "Stulz, Housley, and Wain, tailors, 10 Clifford St., Bond St.") By the time Carlyle wrote of him in *Past and Present* (pp. 215–216) he had already become the abiding symbol of masculine *haute couture*, not to say outright

1. P. 41. All references are to the Riverside edition of *Past and Present* (Boston, 1965), which reprints the text of the first edition.

dandyism: "Your Stulz, with high somerset, vaults from his high shopboard down to the depths of primal savagery,—carrying much along with him!" Hazlitt had mentioned him (*Monthly Magazine*, 1831), as had Bulwer in *Pelham* (1828) and *England and the English* (1833), Thackeray in his *Yellowplush Correspondence* and "Epistle of the Literati" (*Fraser's*, 1838 and 1840 respectively), Carlyle himself in his essay on Scott (*London and Westminster Review*, 1838) —though, oddly, not in *Sartor Resartus*; Samuel Warren in his novel, *Ten Thousand a Year!* (*Blackwood's*, 1839); and Thomas Hood in "Miss Kilmansegg and Her Precious Leg" (1840–1841). By the time of *Past and Present* only the positively illiterate could not have known who Stulz was; Carlyle could allude to him in perfect assurance that the name would carry its intended portion of meaning.[2]

A quack doctor, a fashionable tailor, and now a recalcitrant landowner, the Duke of Newcastle: his name and well-established notoriety, too, served Carlyle as common coinage, but in a more complex and subtle way. The Duke first appears in *Past and Present* on page 11. Though he is unnamed there, every reader would have recognized him behind Carlyle's figure of the "Master Unworker" "coercing, bribing, cajoling; doing what he likes with his own." The latter phrase (Matthew 20:15) had been on derisive tongues ever since 1829, when the Duke had used it in defending himself against criticism in the House of Lords for having evicted two hundred of his tenants at Newark for failing to vote for the Tory candidate. "Is it not lawful," he asked, "for me to do what I please with mine own?" The Duke reappears (p. 57), this time by name, but only as owner of a Suffolk pleasure ground where the Battle of Fornham was fought in 1173. Two pages farther on, Carlyle revives the "doing what he likes with his own" theme to contrast the martyrdom of the benevolent ninth-century King (or Landlord) Edmund with nineteenth-century landowners' abnegation of their social responsibility. Again, Newcastle is not named; the reader's appreciation of Carlyle's irony—his conversion of the phrase, in Edmund's mouth, to allude to a man's inalienable freedom to sacrifice his own life—depends on

2. Stulz's fame persisted for many years. He is referred to in Ruskin's *Modern Painters* (1843); Disraeli's *Coningsby* (1844); Thackeray's *Book of Snobs* (*Punch*, 1846), *Pendennis* (1849), and *The Newcomes* (1853); Bulwer-Lytton's *The Caxtons* (1848); and Reade's *Hard Cash* (1863). Even the putative Sir Roger Tichborne claimed that Stulz had "always" been his tailor; see W. P. Frith, *My Autobiography and Reminiscences* (London, 1887), II, 44.

his responding to the topical allusion of the echo of St. Matthew, which is repeated in later passages (p. 125, again in specific connection with Edmund; and pp. 174, 181).

At the time *Past and Present* was written, the Duke was no longer in the news. Following the burning of one of his residences, Nottingham Castle, by a Reform Bill mob which had not forgotten his ill-advised invocation of Scripture, Newcastle had retired into crusty seclusion. But his name and the indelibly associated tag from St. Matthew still served, a dozen and more years after the event, as a symbol of "landlords' coercion" (p. 80). Carlyle, in effect, did with him what he also did with St. John Long and Stulz: enlarged the character or the sentiment so that it was no longer the attribute of a single historical figure but that of a whole social class or phenomenon —quackery, dandyism, or neglect of *noblisse oblige*.[3]

Because they had been continually in the public consciousness a number of years before their appearance in *Past and Present*, these allusions had a richer resonance than did those of more immediate origin, to which we must now turn, remembering that Carlyle was writing from mid-autumn 1842 to 8 March 1843. (Twice in the later chapters, pp. 259, 265, he speaks of "this Year Forty-Three.") What these references lacked in scope, they made up for in immediacy. "Honour to the name of Ashley" (p. 281) refers to the future Lord Shaftesbury's moving an address to the crown on behalf of the state-aided education of the working class, an event of 28 February. It may well be that Carlyle was writing that very page at that very moment. Ashley's speech was designed to prepare the way for the favorable reception of Sir James Graham's "Factory-Bill" (p. 261) with its crucial provisions for released-time instruction for child workers ("a right Education Bill," p. 262). This was formally introduced into the Commons in the evening of the day that Carlyle wrote the last words of *Past and Present*.

The allusions to "our new friend, the Emperor" (p. 232) and to the treaty of Nanking (p. 264) reflect the end of the Opium War and the enforced reconciliation of China with Britain, news of which had reached London late in November 1842. The focus of the " 'Black or

3. Again like Long and Stulz, the Duke of Newcastle continued to hold a place in the rhetorical vocabulary of Victorian writers, many years after ceasing to be immediately topical. Dinah Maria Mulock recalled his query, in the anachronistic setting of 1800, in *John Halifax, Gentleman* (1856), and Trollope mentioned it in *The Way We Live Now* (1874–1875).

White Surplice' Controversies" (p. 206) was an event of 10 October, the Bishop of London's widely publicized charge to his diocese on a number of questions of ritual, preeminent among which was his recommendation that the preacher wear a surplice at morning service and a black gown at the evening one.[4] Two major literary events of the year are glanced at: Dickens's ("Schnüspel" 's) tour of America from January to June (pp. 60, 246) and the publication of Tennyson's *Poems*, from which a line of "Ulysses" is quoted, in May (p. 41).

As with events, so with contemporary social phenomena. Carlyle's reference to "railway speed" (p. 267) touched a responsive point in the consciousness of the moment, because nothing more acutely induced men's awareness of the new age they were living in than did the sensation of railway velocity, an element in human experience hardly more than ten years old. Even more recent an arrival (in 1840) was the "Stamped Postman" (p. 225). And while extravagant "puffery" (pp. 144, 234) of commercial products was by no means new, it unquestionably was more ubiquitous, and to many observers more objectionable, than ever before: Mill's onslaught, in his essay on "Civilization" (*London and Westminster Review*, 1836), strikingly anticipated Carlyle's. In the literary marketplace, the flamboyant practices of publishers like Bentley and Colburn, who not only touted their books in the usual ways but arranged for favorable reviews in their own periodicals and elsewhere, gave promotion a bad name. Even more offensive, however, were the outdoor advertising devices that burgeoned at this time. The rivalry of two makers of boot blacking, Warren and Day & Martin, was responsible for the defacement by paint or poster of countless pavements and walls. It is alluded to on page 146, along with the famous "seven-feet Hat" (pp. 144, 150, 206, 267) which serves in *Past and Present* as a synecdoche to assimilate all other forms of puffery. Carlyle's readers— the Londoners through daily personal experience, those in the country through the weekly cartoons and expostulations in *Punch*—were aware that at this moment road traffic in the Strand was being choked by vehicles bearing monstrous enlargements of the products advertised. Nor would they have forgotten that in May 1842 the birth of the *Illustrated London News* itself was heralded by the proprietors' turning loose on the crowded sidewalks of central London no fewer than two hundred sign bearers. If the paper's engraving of the line-

4. See Owen Chadwick, *The Victorian Church* (New York, 1966), I, 214–215.

up, in its first issue (14 May), is to be credited, the signs were taller than the men.

The current fame of Morison's pill (pp. 28 ff., 41, 42, 226, 230), acquired both through its manufacturer's extravagant advertising campaigns and through several court cases resulting from fatalities allegedly caused by overdoses, needs no gloss to anyone familiar with the English scene in 1843. It would have been strange indeed if Carlyle had not seized upon Morison's pill, itself (like St. John Long's corrosive mixture) a leading exemplar of quackery in the literal sense, as a central symbol of the pervasive spiritual falsehood to which he extended the same name.[5]

Dominating the allusive fabric of *Past and Present*, of course, were the eventful 1842 session of Parliament, which was prorogued in the middle of August, and the "Manchester Insurrection" which flared in the same month. The latter, taking, in part, the form of the Plug Plot riots from which Carlyle derived the name of Plugson of Undershot, probably makes the greater impression upon the reader, supplying as it does a tempestuous background for the argument. But it actually is depicted in general terms, with little reference to particular incidents. Carlyle is much more specific in his use of the Parliament of 1842. The session had been marked by the head-on confrontation, a decade in the preparing, of the protectionist landowning class and the free-trade manufacturing bloc on the related issues of tariff revision and taxation.

In the large pattern of *Past and Present*, this conflict of vested interests is represented by a sustained interplay of allusions. On the one hand, there are the partridge-shooting, game-preserving dilettantes, of whose activities Carlyle's readers were kept well informed in the press. The *Illustrated London News* for 22 October reported that four gentlemen, shooting at Buckenham, Norfolk, had killed 433 head of game in one day. Only three rabbits were among the casualties; "the greater portion were pheasants and partridges." At the end of the year (31 December) the same paper described a "grand battu" at Dupplin Castle, the seat of the Earl and Countess of Kinnoull. Despite bad weather, the party brought down 176 pheasants, 364 hares,

5. It is not impossible that Carlyle also intended a hidden reference to quack-like adulteration in his "Duke of Logwood" (p. 92). "The alleged use of logwood in colouring spurious or adulterated port wine was at one time a frequent subject of jocular allusion" (*OED*).

27 woodcock, and 275 rabbits. With news like this constantly serving editors as column fillers, Carlyle's diatribes against the Master Unworkers needed no further documentation.

Ranged against the dilettantes were their two large bodies of enemies, the constituency of the Anti-Corn Law League and the Chartists, whose extreme wing was uneasily and fleetingly allied with the corresponding wing of the Manchester free-traders. The Anti-Corn Law League, founded in Manchester in 1838, had gone national the next year, and now it was figuring in the daily news as the most powerful pressure group since Wilberforce's antislavery campaigns. While its leaders were lobbying and propagandizing against protectionism, the Chartists were receiving equal publicity as they handed in the second of their six-point petitions to Parliament (2 May).

When the newly elected Commons met at the beginning of the year, the Peelites had proposed to modify, to the patent disadvantage of the landowners, the sliding scale (pp. 34, 58, 146, 180, 190) built into the Corn Laws with the purpose of making the price of grain responsive to the shifts in supply and demand. The debate, climaxed on 5 April by the passage of the bill embodying the revised scale, inspired Carlyle to a double play on words at one point in his attack on the Idle Aristocracy: " 'sliding,' as on inclined-planes, which every new year they *soap* with new Hansard's-jargon under God's sky, and so are 'sliding' ever faster, towards a 'scale' and balance-scale whereon is written *Thou art found Wanting*" (p. 270).

The opposition to the revised sliding scale was personified by the Duke of Buckingham and Chandos, who had resigned as Lord-Keeper of the Privy Seal early in the session in protest against Peel's ("his Excellenz the Titular-Herr Ritter Kauderwälsch von Pferdefuss-Quacksalber" 's, p. 215) wooing of the Manchester bloc. In May, in tribute to his services in Parliament as "a recognised Farmer's Friend" (p. 58), a group of Chandos' fellow agriculturalists had gathered at Aylesbury to present him with "a piece of plate four feet six inches high, weighing 1800 ounces, and valued at £2000" (*Illustrated London News*, 21 May). Already notorious as an employer of sweated farm labor ("Chandos daydrudges," p. 88; "Chandos Farm-Labourers," p. 188), the Duke almost inevitably joined his fellow peer, the Duke of Newcastle, in the passage (pp. 57–59) already alluded to, as a model of social irresponsibility. In a season of widespread destitution and unrest among the people, Buckingham was thrust into the news by the ill-timed action of his admirers; in an equally tumultuous year, 1831, Newcastle had achieved a doubtful celebrity through the action of his incendiary working-class enemies. Neither, it must be stressed again, is named in this skillful passage; the reader's appreciation of Carlyle's irony depended wholly upon his awareness of what lay behind the allusions to the Farmer's Friend and "doing what one likes with one's own." With that recognition, the two peers merged to exemplify the anti-Edmund, the avatar of game-preserving dilettantism.

The atmosphere and issues of this parliamentary session punctuate the text of *Past and Present* in other ways. In the very first chapter (p. 9), "Mining-Labourer Committees" refers to the shocking report of the Commission for Inquiring into the Employment of Children which resulted in the quick passage of Ashley's act limiting the labor of women and children in collieries and mines. Elsewhere there are allusions to the proposed land property tax (pp. 29, 182) and to tariff revisions (p. 50), also anathema to the landowners, which were passed at the end of June.[6]

Streaked through many of the debates, as we find them reported in Hansard, was the claim of "expediency," cant which Carlyle repeatedly denounced (pp. 14, 24, 92, 152). But it is his iterated use of the word "Conservative" which probably touched his readers' politico-semantic nerve most keenly. In 1843, as applied to a party rather than a broad political philosophy and capitalized rather than set in lower case, the word was but a dozen years old, having first been used in that way by a writer—not John Wilson Croker, as used to be assumed—in the *Quarterly Review* for January 1830. From the outset it had designated the Peelite liberal wing of the Tory party. Now that the Tories were in power after having been in opposition for eleven years (with the exception of the so-called "hundred days" in 1834–1835), the novel name attached to their now dominant Peelite bloc was on everybody's tongue. It is against this background, of a neo-

6. Other events of the parliamentary session to which Carlyle alludes are the passage, at last, of the Talfourd-Mahon Copyright Bill on 24 June (pp. 107, 131, 201), and the "Goulburn-Baring Budget" (p. 208). The latter reference is not entirely clear. Goulburn was the incumbent chancellor of the exchequer, having succeeded Baring when the Tories came to power late in the summer of 1841. They were, of course, on opposite sides during the debate on Peel's financial program. Does Carlyle mean that under present conditions it was a matter of indifference which party, or which chancellor of the exchequer, sponsored a budget?

logism in the process of taking its permanent place in the political lexicon, that Carlyle's uses of the term (pp. 15, 17, 164–166) can most profitably be read. The book's running juxtaposition of past and present is, in a way, epitomized by the recurrence of a single term, whose recently acquired extra function as the label of the party newly in power, one would imagine, caused it to stand out in discourse as if subtly italicized.[7]

This was the session celebrated for the number of constituencies (Harwich, Nottingham, Lewes, Reading, Falmouth, Penryn, Bridport) that were accused of gross electoral corruption. Carlyle's "late Bribery Committee" (pp. 180, 181, 250–254) reported at the end of July. One of the references to the committee and its concern, "Bribery could not be put down" (p. 250), is of more than ordinary interest because, like the use of the Duke of Newcastle's self-justification from Scripture, it exemplifies the Carlylean technique of the submerged allusion. Here he depended upon his readers' recognizing a catch phrase of the moment, the much-derided determination of Sir Peter Laurie, Middlesex magistrate (Alderman Cute in Dickens's *The Chimes*), to "put down suicide." Laurie is not named, but every reader of the newspapers or of *Punch*, which cherished him as a favorite butt, would have responded to the ironical implication.

Laurie's dedication to the antisuicide cause had been expressed in 1841,[8] the year in which several other allusions had their source, among them the Stockport assizes (p. 9) and Chadwick's Report on the Training of Pauper Children (p. 276). Carlyle's allusion to D. F. Strauss (p. 232) was probably more intelligible than it would otherwise have been because of the appearance in the *Foreign Quarterly Review* for July 1841 of a long review of his *Die christliche Glaubenslehre in ihrer geschichtlichen Entwicklung*, published at Tübingen.

---

7. The immediacy of any argumentative work like *Past and Present* is enhanced by the introduction of neologisms, including the author's coinages. According to the *OED*, Carlyle's use of "red tape" attributively (pp. 14, 30, 198, 229) had only very recent precedents, in 1838 (Bulwer-Lytton's *Alice*) and 1840 (Carlyle's own *Heroes and Hero Worship*). "Puseyism" (pp. 119, 133, 163, 292) was equally a novelty: John Sterling had first used it in his *Essays and Tales* (1838) and Mrs. Carus Wilson in 1840. Carlyle's " 'millocracy' so-called" (pp. 143, 174), which he is credited with inventing, was an adaptation of Mrs. Trollope's "millocrat" in *Michael Armstrong* (1839–1840).

8. On Laurie, see Philip Collins, *Dickens and Crime* (Bloomington, Ind., 1968), pp. 184–188. Collins notes that, notwithstanding the widespread persuasion that Laurie had used the precise phrase ascribed to him, there is no solid evidence of his having done so.

Strauss and his doctrines were already known to some British intellectuals, but this review of his new book would have served as a timely reminder. Less intelligible to the generality of readers, one feels, would have been the reference (p. 292) to Brook Farm, which was only two years old in 1843. That Carlyle and his circle were aware of it was due immediately to Bronson Alcott's visit to London in the summer of 1842 (he first called at Cheyne Row on 25 June). But the great experiment had little fame as yet, and Carlyle's allusion would seem to be an example of a topicality whose time had not yet come.

As we move further away from 1842–1843 to events in the middle distance, we necessarily become less confident of the degree to which Carlyle's allusions would have had the impact he desired. Of the continuing currency of some, there can be little doubt. The public would have retained active memories of the Chartists' plan for a general strike, the "Sacred Month" (p. 269), which had been debated, and rejected, at their Birmingham convention in the summer of 1839. Thomas C. Haliburton's *The Clockmaker; or the Sayings and Doings of Sam Slick of Slicksville*, published by Bentley, 1837–1838 et seq., was still being read (pp. 277–278). The Useful Knowledge Society (p. 132), though it had passed the peak of its usefulness, still served as an emblem of the utilitarians' fatuous aim of improving and tranquilizing the masses through instructive books and magazines. The "taxes on knowledge" (p. 89) remained a live political issue, as they had been for more than a decade. So did the agitation for "Church-extension" (pp. 34, 168), which had been revived by the Chartist riots and was, as Carlyle wrote *Past and Present*, intensifying the Church-Dissent controversy that was to doom the education clauses in Graham's factory bill. The Ecclesiastical Commission, appointed in 1835, was still much in the public eye, and its results to date were by no means forgotten, least of all its decision, early in its career, that bishops could live respectably on £4500 a year (pp. 187, 195, 291).[9] Chancery (pp. 126, 133, 258) was still the somnolent symbol of legal inertia that it had been in 1827–1828, when extended book-length attacks had appeared, and in 1840, when Edwin W. Field denounced it afresh.[10] The Bridgewater Treatises (pp. 149–150), published in

9. On the Ecclesiastical Commission and Church Extension, see Chadwick, I, 136, 340.
10. See Trevor Blount, "The Documentary Symbolism of Chancery in *Bleak House*," *Dickensian*, 62 (Winter 1966), 49–51.

1833–1836, were still being read by people anxious to have fresh verification of the truths of natural theology.

We can be less certain, however, of the continuing value, in 1843, of several other references reaching back ten years or more. "Owen's Labour-bank," for instance (p. 204), founded in September 1832, had collapsed only two years later and in all likelihood was now recalled only vaguely as an abortive episode in the early socialist movement. While "the eupeptic Curtis" (p. 157) was unquestionably a man of considerable fame in his lifetime as a by-word for vulgar sensuality and gluttony—Byron had worked him into *Don Juan* (X.86) in 1823—his name probably had vanished from many people's memory. Whatever active disrepute he possessed when he died in 1829 doubtless was soon eclipsed by the larger notoriety of the Duke of Newcastle. And one wonders, too, how much the reference to Hampden's exhumation in 1828 (p. 122) meant to readers fifteen years later. This is an instance in which Carlyle was himself unsure, for he printed a footnote referring to reports of the episode in the *Gentleman's Magazine* and the *Annual Register*.

At all events, the tensions and turbulence of the Reform Bill era were inscribed ineffaceably upon the national memory. In Carlyle's scheme of modern English history, as in that of most of his readers, the years 1830–1832 represented what has recently been called "the most prolonged and dangerous crisis in the country's history since the Revolution of 1688."[11] Two oblique references to this traumatic national experience illustrate Carlyle's technique at its most subtle. The mentions of "heavy wet" beer (pp. 37, 217–218) do not refer merely to the well-known fact that British elections at that time were accompanied by much drunkenness. In addition, Carlyle must have meant to revive a specific though fortuitous association forged between democratic politics and beer in 1830, when, as the Reform fever began to rise, Parliament removed the tax on malt liquor. The coincidence of the Beer Bill and the agitation for the Reform Bill was memorialized in at least two popular songs, one of which was actually titled "Heavy Wet":

> King William and Reform, I say,
>> In such a case who can be neuter?
> Just let me blow the froth away,
>> And see how I will drain the pewter.

11. Norman Gash, *Sir Robert Peel* (London, 1972), p. 38.

> Another tankard, landlord, fill,
>   And let us drink to that ere chap, Broom;
> And then we'll chaunt God save King Bill,
>   And send the echoes thro' the tap-room.[12]

Another instance of double allusiveness is the reference to "the new Downing-Street Schedule A" (p. 251). It was timely, in that it referred to the Peel government's proposed income tax; but contemporary readers, alerted by the word "new," would have recognized that Carlyle was again reaching back to 1831–1832, when there was a Downing Street Schedule A of a quite different sort—the proposed scheme of electoral redistricting.

By such indirect means Carlyle sought to link the present with the immediate past—to suggest that 1843 was witnessing a revival of the crisis conditions of a dozen years earlier. They were troubled years not only in England but in France, with its Three-Day Paris Revolution and the revolt of the Lyons silkworkers, and in Poland (all on p. 20). But looming behind the Reform Bill era was the most crucial event in all modern history; and the conclusion is inescapable that in his handling of topical material Carlyle's overriding motive was to suggest that whatever resemblances might be discovered between the events and issues of 1842–1843 and those of 1830–1832, the combined present-day phenomena of the Manchester Insurrection and Chartism were most ominously suggestive of the French Revolution. "Good Heavens, will not one French Revolution and Reign of Terror suffice us, but must there be two?" (p. 270).

A series of sequential associations artfully spaced throughout the book brings the events of the two epochs, separated by fifty years, into connotative alignment:

Manchester Insurrections, French Revolutions, and thousandfold phenomena great and small [p. 27].

these stormtost seas, French Revolutions, Chartisms, Manchester Insurrections, that make the heart sick in these bad days [p. 40].

no French Revolution or Manchester Insurrection, or partial or universal volcanic combustions and explosions [p. 87].

Chartism, *Bare-backism*, Sansculottism so-called! [p. 125].

12. Charles Hindley, *The Life and Times of James Catnach* (London, 1878), pp. 215–216. See also *Annual Register 1830*, pp. 77–78, 84–86.

in killing Kings, in passing Reform Bills, in French Revolutions, Manchester Insurrections, is found no remedy [p. 140].

Do we wonder at French Revolutions, Chartisms, Revolts of Three Days? [p. 210].

Hence French Revolutions, Five-point Charters, Democracies, and a mournful list of *Etceteras*, in these our afflicted times [p. 214].

To Carlyle, more than any other Englishman perhaps, the French Revolution remained intensely topical in 1842. In *The French Revolution* (1837) he had, in fact, anticipated several of the analogies and relationships he was to exploit, in different form, in *Past and Present*. As the fourth in the series of quotations suggests, his clothes-conscious imagination almost obsessively linked the sansculottism[13] of the 1790's with the bare backs of 1842. Just as breechlessness was the condition of the wretched men who destroyed the *ancien régime*, so shirtlessness—the frequency of its mention (pp. 27, 135, 170, 185, 193, 266) makes it one of the book's leitmotifs—was an omen of the impending revolt of the English masses. Both symbolized the anarchic potential of the oppressed workers. The economy of abundance, as Carlyle climactically showed in the opening paragraphs of the chapter "Over-Production," had caused a glut of both articles of clothing. "We accuse you," he imagined the Governing Class chiding the Workers, "of making above two-hundred thousand shirts for the bare backs of mankind. Your trousers too, which you have made, . . . are they not manifold? . . . Millions of shirts, and empty pairs of breeches, hang there in judgment against you" (p. 172). But the ultimate judgment, Carlyle feared, would be delivered by the shirtless, even as it had been delivered at the tanneries of Meudon, with "the long-naked making for themselves breeches of human skins! May the merciful Heavens avert the omen; may we be the wiser, that so we be less wretched" (p. 180).

There was an implicit association, also, between the shrill, Amazonian *Citoyennes* recurrently seen in *The French Revolution*—"female Jacobins, famed *Tricoteuses* with knitting-needles" (IV, 301) —and the harpy-like "Female Chartists" who explode into the streets

13. Need it be pointed out that Carlyle's rhetoric here (not uniquely) did some violence to history and etymology? *Sans-culottism* in its original usage referred to the masses' egalitarian preference for trousers over knee breeches, not to their total lack of nether garments. But for the sake of a vivid image and the contrast with literal shirtlessness, Carlyle fixed upon the expanded meaning of the word.

of twelfth-century St. Edmundsbury (pp. 69, 91, 95). As historical figures, the shrieking, scolding old women are figments of Carlyle's analogical inventiveness; but the name he gives them creates yet another link between past and present, because many of the most active Chartist organizations in 1842 actually had women's auxiliaries, and at the very moment Carlyle was writing, the newspapers reported meetings of Female Chartists in London (17 October, 5 December). In addition, by arming his Female Chartists with distaffs, the tools of spinners, rather than with the Female Jacobins' knitting needles, Carlyle strengthened the implication that his imagined figures were more modern than medieval. Spinning was the predominant occupation represented in the Manchester Chartist mobs.

Although it was none of Carlyle's doing that the New Poor Law workhouses had acquired the name of Bastille, the accident added a grace note to his allusive pattern. His repeated use of "Poor Law Bastilles" (pp. 7, 163–164, 170, 173, etc.) unobtrusively reinforced the association of the Revolution with the issues of the present moment. "No Bastilles!" had been the slogan of Tory and Chartist alike in the election of 1841, and it was in those hated symbols of latter-day oppression and degradation that "the all-conquering valiant Sons of Toil sit enchanted, by the million" (p. 170). History was indeed repeating itself. It is perhaps not too fanciful to read in his treatment of the Anti-Corn Law League something of the attitude Carlyle maintained toward the Girondists in *The French Revolution*: they were the respectable wing of the Revolution, in contrast to the proletarian Jacobins (1842: Chartists).

Taking Carlyle's employment of the Reform Bill crisis and of the French Revolution in *Past and Present* at its face value, we might conclude that through the public anxieties of 1842 reverberated the still vivid personal memories of 1830–1832 and the residual collective memory, still alive and menacing even among a new generation, of the earlier upheaval across the Channel. Carlyle's rhetoric, it might be assumed, was addressed to a readily receptive mood in his audience, and it therefore succeeded. But this is quite possibly an oversimplification. Might it not be, instead, that the French Revolution meant considerably less to Carlyle's readers than it did to him? Is it not conceivable that he expected a more fervent response to his historical analogies than they were prepared to supply?[14] If so, we may have an additional reason, beyond those usually cited, for his superheated style: its vehemence was designed to reduce the discrepancy he felt between his personal agitation over the resemblances and what he sensed to be the comparative indifference of the public. But it is equally conceivable that Carlyle was unaware of any such discrepancy.

Wherever the truth may lie, our evidence suggests that even if he was not guilty of rhetorical overkill, he sometimes miscalculated. While the majority of his topicalities would have been fully intelligible to most of his readers, a significant number would have produced the maximum intended effect only upon those who enjoyed a prior acquaintance with Carlyle's writings. It is doubtful if the reference to "gigs and flunky 'respectabilities' " (p. 272) would have carried its proposed weight of meaning to anyone not acquainted with Carlyle's fondness for the "gigmanity"-respectability joke he had long ago drawn from a somewhat inaccurate report of testimony at Thurtell's trial and had repeated, most recently, in *The French Revolution* (IV, 245, 322–323). Readers similarly unaware of the role the Female Jacobins played in that book could not have responded fully to their reappearance in *Past and Present* as Female Chartists.

So, too, with elements in *Past and Present* that echo *Sartor Resartus*. Although the pattern of references to dandyism (p. 130) and valethood / valetism (pp. 31, 86, 90, 149–150), like that involving the idle dilettantes, is self-sustaining and self-explanatory, readers who knew *Sartor* would unquestionably have discovered a richer aura of connotation in such passages. The ironies associated with the allusions to the shirtless workers of 1842 vis-à-vis the sansculottes of 1793 were enlarged by an appreciation of the symbolic role which the fancy clothing of the rich played in *Sartor*.[15]

14. How deeply the French Revolution continued to influence the public mind in the early Victorian era is still an open question, deserving of more study than it has yet had. Cf. the somewhat revisionist view of George Watson, *The English Ideology* (London, 1973), pp. 44–46: By the time of *Past and Present* the Revolution "is a fading popular memory which excites ardour, as a political analogy, of an increasingly factitious kind. . . . Most English views of the Revolution itself, though not of the Terror that followed it, are relaxed to the point of acceptance. . . . The bogey of revolution was never accepted as an argument by educated Victorian opinion."

15. As the creator of Diogenes Teufelsdröckh, Carlyle's attention would naturally

From time to time, we may assume, Carlyle's topical references fell short of the mark. But the number of such failures is small when compared with the number of allusions which we can be fairly sure had the effect he desired. Whatever its other attributes, his celebrated idiosyncrasy of style did not include an obscure illustrative vocabulary. In the wisdom of his craft, he largely eschewed private language, at least as far as topicalities were concerned. The great majority of them added substantially to the vividness, force, and immediate applicability that help constitute a successful and enduring tract for the times—lending *Past and Present* the qualities that made it, in Emerson's words, an "immortal newspaper."

---

have been arrested by a speech during the Commons' five-night-long debate on the alleged iniquity of truck shops. On 7 March the fractious member for Knaresborough, Busfield Ferrand, renewed an accusation that the millowners supplied inferior goods to the employees who were obliged to patronize the company shops: "Did they know nothing of the flour paste [used in making calico]; nothing of the shoddy trade; nothing of the old rags and the devil's dust?" Later in the same speech he quoted a letter from an Oxfordshire textile manufacturer, eager to do his northern rivals in, who spoke of "the Yorkshire people always underselling them through the use of 'shoddy' or 'devil's dust.'" Hansard, 3d ser., 61 (1842), cols. 141, 149. Hence the passage in *Past and Present* (p. 143): "The Honourable Member complains unmusically that there is 'devil's-dust' in Yorkshire cloth. Yorkshire cloth, —why, the very Paper I now write on is made, it seems, partly of plaster-lime well-smoothed, and obstructs my writing!" Devil's dust was "the flock to which old cloth is reduced by a machine called a devil" (*OED*).

A *Universal "howl of execration": Carlyle's* Latter-Day Pamphlets *and Their Critical Reception*

MICHAEL GOLDBERG, *University of British Columbia*

Carlyle, said George Meredith, was the "nearest to being an inspired writer of any man in our times," but "when he descends to our common pavement, when he would apply his eminent spiritual wisdom to the course of legislation, he is no more sagacious nor useful nor temperate than a flash of lightning in a grocer's shop. . . . Read the *French Revolution* and you listen to a seer: the recent pamphlets, and he is a drunken country squire of superordinary ability."[1] Meredith's caricature of the visionary seer of 1830–1840 and the inebriated squire of the 1850's–1860's anticipates Augustine Birrell's remark that in "politics there were two Carlyle's" and that "his last state was worse than his first."[2] It also neatly illustrates an important aspect of the changing nineteenth-century response to Carlyle which was largely brought about by his publication of the *Latter-Day Pamphlets*.

Appearing in eight monthly numbers beginning on 1 February 1850, this "offensive and alarming"[3] set of *Pamphlets* with their outspoken attacks on democracy, red-tape officialdom, and philanthropy earned Carlyle "showers of abuse" not only from the "extensive genus Stupid,"[4] as he claimed, but from many perceptive and honest critics. Never before, said David Masson, "was there a publication so provocative of rage, hatred and personal malevolence." He was "cursed by name in open society"[5] and denounced by some sections of the religious press for inflicting the deepest "injuries upon the taste, logic, morals, and religion of his country."[6]

Reviews in the English periodicals were, as Carlyle said, mostly

1. *Letters of George Meredith*, ed. C. L. Cline (Oxford, 1970), I, 411–412. Meredith may have had in mind *Shooting Niagara; and After* (1867) as well as the *Latter-Day Pamphlets*.
2. Augustine Birrell, *Obiter Dicta* (London, 1910), p. 18.
3. H. D. Traill, in the Centenary *Works*, XX, 295.
4. *The Correspondence of Emerson and Carlyle*, ed. Joseph Slater (New York and London, 1964), p. 484.
5. *North British Review*, 14 (Nov. 1850), 4.
6. *Christian Observer and Advocate*, 50 (July 1850), 495.

"scolding and screeching."[7] Even *Punch*, which shared his views on coddling prisoners and his intolerance of democracy, found the *Pamphlets* worth satirizing. Carlyle's rhetoric had degenerated into "barking and froth," observed this journal, while the *Athenaeum* concluded that his "wild and rabid" logic was "little better than raving."[8] The American reprinting of the *Pamphlets* drew quick fire from across the Atlantic, and by 6 September Carlyle had received a forty-eight-page rejection of his views on slavery and capital punishment by Elizur Wright, the father of life insurance and a passionate abolitionist.

Carlyle himself was not taken by surprise at the uproar. A month before the first number of the *Pamphlets* appeared in print he predicted that his "vivid daguerrotype of the times," as Emerson called it,[9] would "occasion loud astonishment, condemnation, and a universal barking . . . from all the dogs of the parish."[10] It was a prediction of remarkable accuracy. Since the "letters of Junius, nothing so sensational in politics had been printed in England,"[11] and one critic advised readers to approach the *Pamphlets* as cautiously as a parcel "reported to contain dynamite."[12] Their immediate effect on public opinion was "convulsive," and if Carlyle exaggerated in claiming that his *Pamphlets* had "turned nine tenths of the world dreadfully" against him, it is true that many even of his "old admirers drew back" after this and "walked no more with him."[13] Carlyle's final estrangement from John Stuart Mill dates from this time, while Thomas Spedding, whom he visited at Keswick in September 1850, along with John Forster, "soon fell away . . . into terror and surprise;—as indeed everybody did."[14] There were, however, notable exceptions. Both Ruskin and Dickens remained loyal to Carlyle, while James Hannay, a lesser-known but no less ardent disciple, responded to W. E. Aytoun's review in *Blackwood's* with a pamphlet of his own in which

7. *The Letters of Thomas Carlyle to His Brother Alexander with Related Family Letters*, ed. Edwin W. Marrs, Jr. (Cambridge, Mass., 1968), p. 692.

8. *Punch*, 18 (Jan.–June 1850), 107; *Athenaeum*, 2 March 1850, p. 228.

9. *Correspondence of Emerson and Carlyle*, p. 461.

10. *New Letters of Thomas Carlyle*, ed. Alexander Carlyle (London, 1904), II, 86.

11. Wilson, *Carlyle*, IV, 237.   12. Birrell, p. 18.

13. Froude, *Carlyle*, IV, 26.

14. *New Letters and Memorials of Jane Welsh Carlyle*, ed. Alexander Carlyle (London, 1903), II, 14. See also Froude, *Carlyle*, IV, 59; *Cornhill Magazine*, 50 (May 1921), 753–754.

he strongly defended Carlyle against the familiar charges of jargon and impracticality. When "almost all the reviews were united in a howl of execration," Mark Rutherford wrote to assure Carlyle of his admiration, and he later recalled his eager journeys to the bookseller "for each successive number,"[15] while Emerson, who clearly had some qualms about them, remarked on the "sturdy tone" of these "wonderful Pamphlets."[16]

Despite such indications of support, Carlyle's *Pamphlets* were assailed from many sides. Philanthropists found his views on emancipation abhorrent and often un-Christian, Utilitarians saw his remedies for social ills as impractical, those of progressive sentiments were repelled by his nostalgia for the bad old days of "feudal bondage and popular ignorance,"[17] while the powerful liberal establishment was shocked by his hostility to democratic beliefs and tended to regard him, in Arnold's current phrase, as a "moral desperado."[18]

This response was altogether to be expected, for the mid-century liberal, whether his liberalism was of the doctrinaire type of Mill or of the commonsense type of Macaulay or of the sentimental type of Dickens, could not, as Saintsbury observed, have failed to regard Carlyle as "something like Antichrist, a defender of slavery," trampling on the "most sacred principles of the Manchester School."[19] To the "liberty men," as Ruskin called them, he appeared as a "legible and steady old signpost saying, That . . . is not the way."[20] Widespread as it was, however, the howl of execration against the *Pamphlets* was not universal. The political left, despite profound disagreements with Carlyle, was far less shocked by the *Pamphlets* than the liberal center, partly because it had always been well disposed to the author whom Engels had singled out as an "honourable exception" to the bourgeois attitudes he castigated in his *Condition of the Working Class*.[21] Even when in 1850, in the *Neue Rheinische Zeitung*,

15. Mark Rutherford, *Pages from a Journal* (London, 1910), p. 2.
16. *Correspondence of Emerson and Carlyle*, p. 461.
17. *Eclectic Review*, 28 (Oct. 1850), 393.
18. *Letters of Matthew Arnold to Arthur Hugh Clough*, ed. Howard Foster Lowry (Oxford, 1932), p. 111.
19. George Saintsbury, *Corrected Impressions* (New York, 1895), p. 210.
20. *The Works of Ruskin*, ed. E. T. Cook and Alexander Wedderburn (London, 1903–1912), XXVII, 179.
21. *Condition of the Working Class*, ed. W. O. Henderson and W. H. Chaloner (Stanford, 1958), p. 331.

Engels repudiated Carlyle's reactionary position on the 1848 revolution and condemned his "unhistorical apotheosis" of the Middle Ages, his hero worship, and the fact that he derived more from Richter than from Hegel, he saluted the "revolutionary" manner in which, in the *French Revolution, Cromwell, Chartism,* and *Past and Present,* Carlyle had taken up the cudgels against the English bourgeoisie.[22] The relatively high regard in which Carlyle was held by revolutionists of the caliber of Marx and Engels may account for the general inattention paid the *Pamphlets* by the Chartist and radical press.[23] Even Ernest Jones, the "Chartist notability" of *Model Prisons,* when he referred to the *Pamphlets* in the *Red Republican* was content merely to deflect Carlyle's jibe about the merits of prison as a place in which to write books with a factual account of the restrictions in the use of pen, paper and ink imposed on him during his term in Tothill Fields jail.[24]

Nevertheless the widespread hostility to the *Pamphlets* reflects a major alteration in the public's view of Carlyle, and a partial eclipse of his reputation began with their publication. Furthermore, the initial reaction helped to entrench two subtly connected and tenaciously held beliefs about the *Pamphlets* which have played an important role in creating an image of the "later Carlyle" as a "virulent old sophist"[25] who in mid-century lost his compassion for humanity. The first is the belief that the *Pamphlets* were composed in great haste and written under acute pressure so that they are frequently regarded as effusions somehow beyond Carlyle's conscious control—a mere discharge of "his black electricities,"[26] or as *Harper's New Monthly Magazine* put it, "the strugglings of a sick giant, whom his friends . . . should compel to take to his bed."[27] The second is the critical view that in the *Pamphlets* Carlyle revealed himself for the first time as a reactionary philosopher. Understandable as it was, this early response was clearly an overreaction, though a highly influential

22. *Aus dem literarischen Nachlass von Karl Marx und Friedrich Engels,* ed. Franz Mehring (Stuttgart, 1930), III, 414–415.

23. Apart from Engel's review of "The Present Time" and "Model Prisons" in the *Neue Rheinische Zeitung,* an important exception is the radical review of "The Present Time" in *The Democratic Review of British and Foreign Politics, History, and Literature,* which was edited by the physical force Chartist G. Julian Harney. See April 1850, pp. 423–425; May 1850, pp. 449–453.

24. *The Red Republican,* 10 Aug. 1850, p. 64.

25. *The Swinburne Letters,* ed. Cecil Y. Lang (New Haven, 1960), IV, 266.

26. Wilson, *Carlyle,* IV, 249.   27. 1 (June–Nov. 1850), 430.

one, one that has had a damaging effect not only on the neglected *Pamphlets* themselves but on Carlyle's reputation as a whole. For one thing, the affront to liberal opinion caused by the *Pamphlets* undoubtedly fostered the tendency to read Carlyle's work essentially for its content and practical value, and especially for its "potential dangers and distortions—a misapprehension" which, said Kathleen Tillotson, "remains an impediment to the understanding not only" of Carlyle "but of the literature of a whole age."[28] The impact of the *Pamphlets* on Victorian readers marks the opening or certainly the intensification of a new phase in the development of Carlyle's reputation. Because of its historical importance, I shall examine the initial reception of the *Pamphlets* and attempt to trace some of the ways in which it has continued to shape later estimates of Carlyle's work.

The first misapprehension about the *Pamphlets*, and the one most easily dismissed, is that they were composed in great haste. They were, it is true, quickly written up and published in their final form, but they were several years in the making. Furthermore, when critics refer to hasty composition they invariably mean to suggest something of the intemperate nature of the end product. Thus haste of composition often stands as a euphemism for Carlyle's assumed derangement, to be included with the other physical and psychological factors which appear so frequently in descriptions of the *Pamphlets'* genesis. The generally accepted account suggests that they were composed under conditions of acute distress, the causes of which are variously listed as general depression, bile, violent anger at the failure of the 1848 revolutions in Europe, events in Ireland and England, and the ebbing of his creative energy after writing *Cromwell.*

Carlyle himself is partly responsible for setting critical hares running in all of these directions. He gave free vent to his preoccupation with his physical condition when in January 1850 he feared to continue with the *Pamphlets* "for my stomach and liver . . . are by no means too strong just now,"[29] a fear he repeated the following month. Again in July he told Sir Charles Gavan Duffy: "My poor *liver* is gone almost to destruction" in completing the *Pamphlets*, and declared he had seldom felt "more entirely worn down."[30] Such re-

---

28. *Novels of the Eighteen-Forties* (Oxford, 1961 [1954]), p. 152.
29. *New Letters*, II, 85.
30. Wilson, *Carlyle*, IV, 303. See also an unpublished letter to Monckton Milnes, 17 Dec. 1850, in the Trinity College Library, Cambridge.

marks have encouraged the "pitiful" attempt, as Chesterton calls it, "to explain his gospel in terms of his liver."[31]

It is also true that Carlyle, when he confronted the task of turning into a coherent whole the masses of notes he had accumulated during the five years since *Cromwell*, was in low spirits. "Shall I begin it?" he wondered, contemplating his draft plan for the *Pamphlets*: "I am sick, lazy, and dispirited."[32] One of the principal causes of his depression was his sense of isolation from the main currents of the time. "How lonely I am now grown in the world" he said, noting how his youthful affections, "mocked, and scourged and driven mad by contradictions," had lain down in a "kind of iron sleep." The "astounding revolutionary time" in which he found himself set him "in dissent from all the world; in black contradiction, deep as the bases of my life, to all the philanthropic, emancipatory, constitutional and other anarchic revolutionary jargon, with which the world, so far I can conceive, is now full."[33]

These comments give apparently impressive sanction to the popular view of his composition of the *Pamphlets*, fostered by Froude and echoed in Garnett's description of Carlyle "in his study, alone with his anger, his grief, and his biliousness."[34] So too do his remarks on the burden of creative effort. But one has to remember that the clamor of almost ceaseless complaint which accompanied all Carlyle's serious writing was mainly the self-dramatizing expression of one who saw the creative process as a heroic struggle to wrest the truth from the hiding places where sham and cant had concealed it.

No one can deny that Carlyle's temperament was exacerbated by what amounted to a crisis in his personal life and in the world as he saw it. His misunderstandings with Jane, the sudden loss in 1848 of Charles Buller, foreshadowing the equally untimely death two years later of his hero Sir Robert Peel, his strong reaction to the European revolutions of 1848, and his painful sense of the dire situation in Ireland, which he had visited in 1849, all contributed to feelings of desperation which undoubtedly had their effect upon his writings. But in approaching the *Latter-Day Pamphlets*, too much has often been made of these factors. Rather than entertain ideas which seem repugnant or even to meet "them on their own grounds," it has often

31. G. K. Chesterton, *Twelve Types* (London, 1902), p. 120.
32. Wilson, *Carlyle*, IV, 23.   33. Froude, *Carlyle*, IV, 21–22.
34. Richard Garnett, *Life of Thomas Carlyle* (London, 1887), p. 130.

seemed "easier and more comforting to posit something wrong with the man who propounded them."[35] Perhaps, as Nietzsche shrewdly observed,[36] liberal-mindedness was so much a part of Victorian thinking that its distinct absence in Carlyle, Ibsen, or Schopenhauer was taken as evidence of a morbid condition. Certainly too much has been read into Carlyle's mind and his habits of work that really derives from a scandalized reaction to the *Pamphlets* themselves. The vigor of their ideas and the intensity of Carlyle's language have driven many critics to argue from effects to causes and to seek these causes in biographical, psychological, and even pathological explanations.

This critical effort has been abetted by well-intentioned Carlyle apologists who sought to deflect the embarrassment caused by the illiberal nature of the *Pamphlets* by suggesting that they were the by-products of haste, pain, or rage rather than works of conscious intelligence. Augustus Ralli's 1920 account is typical in revealing one of the stratagems by which it seemed Carlyle could be rescued from a decline in respect. "With *Latter-Day Pamphlets* more than any other of Carlyle's works," he says, we must "realize the region of his mind whence it came." For misunderstanding "has caused charges of intolerance, even of cruelty to be made against him." The reader is then invited to consider how the "increasing burden of age and care had done its work" in the *Pamphlets* and is warned against taking literally the outbursts most offensive to liberal tastes. Carlyle's "ebullitions of irritability," Ralli concludes, "were superficial, and largely the result of dyspepsia."[37]

Such accounts not only blur the distinction between the man who suffers and the mind which creates, but they also have had the unfortunate effect of isolating the *Pamphlets* from the rest of Carlyle's work, leaving the general impression that they are the brilliant but hectic productions of stress. The notion, however, that Carlyle was propelled into hasty composition by intemperate anger, temporary insanity, or extreme biliousness is not corroborated by the evidence. I should like to test the accuracy of the general assumption that the *Pamphlets* were written in such extremity of spirit as would be possible for only concentrated and limited periods, by examining *Hudson's Statue*—a *Pamphlet* which recommends itself for the pur-

35. G. B. Tennyson, *Carlyle and the Modern World* (Edinburgh, 1971), p. 6.
36. *The Will to Power*, trans. A. M. Ludovic (London, 1909), p. 202.
37. *Guide to Carlyle* (London, 1920), II, 83, 87.

pose as it came from Carlyle's pen with difficulty and was in his view a poor effort, but the *"best* my biliary and other demons would allow."[38]

When Carlyle predicted as early as 1845 that the "railway bubble" was soon likely to burst, he must have had George Hudson, the Railway King, in mind, for in 1845 Hudson was at the peak of his fame. The importance of the date, the year in which Carlyle completed *Cromwell*, can hardly be overstressed, for the dramatic contrast between the two men, which stands as emblematic of the opposing principles of individual worth and collective mediocrity, lies at the heart of his later essay. Cromwell, who for Carlyle more completely than any other man embodied the idea of the hero, was one of those who seemed in Burke's words not so much like a man usurping power as one asserting his natural place in society. What more extreme contrast could there be than Hudson, who to Carlyle was simply the puffed-up idol of sycophants who sought to profit from his association. It seems likely that even as early as 1845, with his head full of the stirring events of Cromwell's life, Carlyle would have noted this contrast between real and apparent worth and how the two men were truly representative of the times in which they lived.

Indeed, by February 1848 he was contrasting moral value and money worth. "How rich" he asked "is Hudson, King of Railways?" since for money he could be induced to stoop so low as to make himself an *"unhangable swindler."*[39] The publication of *Cromwell* had by this time stirred a group of admirers to have a statue raised to the Protector. Writing to his mother in December 1848, Carlyle was quick to note the public's subscription of £25,000 "for a memorial to an ugly bullock of a Hudson" whose only merit had been his wealth, and that, it was now commonly felt, had been arrived at fraudulently. As for Cromwell, Carlyle felt he should be spared public memorials and that people should rather honor him by "learning to be honest men like him."[40] These comments show plainly that Carlyle was aware of Hudson's career from its peak in 1845 through the slide of 1847–1848 to his final collapse the following year, and also that the gist of the 1850 essay was already in his mind. The two statues, and the question of which of them nineteenth-century England best deserved—which is the ironic contrast around which the fierce polemic

---

38. *New Letters*, II, 97. 39. Froude, *Carlyle*, III, 420.
40. Ibid., p. 451.

of the seventh *Pamphlet* is organized—were thus linked in Carlyle's mind for several years before he actually came to write it.

This view is strongly supported by the holograph version of *Hudson's Statue* now in the possession of the Huntington Library. Probably written in 1848 or early 1849, it began, as did the later printed version, with a reference to the prospect of a Cromwell statue at St. Ives in Huntington. Carlyle went on to note how "exceedingly bewildered" the English public then was with statues and further to regret that the monument to Hudson was unlikely to be completed. This ironic regret is based on the notion that a people gets in the matter of statues what it deserves. "Show me the man you honour, I know, by that symptom better than by any other, what kind of man you yourself are. For you show me what your ideal of manhood is; what kind of man you long inexpressibly to be." In this sense Hudson was a real hero to the Mammon seekers of nineteenth-century England, a proper and just "ideal of the Scrip ages."

It is not clear exactly when Carlyle decided that an essay on Hudson would form one of the *Pamphlets*. The Huntington manuscript is, however, a coherent unity, though it represents less than half of the printed version and may therefore have been intended for separate publication. It is not a fragment of the final version, for it is numbered consecutively in Carlyle's hand from pages 1 through 8. When in 1850 Carlyle prepared *Hudson's Statue* for publication he redistributed this material into an introductory and a concluding section, inserting between them a large middle section which forms the bulk of the printed pamphlet.

Furthermore, if one looks at Carlyle's remarks on Hudson chronologically, it appears that his attitude toward the railway tycoon underwent some modification. The earlier references are starkly brutal in pointing out that Hudson is a nonentity and a cheat. On 17 May 1849, however, his Journal contains an account of Hudson's collapse in which Carlyle makes the same point he elaborated in the printed version of the *Pamphlet*: namely, that Hudson was less to be blamed than his idolators. Hudson is seen as a creature of the democratic spirit, raised to bad eminence by public opinion. "King Hudson flung utterly prostrate, detected 'cooking accounts'; everybody kicking him through the mire. . . . The rage of fellow-gamblers, now when he has merely lost the game for them . . . seems . . . a very baseless thing. One sordid, hungry, *canaille* are they all. Why should this, the chief terrier among them, be set upon by all the dog fraternity? One feels a real human pity for the ugly Hudson."[41] This is very close to the argument in the printed *Pamphlet* where Carlyle argues that Hudson was raised to kingly stature by the silent election of the people and, therefore, what is at issue for Carlyle is the whole question of popular suffrage. Hudson's fall into disgrace in 1849 gave Carlyle the chance to cast him as a central character in the general attack on democracy which he had contemplated writing in 1848, but the germ of the idea for *Hudson's Statue* had developed by slow accretion of detail until the draft version of 1848–1849 which was converted, with considerable amplification, into the printed *Pamphlet*. The conclusion seems clear that Carlyle's penultimate *Pamphlet* was the product of slow growth, and not something dashed off in great heat in 1850, under the pressure of depression, rage, or bile.

The 1850 uproar over the *Pamphlets* is in some respects puzzling, for despite a heightened acerbity of tone the subject matter of the *Pamphlets* was not, on the whole, new. Nevertheless, the opinion gained ground that in the *Pamphlets* Carlyle had revealed his true colors as a reactionary philosopher. But there seemed in 1850, as today, to be genuine confusion as to what precisely constituted their novelty or their offense. Some critics claimed with the *Athenaeum* that Carlyle's latest heresies merely reproduced the doctrines of *Sartor Resartus*, *Chartism*, and *Past and Present* in the coarse lumbering folds of his latest style: a "mere seven-fold repetition" of the author's ancient discontent, declared *Harper's New Monthly Magazine*.[42] Others, however, were impressed by a change for the worse in Carlyle's opinions. Some of his earlier writings gave evidence of a "generous sympathy with the poor and the wronged" and a desire to "ameliorate human suffering," but latterly, said Whittier, "like Molière's quack, he has 'changed all that'; his heart has got upon the wrong side."[43] *Blackwood's* too felt that Carlyle's earlier liberal views had been displaced by an "ultra-tyrannical spirit."[44]

The often contradictory charges brought against the *Pamphlets* are united only by their hostility; yet contemporary criticism falls into a few well-defined categories. Depending upon the political persuasion of the critic, the *Pamphlets* are indicted for the harshness

41. Ibid., p. 455.   42. 1 (June–Nov. 1850), 430.
43. John Greenleaf Whittier, *Writings* (London, 1889), VII, 144.
44. *Blackwood's*, 67 (June 1850), 643.

of Carlyle's opinions on slavery, capital punishment, democracy, and the work force, for what was generally assumed to be their despotic character, for the negative quality of his criticisms, and for the vagaries of his style. These objections are met with over and over again. The most predictable response is that of liberal, progressive, and philanthropic readers who were goaded into replying to specific points in the essays. The tone of these varied according as the reader tried to argue the point with Carlyle, to reason with him, to confute his logic, or simply to send him packing with a heap of epithets ringing in his ears.

One of the most sustained and reasoned attacks on Carlyle's view of philanthropy was made in a letter to the editor of *Fraser's*, which had a month earlier published the "Occasional Discourse on the Negro Question." It accused Carlyle of being infected by propaganda of the slavery party before emancipation, and of mistaking for an "affair of sentiment" what was really a "great national revolt of the conscience."[45] Perhaps the most intense reaction was to *Model Prisons* and in particular to Carlyle's remarks on John Howard, his views on capital punishment, and what was called his "damnable" doctrine of servitude. It was on these issues, according to Elizur Wright, that he had bolted into wildest error. On the slavery question Carlyle had made himself an instrument of the devil, declared *Fraser's*, while the *Palladium* in an "unbiassed review" denounced the "brutal and bloody suggestions" of the *Pamphlets* and said *Model Prisons* might have been written by "hangman's hands."[46] *Blackwood's* saw in Carlyle's attitudes a "decided leaning to the whip and the musket as effective modes of reasoning" (p. 643). What cheered the *Athenaeum* was the hope that by their sheer extravagance the *Pamphlets* would break Carlyle's "unwholesome spell." Those readers who "lured by a trick of style . . . followed willingly his argument in exaltation of the lowest form of power—that of physical restraint—so long as it took a hero like Cromwell for its exemplar, will have been startled to find themselves summoned, by corollary, as defenders of the overseer's whip and the hangman's cord, in further illustration of the same bad argument" (p. 228).

This is a fair sample of the humanitarian objections to Carlyle's

45. *Fraser's Magazine*, 41 (Jan. 1850), 26. This unsigned letter was by John Stuart Mill.
46. *Palladium*, 1 (July 1850), 1, 4, 11.

remarks on philanthropy, the treatment of prisoners, and the question of slavery, and it is indicative of the emotional heat generated by the *Pamphlets* that many of his critics in deploring the extremism of his language resorted to it themselves. Democratic sentiments were equally aroused by his political opinions. He ridicules "every species of constitutional or popular government" said one journal;[47] another alleged that his "monstrous" opinions advocated "beyond the possibility of mistake . . . pure unadulterated despotism."[48] His *Downing Street* pamphlet, said *Blackwood's*, was "either downright nonsense, or something a great deal worse." What it took to be worse was that Carlyle looked for the advent of another Cromwell as the sole cure for the ills besetting England, and *Blackwood's* felt persuaded that Cromwellism was "but another phrase for despotism" (p. 646).

Many of these objections gathered around Carlyle's theory of the hero—what the *Prospective Review* called the "perpetual demand for a Captain to give us all the word of command."[49] The very word "heroism," observed the *Southern Literary Messenger*, is for Carlyle's admirers like the "Shibboleth of the Illuminati—it unlocks all" (p. 330). In a more practical vein *Chambers' Edinburgh Journal* noted that the idea of the inspired leader was well enough, but not of much use until Carlyle produced a "recipe how to catch heroes . . . and more especially how to catch masses of people and indoctrinate them with the feeling of obedience" (p. 26). Until then, nations will have to make the best of existing political arrangements.

In view of later attempts to associate Carlyle's hero with the Nazi *Führerprinzip* it is interesting to note that it was essentially cautious Victorian liberalism which promulgated the charge of despotism. Engels, whose view of Carlyle was much more favorable than that of the liberals, objected to Carlyle's hero not because of his unchecked political power but because he was the product of Carlyle's religious outlook on life: a messiah rather than a dictator, a god rather than a man.

Carlyle himself claimed Plato's ideal statesman as the ultimate source of his hero. Writing to Emerson in 1853, he confessed to being much struck with Plato and his ideas about democracy, "mere *Latter-*

---

47. *Chambers' Edinburgh Journal*, 13 July 1850, p. 26.
48. *Southern Literary Messenger*, 16 (June 1850), 339.
49. *Prospective Review*, 6 (May 1850), 228.

day Pamphlet saxa et faces (read *faecas*, if you like) refined into empyrean radiance."[50] And he later recalled reading Plato and finding him "pouring his scorn on the Athenian democracy—'the charming government, full of variety and disorder, dispensing equality alike to equals and unequals'—and hating that set quite as cordially as the writer of the *Latter-Day Pamphlets* hates the like of it now."[51] Thus he was seen by one sympathetic Victorian observer, and may partly have regarded himself, as a "Plato . . . framing ideal aristocracies at a time when matters were ripe for a Macedonian despot."[52] None of this, however, prevented twentieth-century fascists from adopting Carlyle for almost precisely the same reasons that liberals had rejected him for in 1850—and with no greater understanding or regard for what he represented. The process is complex, but the erosion of Carlyle's reputation which made such interpretations possible began with the liberal reaction to the *Pamphlets*. Misgivings about his teaching in 1850 gradually hardened into a fixed belief in a harsh, grating, latter-day Carlyle whose message contained many sinister overtones, a belief which prepared the way for attempts to link Carlyle's doctrines later with Prussian militarism and European facism. In taking this position, Carlyle's critics not only resorted to passages from the *Pamphlets* themselves but either consciously or unconsciously echoed many of the sentiments evoked in response to them by the reviewers of the 1850's.

To complete itself, the process required the debasement of Carlyle's hero and the direct attribution to him of the doctrine of might is right. Considering this doctrine, Professor Grierson echoed G. K. Chesterton when he noted in 1930 that "Carlyle led direct to Nietzsche,"[53] while Bertrand Russell also traced the course of one phase of liberalism from Rousseau and Kant "by logical stages, through Fichte, Byron, Carlyle, and Nietzsche, into Hitler."[54] Thus the Carlylean hero is seen to foreshadow the Nietzschean *Übermensch* as an influence on Nazi theory. It is a double irony that Nietzsche, who regarded Carlyle as a "humbug" and "muddle-head,"[55] should

50. *Correspondence of Emerson and Carlyle*, p. 489.
51. *Harper's New Monthly Magazine*, 62 (May 1881), 906–907.
52. *Fortnightly Review*, 26 (Dec. 1879), 817.
53. H. J. C. Grierson, *Carlyle and Hitler* (Cambridge, Eng., 1933), p. 47.
54. Bertrand Russell, *History of Western Philosophy* (London, 1947), p. 667.
55. Nietzsche, *The Dawn of Day*, trans. J. M. Kennedy (London, 1911), p. 264.

have suffered with him an almost identical fate at the hands of hostile critics and fascist admirers. Not all attempts to see Carlyle as a proto-fascist were so direct. In his 1938 discussion of Carlyle's theory of the hero, for instance, Professor Joad distinguished between German and Italian fascism, and A. R. Orage conceded that Carlyle did not adopt the Prussian error of identifying might with right, though he found Carlyle tainted with the "more subtle error" of thinking that might can only be accumulated by right means, a subtlety that led Carlyle into some "strange company for the moral fanatic he was."[56]

Certainly in early-twentieth-century Europe, topicality had opened a new vein of Carlyle criticism. As early as 1920 Guido Fornelli had published articles on Carlyle's conception of history which served as a basis for his fuller study *Tommaso Carlyle: la nuova aristocrazia.* Carlyle's theories of the hero and of authority quickened a lively interest, and the rapprochements between Carlylean ideas and the theories of the fascists were expressed in a whole series of articles.

If fascist critics claimed him eagerly, the non-fascist world was generally willing enough to accede to the claim. The title of Grierson's 1930 lecture "Carlyle and the Hero" was changed on publication in 1933 to *Carlyle and Hitler* because "the recent happenings in Germany illustrate the conditions which . . . make possible, the emergence of the Hero as Carlyle chiefly thought of him." It is not without significance that this attempt to view Carlyle's opinions in the "perspective afforded by the course of events since the War"[57] should begin with a reference to the *Latter-Day Pamphlets.*

J. E. Baker in "Carlyle Rules the Reich" considered Carlyle the ideal "interpreter" to the mid-1930's of Hitlerian ideals. Much of the article is taken up with the assertion of numerous affinities. Almost all of Hitler's ideas about *Pflichterfüllung* (fulfillment of duty) and his belief in an *aristokratischer Prinzip* rather than *Majorität* "could be expressed in familiar old phrases from Carlyle."[58] While not suggesting that Carlyle would have approved of Nazi practice, Baker does claim that Hitlerian theory is no surprise if interpreted in the context of ideas like those propounded by Carlyle. This is, of course,

56. A. R. Orage, *Readers and Writers* (New York, 1922), p. 22.
57. Grierson, prefatory note to *Carlyle and Hitler.*
58. *Saturday Review of Literature,* 25 Nov. 1933, p. 291.

the view that fascism sought to encourage in its active pursuit of respectability by annexing such eminent writers as Carlyle and Nietzsche.

In a 1945 article J. Salwyn Schapiro relies heavily upon the *Latter-Day Pamphlets* to make the point that, viewed in the light of recent history, Carlyle emerges as a "prophet with a sinister message." His views on social and political problems, "divested of their moral appeal by the march of time, are revealed to be those of a fascist in their essential implications."[59] Though the "relevant" background had changed, many of the initial reactions to the *Pamphlets* recur in Schapiro's analysis, and one wonders how much attempts to link Carlyle with modern fascism would have gained ground had a certain predisposition to see him in a rather sinister light not already existed.

Carlyle's *Pamphlets* also caused him in 1850 to fall foul of those readers who had been touched by Victorian meliorism and the new scientific spirit, and whose sense of pride in Victorian progress was outraged by Carlyle's Cassandra-like view of the age. "We believe," said *Eliza Cook's Journal*, in the "progressive moral amelioration of man," and the reviewer of the *Pamphlets* found "abundant evidence that it does make steady progress at this day." Thus *The Present Time* was "too gloomy" an assessment of the age, being a mixture of "Byron and Diogenes."[60] The *Athenaeum* of 24 August 1850 also refused to be depressed by Carlyle's bleak view of the contemporary world, preferring to believe that the world had improved rather than declined, and that the "true golden age" lay in the future (p. 895).

The most sustained objection, however, came from the utilitarian quarter and concerned the negative character of Carlyle's criticism. In 1850, though not dealing directly with the *Pamphlets*, the *Westminster Review* noted his general failure to offer any "prescriptive rule of life."[61] To *Blackwood's* it appeared that Carlyle had not a shred of "practical ability." If he "were a doctor, and you came to him with a cut finger, he would regale you with a lecture on the heroical qualities of Avicenna, or commence proving that Dr. Abernethy was simply a Phantasm-Leech ... instead of applying a plaster to the wound" (p. 642). *Eliza Cook's Journal* was similarly baffled by

59. *Journal of Modern History*, 17 (June 1945), 97.
60. *Eliza Cook's Journal*, 20 April 1850, p. 398.
61. *Westminister Review*, 52 (Jan. 1850), 397.

Carlyle's thinking. "We are most eager to know. We read on; but, alas! Mr. Carlyle retires into a nebulous maze of thought! We try to reduce his thought, such as it is, into a plan of action; but it escapes us, and instead of a system, we have a phrase of Mr. Carlyle's" (p. 399). The comments are revealing, the "nebulous maze" suggesting Carlyle's transcendentalism and his debts to Romantic philosophy, which are measured against a stern utilitarian requirement of systematic analysis. There is also a strong suggestion that Carlyle's power is almost entirely a matter of rhetoric, or in T. S. Eliot's more contemporary phrasing, that his influence partly depended upon his lack of "precision and completeness of thought."[62]

The insistent demand for practical solutions modulates into frequent impatience with Carlyle's prophetic gloom. By 1883 Trollope could report that it "is simply regarded as Carlylism to say that the English speaking world is growing worse from day to day."[63] While Carlyle "chose to remain vague, mysterious and cloudy," he had said earlier of Dr. Pessimist Anticant in *The Warden*, much was learned from him "but when he became practical, the charm was gone."[64]

The frequency of the objection from the 1850's onward that Carlyle is essentially an iconoclast, far better at pointing out evils than in prescribing remedies, is a new note in Carlyle criticism, and it stems from the triumph of the practical attitudes Arnold was to deplore in his 1864 essay on "The Function of Criticism." Where, he asked distinguishing between the practical and speculative, is that language "innocent enough" to enable us to say to the "political Englishman that the British Constitution itself, which, seen from the practical side, looks such a magnificent organ of progress and virtue, seen from the speculative side,—with its compromises, its love of facts, its horror of theory, its studied avoidance of clear thoughts, . . . sometimes looks . . . a colossal machine for the manufacture of Philistines." Indeed, how was Carlyle to say it without being misunderstood "after his furious raid into this field with his *Latter-day Pamphlets*?"[65]

The attack on Carlyle's impracticality and the belief that the value of the *Pamphlets* was nullified by the lack of any specific remedies for

62. *Selected Essays* (London, 1932), p. 433.
63. Anthony Trollope, *An Autobiography* (Oxford, 1923), p. 323.
64. Anthony Trollope. *The Warden* (London, 1949), p. 139 (chap. 15).
65. *The Complete Works of Matthew Arnold*, ed. R. H. Super (Ann Arbor, Mich., 1962), III, 25.

the conditions they described have been profoundly influential. Thus H. D. Traill, the editor of the Centenary edition of Carlyle's works, echoing Eliza Cook's comment forty years earlier, says the essays "condescend upon particulars to such an extent as to keep the reader in continual expectancy of some definite recommendations of legislative or administrative policy—which never come."[66] And Lord Morley, whose excellent 1921 essay on Carlyle takes issue with the *Pamphlets*, points to the "extreme inefficiency or worse of his solutions," while retaining gratitude for the perspicacity with which Carlyle impressed the world with the urgency of social problems. An "emotional teacher," Carlyle had "increased the fervour of the country, but without materially changing its objects."[67] The earlier reviews in this vein are historically important because they represent the withdrawing from Carlyle of credit for precisely those inspirational qualities for which the young Mill along with many others turned to him with profit. They mark in fact a transition between the Romantic and Victorian estimates of his work.

The charge that Carlyle was a wild Romantic phoenix out of place in the atmosphere of rational sobriety represented by the growing influence of Mill, Spencer, Darwin, and Comte led to a general tendency to regard him as a teacher who in Leslie Stephen's estimate "belonged essentially to a past generation" and whose opinions had "passed into the domain of history."[68] How much this adverse reaction was to solidify, and along the lines of the 1850 reaction, is suggested by George Saintsbury. If they appeared so to few others, Saintsbury regarded the *Pamphlets* as "the very gospel of English politics . . . a sort of modern Politicus in the spirit and tone of which every Englishman should strive to soak and saturate himself." But he acknowledged that by the 1880's an admiration for Carlyle was the very sign of having reached "the fossil stage of intellectual existence."[69] By then the hostility of 1850 had become a comfortably settled attitude. "To-day he is as dead as Macpherson's Ossian,"[70] said Yeats, and Hopkins more vehemently declared, "I hate his principles, I burn most that he worships and worship most that he

66. *Works*, XX, vii.
67. Lord Morley, *Works* (London, 1921), VI, 61.
68. *Hours in a Library* (New York, 1899), III, 254.
69. Saintsbury, *Corrected Impressions*, pp. 212, 209.
70. *Letters of W. B. Yeats*, ed. Allan Wade (New York, 1955), p. 609.

burns,"[71] while Henry James opened his recollections of Carlyle in the *Atlantic Monthly*, just three months after his death, with the curious note: "Thomas Carlyle is incontestably dead at last, by the acknowledgement of all newspapers. I had . . . the pleasure of an intimate intercourse with him when he was an infinitely deader man than he is now."[72]

James was at pains to correct the notion that Carlyle was a "man of ideas." He was an "amateur prophet exclusively," a harlequin in the guise of a Jeremiah, a writer who "valued truth and good as a painter does his pigments, not for what they are in themselves, but for the effects they lend themselves to." Such gifts as he had for "scenic effect and color would not have pushed him to his melancholy 'latter-day drivel' had it not been for those disciples who stimulated his vanity and made him feel himself a god." It was time, James declared, to have done with Carlyle's "rococo airs and affectations; his antiquated strut and heroics."[73] James's attempt to demolish Carlyle as a Romantic *Wahrsager* is directly traceable to the first reviews of the *Pamphlets*, which are frequently characterized by a similar effort to translate Carlyle from Romantic into Victorian terms.

One of the principal effects of the early response to the *Pamphlets* and the critical positions which evolved from it was to drive a wedge between Carlyle's rhetoric and his opinions, to separate form from content, and as a result to foreshorten the critical view of Carlyle by stripping his work to naked assertions of opinion while ignoring the more visionary and poetic aspects of his art. One reflection of this is the perverse tendency of the 1850 reviews to complain when considering his opinions that Carlyle was too explicit and when considering his language that he was too obscure. Several journals actually found it necessary to restate the central arguments of the *Pamphlets* in plain language, as the *Southern Literary Messenger* put it, "free from the exaggerations and obscurities which partially veil them" (p. 339). Thus they adopted the technique of converting Carlyle into the terms by which he could be more readily demolished. What they cut away in the process was the "wholeness," the integral nature of style and content, which as Professor Holloway has admirably demonstrated is the hallmark of the Victorian sage.

71. *The Correspondence of Gerard Manley Hopkins and Richard Watson Dixon,* ed. Claude Colleer Abbott (Oxford, 1935), p. 59.
72. *Atlantic Monthly,* 47 (May 1881), 593.
73. Ibid., 596, 600, 603, 608.

The obverse side of this movement to separate form from content was the tendency to regard Carlyle exclusively as a stylist, a writer whose eloquence was more important than his doctrines—which allowed the critic to admire his effects without being troubled by his meaning. Thus H. D. Traill introduced the Centenary edition of Carlyle's works with the assertion that "Carlyle is neither political prophet nor ethical doctor, but simply a great master of literature who lives . . . by the art which he despised."[74]

A history of their reception makes it clear that in many ways the *Latter-Day Pamphlets* are *the* Carlyle problem. They have exerted a considerable influence over Carlyle's reputation, and the initial response to them has tended to color all subsequent estimates of his work. Yet the *Pamphlets* themselves have been largely ignored, and the issues raised by them dismissed or evaded. A "central work,"[75] for all their extravagance, the *Pamphlets* are still, as Francis Espinasse noted in 1893, "the least read of all Carlyle's writings."[76] Such critical neglect, regrettable in itself, has by fragmenting the otherwise coherent domain of his writing also had a debilitating effect on the full-bodied assessment of Carlyle's work as a whole. In the midst of the storm provoked by their publication, Froude predicted that the *Pamphlets* would survive as a monument to Carlyle's genius, remaining "to be reviewed hereafter by the light of fact."[77] As the centenary of Carlyle's death is less than a decade away, it is to be hoped that the fulfillment of Froude's prediction will not much longer be postponed, for the *Pamphlets* deserve a fate better than simple hostility or indifference. Perhaps more than anything they will require to be approached in the spirit of Walt Whitman, a staunch political opponent of Carlyle's who shrewdly discerned that the final value of the *Pamphlets* lay precisely in launching a "rasping, questioning, dislocating agitation" into the atmosphere of political complacency. "Who cares that he wrote about Dr. Francia, and Shooting Niagara. . . . How he splashes like Leviathan in the seas of modern literature and politics. . . . Never was there less of a flunkey or temporizer. Never had political progressivism a foe it could more heartily respect."[78]

74. *Works*, I, viii.
75. Grierson, p. 18.
76. *Literary Recollections and Sketches* (London, 1893), pp. 177–178.
77. Froude, *Carlyle*, IV, 26.
78. *Specimen Days in America* (New York, 1902), pp. 306, 307, 316.

The Future of Poetry: A Context for Carlyle and Arnold

DAVID J. DeLAURA, *University of Pennsylvania*

I

For poetry, it was the best of times and it was the worst of times. From about 1820, well into the 1850's, the continuous context for the discussion of poetry in England was a fear that it was nearly defunct, combined with sometimes wistful, sometimes extravagant hopes for its future. A kind of mandatory framework is established in contemporary reviews of poetry. The charge is regularly taken up that "poetry is pretty well extinct among us," or that "this is not a poetic age," or that "poetry is worn out forever" and "dead or entranced," and everyone seemed to agree with the booksellers that "poetry will not sell." Then follows, after deploring the contemporary obsession with "facts" and "the Practical," an often sardonic commentary on a string of minor poets—though a Tennyson or, more persistently, a Browning might be caught up in the blanket of contempt—accusing poets of the "twaddle" of empty belletrism, on the one hand, or of an unreal "transcendental" bombast and egotism on the other.[1]

The hopes for poetry are one expression of that widely shared

1. The phrases are from "Past and Present Conditions of British Poetry," *Fraser's Magazine*, 33 (May 1846), 577; "Modern Poets," *English Review*, 4 (Dec. 1845), 259, 260; Elizabeth Barrett [later Browning], *Essays on the English Poets and the Greek Christian Poets* (1st ed. 1863; New York, 1889), p. 116—originally in the *Athenaeum*, 27 Aug. 1842, p. 758; [Herman Merivale], "Southey's Poetical Works," *Edinburgh Review*, 68 (Jan. 1839), 355. See also *Athenaeum*, 16 July 1828, p. 591: "Of late years, poetry has lost its moral value and influence, and has accordingly degenerated into its lighter species"; the author is probably Maurice or Stebbing. Privately, in a letter of March 1841, John Sterling interestingly links the theme to Carlyle: ". . . on the whole poetry is well-nigh dead among us. It counts for nothing among the great working forces of the age, except so far as Wordsworth's idyllic and didactic songs in some slight degree counteract the coarse materialism of society and the superstitious literalism of the church. Carlyle is the great antagonist of these evils, and . . . *Heroes* will perhaps be more widely felt than anything he has done." *Letters from John Sterling to George Webbe Dasent, 1838–1844*, ed. John R. Dasent (Edinburgh: David Douglas, 1914), p. 20. The next year, in reviewing Tennyson (*Quarterly Review*, 70, Sept. 1842, 386), Sterling complained: "the time, among us at least, is an essentially unpoetic one—one which, whatever may be the worth of its feelings, finds no utterance for them in melodious words." A decade later, G. D. Boyle, *North British Review*, 19 (May 1853), 209, echoes the theme: "Poetry is scarce. Our age . . . seems unfavourable to [its] growth. . . ." See also addendum to note 1 on p. 180.

sense of change and transition that we have come to associate with the early Victorians, Carlyle and Mill most famously. As the young G. H. Lewes put it:

Great ideas are in process of incarnation; great changes are taking place within the womb of society; but it is a period of gestation, and we are not yet on the eve of a new birth. . . . In such periods there is an excitement in the public mind favourable to literature—which is the expression of society—and particularly to poetry.[2]

But even Lewes subsides: "In our day . . . few men of remarkable powers have given any labour to poetry," the poet's other great obstacle being that "there is nothing for him to sing!" (p. 493). The hopes and fears—the sheer confusion—are almost amusingly evident in a review of 1853 that blames the poets themselves, who "instead of *writing* poetry, talk about it. The age's want of a poet, what sort of poet is wanted, what his mission is to be, how the age yearns for him, what are to be his characteristics, how he is to lead in the van of progress, and to guide men to an undreamed of perfection, are echoed from one to another."[3] It is precisely this endless circle of debate, with its background of decades of worry about poetry, which Matthew Arnold coolly attempts to jump out of in the Preface of 1853, begun just a few weeks later:

The present age makes great claims upon us: we owe it service, it will not be satisfied without our admiration. . . . [Those who, like Arnold, have habitual "commerce with the ancients"] do not talk of their mission, nor of interpreting their age, nor of the coming poet; all this, they know, is the mere delirium of vanity; their business is not to praise their age, but to afford to the men who live in it the highest pleasure which they are capable of feeling. . . . They are told that it is an era of progress, an age commissioned to carry out the great ideas of industrial development and social amelioration. They reply that with all this they can do nothing.[4]

2. "Robert Browning and the Poetry of the Age," *British Quarterly Review*, 6 (Nov. 1847), 492.

3. "Modern Poetry," *Christian Remembrancer*, NS 26 (July 1853), 167.

4. *The Complete Prose Works of Matthew Arnold*, ed. R. H. Super (Ann Arbor, Mich., 1960–   ), I, 13. Cited below in the text as CPW. Sidney M. B. Coulling's "Matthew Arnold's 1853 Preface: Its Origin and Aftermath," *Victorian Studies*, 7 (March 1964), 233–263, is the best account of the immediate background of the Preface; but he does not give the *Christian Examiner* as a possible source.

Not many early Victorians had been so capable of refusing to share the age's anxieties. Nevertheless, these categories tend to drop out of the reviews after the mid-fifties, as English cultural and intellectual life enters a more decisively naturalistic and relativistic phase. Those incondite but vaguely grandiose hopes for poetry, as we shall see, were almost a function of a special "moment" in English culture, where "creedless Christianity," shading off into Carlyleanism, could hope to inspire a poetry that would offer leadership to an age of (in Arnold's phrase) "bewildering confusion" (CPW, I, 14). That moment was over shortly after 1850; the mid-sixties were to see the rise of new sorts of poetry and new themes in Swinburne, Morris, and Rossetti. The charge of "fleshliness" was to be added to escapism, but neither the poets nor their critics talked very confidently in the seventies about the poet's mission of social and moral regeneration. Arnold's major prophecies were formulated in that later context.

The young Tennyson is probably the clearest and most talented example of an early-Victorian trying on the various styles of singing robes available in the earlier period. The high hopes were fed by the Romantic poets and critics; but by the mid-1820's the Romantic experiment was over, "failed" many were saying, and was perceived to be at an end even by its constantly diminishing band of defenders.[5] Two well-known versions of the poet in *Poems, Chiefly Lyrical* (1830) stand uncomfortably together. "The Poet," born in a "golden clime," is a primitivistic figure who, Apollo-like, seems to bring civilization into being:

> And Freedom reared in that august sunrise
>   Her beautiful bold brow,
> When rites and forms before his burning eyes
>   Melted like snow.
>
>   · · ·
>
> Her [Wisdom's] words did gather thunder as they ran,
>   And as the lightning to the thunder
> Which follows it, riving the spirit of man,
>   Making earth wonder,
>
> So was their meaning to her words.[6]

5. See the important article by R. G. Cox, "Victorian Criticism of Poetry: The Minority Tradition," *Scrutiny*, 18 (June 1951), 2–17. I believe Cox errs only in underestimating the strength of the spreading anti-Romantic critical climate.

6. "The Poet," in *The Poems of Tennyson*, ed. Christopher Ricks, Longmans Annotated English Poets (London, 1969), ll. 37–40, 49–53, pp. 223–224.

But this first or original Poet (the entire poem is in the past tense) is, in his prophetic and apocalyptic character, very much of the nineteenth century, proclaiming Freedom and a new social order while doing away—a "creedless Christian" *avant la lettre*—with outworn "rites and forms." The ideal is Shelleyan, that of

> a Poet hidden
> In the light of thought,
> Singing hymns unbidden,
> Till the world is wrought
> To sympathy with hopes and fears it heeded not.[7]

But the "future" of poetry in such a context is far from Aestheticism and leads instead straight to the visionary politics of Swinburne's *Songs Before Sunrise* (1871). In contrast, the unpleasantly aloof speaker in "The Poet's Mind" seems to repel not only the rationalistic "sophist" but anyone else who would intrude upon his Kubla-Khanian garden. The fountain in the middle sings "a song of undying love"— but that unspecific song lacks any hint of social or moral regeneration. Perhaps it was this very "Aesthetic" poem of Tennyson's—a not so distant precursor of the immurement images in Pater's famous Conclusion—that led his friend Trench to that quintessentially "Apostolic" admonition: "Tennyson, we cannot live in art."[8] At any rate, the premises of "The Poet's Mind" were soon reversed in "The Palace of Art," where the "lordly pleasure-house," with its lawns and fountains, is condemned for a prideful isolation leading to spiritual death. Unfortunately for Tennyson's point (if not for the poetry), his attention is still lavished on the palace, and not on the moralizing coda; but the conclusion, significantly, does not convert the secluded aesthete back into the social prophet of "The Poet," but instead prescribes a morally purgative residence in the humble "cottage in the vale"—in the hope that he will return, "with others," precisely to enjoy the same intellectual and sensual delights. Tennyson's doubts and tergiversations about the vatic and public role of the poet are the persistent doubts of the age about its own deepest needs and aspirations.[9]

---

7. "To a Skylark," ll. 36–40. But not the Shelley of *A Defense of Poetry*; see n. 20, below.

8. Hallam Tennyson, *Alfred Lord Tennyson: A Memoir*, 2 vols. (London, 1897), I, 118.

9. The subject was best opened up in E. D. H. Johnson's *The Alien Vision of*

II

Until recently, surprisingly little attention has been paid to this confused poetic, or antipoetic, climate of the pre- and early-Victorians. It is the unstudied background of Carlyle's attempts, in the twenties and thirties, to mark out a role for poetry. Lionel Stevenson has noted that "about the year 1825 poetry was suddenly faced with an ideological assault that gravely menaced its survival."[10] But his presentation requires a lumping together of Bentham, the "Whig intellectuals" (including Macaulay), and Carlyle, and he regards them as "unanimous in their belief that poetry no longer wielded any real power" (pp. 261–265). There are indeed some shared assumptions about the nature and function of poetry among these diverse spokesmen; but the basis of their alleged antipoetic bias, as well as their different actual valuations of poetry itself, are lost in this scheme. The word "poetry" turns out to be protean, in search of a definition.

Stevenson notes (pp. 263–264) a famous passage in Macaulay's "Milton" (1825) on the "necessary" decline of poetry in a civilized age. The historical scheme controlling that essay, as well as other writings of Macaulay, was part of a much larger debate about the historical fate of poetry. It was an implicit mental framework for the discussion of poetry, well past mid-century, in Matthew Arnold's critical career. It was also a powerful explanatory tool, shared by men of otherwise highly diverse points of view; in its negative, and almost necessitarian, implications, it probably inhibited possibilities for both poetry and criticism.

Notions of inevitable decline in both literature and the fine arts were common in the eighteenth century and had a long earlier history in classical myths of the Golden Age; surprisingly few critics of the eighteenth century looked for linear progress in the arts parallel to progress in knowledge. The uniformitarian standards of the early

---

Victorian Poetry (1952; rpt. Hamden, Conn.: Archon Books, 1963). Two excellent treatments are Lionel Stevenson, "Tennyson, Browning, and a Romantic Fallacy," *University of Toronto Quarterly*, 13 (Jan. 1944), 175–195, and John Lucas, "Politics and the Poet's Role," in *Literature and Politics in the Nineteenth Century*, ed. J. Lucas (London, 1971), pp. 7–43.

10. 'The Key Poem of the Victorian Age," in *Essays in American and English Literature Presented to Bruce Robert McElderry*, ed. Max F. Schulz (Athens, Ohio, 1967), p. 260. The notion of a "decline" in poetry in the writings of Hazlitt, Peacock, and Macaulay is mentioned in Walter E. Houghton and G. Robert Stange's invaluable *Victorian Poetry and Poetics*, 2d ed. (Boston, 1968 [1959]), pp. xv–xvi, 845 n.

eighteenth century, as Lovejoy explained, held "reason" and "nature" to be unchangeable standards, but easily corrupted by traditions and prejudice. More importantly for the present study, the later eighteenth century argued a decline in poetry on the basis of its cult of the primitive bard.[11] Within the broad view that all artistic activities decline after reaching a high point of development, two explanatory theories of civilization were possible. One was that history itself is essentially a continuous alternation between periods of barbarity and refinement, or of action and reflection. Such theories of historic periodicity were of course rife in the nineteenth century, and in one version or another can be found in Coleridge, Mill, Carlyle, and Arnold, among many others. They can explain how periods of "enlightenment" and "expansion" succeed, and are succeeded by, periods of retrogression and "contraction." Such a theory of oscillations can provide, on the Enlightenment's own terms, a comforting panorama of hard-won victories (with dramatic setbacks) of light over darkness; in fact, such "alternations" theories often in the nineteenth century merged imperceptibly into a second or "progressive" theory too.[12] It can, that is, account for Civilization, or Criticism and Culture, or the "march of intellect." But in general it refused to serve as a satisfactory historical theory of poetry. Once committed in the late eighteenth century to the primitivistic notion that in the history of any people "imagination"—the faculty specially associated with poetry—"early reaches a perfection beyond which it cannot advance, and from which it must necessarily decline under the chilling influence of developing reason,"[13] even sympathetic critics were hard put to articulate a role for contemporary poetry.

11. In this material I have relied heavily on John D. Schieffer's article, "The Idea of Decline in Literature and the Fine Arts in Eighteenth-Century England," *Modern Philology*, 34 (Nov. 1936), 155–178. See the equally indispensable study by Lois Whitney, "English Primitivistic Theories of Epic Origins," *Modern Philology*, 21 (May 1924), 337–378.

12. An unusually clear Victorian statement of the alternations theory *without* progressive implications appears in De Quincey's "Style" (1840), in his discussion of "oscillations between the creative and reflective energies of the mind." *The Collected Writings of Thomas De Quincey*, ed. David Masson (London, 1897), X, 201–202.

13. Schieffer, p. 177. Schieffer at one point (p. 157) says such "decline" thinking continued into the nineteenth century, but associates Hazlitt, Macaulay, etc., only with the very general notion of decline-after-excellence. William John Courthope's *The Liberal Movement in English Literature* (London, 1885) is a late but full statement of the inverse relationship of poetry and civilization. Rowland Prothero's review in the *Edinburgh*, 163 (April 1886), 466–498, keenly criticizes the difficulties in Courthope's view "that political and literary movements are different manifestations

Apparently the first to see *almost* the full cultural implications of this view of poetry and imagination was not Wordsworth or, as one might suspect, Coleridge, but Hazlitt, in two of his *Lectures on the English Poets* (1818). The well-known lecture "On Shakspeare and Milton" presents an already familiar contrast between a "'progressive" science and other intellectual and critical modes of inquiry, as against poetry and the imitative arts. Science and its cognate activities have in them "no principle of limitation or decay," whereas the greatest poets and artists "appeared soon after the birth of these arts, and lived in a state of society which was, in other respects, comparatively barbarous. Those arts, which depend on individual genius and incommunicable power, have always leaped at once from infancy to manhood, . . . and have in general declined ever after."[14] But something rather different, and I think unprecedented, is going on in the introductory lecture, "On Poetry in General." Hazlitt is close to the language of Wordsworth when he describes imagination as involved in the different ways in which things strike the observer, depending on his varying "interest" in them. In this way poetry, intent on "appearances" and even "illusions," "is one part of the history of the human mind, though it is neither science nor philosophy."[15] But suddenly Hazlitt veers off to inspect a darker landscape:

It cannot be concealed, however, that the progress of knowledge and refinement has a tendency to circumscribe the limits of the imagination, and to clip the wings of poetry. The province of the imagination is principally visionary, the unknown and undefined: the understanding restores things to their natural boundaries, and strips them of their fanciful pretensions. Hence the history of religious and poetical enthusiasm is much the same;

---

of analogous causes" (p. 469). The *Wellesley Index*, vol. 1, reveals that Courthope, in his numerous and severe reviews in the *Quarterly* in the seventies and eighties, virtually single-handedly maintained the reactionary literary mood detected there by R. V. Johnson, in "Pater and the Victorian Anti-Romantics," *Essays in Criticism*, 4 (Jan. 1954), 42–57.

14. *The Complete Works of William Hazlitt*, ed. P. P. Howe (London, 1930–1934), V, 44–45.

15. A note sounded by Wordsworth as recently as the "Essay, Supplementary" of 1815 (William Wordsworth, *Selected Poems and Prefaces*, ed. Jack Stillinger, Riverside Editions [Boston, 1965], p. 471): "The appropriate business of poetry, . . . her privilege and her *duty*, is to treat of things not as they *are*, but as they appear; not as they exist in themselves, but as they *seem* to exist to the *senses*, and to the *passions*. What a world of delusion does this acknowledged obligation prepare for the inexperienced!"

and both have received a sensible shock from the progress of experimental philosophy. . . . There can never be another Jacob's dream. Since that time, the heavens have gone farther off, and grown astronomical. They have become averse to the imagination, nor will they return to us on the squares of the distances, or on Dr. Chalmers's Discourses. . . . It is not only the progress of mechanical knowledge, but the necessary advances of civilization that are unfavourable to the spirit of poetry. We not only stand in less awe of the preternatural world, but we can calculate more surely, and look with more indifference, upon the regular routine of this [p. 9].

Still, though Hazlitt stands on the verge of a genuine "theory" of modern cultural history, he stops short, just at this point, and drops the subject. Like Coleridge, he senses the danger to the life of the imagination, as well as to religion, in the gradual emergence of a full-blown mechanism and naturalism. What Hazlitt lacks, almost as much as Coleridge, is a decisive theory of modernity, which would go beyond seeing their own period as one further stage in the gradual elimination of heroes, monsters, and giants—in short, the dramatis personae of the undefined "preternatural" world given over to passion, imagination, enthusiasm, fable, illusion, and (as Hazlitt says at one point) "religious faith" (p. 11).

What enabled Hazlitt to go even so far as he did in formulating his view was his essentially negative judgment of contemporary poetry, though the latter was not yet apprehended so compactly as the later phrase "Romantic movement" was to imply. Even Hazlitt's favorable treatment of poetry as a world of "appearances" and "illusions" whose sphere is the visionary and the preternatural, a world of dream and fancy, is rather disturbingly touched by the skeptical spirit and somehow confines poetry to an inner and insubstantial world. His own skepticism about the "truth" of poetry seems to govern his not fully coherent attacks on Romantic subjectivity. Referring to "the Lake school of poetry," but meaning Wordsworth more than Coleridge, Hazlitt disapproves it, as "an experiment to reduce poetry to a mere effusion of natural sensibility; or what is worse, to divest it both of imaginary splendour and human passion, to surround the meanest objects with the morbid feelings and devouring egotism of the writers' own minds." Milton and Shakespeare "did not do all they could to get rid of" nature and art and "to fill up the dreary void with the Moods of their own Minds." Instead, they had "a deeper sense than others of what was grand in the objects of nature, or affecting in the events of human life"; whereas to the moderns, "there is nothing interesting, nothing heroical, but themselves" (p. 53). This charge of egotism is extended ad libitum to Byron, seen as a figure of "un-accommodating selfishness," cherishing his "intellectual diseases" (p. 153).[16] In short, Hazlitt seems to be the first critic, not merely a *Quarterly* or *Edinburgh* reactionary, to see in Romanticism a great wrong-turning in the history of culture and of human expression. Though he does not clearly tie the two lines of thought together, the Wordsworthian experiment, expanded now by Byron's variety of egotism, seemed to have collaborated all too successfully with the irreversible direction of modern civilization. Science and the modern skeptical "understanding" have banished from the contemporary mind and imagination all traces of the preternatural, the visionary, and "illusion"; the Romantic poets go further along the same line by renouncing the splendor of nature, as well as heroic action and passion. The new poetic, with its concentration on the "meanest objects" and its method of "morbid" subjectivity and egotism, closely parallels the confinement of the mind to "the regular routine" of things endorsed by modern mechanism and utilitarianism. In the terms of Hazlitt's historical scheme, the poetics of "mere sentiment" was a sort of dangerous trafficking with the enemy.

III

The important fact is that, if Hazlitt shrank from drawing the logical conclusions from his own premises, others did not. The first to see that Hazlitt's version of the inverse relationship of poetry and civilization, combined with a profound disapproval of the direction taken by contemporary poetry, offered an unprecedented threat to poetry and the life of the imagination was Thomas Love Peacock.[17]

16. Hazlitt's campaign against Wordsworth's "egotism" (picked up by Keats as "the wordsworthian or egotistical sublime," by October 1818) began as early as his 1814 review of *The Excursion*, later in the *Round Table*, 1817 (Howe, IV, 112–116, and 92). The charges against Wordsworth and his "school" are amplified in *Table Talk*, 1821–1822 (Howe, VIII, 43–45) and *The Spirit of the Age*, 1825 (Howe, XI, 69, 71, 94–95). Coleridge was of course much earlier aware of the danger of "Self-involution" in Wordsworth, and feared "lest a film [of egotism] should rise and thicken on his moral Eye" (letter to Poole, 14 Oct. 1803), but he had not brought the issue to a focus in the *Biographia* (1817).

17. Both of the major modern studies of Peacock see Hazlitt as the immediate background. See Howard Mills, *Peacock: His Circle and His Age* (Cambridge, Eng.,

But because his satirical instinct perversely led him to adopt a mock-utilitarian and seemingly antipoetic point of view, Peacock's *Four Ages of Poetry* (1820) has remained something of an enigma into our own day. It is clear, however, that Peacock is very far from equating poetry with push-pin, and that, as a poet himself and a lover of the older poets, his near-despair over the future of poetry is the reflex of his sense that the new expressive theories of poetry, with their "new conception of the sources and purposes of poetry," have wrongly excused poetry from its social and political responsibilties and reduced it to a form of "cryptic and private communication."[18] It was precisely this threatened social dimension of poetry that Shelley, in response, took up in his *Defense of Poetry* a few months later.[19] But even there, although "prophecy" is "an attribute of poetry" and poets are "the *unacknowledged* legislators of the world," they are (in a splendid image) "the mirrors of the gigantic shadows which *futurity* casts upon the present" (Jordan, pp. 32, 80; my emphases): poets (who always live "now" and not in the future) have a high destiny but a quite unclear contemporary function. At any rate, for the present and the foreseeable future, the poet must be content to write (in Shelley's phrase) "simply for the esoteric few" (Dawson, p. 84).

But the essays of Peacock and Shelley, though in very different ways acknowledging the profound crisis of "modern" poetry, play no real part in the cultural polemics of their own period, since both were unavailable for many years.[20] It was obviously Macaulay who, from the highly visible platform of the *Edinburgh Review*, developed between 1825 and 1830 the full implications of Hazlitt's views of the crisis of poetry into a full-blown historical theory of the "laws on which depend the progress and decline of poetry" and the other arts,

---

1969), p. 42; and Carl Dawson, *His Fine Wit: A Study of Thomas Love Peacock* (Berkeley and Los Angeles, 1970), p. 95.

18. See Dawson's treatment (pp. 78–79, 84, 88–94), by far the most penetrating we have. The quoted phrases are Dawson's, pp. 91 and 84.

19. A reliable text of both men's essays, along with an expert Introduction and notes, is to be found in John E. Jordan's edition in the Library of the Liberal Arts (Indianapolis, 1965), cited below as Jordan.

20. Peacock's essay appeared anonymously in Ollier's *Literary Miscellany*, an obscure and short-lived journal, and was not reprinted until 1863 (and then privately). Shelley's *Defense* did not see the light until 1839 (dated 1840). Of course Peacock's judgment of the "morbidities" of modern literature was perfectly evident in *Nightmare Abbey* (1818), with its portraits of Flosky (Coleridge), Scythrop (Shelley), and Cypress (Byron).

laws as invariable as those governing "the periodical returns of heat and cold."[21] In the landmark essay on Milton (1825) and the less well known one on Dryden (1828), Macaulay treats poetry more or less incidentally as part of his straight-line theory of the "natural progress of society": from the seventeenth century on, "One after another phantoms which had haunted the world through ages of darkness fled before the light."[22] Though by no means a Benthamite enemy of the imagination, Macaulay, reluctantly perhaps but dry-eyed, presents poetry as the vanishing product of the phantom-haunted and now irrecoverable "dark" origins of human consciousness. The terms are familiar to all readers of Macaulay. On the one hand there is civilization, enlightenment, science, philosophy; they all work for "the clear discernment of truth" by means of reason, analysis, dissection, classification, comparison, wit, judgment, memory, taste, eloquence—in short, an "examining" frame of mind. Poetry, under "the despotism of the imagination," is variously the product of deception, illusion, "unsoundness of mind"; its truth is "the truth of madness" and requires "a degree of credulity which almost amounts to a partial and temporary derangement of the intellect." Its intense emotions (as strong as agony and ecstasy) require

21. "John Dryden," in *Lays of Ancient Rome and Miscellaneous Essays and Poems*, Everyman's Library (London, 1910), p. 42; originally in the *Edinburgh* for January 1828. I single out Hazlitt, though I am fully aware of the large group of "primitivists" in the background: see Terry Otten, "Macaulay's Secondhand Theory of Poetry," *South Atlantic Quarterly*, 72 (Spring 1973), 280–294. (Otten has excellently summarized Macaulay's position, in "Macaulay's Critical Theory of Imagination and Reason," *Journal of Aesthetics and Art Criticism*, 28 [Fall 1969], 33–42.) Except for Hazlitt, all of these sources (including Otten's other new candidate, Jeffrey) lack a view of the *decisive* demise of poetry, its confirmation in the history of the Romantic experiment, and a relation to the decline of religion and "belief" in the age. Both P. L. Carver, "The Sources of Macaulay's *Essay on Milton*," *Review of English Studies*, 6 (Jan. 1930), 49–62, and Frederick L. Jones, "Macaulay's Theory of Poetry in *Milton*," *Modern Language Quarterly*, 13 (Dec. 1952), 356–362, suggest Hazlitt as a source. But Jones's view that Macaulay "drew his theory almost in toto" from Peacock is rendered improbable by the evidence in n. 20, above. There is no external evidence of Macaulay's knowing Peacock's *Four Ages* (Macaulay was still an undergraduate at Cambridge when the anonymous essay appeared so quietly), and the internal evidence presented by Jones does not, in my judgment, favor Peacock over Hazlitt. Other evidence (not to my knowledge suggested before) of Macaulay's indebtedness to Hazlitt might be found in a close parallel examination of Macaulay's essays on Byron and Southey (both 1830) and Hazlitt's chapters on the two men in *The Spirit of the Age* (1825). In any case, my description of the climate of the twenties remains, I think, valid, whether or not Peacock actually enters the scene as a "source."
22. "Southey's Colloquies" (1830), in *Critical and Historical Essays*, Everyman's Library (London, 1907), II, 22; and the third chapter of vol. 1 of *The History of England* (begun in the late thirties), in Everyman's Library (London, 1906), I, 308.

a "plenitude of belief" unavailable to the modern cultivated mind. This is, after all, nothing short of "the law of our nature. Our judgment ripens, our imagination decays." We are not surprised at the conclusion that in such modern and civilized conditions, the sciences and "criticism" advance, "but poetry, in the highest sense of the word, disappears."[23] What is less evident at first glance is the fact that this view of the irrevocable extinction of poetry and its vehicle, the imagination allied to "belief," is shared not only by Benthamites, rationalists, and Whig intellectuals—but also by Thomas Carlyle.

Up to about 1830, at the height of his always tentative commitment to the "German" doctrine of Poetry and Art, Carlyle could insist that the highest poetry demands "a certain Infinitude, and spiritual Freedom; that elevation above the Fate and Clay of this Earth, in which alone, and by virtue of which, Poetry, soul-Music, is possible."[24] But the crisis of his own career, as of his poetics, was his intense realization in the early thirties that if true poetry, which is always "sacred or divine, and inspired," inevitably demands "Belief," then even the "tolerable semblance" of poetry is impossible in this unbelieving era. The Poet or Seer to discern these "proper Realities"

23. Throughout this paragraph I have quoted from "Milton," *Critical and Historical Essays*, I, 150–194, and "Dryden," pp. 39–77. The notion of decline-with-crisis is almost casually mentioned by Arthur Hallam in his 1831 review of Tennyson's poems: ". . . the age in which we live comes late in our national progress. The first raciness and juvenile vigor [sic] of literature . . . is gone, never to return. Since that day we have undergone a period of degradation. . . . With the close of the last century came an era of reaction, an era of painful struggle to bring our over-civilised condition of thought into union with the fresh productive spirit that brightened the morning of our literature. But repentance is unlike innocence." *The Writings of Arthur Hallam*, ed. T. H. Vail Motter (New York, 1943), pp. 189–190. Macaulay's view of poetry was occasionally attacked, e.g., by R. H. Horne (with possible help from Elizabeth Barrett), in *A New Spirit of the Age* (London, 1844), II, 40 ff., and very ably by G. H. Lewes, *British Quarterly Review*, 9 (Feb. 1849), 20 ff. The only "progressive" review of poetry that I have found in the era—that "the great principle of human improvement is at work in poetry as well as everywhere else"—occurs in W. J. Fox's naively utilitarian review of Tennyson (*Westminster Review*, Jan. 1831); rpt. in *Tennyson: The Critical Heritage*, ed. J. D. Jump (London, 1967), p. 213.

24. *Carlyle's Unfinished History of German Literature*, ed. Hill Shine (Lexington, Ky., 1951), p. 87; written in 1830. A. Abbott Ikeler's *Puritan Temper and Transcendental Faith: Carlyle's Literary Vision* (Columbus, Ohio, 1972) is valuable in providing the fullest survey of Carlyle's literary opinions. But his approach largely ignores the contemporary English context and in my judgment overly polarizes the two elements in Carlyle's career signified in his title—while underestimating the way in which Carlyle's lifelong religious quest tends to move the themes toward a common and unifying center. Ikeler takes Carlyle's interest in German thought too literally and misreads the theological implications of Carlyle's retreat to a "Calvinist" position after the early thirties. Ikeler is also unaccountably indifferent to the fact and the significance of Carlyle's "prophetic" view of poetry.

is wanting, and it may take centuries to produce him (*Works*, XXVIII, 49–52, "Biography," 1832). Carlyle knew by 1832 that he was not and was not to be such a poet: "To imagine: *bilden!* That is an unfathomable thing. As yet I have never risen into the region of creation."[25] Instead, abjuring Fiction and Invention, he will work "more and more on REALITY" and evolve "*its* inexhaustible meanings." This "new Truth" or "Revelation," derived from history or biography and based on a newly contracted "*Belief*" in ascertainable Fact, would yield its own poetry (*Works*, XXVIII, 53–54; see p. 178).[26]

This fundamental change of front is what Carlyle referred to in 1833 as his new view "that all Art is but a reminiscence now, that for us in these days *Prophecy* (well understood) not Poetry is the thing wanted; how can we *sing* and *paint* when we do not yet *believe* and *see?*" Even Goethe "is not to have any follower, and should not have any."[27] The attempt to find a spiritual truth in history would obviously be a painful struggle to gain diminished and distant glimpses of an ultimate religious interpretation of reality that poets had once sung of freely. As he told Mill, "melodious Art" has "fled . . . far away; not in Poetry, but only if so might be in Prophecy, in stern old-Hebrew denunciation, can one speak of the accursed realities that now, and for generations, . . . weigh heavy on us!"[28] Carlyle's own ·experiment at last flagged and failed: History did not furnish the anticipated "Revelation" of the divine. "He does nothing," he bitterly concluded.[29] He continued to praise the true poet who "transports us into a holier and higher world than our own"; his "enchantments . . . are strong enough to silence our scepticism" (*Works*, XXV, 78, *Life of Schiller*, 1825). But poetry and the poet were now for the unknowable future; Carlyle was forced to settle for the Prophet's limited vision and his role of stern denunciation. The point here is that the historical scheme of poetry followed by Carlyle, and the

25. Froude, *Carlyle*, II, 283.
26. A process best studied in Hill Shine, *Carlyle's Fusion of Poetry, History, and Religion by 1834* (1938; rpt. Port Washington, N.Y., 1967), and in Carlisle Moore, "Carlyle's 'Diamond Necklace' and Poetic History," *PMLA*, 58 (June 1943), 537–557 —although both works are oddly absent even from Ikeler's bibliography. See also a letter to Mill of 17 Dec. 1833, in A. Carlyle, *CMSB*, p. 87, and one to his brother John of 24 Dec., in Froude, *Carlyle*, II, 386.
27. *Letters of Thomas Carlyle, 1826–1836*, ed. Charles Eliot Norton (London, 1889), p. 378.
28. 18 April 1833, A. Carlyle, *CMSB*, p. 48.
29. Froude, *Carlyle*, II, 260.

causes of its decline, followed very closely a pattern already well established in the period. The genius of Carlyle, and a central source of his great power, lay in his development of this insight into a comprehensive view of the maladies and responsibilities of the modern situation. The eclipse of poetry was a symptom and an index of the disease of modernity; the reappearance of poetry would be a sign of regained spiritual health.

IV

For poetry, then, it seemed the worst—and very nearly the last—of times. But what are we to make of the bewildering range of claims for, and predictions about, poetry that run through the century? For in one sense, the "status" and "standing" of poetry—or at least poetry as it might someday be—had never been higher. My special interest here is to suggest where in the range of possible predictions two famous prophecies stand: Carlyle's "Literature is but a branch of Religion, and always participates in its character: however, in our time it is the only branch that still shows any greenness; and, as some think, must one day become the main stem" (1831; III, 23), and Arnold's "The future of poetry is immense. . . . The strongest part of our religion to-day is its unconscious poetry" (1880; CPW, IX, 161). What is most obvious in such predictions is not merely the high and religious claims made for poetry but the fact that the unprecedented elevation of poetry is correlative to a broadly conceived religious and spiritual crisis, seen as the central and characteristic experience of the century. An important corollary of this widely shared and emergent view is the rise of poetry as an "independent" power, a new and distinct source of value in a disintegrating cultural situation. All critics recognized this new and insistent "presence" of poetry, or at least of the *theory* of poetry, even when they deplored it. In effect, men of all parties sought to claim poetry for their own purposes, to compel it to serve their own vision of social and personal need—in short, to assign poetry a role in a new and quickly emerging vision of the human future. If we are not extremely discriminating about the century's promiscuous use of the term "religion," we end in the seeming double-talk of saying that "Religion . . . not only became a part of poetry, but a product of it as well," or that the "majority" of critics tend to regard poetry as "religion itself."[30] The majority did nothing of the sort; and although it would take a book to discriminate all the possible relationships between poetry and religion, some major possibilities can be defined.

One might imagine a long double spectrum: a horizontal line would stand for religious and philosophical orthodoxy; another, nearly touching the first at one end and gradually widening the distance, would represent the growing independence of poetry from such traditional standards. At the closed end would stand those (especially but not exclusively High-Churchmen and Roman Catholics) who place a high premium on credal and doctrinal correctness; for these the judgment of poetry would only with difficulty be separated from identifiably orthodox standards of both piety and "truth." (But there is always some play, a falling short of coincidence; even Newman, while of course viewing poetry as certainly subordinate to revelation, saw poetry as a cooperating but distinct source of religious value: "the taste for poetry of a religious kind [he says in 1839] has in modern times in a certain sense taken the place of the deep contemplative spirit of the early Church. . . . Poetry . . . is our mysticism.")[31] As one moves along the scale and away from the demands of traditional orthodoxy, the gap between the autonomous value of poetry and the truth of traditional philosophy and theology grows ever wider. This, the major segment of the spectrum, moves from more or less liberal but still consciously orthodox Christian spokesmen on to either theists who (like Carlyle) stand outside Christianity, or an agnostic like Matthew Arnold whose spiritual synthesis retains conscious links to the older theology. This portion includes the bulk of Victorian critics. Only a small though sometimes highly talented remainder, at the far extreme, simply deny or ignore or invert the relationship of poetry to the endangered but somehow still authoritative historical synthesis of philosophy, theology, and piety: extreme utilitarians and positivists, who tend to have difficulty justifying poetry anyway, and the more daring aesthetes, who,

30. See Lawrence J. Starzyk, " 'That Promised Land': Poetry and Religion in the Early Victorian Period," *Victorian Studies*, 16 (March 1973), 281, 271. Again, a valuable collection of materials, but seriously deficient in discriminating the varied meanings of its two major terms and lacking in a sense of the mitigating contexts in which provocative statements are frequently made.

31. *Essays Critical and Historical* (1871; London, 1887), I, 290–291. The High-Church and Roman Catholic position is not so simply that poetry is the "handmaiden" of theology as Starzyk (pp. 269, 270, 289) and others have implied.

though repudiating the substance of philosophy and theology, want the "perfume" of the old religion to pervade their "new" art. The majority of Victorian critics, including most aesthetes and excluding only the most intellectually radical, have in this sense a "conservative" view of poetry's past—and its future: poetry's fate, and its role, is a function of what may be salvaged in the coming universal shipwreck of the older European synthesis.

A central effort of nineteenth-century religion, apart from the severer forms of orthodoxy, is that of separating the "kernel" of spiritual truth from the "husk" of its various historical embodiments; the "idea" will somehow survive its diverse and erroneous formulations and cultural embodiments. A typical statement is that of F. W. Newman, a non-institutional Christian:

Religion can never resume her pristine vigour, until she becomes purely Spiritual, and, as in apostolic days, appeals only to the Soul; and the real problem for all who wish to save cultivated Europe from Pantheism, Selfishness, and Sensuality, (such as flooded and ruined ancient Greece,) is,— to extract and preserve the heavenly spirit of Christianity, while neglecting its earthly husk.[32]

This is the great modern attempt to save the "religious" consciousness of mankind from religion's own imperiled institutional, philosophical, theological, and mythological past—to rescue the precious cargo before the ship goes down. The notion is, in an important sense, un- and anti-historical, and goes back to the rationalism of the eighteenth century.[33] It lies behind Arnold's 1880 prophecy, when he says that traditional religion has propped itself up with creeds, dogmas, and traditions that have proved to be "illusions." Once religion detaches itself from these now discredited assertions, it can identify itself with the underlying spiritual and moral "idea," which is the *real* fact of religion. Conscious poetry can now provide what traditionally

32. *The Soul, Its Sorrows and Aspirations* (1849; London, 1862), p. 158. F. W. Newman's own views of art comprehend two familiar themes of the age: on the one hand (*The Soul*, pp. 22–23) he is almost Evangelical in speaking of "the danger besetting those who allow themselves to cultivate devout feeling by aid of human art," and he assigns "an exceedingly subordinate place in religion" to the fine arts. Yet on the next page (24) he can trumpet "the glorious effect of high poetry, and of all that excites pure and beautiful imagination, on the youthful mind."

33. See Schiller's "On the Use of the Chorus in Tragedy," prefixed to *The Bride from Messina*, trans. Charles E. Passage (New York, 1962), p. 12: "Beneath the husk of all religions lies religion, the idea of a divinity, and a poet must be allowed to express this in whatever form he finds most convenient and most fitting."

in religion has been merely "unconscious poetry" (CPW, IX, 161, 63).
But whether the religious consciousness can indeed survive its own
history is, though crucial, a separable question. What is important
here is that the defense of poetry in the nineteenth century (and in
more inchoate ways, the defense of the humanities in our own time),
the high and escalating prophecies and predictions about poetry's
"religious" future, are the indices of a profound doubt and fear about
the survival of a residue of human values in general.

It is evident that talk about the religious character of art, as well as
of "the religion of art," had become troublesome and nearly epidemic
long before the confusion of Art and Religion that T. S. Eliot so deplored in Arnold and Pater.[34] By mid-century it was the small talk of
poets and critics. Charles Kingsley, himself a very "broad" church-
man, explosively linked the pestilential chatter about the "divine"
imaginings of poetry with the drift of modern theology. He addresses
a typical poetaster: "Not that you meant to be blasphemous; no, you
used 'Divine' just as you would intense, or gorgeous, or 'utterless,' or
any other word from the stock-cant vocabulary":

True, you are not the only offender. Older and cleverer men than you, with
false prophet Emerson at their head, bandy about in their new Every-man-
his-own-God-maker-cant, the most holy and awful words, and apply un-
blushingly to man the attributes of Almighty God, little knowing how thin
a paper-wall parts their Autotheism from sheer, blank, honest, manful Atheism,—honest and manful, because it wears no rouge, and has courage to
look steadily at the reflection of its own skeleton-face. . . .
. . . the prevalence of—what shall we call it?—Pseudo-Spiritualistico-Eclec-
tico-Hypoplatonico-Pantheistico-Pamborborotaractic Sentimentalism, infecting the greater part of our bad poetry, and too much of our good, is an
ugly sign of the "unreality" . . . which is abroad in the world . . . in the very
sanctuary of God, as poetry once was, and will be again.[35]

34. "Arnold and Pater" (1930), in Selected Essays, 3d ed. (London, 1951), pp.
431–443.
35. "The Prevailing Epidemic," Fraser's Magazine, 43 (May 1851), 497, 498.
Kingsley had made boisterous fun of the art talk of the period at several points in
Yeast (1848), notably in chap. 3. No doubt he was also thinking of the numerous
artist novels of the period (see n. 57 below). In this review, Kingsley may well have
taken his cue from "Jesuitism" (Aug. 1850), where Carlyle is unusually ambiguous
on the " 'Worship of the Beautiful,' " moving in a short compass from the balanced
view that the Fine Arts, "if not religion," are "indissolubly united to it," to a ferocious
denunciation of contemporary art as "divorced entirely from Truth this long while"
and in "an insane condition" (Works, XX, 318–323).

It should be remembered that the defense of a high and "truly" religious poetry—whether in Kingsley or in the even less orthodox Carlyle and Arnold—is, in a crucial sense, *anti-*"aesthetic," in necessarily deprecating what Carlyle called the new insistence that "a man of culture shall understand and worship Art," one of the loudest of the "windy gospels" of the century (*Works*, XI, 174, *Life of Sterling*, 1851).

Still, most of even the more serious critics were not so troubled as Kingsley was by this "blasphemous" new attitude toward art and the artist—and their future. Even the analogy of poetic and religious experience had a long history in the Christian tradition, going back through the Christian Platonists of the Renaissance to the Fathers of the Church. The Oxford Movement itself sponsored, for a few years, a very "high" and hopeful theory, according to which a new Christian poetry, though not quite emancipated from its traditional role as handmaiden to piety and doctrine, would act to some extent independently as the restorer of a disappearing religious consciousness.[36] More typically, no doubt, a liberal Anglican and popular preacher like Frederick Robertson expresses an increasingly widespread view of poetry as the guardian of a "vague" numinousness under threat from science. "Science destroys Poetry [he explains]: until the heart bursts into mysticism, and out of science brings Poetry again; asserting a wonder and a vague mystery of life and feeling beneath and beyond all science, and proclaiming the wonderfulness and mystery of that which we seem most familiarly to understand."[37] This is

36. This line of argument, involving a still influential and polemical view of the history of English culture, can be found not only in the writings of leaders like Newman and Keble, but throughout the High Church journals. It has received virtually no close attention. M. H. Abrams, in *The Mirror and the Lamp* (1953; rpt. New York, 1971), pp. 330, 332, correctly locates in Wordsworth, as well as in Shelley and De Quincey after him, the "substitution of a predominantly emotional for a predominantly doctrinal culture"—but then narrows this to mean "the turn from the rational and calculative ethics of Bentham and the early Godwin to other eighteenth-century theorists who put sensibility and sympathy at the center of morality." My own subject here is the shift away from "doctrine" in a wider sense: from the not easily grasped but nevertheless interrelated congeries of theological and philosophical ideas historically associated with Christian culture and couched in Hellenic categories. It should be borne in mind, of course, that leaders of thought as well as most creative artists among the early- and mid-Victorians were more overtly conscious of a revived "Christian" ambience than the bulk of the English and Continental Romantics had been.

37. "Two Lectures on the Influence of Poetry on the Working Classes" (1852), in Robertson, *Lectures, Addresses and Other Literary Remains* (1858; London, 1906), p. 83.

"vague" to the point of fustian; but the broader-than-Broad-Church Robertson can startle when he makes clear (p. 113) that he is speaking of a religion "separate from some particular form, either of words or ritual." But the asserted religious quality of poetry loses almost all definable intellectual content, and renounces virtually all relationship to any discernible religous tradition when a Shelley declares that the poet draws "into . . . a certain propinquity with the beautiful and the true, that partial apprehension of the agencies of the invisible world which is called religion," or when a *Westminster* reviewer announces that "Men feel that religion is generally safe in the hands of a poet; for religion is the enduring poetry of the human race," or when the positivistic G. H. Lewes defines poetry as "the metrical utterance of emotion, having beauty as its result, and pervaded by a religious Idea which it thereby symbolizes."[38]

The confusions and extravagances about poetry-and-religion, then, are pervasive from about 1830 onward. But like many other "radical" elements in English life and culture, the effect of the new claims was rather muted and rarely brought to a clear intellectual focus. The result is that, even in our time, early- and mid-Victorian statements about the religious character of poetry are frequently read, in passing, as harbingers of Aestheticism, or art for art's sake, or "the religion of art."[39] But in general the more aggressive "Aesthetic" statements about the independently religious quality of poetry tend to distinguish themselves from what has been described as the new moral and

38. Jordan, p. 31; "The Poets of the Age, Considered as to Their Philosophical Tendencies," *London and Westminster Review*, 25 (April 1836), 62; Lewes's 1842 Hegel essay, cited in Alice R. Kaminsky, *George Henry Lewes as Literary Critic* (Syracuse, N.Y., 1968), p. 48. The *Westminster* reviewer's description of poetry as "this retreat for wounded spirits" became all too familiar; it is a central conception in Keble's Oxford lectures on poetry in the 1830's and lingers in Arnold's "The Study of Poetry" ("stay," "console," "sustain": CPW, IX, 161–163). Lewes explains *his* notion of the religious idea as "the formula of any truth leading to new contemplations of the infinite or to new forms in our social relations" (Kaminsky, p. 49). Starzyk, *Victorian Studies*, 16, pp. 272, 287–290, makes in my judgment a serious mistake by in effect taking this "empty" and unhistoric sense of the term (referring, as Kaminsky says, to "such concepts as liberty, equality, humanity and morality") as the "majority" view of the period.

39. Johnson, *Alien Vision*, pp. 163, 165, 218; A. Dwight Culler, *Imaginative Reason: The Poetry of Matthew Arnold* (New Haven and London, 1966), p. 75; Alba H. Warren, *English Poetic Theory, 1825–1865* (1950; rpt. New York, 1966), p. 155; and William A. Madden, *Matthew Arnold: A Study of the Aesthetic Temperament* (Bloomington, Ind., 1967)—on which see my review, *Modern Philology*, 66 (May 1969), 345–355.

social "burdens" of art.[40] And a highly polymorphous Aestheticism itself can move in somewhat different directions. It can, first, in retreat and withdrawal, immure itself within (in the terms of Pater's Conclusion) the "thick wall of personality," "the narrow chamber of the individual mind." There, art will have no responsibilities except "to itself"; concentrating on the formal aspects of its own activity, it will abjure the historic Western search for "ends" of any sort: it moves toward the disjunction of art from "meaning" in any ordinary sense of the term. Or more ambitiously, the claim can be made that aesthetic experience (whether the experience of the creating artist or, increasingly, that of the observer of art) is the supreme form of human activity, superseding and now free to draw upon all of the once-meaningful human activities. This is what John Morley, himself a rationalist and moralist and no aesthete, referred to when he said that in endorsing art for art's sake Pater had "raise[d] aesthetic interest to the throne lately filled by religion."[41] Pater's most daring formulation of this view in his early writing is to suggest that precisely the "religious graces" of the older culture, embodied in the highest literature and art, will be the most apt *material* for this "higher" consciousness, a morality-above-morality. The supreme productions of the "faith" and "belief" of all past cultures will be the finest stimulants for the skeptical self-culture of "special souls."[42]

But only the early Pater developed these daring strategies into a comprehensive vision of a newly coordinated and perfected life. Even in the nineties, for the most part, this important double notion—that art usurps the once unchallenged paramountcy of religion, but that the highest art itself draws its materials from the historic religious consciousness and somehow conducts itself in the spirit of religion—remains muffled and somewhat indistinct, and much less "existentially" challenging than Pater's seductive formulations. The culmination of such claims can be seen in Arthur Symons' assertion, in 1899, about the "new literature": "in speaking to us so intimately,

40. See William A. Madden, "The Burden of the Artist," in *1859: Entering an Age of Crisis*, ed. P. Appleman, W. Madden, and M. Wolff (Bloomington, Ind., 1959), pp. 247–268.

41. Review of *Studies in the History of the Renaissance*, *Fortnightly Review*, NS 13 (April 1873), 476.

42. See my *Hebrew and Hellene in Victorian England: Newman, Arnold, and Pater* (Austin and London, 1969), pp. 192–255, 342–343.

so solemnly, as only religion had hitherto spoken to us, it becomes itself a kind of religion, with all the duties and responsibilities of the sacred ritual."[43]

v

These last quotations belong to a later and rather fatigued stage of Victorian experience, when poetry had given up some of its own engagements with the culture at large. The struggles between Culture and Religion, or between Hellenism and Hebraism, especially as they came to high visibility in the sixties and seventies in Arnold and Pater, have been studied in much greater detail in recent years—though a consensus on the exact mutual bearing of the various entangled elements has not yet been reached.[44] But what the bulk of the *early*-Victorian citations gathered here suggests is that a less well defined encounter, a "first round" of a large cultural dialectic, had been gone through in the years after 1820 and had subsided by mid-century without coming to any distinct conclusion or an authoritative statement of the issues. Educated Englishmen were simply not yet ready for the challenge of Aestheticism and Culture, certainly not as ready as some in the French and German intellectual classes were. The crucial contributory stream, not referred to directly so far in this essay, is that of what the reviewers nervously referred to as "German thought"—above all, the thought of Goethe.[45] But as Professor Bruford reminds us, though Goethe played a role in the formation of the secular humanism of a number of important Victorians, his "aesthetic" thought even among his admirers was generally played down in favor of his "wisdom." Bruford concludes that Goethe's "influence in England even in Victorian times was never really fundamental."[46] The "Art" issue was usually submerged in a larger battery of suspicion directed against Goethe's "immoral" treat-

43. *The Symbolist Movement in Literature* (1st ed. 1899; New York, 1919), p. 5. Symons' Introduction itself is a somewhat coarser parody of Pater's Conclusion.

44. See Madden and my review, n. 39, above; *Hebrew and Hellene*, n. 42, above; and Madden's important article, "The Divided Tradition of English Criticism," *PMLA*, 73 (March 1958), 69–80.

45. The most frequent use of the word "German" by Victorian critics and reviewers was as a sign of theological panic or as an instrument of rabble-rousing. What is at stake in the present essay is not what Kant, Schiller, Goethe, and the Idealists "really" meant, but how they were perceived by the Victorians.

46. See W. H. Bruford, "Goethe and Some Victorian Humanists," *Publications of the English Goethe Society*, NS 18 (1949), 34–67, esp. p. 64.

ment of women, his dubious religious views, and his withdrawal from the pressing social and political questions of his time. Until Lewes's *Life* in 1855, Goethe was conceived even among the literary and the intellectual as the author of *Werther, Götz,* the still enigmatic *Faust,* Part I—and, with more important direct results for some, *Wilhelm Meister.* But in the absence of translations of important works of Goethe's until the forties and fifties,[47] and in the ignorance before Lewes of the fuller scope and the varying phases of Goethe's career, key ideas and citations were regularly considered askew and out of context.

The most important cause of distortion was certainly Carlyle's powerfully attractive and insistent portrait of Goethe as the "exemplary" modern man who had struggled through the various phases of doubt and had emerged into the clear calm "victorious" light of spiritual serenity. This reading was reinforced by Carlyle's general strategy of presenting "the higher Literature of Germany," not as exalting Art, but as "the beginning of a new revelation of the Godlike" and as permitting "a Faith in Religion" (III, 41).[48] Though Carlyle's Notebooks of the twenties and thirties reveal that the prospect opened up by Schiller and Goethe of an inversion of the traditional relationship between the Good and the Beautiful both troubled and fascinated him, in the printed works such anticipations are carefully distanced. When he says that Goethe "intimates" that "The Beautiful is higher than the Good," he at once hedges by calling it "a saying . . . which has staggered several" and then by insisting that what is meant is the "*true* Beautiful" (*Works,* V, 81, *Heroes*). Even the now much quoted prediction about Literature and Religion (III, 23) is a surprisingly full synopsis of Carlyle's complex indecision on the issues. Above all, the seemingly daring prophecy is hedged: "as some think." Moreover, the opening, "Literature is but a branch of Religion," comes very close to the traditional subordination of Literature and Religion; whereas the next phrase, "it is the only branch that still shows any greenness," suggests a contemporary shift in

47. *Dichtung und Wahrheit* had been translated from a faulty French version in 1824; the first translation from the German was in 1848. Other first translations: *Theory of Colours,* 1840; *Egmont,* 1841; *Correspondence Between Schiller and Goethe,* 1845; *Letters from Switzerland,* 1849; *Elective Affinities,* 1854; *West-Östlicher Divan,* 1877.

48. This is in 1831. Parallel citations of that same year linking German literature and "the rudiments of a new spiritual era" are qualified by phrases like "perhaps," "may," and "say some": see *Works,* XXVII, 346, and *Letters . . . 1826–1836,* p. 266. See also Shine, *Carlyle's Unfinished History of German Literature,* p. 11.

which Literature emerges, among man's various spiritual activities, if not exactly as a rival to Religion (at best a cooperating but independent force), at any rate as no longer deriving its vitality and authority from the defunct parent stem. And finally, the bold-but-hedged prophecy, that Literature "must one day become the main stem," changes the character of the necessarily subordinate "branch" not only into a self-sustaining main stem but into a uniquely authoritative source of spiritual value. But the phrase may actually imply *either* of the two main Victorian positions. First, and probably closer to Carlyle's more or less conscious intentions, Literature, once the agent or handmaiden of Religion, must now become the chief and authoritative source of spiritual insight and "revelation," bearing in a non-dogmatic way the religious and moral burdens once shouldered by a now decaying institutional Christianity.[49] Or there may, just for a moment, flash upon the retina of the prophet a more dazzling vision, in which Literature announces its own self-sufficiency, an independence even of a broadly conceived "Religion": it may yet become "the main stem" of human consciousness.[50]

But few of the small number of Englishmen who took Goethe seriously, and certainly not Carlyle, opened themselves very fully to the "aesthetic" possibilities of discipleship. It is too often overlooked that even Matthew Arnold, who obviously in the forties absorbed certain aspects of Carlyle's portrait of Goethe, *objected* in 1850 to the view he attributed to Goethe: *"The end is everywhere, / Art still has truth, take refuge there!"* ("Memorial Verses," 27–28) —on the ground that it implied an indifference to the terror and distress of less privileged mortals. John Sterling was perhaps the only Englishman of even minor creative talents who submitted to the aesthetic side of what might be called the Goethe-"temptation." And although he died in 1844 at thirty-eight, the evidence was not available until J. C. Hare's effort to capture Sterling for the liberal

49. For another direct prophecy about the "high destinies which yet await Literature," see *Works*, XXVIII, 178. The term Literature in all the citations is a compendious one only problematically containing Poetry; it often includes critical-cultural expression in general as well as more creative activity. But the discriminations would require a separate essay, and Carlyle's predictions of this period about Literature certainly carry along with them the more limited term Poetry.

50. Only once or twice in Carlyle's career does this final and seraphic prospect open up, notably in an apparently late remark to Espinasse on "the ultimate supremacy of the beautiful," as illustrated in the visions of the medieval saints. "In time, he prophesied, beauty would be all-in-all." Francis Espinasse, *Literary Recollections and Sketches* (London, 1893), pp. 197–198.

Christian camp in 1848, and Carlyle's counterattempt in 1851 to claim Sterling for a post-Christian and "aesthetic" position that Carlyle himself was far from accepting.[51] But even then the elements for judgment were too inadequately articulated to allow most readers to see the issues clearly, and by then it was, culturally speaking, too late for anyone (including the younger poets who had come to maturity in the forties, like Arnold and Clough) to live out the premises of Sterling's life, and too early for the much more public shift of taste we associate with Swinburne, Morris, Rossetti, and Pater, which by about 1870 was to present English culture with one of the most decisive crises in its history.

Undoubtedly more typical of the few who in Sterling's generation saw the "German" aesthetic temptation clearly was F. D. Maurice, Sterling's fellow "Apostle" at Cambridge and in some ways the closest friend of his life. Sterling slowly moderated a very "Apostolic" view of Goethe as an alluring but dangerously Mephistophelean "bad man" who praised art over religious devotion; only late, about 1840, did he succumb.[52] In contrast, Maurice, though only a year older, had already moved decisively in an opposite direction. His semi-autobiographical novel, *Eustace Conway*, appeared in 1834; finished by early 1830, it is in effect a more Christianized version of *Sartor Resartus*, though written *before* it. It is an English counter-*Bildungsroman* that takes up, in order to *refute*, the arguments in favor of a many-sided secular self-development that is central to *Wilhelm Meister*.[53] Maurice (then only twenty-nine) was not of course the well-known and controversial theologian he was to become, and the

51. A good contrast between Hare's "Memoir of John Sterling," prefixed to *Essays and Tales of John Sterling* (1848), and Carlyle's *Life* (1851) can be found in William Blackburn, "Carlyle and the Composition of *The Life of John Sterling*," *Studies in Philology*, 44 (Oct. 1947), 672–687.

52. See Anne Kimball Tuell, *John Sterling: A Representative Victorian* (New York, 1941), pp. 195, 160–161.

53. Maurice's novel was written in conscious competition with Sterling's *Arthur Coningsby* (1833); the friendly plan was settled upon perhaps as early as 1828. *The Life of Frederick Denison Maurice*, ed. Frederick Maurice (London, 1884), I, 90. Maurice finished the first draft of his novel (which was later condensed) by February 1830 (ibid., p. 104), and Sterling's novel was also finished well before the publication date. As Susanne Howe makes clear, in *Wilhelm Meister and His English Kinsmen* (1930; rpt. New York, 1966), pp. 210–220, Sterling's novel was written well *before* he came under the spell of Goethe—or even Carlyle. (See also Tuell, pp. 160, 176–178.) It is, then, puzzling that Howe should devote so much attention to Sterling, while totally neglecting Maurice, whose *roman à thèse* intelligently raises the "Goethe-problem" in a characteristic and significant pattern of experience—though reversing the usual *Meister* pattern.

novel caused a ripple or two mostly because of the accidentally wounded feelings of Captain Marryat (*Life*, I, 163–164); but in an England not yet ready to understand, it took up a surprising number of the themes about "Culture" debated by Matthew Arnold and his more orthodox critics in the late sixties. The novel in effect explains Maurice's conversion and his decision to take Anglican orders; in its religious rejection of "German" thought and its comprehensive survey of modern alternatives, it is strikingly parallel to the experience of Kierkegaard (whom the early Victorians did not of course know) and the latter's attack on Hegel.

As Conway, Maurice's hero, approaches the resolution of his doubts in the third volume, he debates in his journal "the connexion between poetry and religion," insisting that "the operations of the soul is [sic] the only *subject* of poetry, however numerous may be its objects."[54] Though "Mr. Wilmot," the enigmatic clergyman who acts increasingly as Conway's spiritual guide, praises the "solid wisdom" of the best poets, Conway is shocked when Wilmot "absolutely" denies his own apparent sentiment, that "poetry is religion" (p. 39). Wilmot contrasts poetry ("an outgrowth of our own mind") to religion, "a process by which the soul is re-united to a Being greater than itself, from whom it has been separated"; the only affinity will be in matters of "devotion," which refers to "an effort of the [human] mind" (pp. 39–40). Wilmot offends Conway by abusing "German spiritualism" and any other "vague, shadowy belief of a great spirit" (p. 40). Wilmot's objection is that the German doctrine that the "cultivation of the faculties [is] the main business" of life destroys the distinction between "the powers of man and the soul of man" (p. 53). Even Conway's retort, that the will is to "correct, guide and govern" the imagination and the intellect, does not satisfy Wilmot, who insists, "so long as we are the cultivators, something will remain to be cultivated still" (p. 54).

At a later stage of Conway's progress toward a still formative Mauricean Christianity, Wilmot tells him of his own spiritual history. Twenty-five years earlier, in the first decade of the century, Wilmot had turned to the rising school of poets for inspiration—presumably Wordsworth, Coleridge, Scott, and Southey—at a time when very few

54. *Eustace Conway; or, The Brother and the Sister*, 3 vols. (London, 1834), III, 39. All further quotations from the novel are from vol. 3, and will be cited parenthetically by page alone.

saw "any deep significance" in art, and he even made proselytes to this "poetic" line taken up against "the low worldly notions of our opponents" (p. 79). But Wilmot eventually wearied of loose talk about poetry and its powers, and returned to his "masters," presumably the sources of his earlier religious inspiration (p. 81). Wilmot underwent, again *before* "The Everlasting No" and "The Centre of Indifference" were written, a severe illness and a kind of collapse of will, a state in which he found everything "dead and motionless" (p. 81). His reason harassed him "with agonizing questions about myself and my own identity." In the following "time of distracting doubt and disquietude," he became "an infidel, an Epicurean." To his own pressing question, "what am *I*?" he receives no answer from —in succession—physical science, metaphysics ("not even Fichte, with his *Ich*, and his *Nicht, Jah* [sic!]"), and poetry (pp. 81–82). At any rate, within three months Conway, the disciple, himself came round to the view that it is *not* "the main business of life to cultivate the faculties" (p. 105).

Though he was not in fact a close student of the German sources, and though he moralizes the issues excessively, Maurice's version of the new "temptation" and of the cultural issues involved comes near to being the fullest and soberest of the period. The issues were certainly understood, at least skeletally, and debated by the earnest young men at Cambridge for a few years. In August 1831 Arthur Hallam had defended Tennyson's "worship of beauty" (however mixed it was with "a strange earnestness") as leading to a single-minded desire "to communicate the love of beauty to the heart." Tennyson's poetry that "is a sort of magic" is simply "art free and unalloyed."[55] But by December Hallam had so far recoiled from this first bold aproach in England to aestheticism and symbolism as to throw doubt on the view of the "Germans"—Schiller and Goethe are singled out—"that the worship of Beauty [the very phrase of the Tennyson review] is a vocation of high and mysterious import, not to be relegated into the round of daily amusements." "I do not hesitate [Hallam continues] to express my conviction, that the spirit of the Critical philosophy, as seen by its fruits in all the ramifications of art, literature, and morality, is as much more dangerous than the spirit of Mechanical philosophy, as it is fairer in appearance, and

55. Review of Tennyson's 1830 *Poems, Chiefly Lyrical*, in Hallam, *Writings*, pp. 191, 192, 187, 188.

more capable of alliance with our natural feelings of enthusiasm and delight."[56] This is exactly the climate in which Tennyson's "Palace of Art" (glanced at earlier in this essay) was written. Trench's similarly earnest admonition, "Tennyson, we cannot live in art," must have been contemporaneous, since Tennyson's poem was begun after October 1831 and finished by April 1832. The dedicatory poem to Trench describes the subject in terms very close to those of a current caricature of Goethe—as a "glorious Devil, large in heart and brain," who loved "Beauty only," and "Knowledge for its beauty," and shut Love out.

The point is that among a significant portion of the probably small number of Englishmen seriously interested in the question, Carlyle's version of Goethe as the moral sage, a portrait in which the aesthetic question was consistently veiled in the rhetoric of finding in "the higher Literature of Germany . . . the beginning of a new revelation of the Godlike" (III, 41), was *not* immediately and decisively influential. It should be remembered that "Characteristics," in which this prediction is made, appeared in December 1831, at the very time when the solemn debate among the Apostles was leading to very different conclusions. I suggest, in fact, that though Carlyle was to be of great and pervasive influence as a spiritual guide and social critic for a decade after 1839 (the year of *Critical and Miscellaneous Essays*), the specifically "aesthetic" side of his early message, his special version of literature-and-religion, had surprisingly little discernible influence on the susceptible young of the late twenties and early thirties, or even on the Arnold-Clough generation of the forties.[57] Arnold alone later attempted to revive and extend

56. "The Influence of Italian upon English Literature," in Hallam, *Writings*, p. 232. Delivered as an address in December 1831 in Trinity College Chapel; printed as a pamphlet in 1832. W. D. Paden suggests that Maurice confirmed Tennyson's "high" view of the poet's function: *Tennyson in Egypt: A Study of the Imagery in His Earlier Work*, Univ. of Kansas Publications, Humanistic Studies, No. 27 (Lawrence, 1942), pp. 149–50.

57. This was also the period of the first two full-blown "art novels" in English: Disraeli's *Contarini Fleming* (1832), and Bulwer-Lytton's *Ernest Maltravers* (1837). Both novels, significantly, follow the "Palace of Art" pattern by condemning the artist who turns his back on society and dwells in isolation apart from human sympathy. See Maurice Beebe, *Ivory Towers and Sacred Founts: The Artist as Hero in Fiction from Goethe to Joyce* (New York, 1964), pp. 79–84, and Howe, pp. 161–170, 190–195. Bulwer-Lytton himself misleadingly explained (Howe, pp. 161–162) that whereas in *Meister* "the apprenticeship is . . . that of theoretical art," the apprenticeship in *Maltravers* "is rather that of practical life."

Carlyle's *kind* of prophesying about the "religious" future of poetry.[58]

There was of course a logical third alternative: a more straightforward approval of the vista for art and poetry opened up by Schiller and Goethe. Before Lewes's 1855 volume, itself fairly defensive on the issue, perhaps the most important single source of information on Goethe in English was the three-volume *Characteristics of Goethe*, compiled in 1833 by Sarah Austin, the bulk consisting of translations from various Germans who had defended Goethe against his already numerous German critics. A passage on the influence of *Wilhelm Meisters Lehrjahre* in the 1790's presents the new category-shuffling in a rather dizzying form:

Not only did novels of Art follow in great number, but the life of an artist assumed a higher import, and an aesthetic system arose, such as antiquity had divined but had never developed. Aesthetics appeared as the Perfecter of life and of philosophy. Ethics, or morals, took a subordinate station; but religion, which had been made merely subservient to morals, rose above them, inasmuch as she was one with aesthetics. By aesthetics the mind was enabled to soar to religion;—and it was impossible to be religious without being aesthetical; and a finely constituted soul (*eine schöne Seele*) could exist only in this state of profound aesthetico-religious feeling.[59]

The passage approaches self-parody. It seems agreed that ethics and morals must, once for all, take a back seat or the bottom rung. But the relationship of religion and aesthetics is teasingly ambiguous: religion is "one with aesthetics," but aesthetics is also the *means* to enable the mind to "soar" to a presumably superior "religion." Most of the confusions of the century on the issue are generously heaped up here. Except for the Arnold-Pater "moment" in the late sixties and the seventies, most later positive statements about the newly elevated status of poetry and art seem equally unsure about their own premises.

VI

Much of the prophecy about poetry settles for this undifferentiated "state of profound aesthetico-religious feeling." It was a heartfelt

58. I have discussed Arnold's attitudes toward poetry and religion in the chapter "Arnold and Literary Criticism: Critical Ideas," forthcoming in *Matthew Arnold*, ed. Kenneth and Miriam Allott, Writers and Their Background (London, 1975).

59. London, 1833, III, 223–224; cited from the *Conversations-Lexicon*, and Supplement.

ambition of a century struggling confusedly to cope with the breakdown of the older metaphysics and theology, while also nervously
questioning traditional "ethics and morality," now perceived to be
negative and (in twentieth-century terms) no longer life-enhancing.
Prophecies about the future of poetry were no doubt indistinct; but
they were not usually so incautious as one might suppose. Wordsworth's prediction, in the Preface to *Lyrical Ballads*, that the poet
"will lend his divine spirit to aid the transfiguration" of science into
the categories of ordinary consciousness, is obviously developed in
a limited context.[60] The rhetoric of the "Essay, Supplementary" of
1815, in the view that a certain kind of modern poetry (apparently
Wordsworth's own) "is at once a history of the remote past and a
prophetic enunciation of the remotest future," seems to have provided
a model for the language of Shelley's *Defense*.[61] But Wordsworth's
development of "the affinity between religion and poetry" is notably
restrained.[62] Carlyle's and Arnold's prophecies have, finally, to do
with the use of a small group of "high" poets *of the past*—poets of
the order of Homer and Shakespeare—as the adequate vehicles, as
the Church no longer is, of a residual moral-emotional synthesis in
the collapse of the older intellectual scaffolding. For both men, the
hope that such an adequate poetry can be written *today*, though
fitfully maintained for a while and given plausibility by the example
of Goethe, is finally either abandoned or relegated to a far-distant
future.

What Carlyle (and Arnold after him) did not clearly recognize
was that one major Victorian poet, after a thorough exploration of
the impasse of the post-Romantic poet, was struggling for a new
kind of poetic "prophecy," based on religious and aesthetic principles
strikingly consonant with Carlyle's own. After confusedly canvassing
in his early long poems the various political, social, and moral possibilities open to the modern poet, Robert Browning after 1845
moved toward acceptance of the Christian doctrine of the Incarnation, a movement first fully expressed in *Christmas-Eve and Easter-*

60. For the background, see Roger Sharrock, "The Chemist and the Poet: Sir
Humphry Davy and the preface to *Lyrical Ballads*," *Notes and Records of the
Royal Society of London*, 17 (1962), 57–76.
61. B. R. McElderry, Jr., treats "Common Elements in Wordsworth's 'Preface' and
Shelley's *Defense of Poetry*," *Modern Language Quarterly*, 5 (June 1944), 175–181,
but suggests no parallel with the 1815 Essay.
62. *Selected Poems*, ed. Stillinger, pp. 455–456, 480, 474.

Day (1850) and finding its adequate poetic embodiment in the dramatic monologues of *Men and Women* (1855). In the terms of the Shelley essay of 1852, the "whole poet" seeks to fuse the roles of the "objective" poet (the "fashioner") and of the "subjective" (the "seer") by combining a minute attention to the "raw material" of actual life with a continuous concern for "spiritual comprehension."[63] When Browning (with a strong implicit reference to himself) presents Shelley's poetry "as a sublime fragmentary essay towards a presentment of the correspondency of the universe to Deity, of the natural to the supernatural, and of the actual to the ideal" (Collins, p. 118), he seems almost the echo of the Carlyle for whom in the high poetry of the past "Spirit mingled . . . in trustful sisterhood with the forms of sense" (*Works*, XXI, 266, *German Romance*), who had explored in *Sartor* the necessary blending of "transcendental" and "descendental" aspects of reality, and for whom in 1832 "The Whole Creation seems more and more Divine . . ., the Natural more and more Supernatural" (Froude, *Carlyle*, II, 319).

In fact, Carlyle's rationale of "poetic" history, in "Biography" (1832), which we looked at earlier, closely resembles the principles Browning was later to work out for himself. Carlyle of course insisted that the Poet or Seer who could discern the "Godlike" was still "utterly wanting, or all but utterly," and he himself turned from Fiction to the Fact of history and biography. But although Browning moved more directly into the interior arena of his subjects, often in a well-researched but less than fully historical setting, he too sought a "Revelation," a "new Truth," by "working more and more on REALITY, and evolving more and more *its* inexhaustible meanings" (*Works*, XXVIII, 52–54). Browning's integrity, and perhaps his closest resemblance to Carlyle, lay in his attempt to preserve the irreducible contrariety of the "imperfect" and finite actual world, and to insist that in our present state the intimations of "perfection" and of the infinite remain only Blougram's scattered hints and guesses. Indeed, Carlyle's description of the highest kind of poetry conveys almost exactly the sense of the "confused multitudinousness" (as the hostile Matthew Arnold called it), brought under an almost violent pressure to achieve unity and a "spiritual" viewpoint, that we experience in Browning's

63. The development of Browning's poetics is most conscientiously detailed in Thomas Collins, *Robert Browning's Moral-Aesthetic Theory, 1835–1855* (Lincoln, Neb., 1967), especially chaps. 5 and 6.

best poetry. Goethe's poetry, Carlyle explained in 1827, renders the
real world "holier"; poetry "must dwell in Reality," and in Goethe
and to a lesser extent in the other Germans "the Nineteenth Century
stands before us, in all its contradictions and perplexity; barren, mean,
and baleful, . . . yet here no longer mean or barren, but enamelled
into beauty in the poet's spirit" (*Works*, XXVI, 65–66, "State of
German Literature"). Similarly, Shakespeare's "high *vates* talent"
is exactly that of "interpreting confused actualities" (*Works*, XX,
326, *Latter-Day Pamphlets*, 1850). More problematically, Carlyle
may also have approved Browning's shift to a more explicit moralism
and didacticism after 1850; presumably he never gave up the view
that, as against the "jingle" of most poetry, "My greatly most delightful reading is, where some Goethe musically *teaches* me."[64]
Finally, Browning himself reported in October 1851 that the Shelley
essay had reference to "opinions" of Carlyle, and Carlyle seemed to
see that the "objective" poet in "How It Strikes a Contemporary"
came close to being a flattering portrait of himself.

Still, though in Browning's case Carlyle seemed to relent somewhat in his admonition that in the confused modern era poets should
turn to prose,[65] Carlyle never fully penetrated Browning's intentions.
The reasons for his resistance are revealing: his general repugnance
for the mere "musical psalmody and fiddling" of contemporary poetry
(*Works* XI, 196, *Life of Sterling*, 1851); the obscurity and roughness
of Browning's poetry, so much like the surface texture of Carlyle's
own prose; and perhaps above all (and here Arnold would concur),
Browning's accommodation by 1850 to an explicitly Christian, if
broad, interpretation of reality. Carlyle never gave up the view that
Poetry in the modern world would have to wait—perhaps for two
"agonistic" centuries—until "Religion" could be "discriminated from
the New and Old Light *forms* of Religion" (*Works*, XXVI, 313–314,
"Burns," 1828). Thus did men of similar mind misunderstand one

---

64. *Two Note Books of Thomas Carlyle*, ed. Charles Eliot Norton (New York,
1898), p. 151; spring 1832.

65. The personal relations of the two men, and some of their similarities in
doctrine and outlook, are admirably treated in two essays by Charles Richard Sanders:
"Carlyle, Browning, and the Nature of a Poet," *Emory University Quarterly*, 16 (Winter
1960), 197–209, and "Some Lost and Unpublished Carlyle-Browning Correspondence,"
Journal of English and Germanic Philology, 62 (April 1963), 323–335. For some crucial
differences as well, and on Browning's growing didacticism, see William Clyde
DeVane, Jr., *Browning's Parleyings: The Autobiography of a Mind* (New Haven,
1927), chap. 1, and 120–121.

another in the "nightmare wilderness, the wreck of dead-men's bones, this false modern world" (*Works*, XX, 313).

Whatever Carlyle's deafness to the parallel creative efforts going on about him, at least one astute observer of the age saw the caution in Carlyle's own prophecies and blamed him for falling short of the "new religion" of poetry. In 1864 Walter Bagehot credited Carlyle with having, thirty years before, "most rudely contradicted" the "doctrine that poetry is a light amusement for idle hours, a metrical species of sensational novel":

> But perhaps this is about all that he has done. He has denied, but he has not disproved. He has contradicted the floating paganism, but he has not founded the deep religion. All about and around us a *faith* in poetry struggles to be extricated. . . . Some day, at the touch of the true word, the whole confusion will by magic cease; the broken and shapeless notions cohere and crystallize into a bright and true theory. But this cannot be yet.[66]

Coming from the studiedly disillusioned and far-from-aesthetic Bagehot, the statement can still startle and even move. It testifies to a kind of secret yearning in the hearts of many nineteenth-century men and women for some sort of decisive and "magical" deliverance from the "whole confusion" of modern thought. In its almost evangelical use of "the true word" and "*faith*" it is strangely parallel to the apocalyptic tone of nineteenth-century radical attempts to "solve" the burden of human nature and history by a root-and-branch reformation of society or the reconceiving and reordering of human nature itself.[67] Bagehot was unduly restrictive in describing the actual scope

66. "Wordsworth, Tennyson, and Browning; or, Pure, Ornate, and Grotesque Art in English Poetry," in *The Collected Works of Walter Bagehot*, ed. Norman St. John-Stevas (Cambridge, Mass., 1965), II, 323. These highest hopes for poetry, and the concurrent theme of the low actual estate of poetry, are given a historical basis, when Bagehot comments that English poetry and criticism have never "recovered the *eruption*" they both made in the Romantic period, mostly because poets like Byron and Moore, lacking high thought and feeling, degraded the art and so are no longer read (as Wordsworth and Shelley deserve to be read). The result is that genuine poetry today is reduced to "a still small voice": "The mere notion, the bare idea, that poetry is a deep thing, a teaching thing, the most surely and wisely elevating of human things, is even now to the coarse public mind nearly unknown" (II, 321–23). As late as 1869 the querulous Alfred Austin bewails: "[This age] produces great speculators, great contractors, great millionaires, great manipulators and mountebanks. But poets! Alas! none of these. How can it? It cannot give what it has not got; and it has not got the divine *afflatus*." See *Matthew Arnold: The Poetry. The Critical Heritage*, ed. Carl Dawson (London and Boston: Routledge and Kegan Paul, 1973), pp. 207–208.

67. Such almost millennial hopes for human renewal through the agency of poetry may in fact be read as late and even more extreme survivors of the final and internalized "faith" in M. H. Abrams' three-phase history of Romanticism: "faith in an apocalypse

and intent of Carlyle's views of poetry's future; but he was correct in saying that Carlyle did not endorse the new *"faith* in poetry" struggling for both formulation and embodiment. Bagehot, of course, literally did not know what he meant. In 1864 he could not see what the new generation of Swinburne and Morris and Rossetti were already bringing forth, still less the generation of Wilde, Dowson, Johnson, and the early Yeats. It is hard to imagine that he would have approved of either.

---

by revelation had been replaced by faith in an apocalypse by revolution, and this now gave way to faith in an apocalypse by imagination or cognition." See *Natural Supernaturalism: Tradition and Revolution in Romantic Literature* (New York, 1971), p. 334. On p. 347 Abrams mentions Carlyle, but Carlyle—like Abrams' major Romantics —stresses the social and moral benefits of "poetry," whereas Bagehot, like the Pater he could not yet know, seems to be groping for a reality and a dynamism peculiar to the aesthetic act itself.

Addendum to note 1, p. 148: Charles Kingsley, in the very act of denying it ("We cannot refute their arguments."), gives a very full version of the current view that "lofty" and "living" poetry "has henceforth become impossible for man." "Poems of Matthew Arnold," *Fraser's Magazine,* 49 (Feb. 1854), 140–141.

Illustrations

1. Thomas Carlyle, c. 1845. Pencil and wash drawing by Samuel Laurence. *(Courtesy of Dr. Gordon N. Ray)*

2. Birthplace of Thomas Carlyle, Ecclefechan. This is the *Entepfuhl* (Duckpond) of *Sartor*, with its *Kuhbach* (Cowbrook) visible in the foreground. Photograph by John Patrick taken about 1890. (*Courtesy of the University of Edinburgh*)

3. Main street of Ecclefechan, about 1890. Photograph by John Patrick. (*Courtesy of the University of Edinburgh*)

4. Jane Welsh Carlyle, c. 1838. Pencil drawing with touches of white and red crayon by Samuel Laurence, now in the Carlyle House, Chelsea. (*Courtesy of the National Trust*)

5. Cheyne Row in the 1890's, with No. 5 (renumbered 24 in the 1870's) in the middle. The Carlyles moved to then unfashionable Chelsea in 1834 and lived in the same house the rest of their lives. The bronze replica of Boehme's statue of Carlyle is visible on the Thames embankment at the end of the street. Photograph by John Patrick. *(Courtesy of the University of Edinburgh)*

6. Godefroy Cavaignac, 1834, a few years before he met the Carlyles. Medallion by P. J. David d'Angers. (From *Les Médaillons de David d'Angers*, Paris, 1883)

7. "How to make culprits comfortable; or, Hints for prison discipline." *Punch* anticipated with great exactness some of the sentiments about the mild treatment of prisoners
which Carlyle expressed in *Model Prisons*, the second of his *Latter-Day Pamphlets.* (*Punch,*
16, Jan.–June 1849, 68)

OFF THE RAIL.

8. "Off the Rail"—*Punch*'s parody of George Hudson, the Rail-king. In *Hudson's Statue,* the seventh of his *Latter-Day Pamphlets,* Carlyle contrasted the railway speculator Hudson with the Puritan hero Cromwell—much to Hudson's disadvantage. (*Punch,* 16, Jan.–June 1849, 191)

9. George Henry Lewes, November 1840. From a pencil drawing by Anne Gliddon. *(Courtesy of the National Portrait Gallery)*

10. Agnes Jervis Lewes, George Henry Lewes, and Thornton
Leigh Hunt, c. 1844. From a pencil sketch by W. M. Thackeray, whose face appears in the top right-hand corner and his
pseudonym "Smithers" in the bottom left-hand corner. *(Courtesy of the National Portrait Gallery)*

11. Carlyle in 1851. Medallion modeled by Thomas Woolner. Woolner, the sculptor-poet of the Pre-Raphaelite Movement, captures the projecting lower lip—a physiognomical trait
Carlyle valued as signifying determination. The medallion recalls Lady Eastlake's description of Carlyle: "The head of a
thinker, the eye of a lover, and the mouth of a peasant." *(Courtesy of the Scottish National Portrait Gallery)*

12. George Eliot, "the strong minded woman," in 1858.
From a photograph by John Edwin Mayall.

13. "Work" (1852–1865). Allegorical painting by Ford Maddox Brown. Standing at the extreme right are Carlyle and the Rev. Frederick Denison Maurice. Carlyle's ethos of work—the "Produce! Produce!" of *Sartor*—powerfully influenced many contemporaries. (*Courtesy of City Art Gallery, Manchester*)

14. John Ruskin, c. 1858. This photograph, taken shortly
before the publication of *Unto This Last*, captures a certain
boyish, disheveled, strangely personal quality in Ruskin—
a quality which fits in with the impression we often receive
in reading his letters to Carlyle. (*Courtesy of the Radio
Times Hulton Picture Library*)

15. James Anthony Froude in the 1880's. "His presence
was striking and impressive," John Skeleton wrote of Froude
a year after his death in 1894, "—coal-black eyes, wonderfully lustrous and luminous . . . ; coal-black hair, only latterly streaked with grey; massive features strongly lined,
—massive yet mobile, and capable of the subtlest play of expression. For myself I can say without any reserve that he
was, upon the whole, the most interesting man I have ever
known." From an unpublished photograph in the possession of the editor.

16. Carlyle in 1877. From the painting in oils by John Everett Millais. Carlyle's verdict on it was, as Froude notes, "modestly uncertain." To his brother John Carlyle he wrote in June 1877: "The picture I think does not please many, nor in fact myself altogether; but it is surely strikingly like in every feature & the fundamental condition was that Millais should paint what he himself was able to see there." *(Courtesy of the Scottish National Portrait Gallery)*

The Carlyles and the Leweses

GORDON S. HAIGHT, *Yale University*

On 10 October 1851 John Chapman, who had just completed the purchase of the *Westminster Review*, called at 5 Cheyne Row to ask Carlyle to write an article on the peerage for his first number. Carlyle declined, "being clear for silence at present." But as soon as Chapman had gone, he sent off a letter to Robert Browning, describing Chapman as "really a meritorious, productive kind of man, did he well know his road in these times. . . ; his intense purpose now is, To bring out a Review, Liberal in all senses, that shall charm the world. He has capital 'for four years' trial,' he says; an able Editor (name can't be given), and such an array of 'talent' as was seldom gathered before."[1] He was reluctant to give the name of his "able Editor" because she was a woman—Marian Evans, who had lately come from Coventry to board at Chapman's house at 142 Strand. While he interviewed Carlyle, she was wandering up and down Cheyne Walk, passing more than once the house at number 4 where she was to die in 1880.

Marian Evans had long admired Carlyle's books. In 1841 she wrote to a schoolmate: "He is a grand favourite of mine, and I venture to recommend to you his *Sartor Resartus*. . . . His soul is a shrine of the brightest and purest philanthropy, kindled by the live coal of gratitude and devotion to the Author of all things. I should observe that he is not 'orthodox.' "[2] In 1848, having herself quite abandoned orthodoxy, she sympathized heartily with Carlyle's enthusiasm for the French Revolution.[3] But by the time she came to live in London, her natural conservatism was beginning to reassert itself, and she was willing to acknowledge some truth in the hostile notice of *The Life of John Sterling* in the *Times*—though it was unfair to the book, which she had read with great pleasure, "not for its presentation of Sterling

---

1. Gordon S. Haight, *George Eliot and John Chapman*, 2d ed. (New Haven and London, 1969 [1940]), pp. 41–42.
2. *The George Eliot Letters*, ed. Gordon S. Haight, 7 vols. (New Haven and London, 1954–1955), I, 122–123.
3. Ibid., I, 252–253.

but of Carlyle. There are racy bits of description in his best manner and exquisite touches of feeling."[4] In 1855, reviewing a volume of selections from Carlyle's works, Miss Evans carefully distinguished his ideas from his influence:

It is an idle question to ask whether his books will be read a century hence; if they were all burnt as the grandest of Suttees on his funeral pile, it would be only like cutting down an oak after its acorns have sown a forest. For there is hardly a superior or active mind of this generation that has not been modified by Carlyle's writings; there has hardly been an English book written for the last ten or twelve years that would not have been different if Carlyle had not lived. . . . And we think few men will be found to say that this influence on the whole has not been for good.[5]

In saying that "many of the men who have the least agreement with his opinions are those to whom the reading of *Sartor Resartus* was an epoch in the history of their minds" she was glancing at her own experience.

Though Carlyle called more than once at 142 Strand while Marian Evans was living there, I have found no record of their meeting. In November 1851 he came, "strongly recommending Browning the poet as a writer for the Review, and saying 'We shall see' about himself."[6] It is not clear whether he spoke to her as well as to Chapman. Nor has Carlyle's letter been found which she sent to Sara Hennell as an autograph, saying, "He is a naughty fellow to write in the Keepsake and not for us— after I wrote him the most insinuating letter, offering him three glorious subjects."[7] Perhaps, as in other cases, she had merely drafted a letter for Chapman to copy. Her Coventry friends were sometimes regaled with stories about Carlyle. For example, when he met FitzBall one day, Carlyle asked, "How is it I never see your name as a dramatic author now?" FitzBall replied, "Oh" (very much through the nose) "I'm comfortable now; *my mother's dead.*"[8]

This sort of gossip, comically rendered, probably came to her from George Henry Lewes, with whose life her own was soon to be joined.

4. Ibid., I, 372. See also her review of Carlyle's *Sterling* in *Essays of George Eliot,* ed. Thomas Pinney (New York and London, 1963), pp. 46–51.
5. *Leader*, 6 (27 Oct. 1855), 1034. Rpt. in Pinney, pp. 213–215.
6. *The George Eliot Letters*, I, 376.
7. Ibid., I, 376.
8. Ibid., II, 139.

Born in 1817, he had become one of Carlyle's "young men" perhaps as early as March 1835, for he told John Fiske that he had gone to Cheyne Row a few days after the burning of the manuscript of *The French Revolution* and "found Mill on the sofa in paroxyms of weeping and sobbing, while Carlyle was trying to comfort him."[9] If this account can be accepted, it seems probable that Carlyle introduced Lewes to Leigh Hunt, who lived only a few doors away in Upper Cheyne Row, for in the summer of 1835, when Lewes submitted a story called "Mary Altonville" to *Leigh Hunt's Journal*, he had no personal acquaintance with Hunt.[10] Their warm friendship grew from a passionate interest in Shelley, whose biography Lewes was determined to write; he sought information from both Hunt and his son Thornton. A highly premature announcement of the book as "In the Press" appeared four times in the *National Magazine* from January to April 1838.

In their parlor the Carlyles had a "reminiscent" bust of Shelley by Marianne Hunt,[11] given to them in 1836; but Carlyle considered his poetry "all a shriek merely,"[12] the man "a poor, thin, spasmodic, hectic, shrill and pallid being," and his revolutionary ardor the ghost of extinct, obsolete Robespierrism.[13] Carlyle's "universal man," of course, was Goethe, whom he wanted to choose in 1840 for his Hero as Man of Letters. "But at present," he told the audience, "such is the general state of knowledge about Goethe, it were worse than useless to attempt speaking of him in this case. . . . Him we must leave to future times." The man who was to do most to make Goethe known to the English-speaking world was Carlyle's eager disciple George Henry Lewes. Stirred by Carlyle to learn German, Lewes set out for Berlin in July 1838, bearing from its author a presentation copy of *Sartor Resartus* to be delivered to Varnhagen von Ense and a letter of introduction for himself.

9. *The Letters of John Fiske*, ed. Ethel Fiske Fisk (New York, 1940), p. 300.

10. George Henry Lewes to Leigh Hunt, 2 Oct. 1835, MS: British Museum, Add. 29,755.143.

11. Newman Ivey White, *Shelley*, 2 vols. (New York, 1940), II, 521; Charles Richard Sanders, *The Correspondence and Friendship of Thomas Carlyle and Leigh Hunt* (Manchester, 1963), p. 44, and "Carlyle, Poetry, and the Music of Humanity," *Western Humanities Review*, 16 (Winter 1962), 63.

12. *William Allingham: A Diary*, ed. H. Allingham and D. Radford (London, 1907), p. 242.

13. A. Carlyle, *CMSB*, p. 292.

Varnhagen, who had corresponded with Carlyle but not yet met him, was the author of a book on Goethe, whom his late wife Rahel had known and adored. He received the young man kindly and introduced him to the best literary circle in Berlin. Lewes worked hard at his German, "reading *Faust* in the original—no easy task—and translating Goethe's *Torquato Tasso*." He also worked sporadically at his life of Shelley, finding his old views much changed since he came to Germany and "feeling the necessity for a deep aesthetical exposition of his poems and philosophy." At the same time, he wrote, "I am going regularly through Byron's works for the parallel I intend to draw between him and Shelley, but I get on slowly." Was he perhaps haunted by Carlyle's stern injunction, "Close thy *Byron*; open thy *Goethe*"?[14] He asked Hunt to inquire of John Stuart Mill whether an article on Carlyle—"a general criticism of his whole works, their tendency, influence, force, and weakness, would be acceptable for the London and Westminster? as I have been preparing such a thing."[15] Nothing came of it, however, Mill having already commissioned John Sterling's article, which appeared in the October 1839 number.

Lewes's interest in Goethe, inspired by Carlyle, grew stronger during his residence of more than a year in Berlin and Strassburg. After a few months at home, he returned to the Continent in July 1840 and lived for six months in Vienna, where he knew Franz Liszt. The first fruit of his study was a long anonymous article, "The Character and Works of Göthe," written in February 1842 and published a year later in the *British and Foreign Review*. There Lewes declared that Carlyle's "fervent and eloquent Essays . . . give no definite image of the man," though, he conceded, "they are exquisite exhortations to study, rather than information of what the student will find, or how to seek it."[16] According to Francis Espinasse, who may betray a touch of jealousy, Carlyle thought Lewes's article "wide of the mark."[17] It certainly includes much with which Carlyle must have disagreed. To Lewes, Goethe was a man like Shakespeare with no dogmatic philosophy, a Spinozist in individuality, pursuing self-

14. Harrold, *Sartor*, p. 192.
15. G. H. Lewes to Leigh Hunt, 15 Nov. 1838, MS: British Museum, Add. Mss. 29,755.182.
16. *British and Foreign Review*, 14 (March 1843), 80.
17. Francis Espinasse, *Literary Recollections and Sketches* (London, 1893), p. 282.

culture without restraint of duty. Despite some youthful exaggeration, later moderated, and with no undue humility, Lewes's eloquent defense was a preliminary sketch for his *Life and Works of Goethe* (1855), a pioneer biography.

While in London in May 1840, between his German visits, Lewes attended Carlyle's lectures *On Heroes and Hero-Worship*. In June, having abandoned all hope of securing through Hunt's intercession the family's consent to a biography, he wrote for the *Westminster Review* a long article on Shelley. In it he quoted from "The Hero as King":

Carlyle, speaking of Johnson, said, "If he had been asked to be Lord Chancellor, he would have felt uneasy at the great weight to be put on his shoulders. What did he care for riding in gilt coaches from Westminster to Whitehall? . . ." We quote from memory (out of his eloquent Lectures on 'Heroes and Hero-Worship' delivered last May).[18]

In the lecture Carlyle, defending Cromwell from the charge of ambition, wrote that a *great* man would not sell himself to falsehood "that he might ride in gilt carriages to Whitehall. . . . What could gilt carriages do for this man?" Then, turning to Johnson for comparison, he added: "Old Samuel Johnson, the greatest soul in England in his day, was not ambitious. 'Corsica Boswell' flaunted at public shows with printed ribbons round his hat; but the great old Samuel stayed at home."[19] Though Carlyle revised his lectures extensively for publication, this variation is probably due to Lewes's faulty memory.

John Stuart Mill, though no longer editor of the *Westminster*, read the manuscript for his "young friend" Lewes and objected—quite rightly—to its lack of unity:

I think you should have begun by determining whether you were writing for those who required a *vindication* of Shelley or for those who wanted a *criticism* of his poems or for those who wanted a biographic Carlylian *analysis* of him as a *man*. I doubt if it is possible to combine all these things, but I am sure at all events that the unity necessary in an essay of any kind as a work of art requires at least that one of these should be the predominant purpose & the others only incidental to it.[20]

18. *Westminster Review*, 35 (April 1841), 303–344, at 317.
19. "The Hero as King," *Works*, V, 223, 223–224.
20. *The Earlier Letters of John Stuart Mill, 1812–1848*, ed. Francis E. Mineka, (Toronto, 1963), II, 449. For Lewes's early collection of Mill's articles see Geoffrey Tillotson, "A Mill-Lewes Item," *Mill Newsletter*, 5 (1969), 17–18.

As eventually published in April 1841 Lewes's article is still open to objection on this score. A more serious fault is the obvious imitation of Carlyle's style. In earlier days Mill himself had undergone the same temptation and had overcome it. A paper of his "On Genius," published in W. J. Fox's *Monthly Repository* in 1832 under a pseudonym, Lewes had ferreted out, probably tipped off by Fox. Commenting on it in the same letter to Lewes, Mill wrote:

The "Genius" paper is no favorite with me, especially in its boyish stile. It was written in the height of my Carlylism, a vice of style which I have since carefully striven to correct & as I think you should do—there is too much of it in the Shelley. I think Carlyle's costume should be left to Carlyle, whom alone it becomes & in whom it would soon become unpleasant if it were made common—& I have seen as you must have done, grievous symptoms of its being taken up by the lowest of the low.

This was a timely warning for Lewes, whose early articles frequently imitated Carlyle's worst mannerisms. For example, in defending Goethe against the charge of charlatanism, he wrote sarcastically: "O ye poor sheep! ye Göthe-humbugged! whither have ye been straying? into what black bogs of murkiest folly have ye been floundering, led by this stolid bell-wether? Think upon your condition!"[21]

That nothing quite so bad survived in his Shelley paper Lewes probably owed to Mill's tactful hint. Yet the influence of Carlyle is apparent throughout the essay, however widely Lewes may differ from him in opinion. Presenting Shelley as one of the "two most memorable men of this nineteenth century" (the other was Jeremy Bentham!), Lewes asks:

Where, among his contemporaries, shall we find in so eminent a degree the qualities which Carlyle says constitute the "original man—the hero"? In commanding intellect, in large-heartedness, but above all, in his heroic preaching and fighting for all that was to him Truth, at grievous personal cost, but with unabated energy,—he stands out as the most memorable man of his day (a day not wanting in heroism or endurance), calling forth our hero-worship. . . . Shelley arose in such an era to proclaim to the world that "by lies and formulas it could not get on, but must take up some truth and vital energy, if it would live."[22]

21. "Character and Works of Göthe," *British and Foreign Review*, 14 (March 1843), 78.
22. *Westminster Review*, 35 (April 1841), 316.

Lewes's heroes were not Carlyle's, and while Carlyle undoubtedly saw the article, it did nothing to soften his unfair opinion of Shelley. Neither did it cool the cordial regard Carlyle and his wife both showed to young Lewes. His amusing stories, told with "first-rate mimicry," are often recalled in their letters, and though on account of his appearance they referred to him as "the Ape," Lewes was always welcome at Cheyne Walk. Carlyle admitted his diligence in compiling the *Biographical History of Philosophy*, but (according to Espinasse) grumbled at the absurdity of thinking he "could learn anything about philosophy from that body Lewes."[23] The biographical element of the book, which was begun in 1837 as a series of lectures at W. J. Fox's Chapel in Finsbury, may suggest the influence of Carlyle. At the end of one chapter Lewes quotes from the tribute to Fichte in Carlyle's essay on the "State of German Literature."[24]

As a novelist Lewes pleased neither Thomas nor Jane Carlyle. In 1848 he sent them his *Rose, Blanche, and Violet*, which Jane took with her to Addiscombe on a visit to Lady Harriet Baring. In a letter to Thomas she pronounced it "execrable."

I could not have suspected even the ape of writing anything so silly. Lady H. read it all the way down, and decided it was "too vulgar to go on with." I myself should have also laid it aside in the first half volume if I had not felt a pitying interest in the man, that makes me read on in hope of coming to something a little better. Your marginal notes are the only real amusement I have got out of it hitherto.[25]

Espinasse gives a detailed account of Lewes's efforts to discover Carlyle's opinion of the novel.

Carlyle had read it, but the adventures of Mesdemoiselles Rose, Blanche, and Violet were not, as chronicled by Lewes, of a kind to interest him, yet here was the author bent on discovering his opinion of it! It was amusing, at least to me, to see how Carlyle fenced with the anxious inquirer. The author could extract little more from the reluctant critic than that *Rose, Blanche, and Violet,* showed "more breadth" than its predecessor, *Ranthorpe*. However, by way of soothing his visitor, Carlyle added that Mrs. Carlyle had taken the book with her to the country, to be read not only by

23. Espinasse, *Literary Recollections*, p. 282.
24. *A Biographical History of Philosophy*, 4 vols. (London, 1845–1846), IV, 154, quoting *Edinburgh Review*, 46 (Oct. 1827), 344.
25. *Letters and Memorials of Jane Welsh Carlyle*, ed. J. A. Froude, 3 vols. (London, 1883), II, 34.

herself, but by "a very high lady," the Lady Harriet Baring, who became soon afterwards Lady Ashburton. Carlyle commenting in a depreciatory way on the amount of lovemaking in modern novels, Lewes retorted by referring to the amatory episodes in *Wilhelm Meister*. Carlyle rejoined that there was no more of that sort of thing in *Meister* than "the flirtation which goes on in ordinary life," a very different verdict from Wordsworth's and De Quincey's. "I would rather have written that book," Carlyle said, "than a cartload of others," and he went on to speak of Goethe's "Olympian silence" and other transcendent qualities. With admirable persistence Lewes took advantage of a pause to ask if some gaming-house scenes in *Rose, Blanche, and Violet* were not to be commended. Instead of answering the question, Carlyle launched into a description of a gaming-house in Paris, to pay a visit of curiosity to which he had been taken, by the late Sir J. Emerson-Tennent, I think, and said that he remembered the faces of the players at the gaming-table so vividly that if he were a painter he could reproduce them even after that long lapse of years. Abandoning his fruitless quest, Lewes spoke of a life of Robespierre, which, as well as his life of Goethe, he had then on the anvil. Seeing that I was surprised at the conjunction of two such tasks, Carlyle said genially: "Lewes is not afraid of any amount of work."[26]

Espinasse was then a comparatively new acquaintance of Carlyle, and the edge of ridicule discernible in this account may be attributed to his annoyance at having been interrupted as he was preparing to tell Carlyle about the Chartist gathering that day on Kennington Common. There is no trace of dislike in the letter Jane wrote about him to her cousin Jeannie Welsh:

But what I took up my pen to tell you is that little Lewes—author of Rose Blanche &c., &c. is going to lecture in Liverpool—one of these days and I have given him my card for you—and you *must* try and introduce him to my Uncle; for he is the most amusing little fellow in the whole world—if you only look over his unparalleled *impudence* which is not impudence at all but man-of-genius-*bonhomie*—either you or Helen saw him here—and his charming little wife. He is [the] best mimic in the world and full of famous stories, and no spleen or envy, or *bad* thing in him, so see that you receive him with open arms in spite of his immense ugliness.[27]

The "charming little wife," Agnes Jervis, whom Lewes married in 1841, had borne him four sons, the youngest of whom was less than

26. Espinasse, *Literary Recollections*, pp. 279–280.
27. [5 Feb. 1849], in *Jane Welsh Carlyle: Letters to Her Family*, ed. Leonard Huxley (London, 1924), pp. 319–320.

a year old when Mrs. Carlyle wrote this description. In addition to doing scores of articles, writing plays, acting, and lecturing, Lewes was traveling about the country to gather support for the *Leader*, the radical weekly which he and Thornton Hunt were to edit jointly. Carlyle thought highly of Lewes's part of it and called him "the Prince of Journalists."[28] During the few weeks he was away from home at this time Mrs. Carlyle's keen eye detected a distinct change. A postscript to a note to John Forster of 20 March 1849 added: "The Leweses were here last night. '*Great* God'! as *you* say. Poor Lewes looks to me going rapidly to you know whom."[29] Writing again to Jeannie Welsh, she said:

Little Lewes came the other night with his little wife—speaking gratefully of you all—but it is Julia Paulet who has taken his soul captive ! ! he raves about her "dark luxurious eyes" and "smooth firm flesh"—! his wife asked "how did he know? had he been feeling it?" In fact his wife seems rather *contemptuous* of his raptures about all the women he has fallen in love with on this journey, which is the best way of taking the thing—when one can.

I used to think these Leweses a perfect pair of love-birds always cuddling together on the same perch—to speak figuratively—but the female love-bird appears to have hopped off to some distance and to be now taking a somewhat critical view of her little shaggy mate!

In the most honey-marriages one has only to *wait*—it is all a question of time—sooner or later "reason resumes its empire" as the phrase is.[30]

In this marriage she had not long to wait. Within a year, on the 16th of April 1850, soon after the *Leader* began publication, Agnes gave birth to a fifth son, whose father was Lewes's friend and co-editor Thornton Hunt. Unwilling to stigmatize the child as illegitimate, Lewes registered him as his own, giving him, with perhaps a sardonic glance at the bastard in *King Lear*, the name of Edmund. By condoning the adultery, he precluded all possibility of asking for a divorce.

Agnes's relation with Hunt was no passing affair. In October 1851 she bore him a daughter, Rose Agnes, and in October 1853 another daughter, Ethel Isabella Lewes, both within weeks of the birth of

28. Espinasse, *Literary Recollections*, p. 282.
29. [20 March 1849], MS: NLS, 604.279.
30. [4 April 1849], *JWC: Letters to Her Family*, p. 329.

two of Hunt's ten children by his own wife. There was a marked contrast between the rosy, blond Lewes boys and the other children, all of whom showed the dark complexion of the Hunts—"a trace of the African, I believe," Carlyle remarked.[31] He referred to Thornton as a "little brown-skinned man."[32] Carlyle had at this time no high opinion of the Hunts, once his feckless neighbors in Cheyne Row. "They are a generation of fools," he said.[33] But the young George Leweses were different. Late in life he spoke of them to Allingham; he noted that

Lewes and *his wife* lived in Carlyle's memory in the magic light that surrounded all those who were friends or *friendlies* of the house in Cheyne Row in Mrs. Carlyle's time. "They used to come down," he often said, "of an evening to us through the lanes from Kensington, and were as merry as two birds."

"She was a bright creature," he said one day, "and far cleverer than——." Here he suddenly paused and said no more, a most unusual thing with him; but I could guess the course of his thoughts.[34]

They led, of course, to the editor of the *Westminster Review*, "the strong minded woman" Marian Evans. As soon as it was known that she and Lewes had gone to Germany together, gossips were accusing her of having "run away" with Agnes's husband. Actually the marriage had collapsed long before Marian ever saw him, and Agnes, who had no intention of giving up Thornton Hunt, expressed the wish that George "could marry Miss Evans."[35]

At Weimar, where they were living while Lewes worked at his biography of Goethe, Marian noted in her Journal, 11 October 1854: "A painful letter from London caused us both a bad night." It came from Carlyle, who had been driven by the gossip-mongers to inquire about the scandal. In the morning Lewes wrote to him, "explaining his position." Neither letter has been found; but on the envelope containing Lewes's (now in the Parrish Collection at Princeton), postmarked 13 October 1854, Carlyle wrote: "G. H. Lewes and 'Strong minded Woman.'" His reply, described by Marian as "a letter of

31. *Reminiscences,* I, 175.
32. *New Letters of Thomas Carlyle,* ed. Alexander Carlyle, 2 vols. (London, 1904), II, 93.
33. To John A. Carlyle, 22 June 1840, MS: NLS, 523.88.
34. William Allingham, Note on Carlyle and George Eliot, MS: NLS, 3823.
35. G. S. Haight, *George Eliot: A Biography* (New York and Oxford, 1968), p. 179.

noble sympathy," is also missing, and we can only infer its contents from the tone of Lewes's answer.

Weimar Thursday night [19 October 1854].

My dear Carlyle

Your letter has been with me half an hour and I have not yet recovered the shock—delightful shock—it gave me. One must have been, like me, long misjudged and harshly judged without power of explanation, to understand the feelings which such a letter creates. My heart yearned towards you as I read it. It has given me new courage. I sat at your feet when my mind was first awakening; I have honoured and loved you ever since both as teacher and friend, and *now* to find that you judge me rightly, and are not estranged by what has estranged so many from me, gives me strength to bear what yet must be borne!

So much in gratitude. Now for justice: On my *word of honor* there is no foundation for the scandal as it runs. My separation was in nowise caused by the lady named, nor by any other lady. It has always been imminent, always *threatened*, but never before carried out, because of those assailing pangs of anticipation which would not let me carry resolution into fact. At various epochs I have explicitly declared that unless a change took place I would not hold out. At last—and this more because some circumstances into which I do [not] wish to enter, happened to occur at a time when I was hypochondriacal and hopeless about myself, fearing lest a chronic disease would disable me from undertaking such responsibilities as those previously borne—at last, I say, the crisis came. But believe me the lady named had not only *nothing* whatever to do with it but was, I solemnly declare, ignorant of my own state of mind on the subject. She knew the previous state of things, as indeed others knew it, but that is all.

Then as to the "letter to Miss Martineau"—not only is she totally incapable of anything she justly considers so foolish and unworthy; but in fact she has *not* written to Miss Martineau at all— has had no communication with her for twelvemonths—has sent no message to her, or any one else— in short this letter is a pure, or impure, fabrication—the letter, the purport, the language, all fiction. And I shall feel doubly bound to you if you will, on all occasions, clear the lady from such unworthy aspersions and not allow her to be placed in so totally false a position.

Thus far I give you a solemn denial of the scandal. Where gossip affects a point of honour or principle I feel bound to meet it with denial; on all private matters my only answer is *silence*.

Marshall, who has been absent since my arrival until within the last few days, I find a very agreeable friendly fellow, whom I should have been glad to see earlier. However there has been no end of kindness shown me here, and I have gained such materials for Goethe as could only have been gained *here*. I go to Berlin shortly, and think of wintering there, and quietly finishing my work.

Wilson seems to pine for London, although they do everything they can to make Weimar agreeable to him. Eckermann is very feeble, and his intellect going fast.

With kindest regards to your wife, Believe me, dear Carlyle,

> Your very grateful
> G. H. Lewes.[36]

At the end of this letter Carlyle has added:

Alas, alas!—I had (at his request) approved unequivocally of parting *such a marriage*; and advised to contradict, if he could, on his word of honour, the bad rumours circulating about a certain "strong minded woman" and him. He assures me, on his word of honour, the strong minded did not *write* etc.: as well assure me her stockings are both of one colour; that is a very insignificant point!—No answer to this second letter.

Writing to his brother John, Carlyle was more explicit:

Lewes, *Ape* Lewes, or "hairy Lewes," as we called him, has not only gone to Weimar, but is understood to have a "strong minded woman" with him there, and has certainly cast away his Wife here,—who indeed deserved it of him, having openly produced those dirty sooty skinned children which have Th[ornto]n Hunt for father, and being ready with a *third*; Lewes to pay the whole account, even the money part of it!— Such are our sublime George-Sand Philosophies teaching by experience. Everlasting peace to them and theirs,—in the Cesspool, which is their home.[37]

If, as this letter suggests, Agnes was pregnant in 1854, the child must have been stillborn, for it was not registered. Carlyle apparently believed that she was then the mother of two, and not three, children by Hunt. Their fourth, Mildred Jane Lewes, was born 21 May 1857, and the liaison continued some years more.

After Lewes returned to London in March 1855, he consulted Carlyle about the *Goethe*, which was ready for the printer in June. Carlyle read some of the first proofs while the book was in the press and wrote Lewes a remarkably interesting letter about it:

---

36. *The George Eliot Letters*, II 176–178, MS: Princeton.
37. 2 Nov. 1854, MS: NLS, 516.86.

Chelsea, 7 August 1855

Dear Lewes,—

I go into Suffolk tomorrow, and am likely to be wandering about for some time; so that I find it will only be a bother to you, and a delay *without* advantage, to shoot those Proofs after me in my erratic course. I found it an amazing thing to read them in the evening, under the cloud of a quiet pipe in the Garden here: I had, as it were, *nothing* to suggest; and felt that my remarks, had they even been of value, came too late.

The Book goes on rapidly (Printer and all), and promises to be a very good bit of Biography; far, far beyond the kind of stuff that usually bears that name in this country and in others.— I desiderate chiefly a little change of *level* now and then; that you could sit upon some height, and shew us rapidly the contours of the region we are got into, from time to time,—well abhorring to be drowned in details as Viehof and Co. are, or to swim about (not quite drowned, but drowning) in endless lakes of small matters which have become "great" only by being much talked about by fools for the time being.

You missed the *Malefactor's scull* that was on one of the steeples of Frankfort; no great matter. I found out, the other year, *who* the proprietor had been (a foolish *radical* about 1600 or so); but have already almost forgotten again, a proof there was not much for you in the story of him.

Slightly more important for you was another thing I remembered in the reading over of the Proofs, but did not then see how you were to get in: the "Visitation of Wetzlar," through *Overhauling* (with an eye to repair) of that "German Court of Chancery," which had been ordered by the Diet, and was just then *beginning*, about the time Goethe went. That was thought a great chime for a young lawyer,—to witness the very *dissection* of Themis. It came as other "Visitations" had done, to *nothing*. If you make an Appendix, there might be some notice taken of this—, though whither to go for summary information I cannot at this moment direct you. My Pfeffel's Abrégé (in Brit. Mus.) which has an Index, could let it lie altogether! — Best speed to you, dear Lewes.

Yours always truly
T. Carlyle[38]

The Life and Works of Goethe: with Sketches of His Age and Contemporaries, from Published and Unpublished Sources, to give the book its full title, was published 30 October 1855, dedicated in all sincerity to the man who had inspired it: "To Thomas Carlyle, who

38. MS: Fitzwilliam Museum, Cambridge.

first taught England to appreciate Goethe, this work is inscribed, as a memorial of gratitude for intellectual guidance, and of esteem for rare and noble qualities." Here is Carlyle's acknowledgment:

Chelsea, 3 November 1855

Dear Lewes,

I am sorry to hear you still complain of health; bad health is a very miserable adjunct to one's burden, tho' not an uncommon one to poor wretches of this craft! *Festina lentè*: don't work *too much* (which proves always *too little* by and by): that is the one way of procuring some abatement, if abolition of the misery is not possible.

I know your clean finger in *The Leader* weekly as heretofore; one of the few writing fingers of this epoch which are not dog's paws, or cloven hoofs of mere human swine. Pah!—

Furthermore I got the *Goethe* the other night, almost at the same time with your Note. Every night since, in my reading hours, I am dashing athwart it in every direction; *truanting*; for I won't wait a time to read the work with such deliberation as I well see it deserves. My conviction is, we have here got an excellent Biography,—altogether transcendently so, as Biographies are done in this country. Candid, well-informed, clear, free-flowing, it will certainly throw a large flood of light over Goethe's life, with many German things which multitudes in England have been curious about, to little purpose, for a long while. It ought to have a large circulation, if one can predict or anticipate in regard to such matters. On the whole, I say *Euge*, and that heartily,—tho' dissenting here and there. I ought also to be thankful, and am, for the fine manful words you have seen good to say about my poor self: good words go about too, as well as evil;—and all words go to nothing except they be the copies of things:

Denn geschwätzig sind die Zeiten,
Und sie sind auch wieder *stumm*.

Ach Gott ja, most dumb indeed;—and we read with pain in M. Thiers and the like, *femme alors celèbre*, homme alors etc.

I returned from my wanderings, which never went very wide, some three or four weeks ago; and am here in my garret, again, up to the chin in Brandenburg *marine-stores*; uncertain whether I shall not sink dead, and be buried under them, one day; but struggling to hope not.

Once more, *Well-done*, and thanks; and let me see you soon.

Yours always truly
T. Carlyle[39]

To his brother John, Carlyle wrote:

39. MS: Yale.

I would at once send you *Lewes's Goethe*, tho' I know not whether so much weight (probably 4 lbs. or so) were worth carrying so far: but Tait has it on loan; . . . so that we must wait till his turn is past. The Book is decidedly good as such Books go, but by no means very interesting if you have a strict taste in Books.[40]

When all the correspondence is collected, it will be possible to determine Carlyle's real opinion of the *Goethe* more positively. Moncure Conway is the source of a story that early in 1878, when Bayard Taylor told Carlyle he was gathering materials for a life, Carlyle said: "But are there not already Lives of Goethe? There is Lewes's *Life of Goethe*. What fault have you to find with that?" The tone seemed to suggest that Lewes had exhausted the subject. Taylor "began pointing out errors here and there in the biography," and Carlyle interrupted him "with a ringing laugh" and cried: "I couldn't read it through."[41] No such disparaging remarks are recorded earlier. Carlyle's relations with Lewes after publication of the book were cordial. A letter to Lewes of 7 December 1857, discussing the price offered by Tauchnitz for reprinting the first two volumes of *Frederick the Great* in Germany, ended:

I have had such a 14 months as was never appointed me before in this world,—sorrow, darkness and disgust, my daily companions; and no outlook visible except getting a detestable business turned off, or else being driven mad by it.— In a three months more, I hope to be at large again, and capable of seeing those I like.[42]

Quoting the first of these sentences in a letter to Sara Hennell, Marian wrote:

That is his exaggerated way of speaking, and writing is always painful to him; but he has been specially tormented by the shortcomings of German commentators and book-makers, on whom he has depended as authorities. Do you know he is 62! I fear this will be his last book.[43]

Her information must have been supplied in part by Lewes, who called occasionally at Cheyne Row, alone or with friends to introduce to the Carlyles—Bodenstedt, W. G. Clark, and Anthony Trollope, for example. Marian Evans, now living at Richmond and calling herself Mrs. Lewes, was not among them. Soon after she and Lewes "took up

---

40. *New Letters of Thomas Carlyle*, II, 177.
41. Wilson, *Carlyle*, VI, 425.   42. MS: McGill.
43. *The George Eliot Letters*, II, 412, MS: Yale.

with each other," Wm. Allingham reported, Carlyle on one of his daily rides called and "made her acquaintance. My impression is that they met very few times altogether, and that Carlyle went no further than tolerant civility, and even so far against the grain."[44]

It was probably at Lewes's suggestion that, when *Scenes of Clerical Life* was issued in 1858, reprinted from *Blackwood's*, Mrs. Carlyle's name was on the list of nine persons to receive copies of it "From the Author." A few days later she sent the unknown George Eliot the following letter:

> 5 Cheyne Row Chelsea
> 21st January /58.

Dear Sir,

I have to thank you for a surprise, a pleasure, and a—*consolation*(!) all in one Book! and I *do* thank you most sincerely. I cannot divine what inspired the good thought to send *me* your Book; since (if the name on the Title Page be your real name) it could not have been personal regard; there has never been a *George Eliot* among my friends or acquaintance. But neither I am sure could *you* divine the circumstances under which I should read the Book, and the particular benefit it should confer on me! I read it—at least the first volume—during one of the most (physically) wretched nights of my life; sitting up in bed, unable to get a wink of sleep for fever and sore throat; and it helped me through that dreary night, as well—better than the most sympathetic helpful friend watching by my bedside could have done!

You will believe that the book needed to be something more than a "new novel" for me; that I *could*, at my years, and after so much reading, read it in positive torment, and be beguiled by it of the torment! that it needed to be the one sort of Book, however named, that still takes hold of me, and that grows rarer every year—a *human* book—written out of the heart of a live man, not merely out of the brain of an author—full of tenderness and pathos without a scrap of sentimentality, of sense without dogmatism, of earnestness without twaddle—a book that makes one *feel friends*, at once and for always, with the man or woman who wrote it!

In guessing at why you gave me this good gift, I have thought amongst other things: "Oh, perhaps it was a delicate way of presenting the *novel* to my Husband, he being head and ears in *History*." If that was it, I compliment you on your *tact!* for my Husband is much lik[e]lier to read the *Scenes* on *my* responsibility than on a venture of his own—though, as a

44. MS: NLS, 3823.

general rule, never opening a novel, he has engaged to read this one, whenever he has some leisure from his present task.

A severe Influenza, which fell on me the same day I had the windfall of the book, and from which I am but just *beginning* to recover, must excuse the tardiness of my acknowledgements.

I hope to know someday if the person I am addressing bears any resemblance, in external things to the Idea I have conceived of him in my mind—a man of middle age, with a wife from whom he has got those beautiful *feminine* touches in his book, a good many children, and a dog that he has as much fondness for as I have for my little Nero! for the rest, not just a clergyman, but Brother or first cousin to a clergyman!— How ridiculous all this *may* read, beside the reality!

Anyhow, I honestly confess I am very curious about you, and look forward with what Mr. Carlyle would call "a good, healthy, genuine desire" to shaking hands with you someday. In the meanwhile I remain your obliged

Jane W. Carlyle.[45]

The delicious irony of Jane's *"feeling friends"* with the "strong minded woman" was surely not lost on Marian Evans. Her pseudonym was still intact in February 1859, when a copy of *Adam Bede* arrived at Cheyne Row, inscribed again by the publisher's clerk: "Mrs. Thomas Carlyle from the Author."[46] It brought what she called in her Journal a "letter of warm acknowledgement":

5 Cheyne Row Chelsea | 20th February / 59.

Dear Sir

I must again offer you my heartiest thanks. Since I received your *Scenes of Clerical Life* nothing has fallen from the skies to me so welcome as *Adam Bede, all to myself,* "from the author."

My Husband had just read an advertisement of it aloud to me, adding; "*Scenes of Clerical Life? That* was *your* Book wasn't it?" {The '*your*' being in the sense not of possession but predilection} "Yes," I had said, "and I am so glad that he has written another! *Will* he send me this one, I wonder?"—thereby bringing on myself an utterly disregarded admonition about "the tendency of the Female Mind to run into unreasonable expectations"; when up rattled the Parcel Delivery cart, and, a startling double-rap having transacted itself, a Book-parcel was brought me. "There it is!" I said, with a little air of injured innocence triumphant!—"There is *what*, my

45. *The George Eliot Letters*, II, 425–26, MS: Frederick W. Hilles.
46. At Yale.

Dear?"—"Why, *Adam Bede* to be sure!"—"How do you know?" {I had not yet opened the parcel} "By *divination*."—"Oh!—Well!—I hope you also *divine* that *Adam Bede* will justify your enthusiasm now you have got it!" —"As to *that*" {snappishly} "I <don't> needn't have recourse to divination, only to natural logic!"——Now; if it had turned out *not Adam Bede* after all; where *was* my "diminished head" going to have hidden itself?— But Fortune favours the Brave! I had foretold aright, on both points! The Book was actually *Adam Bede*, and *Adam Bede* "justified my enthusiasm"; to say the least!

Oh yes! It was as good as *going into the country for one's health*, the reading of that Book was!— Like a visit to Scotland *minus* the fatigues of the long journey, and the grief of seeing friends grown old, and Places that knew me knowing me no more! I could fancy in reading it, to be seeing and hearing once again a crystal-clear, musical, Scotch stream, such as I long to lie down beside and—*cry* at (!) for gladness and sadness; after long stifling sojourn in the South; where there [is] no *water* but what is stagnant or muddy!

In truth, it is a beautiful most *human* Book! Every *Dog* in it, not to say every man woman and child in it, is brought home to one's 'business and bosom,' an individual fellow-creature! I found myself in charity with the whole human race when I laid it down—the *canine* race I had *always* appreciated—"not wisely but too well!" —the *human*, however,—Ach!— *that* has troubled me—as badly at times as "twenty gallons of milk on one's mind"! For the rest; why you are so good to *me* is still a *mystery*, with every appearance of remaining so! Yet have I lavished more childish conjecture on it than on anything since I *was* a child, and got mistified about— a *door* (!) in our dining-room. What *did* that door open into? Why had I never seen it opened? Standing before it, "as in presence of the Infinite," I pictured to myself glorious possibilities on the other side, and also horrible ones! I spun long romances about it in my little absurd head! I never *told* how that door had taken hold of me, for I *"thought shame";* it was a curiosity too sacred for speech! But I lay in wait to catch it open some day; and then I somehow—forgot all about it!—till long after (a year or so) that the recollection of my door-worship occurred to me "quite promiscuously," and in the same instant, the whole fact as to the door smote me, like a slap on the face! It was a door into—*nothing!* Make-believe! *There* for uniformity! Behind it was bare lath and plaster; behind *that* the Drawing-room with its familiar tables and chairs! Dispelled illusion No. I! and epitome "of *much!*" {as Mr. Carlyle might say}

Perhaps *could* I penetrate my little mystery of the present date; I should arrive at the same sort of lath-and-plaster results! and so—I give it up; just "taking," gratefully and gladly, "the good the gods {under the name of George Elliot} have provided me."

Now, Heaven knows if such a long letter to read be not illustrating for *you* also "the tendency of the female mind to run into unreasonable expectations"! But just consider! Is it possible that, with my opportunities, I should not know perfectly well, what a "distinguish-author" *does* with letters of compliment *that bore him;* either by their length or their stupidity? He lights his pipe with them or he makes them into spills; or he crushes them into a ball, and pitches them in the fire or waste-paper basket; does anything with them *except read them!* So I needn't take fright about having *bored* you; since, long before it came to that, I should have, or shall have been slit up into spills, or done good service in lighting your pipe! It is lawful for *Clergymen* to smoke, I hope,—for their own sakes? The newspaper critics have decided you are a Clergyman, but I don't believe it the least in the world. You understand the duties and uses of a Clergyman too well, for *being* one! An old Lord, who did not know my Husband, came up to him once at a Public meeting where he had been summoned to give his "views" {not *having* any} on the "Distressed Needle Women," and asked; "pray Sir, may I inquire, are *you* a Stock-Broker?"—"A Stock-Broker! certainly not!"—"Humph! Well I thought you *must* be a Stock-Broker; because, Sir, you go to the root of the matter." —If that be the signal of a Stock-Broker I should say you must certainly be a *Stock-Broker*, and must certainly *not* be a *Clergyman!*

Respectfully and affectionately yours, whatever you be,

Jane W. Carlyle.[47]

In forwarding it to Blackwood George Eliot wrote:

Mrs. Carlyle's ardent letter will interest and amuse you. I reckon it among my best triumphs that she found herself "in charity with the whole human race" when she laid the book down. I want the philosopher himself to read it because the *pre*-philosophic period—the childhood and poetry of his life—lay among the furrowed fields and pious peasantry. If he *could* be urged to read a novel! I should like, if possible, to give him the same sort of pleasure he has given me in the early chapters of *Sartor*, where he describes little Diogenes eating his porridge on the wall in sight of the sunset, and gaining deep wisdom from the contemplation of the pigs and other "higher animals" of Entepfuhl.

Your critic was *not* unjustly severe [on] the Mirage Philosophy —and I confess the "Life of Frederic" was a painful book to me in many respects;

47. *The George Eliot Letters*, III, 17–19, MS: Yale.

and yet I shrink, perhaps superstitiously, from any written or spoken word which is as strong as my inward criticism.

A postscript added:

I have reopened my letter to ask you if you will oblige me by writing a line to Mrs. Carlyle for me. I don't like to leave her second letter (she wrote a very kind one about the C.S.) without any sort of notice. Will you tell her that the sort of effect she declares herself to have felt from "Adam Bede" is just what I desire to produce—gentle thoughts and happy remembrances; and I thank her heartily for telling me so warmly and generously what she has felt. That is not a pretty message—revise it for me, pray, for I am weary and ailing and thinking of a sister who is slowly dying.[48]

Annie Thackeray, calling on Mrs. Carlyle some weeks later, found her

speaking enthusiastically of *Adam Bede*. She has written some of her enthusiasm off to George Eliot and had grateful messages in reply. Mr. Carlyle quite declines reading the book, and when Mrs. Carlyle hoped it might be sent to her, he said, "What should George Eliot send it to you for?" "Why shouldn't he, as he sent me his first book?" says she. "You are just like all weemen," (Mr. Carlyle always calls them weemen). "You are always forming unreasonable expectations," growls he, and at that moment ring at the bell and in comes the maid with a brown paper parcel containing the book![49]

In spite of Carlyle's disclaimer, *Adam Bede* was one of George Eliot's novels that he read. More than twenty years later he told Wm. Allingham: "I found out in the first two pages that it was a woman's writing —she supposed that in making a door, you last of all put in the *panels!*" Wm. Allingham adds: "I think this comment (perhaps not well-grounded) was the only one I ever heard him make on George Eliot or her works!"[50] His ex post facto opinion should be weighed against Blackwood's account of how his manager George Simpson took a set of the sheets of *Adam Bede* home to his brother, a cabinet-maker in Edinburgh, who read them with great admiration, and maintained that "the writer must have been bred to the business or at all events passed a great deal of time in the workshop listening to

48. *The George Eliot Letters*, III, 23, MS: NLS.
49. *Letters of Anne Thackeray Ritchie*, ed. Hester Ritchie (London, 1924), p. 110.
50. MS: NLS, 3823.

the men."[51] Carlyle told John Churton Collins that "the best thing she ever wrote was, in his opinion, her article on Young in the *Westminster Review*. He had, he said, come across *Middlemarch* at a friend's house and "found it neither amusing nor instructive, but just dull."[52]

Jane's admiration of the books was quite genuine. Under other circumstances she would probably have enjoyed knowing their "strong minded" author. But, as Queen Caroline remarked to the Duke of Argyle when Jeanie Deans made her unfortunate allusion to the Seventh Commandment, "The Scotch are a rigidly moral people." Thomas Carlyle would never in the Leweses' case overlook the impediment to their union. He would more readily have excused the life of George Sand, about whom (he later confessed to Espinasse) there was "something Goethian."[53] Gavan Duffy reports a conversation linking the two Georges:

Mrs. Carlyle, who was present, said we had small right to throw the first stone at George Sand, though she had been caught in the same predicament as the woman of old, if we considered what sort of literary ladies might be found in London at present. When one was first told that the strong woman of the *Westminster Review* had gone off with a man whom we all knew, it was as startling an announcement as if one heard that a woman of your acquaintance had gone off with the strong man at Astley's; but that the partners in this adventure had set up as moralists was a graver surprise. To renounce George Sand as a teacher of morals was right enough, but it was scarcely consistent with making so much of our own George in that capacity. A marvellous teacher of morals, surely, and still more marvellous in the other character, for which nature had not provided her with the outfit supposed to be essential.

The gallant, I said, was as badly equipped for an Adonis, and conqueror of hearts. Yes, Carlyle replied, he was certainly the ugliest little fellow you could anywhere meet, but he was lively and pleasant. In this final adventure it must be admitted he had escaped from worse, and might even be said to have ranged himself. He had originally married a bright little woman, daughter of Swinfen Jervis, a disreputable Welsh member; but every one knew how that adventure had turned out. Miss Evans advised him to quit a household which had broken bounds in every direction. His pro-

51. *The George Eliot Letters*, III, 23.
52. *Life and Memoirs of John Churton Collins*, ed. L. C. Collins (London, 1912), p. 44.
53. Espinasse, *Literary Recollections*, p. 224.

ceeding was not to be applauded, but it could scarcely be said that he had gone from bad to worse.[54]

Though he would defend Lewes to this extent, Carlyle would allow no intimacy with George Eliot.

I cannot explain Jane's remarks in a letter to Carlyle of 20 August 1860 about engaging a servant, "who is really promising (the woman Miss Evans wanted to have)."[55] During her search Jane had gone twice to Richmond, where the Leweses were then living, but there is no indication that the ladies met. On 26 July 1861, however, going to the Princess's Theatre to see Fechter as Hamlet, Jane wrote: "[I] found myself between Lewes and Miss Evans!—by Destiny and *not* by my own Deserving. At least Destiny in the shape of Frederick Chapman who arranged the thing. Poor Soul! there never was a more absurd miscalculation than *her* constituting herself an improper *woman*. She looks Propriety personified! Oh so *slow!*"[56] To other correspondents—Mrs. Oliphant, for example—Jane declared that Miss Evans "has mistaken her rôle—that nature intended her to be the properest of women, and that her present equivocal position is the most extraordinary blunder and contradiction possible."[57] If during the intervals of *Hamlet* Jane Carlyle was able to voice her admiration of those "most *human* Books," which had made her "*feel friends*, at once and for always" with their author, no record of the conversation has been preserved. It would be strange if the attraction felt for George Eliot by so many intellectual women had failed to touch Jane Carlyle in this accidental encounter. In 1866, hardly a week before she died, Jane wrote to Thomas about Lady Lothian, who wanted her "to 'come some day before luncheon, and then we could go somewhere.' To Miss Evans is where we should go still, if you would let us."[58] I find no reference in the Lewes papers to either Lady Lothian or Mrs. Carlyle as visitors, and should be tempted to suspect a different "Miss Evans" had Carlyle not scornfully glossed the name: "Famous 'George Eliot' (or some such pseudonym.)" A month before his death he said to Browning: "What a world of pity

54. Sir Charles Gavan Duffy, *Conversations with Carlyle,* (London, 1892), pp. 222–223.

55. *Letters and Memorials,* III, 300.

56. To Alexander Gilchrist, 31 July 1861, in *Anne Gilchrist,* ed. H. H. Gilchrist, 2d ed. (London, 1887), pp. 85–86.

57. *The Autobiography and Letters of Mrs. M. O. W. Oliphant,* ed. A. L. Coghill (New York, 1899), p. 180.

58. *Letters and Memorials,* III, 329.

she should come up to London and fall in with *anti-Christ* Chapman and his set."[59] Though his hostility to her was unrelenting to the end, George Eliot always spoke charitably of Carlyle. When Madame Bodichon reported one of his outrageous remarks, she wrote: "That speech of Carlyle's, which sounds so odious, must, I think, have been provoked by something in the *manner* of the statement to which it came as an answer—else it would hurt me very much that he should have uttered it."[60]

As Carlyle's eightieth birthday approached, a group of his friends proposed a tribute to him. Boehm was commissioned to cut a medallion portrait, which was struck in gold for Carlyle, in bronze for the subscribers. David Masson and John Morley collected 119 signatures of friends and admirers to be appended to an address they had composed. Masson sent two of the programmes to Lewes for signature. "A most felicitous idea!" he replied. "Repeats his own tribute to Goethe,"[61] alluding to the carved seal that "Fifteen Englishmen"— Carlyle among them—had sent to Goethe on *his* eightieth. Lewes signed one programme and returned it. When Masson inquired about George Eliot's, he wrote that she "was very desirous to pay her tribute, but did not suggest it lest women should have been excluded. Herewith her signature!" Then he added a postscript: "I find she has written her signature so badly that I will ask you to send another prospectus on which she may improve!"[62] A few days later Lewes wrote again:

Madonna is distressed and "can't think" what you will think of her stupidity and carelessness when you hear that she has blurred and spoiled the second programme you sent for signature. Enclosed is a clean one on a piece of paper. If that won't do, but if it must be on the programme, forgive the trouble, and send a third! But I suppose this will do as well?[63]

It did. All the signatures were clipped out and mounted in alphabetical order on a single sheet beneath the engrossed address, which can be seen at Ecclefechan. "Shall we present the memorial in person?" Lewes asked. Perhaps the prospect of seeing his old friend accounts for his rereading *Heroes and Hero-Worship* at this time;

59. *Life and Memoirs of John Churton Collins*, p. 47.
60. *The George Eliot Letters*, IV, 65.
61. G. H. Lewes to David Masson, MS: NLS, 1778.114. For details of the medal see *New Letters of Thomas Carlyle*, II, 119, and Wilson, *Carlyle*, VI, 372–374.
62. MS: NLS, 1778.111.   63. MS: NLS, 1778.112–113.

and her sense of Carlyle's hostile feeling may account for George
Eliot's agitation in signing the memorial. It is unlikely that she would
have attended the presentation in any case. When the birthday came
round, there was snow and fog so intense that they did not even
venture out to the concert.

Carlyle's opinion of George Eliot cropped out when he was collecting and arranging his wife's letters after her death in 1866:

As to "talent," epistolary and other, these *Letters*, I perceive, equal and
surpass whatever of best I know to exist in that kind; for "talent," "genius,"
or whatever we may call it, what an evidence, if my little woman needed
that to me! Not all the *Sands* and *Eliots* and babbling *cohue* of "celebrated
scribbling women" that have strutted over the world, in my time, could,
it seems to me, if all boiled down and distilled to essence, make one such
woman.[64]

But the object of his scorn still held the generous view of Carlyle
given in her article in the *Leader*:

When he is saying the very opposite of what we think, he says it so finely,
with so hearty conviction—he makes the object about which we differ stand
out in such grand relief under the clear light of his strong and honest intellect—he appeals so constantly to our sense of the manly and the truthful
—that we are obliged to say 'Hear! hear!' to the writer before we can give
the decorous 'Oh! oh!' to his opinions.[65]

64. *Reminiscences*, I, 209.
65. *Leader*, 6 (27 Oct. 1855), 1035. Rpt. in Pinney, p. 214.

Carlyle and Trollope

RUTH apROBERTS, *University of California, Riverside*

Thomas Carlyle and Anthony Trollope are so remote in temper, in office, in kind, it may seem a very unlikely task to link them at all. And yet as we find more and more that to understand the Victorians better is to return more and more to Carlyle, it may be that to trace some links between Carlyle and even such a man as Trollope will help to reveal and define that radical *basso continuo* of Carlylean thought. The relationship defines itself with some nicety even in Carlylean terms. Carlylean process-thinking, the fire, the flux, takes shape at one notable point in a figure of "Organic Filaments," and he speaks of

the venous-arterial circulation, of Letters, verbal Messages, paper and other Packages . . . not Life only, but all the garniture and form of Life . . . flow on those main-currents of what we call Opinion; as preserved in Institutions, Polities, Churches, above all in Books. Beautiful it is to understand and know that a Thought did never yet die; that as thou, the originator thereof, hast gathered it and created it from the whole Past, so thou will transmit it to the whole Future.[1]

Now, in this program I think there may be seen a division of labor. Trollope is very active indeed in the "venous-arterial circulation," and Carlyle is close to the center, as the originator and transmitter of the "Thought."

Trollope's primary activity in the "venous-arterial circulation" is by way of his many novels, many of them continuously in print; Carlyle's figure works out especially well if one thinks of them as a kind of vintage wine functioning as a vascular stimulant. But first I want to call to mind that aspect of Trollope's life (Carlyle said Biography is our proper study) where he is literally the stimulant, custodian and protector of real Letters, his work in the Post Office. When he first began his work there it was only *faute de mieux*, a position arranged through influence for an unpromising young man. There has been a tendency to think of Trollope as a *mere* civil servant: the Post

---

1. Harrold, *Sartor*, pp. 245–247, passim.

Office was just a job, and he was a drudge. And sometimes thoughtless people have felt his novels were just a job, and as novelist he is a drudge. But in fact as he continued his work in the service, it changed in his mind and became important. He became impassioned and devoted. "I was attached to the department, had imbued myself with a thorough love of letters,—I mean the letters which are carried by the post,—and was anxious for their welfare as though they were all my own."[2]

His accomplishments in the department, for thirty-three years, were considerable. He traced out actual routes of rural letter-carriers. (He did not walk, however; it was permissible to do the tracing on horseback, and this fortunately tied in with another passion of his— fox-hunting. If you rode a certain number of miles or hours in your line of work you were allowed two horses rather than one, and Trollope worked furiously and well, kept up his mileage, and his second horse was a hunter.) He instituted that invaluable thing, the pillar-box, without which even an ivory tower is scarcely livable. "Neither from within comes there question or response into any Postbag; thy thoughts fall into no friendly ear or heart . . . : there has a Hole fallen out in the immeasurable universal World-tissue. . . ."[3] If you want to put your poems in the coffin of your dead love, you'd better keep copies and somehow get them in the mail. At the highest level,

---

2. Anthony Trollope, *Autobiography*, ed. Bradford A. Booth (Berkeley and Los Angeles, 1947), p. 233.

3. Harrold, *Sartor*, p. 245. My attention has been drawn to several other interesting tributes to the Postbag. In one Goethe writes to Carlyle, gratified that Carlyle's last letter has reached him quickly: "Es ist wirklich höchst erfreulich dass die Einrichtungen unsrer gesitteten Welt, nach und nach, die Entfernung zwischen Gleichgesinnten, Wohldenkenden geschäftig vermindern, wogegen wir derselben manches nachsehen können." Charles Eliot Norton translates: "It is certainly highly gratifying that the distance between well disposed persons . . . is being steadily diminished, owing to the arrangements of our civilised world, in return for which we may excuse much that is amiss in it." Carlyle, in turn, expresses to Goethe some months later his satisfaction "that hitherto our messages pass safely, over rough seas and tumultuous lands, and do not once miss their road. Among the many wonders of modern society, such a benefit is not the least wonderful; and ought, indeed, as you once remarked, to make amends for much that we could wish otherwise." *Correspondence between Goethe and Carlyle*, ed. C. E. Norton (London and New York, 1887), pp. 193, 200, 237. The letters quoted are of June and November 1830. It is pleasant to think that we owe the safeguarding of this important correspondence to such devoted civil servants as Trollope. Although he did not actually join the Post Office until 1834, the new efficient administration, which he was to help establish, had already begun under Sir Rowland Hill. We may also notice the way in which Carlyle announced the spreading across France of the news of the King's flight to Varennes ("the electric news" radiating forth in "all Mail-bags") in *The French Revolution, Works*, III, 166–167.

Trollope had a good deal to do with arranging international postage routes and international postage treaties, and no Federation of the World is going to be accomplished without *them*. So he was vitally engaged in the venous-arterial circulation on which correspondences depend: for instance, a certain immeasurably precious set of letters involving Annandale and Ecclefechan and Edinburgh and London. It is worrisome to see how at times it was at the mercy of a hopelessly laggard comic rustic.

Trollope's high sense of the value of his postal work finds a nice motto in one of his favorite quotations from Cicero:

Omne officium, quod ad conjunctionem hominum et ad societatem tuendam valet, anteponendum est illi officio quod cognitione et scientia continetur.

Trollope's own translation is as follows:

All duty which tends to protect the society of man with men is to be preferred [in the old sense of given "precedence"] to that of which science is the simple object.[4]

The passage is from the *De Officiis*, that book of Cicero's that Trollope loved above all, *Concerning Duties*, or *offices*, even that of a Post Office *official*. How well it points to all those humane values that are the essence of the *polis* and are protected by the efficient, cheap, and safe interchange of Letters, verbal Messages, paper and other Packages.

In Trollope's novels there are many little in-joke references to the Post Office, and one novel, *John Caldigate*, has a plot which uses his knowledge of the workings of the Australian Post Office. There is also a high incidence of letters in the texts, and a sense of their importance in the events of people's lives. They are especially fine instances of the novelist's art too, as highly characteristic as the best dialogue, often articulating an important crux or shift in action in a way vital to the essence of the novel. But all this letter-stuff in the novels, and Trollope's own activity in the Post Office, take on, as we consider his life work, a symbolic significance. Those letters (and paper and other packages) which constitute his œuvre, all forty-seven novels and all the other books, what a contribution they are themselves to the life-giving circulation, the humane interchange,

---

4. Anthony Trollope, *Cicero* (London, 1880), II, 323; *De Officiis*, lib. I, ca. xliv.

that connects us to each other now, to times past, and in all likelihood to times to come.

The practical life-giving circulation as evidenced in actual Institutions, Polities, Churches—and as I think in the record of test cases,
the arena of behavior where we have to make decisions that imply,
whether we will or not, some ethical principle—that is Trollope's
business. In Carlyle's "*Thou*, the originator of a Thought," who has
"gathered it and created it from the whole Past, so thou wilt transmit
it to the whole Future," I think that there we see Carlyle himself. He
fulfills his own humanist program. To read the beautiful Duke-
Edinburgh edition of his Letters, just as far as we have them now, is
to be freshly impressed with that great dynamo that he was, his
marvelous zest and resilient earthy humor, his piety and tenderness,
his great hunger and thirst after righteousness, but above all let me
especially note for now, the vastness of his learning. Was there any-
body else in this time of enormous reading quite so learned as Carlyle? He seems a later John Donne: "Poor intricated soul," certainly, "Riddling, perplexed, labyrinthical soul," but driven like
Donne with "an hydroptique immoderate desire of humane learning and languages." But more yet like a Milton, in gathering, creating and transmitting. His early devotion to mathematics is eloquent evidence of the creative and synthesizing power of his mind, of
his purity and disinterestedness. He seems, like Pascal, to have pushed
mathematics to its limit and to have gone beyond: "Logic is good,
but it is not the best"; "Metaphysics is the attempt of the mind to rise
above the mind; to environ and shut in, or as we say, *comprehend*
the mind."[5] How peremptory his demands on himself, to *comprehend*, and how proportionately great his disgust, with pedagogy, with
geology, with law, with theology! What perseverance, through the
Rue St. Thomas de l'Enfer, through the numb Centre of Indifference,
and how heroic, how Promethean he emerges, the "originator of a
Thought," a prize, a fire at which we may still warm ourselves. His
thought represents a gathering from the "whole" past, at least much
more whole than ours with our fragmented learning, and his work is
the making that thought available to the future, his age, and ours
too. He, in our vulgar but practical phrase, "gets it all together," gets

5. "Characteristics," *Works*, XXVIII, 6, 27. "Metaphysics" is not a very respectable
word in philosophy these days, but the concept here is modern, very much in
line with Chomsky on language, with Gödel on limitations.

more of it together than anyone else does, taking account of just about all extant learning, and shapes the thought of his age into a mode one can abide by in a post-enlightenment, progress-ridden iron time. Arnold spoke of "wandering between two worlds, one dead, / The other powerless to be born," and his rhetoric is so authoritative and seems somehow to speak so straight to our twentieth-century values, that no one dares contradict. He is right, of course, with poetic truth. But there is a sense in which Carlyle made an in-between world, and most thinking men lived in it. Arnold survived, and we like to think may yet prevail in some measure.

It seems to me that Carlyle's title "Characteristics" is a failure to translate the *Grundzüge* which are his subject, although I don't know how he might have done better. But Carlyle gives us a world that is process, flow, *Züge*, while "characteristics" has a rather static sense. He tells us what the ground swells are, the main processes, but the main thing he teaches is the fact of flux, or relativity; he was even able to see time and space as fictions, mere "Forms of Thought" as he called them, and he gives us a continuum, a process where the outward forms, the garments change, but the mystery underneath is whole and complete. Poor man, while the vulture Dyspepsia ate at his innards, he enabled us to see, to be, and above all to do. The sages, Arnold, Newman, Ruskin, Pater, move and have their being in his light.

From this guru of gurus, the organic filaments extend even to novelists, and to Trollope in a very special way. It has not perhaps been sufficiently noted that Trollope is not part of the classically Victorian pattern of Belief–Doubt–Loss of Faith. You have to be evangelical-literalist-puritan to have a really rousing Victorian crisis of faith, and then you work through it to establish some new basis for spiritual survival. Examples one might call classical in this sense are George Eliot, Browning, and Mark Rutherford. Carlyle's own crisis is positively archetypal, and his hard-won new ground the new life-giving "mythos" of *Sartor*. Trollope comes out of an intellectual milieu more sophisticated than the evangelical. His mother may seem rather a figure of fun, as "indomitable" women tend to do, and his father seems a monster of learned gloom; but the essential cultural fact is that they were High Anglicans, anti-evangelical (Mrs. Trollope's novels passionately so), and *au courant* in the cultivated world. I think ultimately this shows in his novels; even more than Thackeray he writes in awareness of a literary tradition. And I think it exempted him from religious crisis; his period of *Sturm und Drang* was especially agonizing, but none of the agony appears to have stemmed from religious insecurity. As he became more learned, self-taught, after his school phase, based in old High Anglican non-literalism, he was the better equipped to appreciate Carlyle's achievement in a relatively cool manner. He discriminates, acclaiming some of Carlylean thought, and rejecting some. His negative appraisals of Carlyle are each carefully prefaced with a tribute, and there is no reason not to take these tributes at face value. In *The Warden* he says, "We all of us could, and many of us did, learn much from the doctor" (XV). He admires "the genius, honesty, and courage of Mr. Carlyle, [and he is among] the number of students who have sat at his feet believing, trusting, and learning."[6] Carlyle is the man "whom I have ever revered as a thinker, and valued as an author, and whom I much esteem as a man, —one from whom, perhaps, I have myself learned more than from any other English writer."[7]

What did Trollope learn from Carlyle? The most obvious answer is the doctrine of work, with a vengeance. In an age of astonishing productivity, perhaps no one outdoes Trollope in doing what lies to hand with his whole might. Produce! Produce! Forty-seven novels. Sixty-seven books, in all. Innumerable magazine pieces, lectures, editings, Post Office reports, letters, travel books, an exhaustive study of Cicero, and a translation of Caesar's *Commentaries*. Less obviously, I think one may trace in the *Autobiography* his own emergence out of a particularly miserable lost youth, out of a chaos, by means of a gradual achievement of a Carlylean discipline of work, making order for himself out of doing the clerkship at hand, rising above the discouragement, the dissipation, the moneylenders and the loneliness by reading and study on his own. He is wonderfully victorious in what Carlyle described as that "struggle of human Freewill against material Necessity, which every man's Life, by the mere circumstance that the man continues alive, will more or less victoriously exhibit."[8] The Latin he had failed in at school, he now works at by himself, and he becomes a good scholar. The urbane tone of Horace becomes something of his own. He recognizes in Cicero the passion-

---

6. "An Essay on Carlylism," *St. Paul's*, 1 (Dec. 1867), 292.
7. From Trollope's projected "History of Fiction" transcribed from the MSS by Michael Sadleir, Appendix III to *Trollope: A Commentary* (New York, 1947), p. 423.
8. "Biography," *Works*, XXVIII, 44–45.

ate concern with morals and their practical working out in institutions and behavior, welcomes Cicero's zest for life and engagement, his ultimate optimism about man's fate in spite of frequent ill bodings, his concern with the philosophy and practice of law, and political action—all those concerns that are so conspicuous in the novels; and in his ironic position as narrator, he is to maintain much of the Ciceronian irony and "humane grace." The extent of his organized reading—all English novels from *Arcadia* on, and no less than two hundred and fifty-seven Elizabethan and Jacobean plays all annotated, for instance—makes him appear somewhat "hydroptique" and "immoderate" himself, in his love of humane letters. Ultimately, out of the "dark wasteful Chaos," he is to create the order of Barchester, and later the larger and more sophisticated world of Whitehall, and Glencora and Plantagenet Palliser. The night cometh in which no man can create fictions. "My only doubt as to finding a heaven for myself at last arises from the fear that the disembodied and beautiful spirits will not want novels."[9]

On the matter of religion, I think Trollope valued Carlyle's teachings and found in them the courage of his non-conviction. Coming from a High Church ambiance, as I have said, he had not languished in what Arnold calls the prison of Puritanism, and his writing is remarkably free from religious stress. In fact, it is only because he is so free of involvement in the crises of Faith and Doubt that he can write so wittily and detachedly of High and Low, Oxford Movement and "The Clergyman Who Subscribes for Colenso."[10] Carlyle's hard-won and finely wrought declaration of religious values as not dependent on orthodox supernaturalism must have sustained him in his non-literalism. He calls Carlyle "Our dear English Homer"[11] (only, it is true, to add that he is a Homer "in prose," and to make the point that he "nods"), and I think his sense of him as Homer is a sense of his grandeur and of how he constitutes the base and theory of the moral values of an age.

Trollope's writing about religion is quite remarkably devoid of orthodox supernaturalism. Especially in the "Clergymen" essays, he writes of how difficult it is even to define belief, of what constitutes

9. *Letters*, ed. Bradford A. Booth (London, 1951), p. 286.
10. The last essay in the series "Clergymen of the Church of England," published originally in the *Pall Mall Gazette*, 1865–1866, and reprinted (1974) in the Victorian Library of Leicester University Press.
11. Quoted from Sadleir's *Trollope: A Commentary*, p. 423.

the act of believing, and of how ill we can define what we do believe. I think he would have heartily approved the Carlyle who in the *Life of John Sterling* advocated a

Speedy end to Superstition. . . . What can it profit any mortal to adopt locutions and imaginations which do *not* correspond to fact; which no sane mortal can deliberately adopt in his soul as true; which the most orthodox of mortals can only, and this after infinite essentially *impious* effort to put-out the eyes of his mind, persuade himself to "believe that he believes?"[12]

Variations of this rather remarkable locution are current in Trollope: "We think that we think . . . we believe that we believe."[13] In *Marion Fay* the progressive young Lord Hampstead speaks of religion as a "tone of mind" (XVI). Miss MacKenzie and her friend have a "strong faith in the need for the comfort of religion" (*Miss MacKenzie*, IX). Josiah Crawley, one of Trollope's most learned clergymen, as well as most unfortunate and contrary, has this insight: "It is in his perfection as a man that we recognize the divinity of Christ. It is in the imperfection of men that we recognize the necessity for a Christ" (*Last Chronicle*, LXVIII). The pagan Cicero, for Trollope, understood it all pretty well even without Christ; Cicero is "a man whom you might accompany across the village green to church, should he be kind enough to stay with you over the Sunday. The urbanity, the softness, the humanity, the sweetness are all there."[14]

"Custom," says Teufelsdröckh, "doth make dotards of us all." And Carlyle would loose the bonds of Custom, and awaken us to the astounding mystery that existence itself is, and to the wonder proper to us in the face of the mystery. It is a poor reader of Trollope, I think, who finds only custom and the ordinary in the novels. In Trollope's loving, detailed anatomies of custom and its interplay with the endless variations, depths, inventions and ingenuities of the human psyche, Trollope himself fosters the sense of wonder in existence. His own Natural Supernaturalism is revealed to us, not like Carlyle's in poetry and theory, but in the mysterious variety of "real" human behavior, the mystery of evil in Melmotte, the mystery of a Dostoyevskian kind of contrariety in Josiah Crawley, in Louis Trevel-

12. *Works*, XI, 51.
13. See my *Trollope: Artist and Moralist* (London, 1971); in the U.S., *The Moral Trollope* (Athens, Ohio, 1971), pp. 100–101.
14. *Cicero*, II, 325–326.

yan, and most astounding of all, perhaps, the occurrence of real goodness in, say, Mr. Harding or the priest in *The Macdermots* or Plantagenet Palliser. "The natural goodness of some men is a problem which we cannot solve," Trollope declares forthrightly in a gloss on Bacon's *Essays*.[15] It is for him a mystery, and his feeling for it is a Carlylean kind of religious feeling.

These attitudes of Trollope's, fostered if not formed by Carlyle, are so much a part of him as to be unconscious. But throughout his career he stands in a special relationship to Carlyle, in the way of actual comment, or parody, or rebellion, or adaptation.[16] Everyone remembers the caricature of Dr. Pessimist Anticant in *The Warden*, and some object to it as heavyhanded or wrong in tone. However that may be, it is significant in Trollope's work. In *The Warden*, Trollope was in process of self-discovery as an artist, and the two parodies, of Carlyle and of Dickens, are self-definitions by negatives. Dr. Anticant in a Past-and-Present-style analysis of the case of Hiram's Hospital makes it all black and white. He was grand in theory, but when he gets down to cases the theory is no good. The difficulty is that right and wrong are much mixed together; *The Warden* is the classical case, the very paradigm of ambivalence. For the same reasons, Dickens's artistic simplifications are not Trollope's business. His concern is to examine complications—in Bishop Butler's phrase, "the doubtfulness things are involved in."

One might think that with the Carlyle parody in *The Warden*, Trollope had dismissed the matter. But to the astonishment of the publisher's reader, the next thing he offered Longmans was a big Condition-of-England MS, an imitation, no less, of the *Latter-Day Pamphlets*, called *The New Zealander*.[17] This sorts oddly with his letter to his mother at about the same time:

I have read—nay, I have bought!—Carlyle's *Latter Day Pamphlets*, and look on my eight shillings as very much thrown away. To me it appears that the grain of sense is so smothered up in a sack of the sheerest trash, that the former is valueless. . . . He has one idea—a hatred of spoken and acted

15. Michael Sadleir, "Trollope and Bacon's Essays," *Nineteenth-Century Fiction*, [then *The Trollopian*], 1 (Summer 1945), 21–34.

16. There is a good overview of their relationship in "Trollope and Carlyle" by N. John Hall, *Nineteenth-Century Fiction*, 27 (Sept. 1972), 197–205.

17. Trollope's own revision of this has recently been published for the first time, edited by N. John Hall (Oxford, 1972). Hall argues that the Ur-*New Zealander* must have been still more Carlylean than the extant form.

falsehood; and on that he harps through the whole eight pamphlets. I look on him as a man who was always in danger of going mad in literature and who has now done so.[18]

I think I detect here a trace of an effort at literary smart-talk, to impress the old lady. Surely he exaggerates a little, being in the very act of paying Carlyle the compliment of imitation. But it is imitation *and* modification. He keeps some of the Carlylean rhetoric, most unfortunately, and discourses over a wide range: Politics, Press, Law, Medicine, Army and Navy, Church, Monarchy, Society, Literature, and Art. But it is his nature to qualify and discriminate, and he says we are not in fact all going down the drain. How interesting it is, however, that he should even try this mode; and it can serve to remind us of the solid intellectual basis upon which the novels rest.[19] Many parts of the rejected *New Zealander* turn up in one guise or another in the novels, and the assessment of Carlyle himself is more or less restated in Trollope's "Essay on Carlylism" much later, in 1867.[20]

In that essay, Trollope acclaims Carlyle's early literary greatness, but deplores his later tendency to overplay the prophet of doom. He declares Carlyle has resorted to the rhetoric of the pulpit, understanding this as an exhortation for a total change of heart in the hope of achieving some little moral improvement; but Carlyle really believes we are going to the devil. Who, Trollope wonders, is *we*? Of course all countries grow, flourish, and decline; England may look to its colonies for the future and an improved society. Meantime, what does the individual do? Carlyle's chief answer Trollope finds altogether too simplistic: it is the mere commonplace of the old song, "It is good to be honest and true." But everything around us is bad, Carlyle would say. Chiefly, one, the power is in the hands of the government; two, manufacturers produce shoddy goods; three, maidservants give notice. These horrible things are not all bad, Trollope says, and speculates mildly that although there isn't enough evidence to prove anything, there may have been some improvement since olden times. There is probably more education and less governmen-

---

18. *Letters*, pp. 14–15.
19. See *Times Literary Supplement*, 28 July 1972, p. 862, for a review essay; and my review in *Nineteenth-Century Fiction*, 27 (March 1973), 472–477.
20. *St. Paul's Magazine*, 1 (Dec. 1867), 292–305.

tal corruption; Cromwell's period may not have been the only good time. Leaders like Russell, Derby, and Gladstone are infinitely better than the courtiers of the Tudors and Stuarts. The literature of the time, which Carlyle puts on a par with the shoddy, is developing in fact a new honesty, a new truthfulness. And behind this last claim of Trollope's we may think of his own progressive achievement in a new psychological realism.

Before writing *The Warden*, Trollope had written one historical novel, *La Vendée*. Since it deals with a phase of the French Revolution, it invites inspection for Carlylean influence, such as there is with Dickens's *Tale of Two Cities*. But although there are some Carlylean concepts, Trollope has none of Carlyle's prophetic way. Trollope's own monarchic ideas had probably developed, anyway, out of his parents' personal acquaintance with Lafayette. He might conceivably have known Balzac's *Les Chouans*, which covers the same story, the Vendean counterrevolt, but there is no evidence that he did. In style *La Vendée* is more like Scott than Carlyle, and it imitates the worst of Scott more successfully than the best. It has some vigorous and dramatic scenes, tersely and objectively done. Perhaps most promising is the part where Trollope warms to the enigma of Robespierre's character:

He attempted, unassisted, to be perfect among men, and his memory is regarded as that of a loathsome plague, defiling even the unclean age in which he lived. . . . He seems almost to have been sent into the world to prove the inefficacy of human reason to effect human happiness [XXII].

It is a Carlylean idea, but not Carlylean rhetoric. Again, Trollope has something of his own to say on the theory of history:

Public men are like soldiers fighting in a narrow valley: they see nothing but what is close around them, and that imperfectly, as everything is in motion. The historian is as the general, who stands elevated on high ground, and with telescope in hand, sees plainly all the different movements of the troops [XXIII].

Carlyle interests himself in this kind of irony, but I think here it is Trollope's own, and a hint of the ironic stance of the narrator that Trollope was to develop. It is remarkably reminiscent of the typically ironic Lucretian *suave mari magno*, with which Trollope would have been familiar from Bacon's translation in "Of Truth." One cannot help but think too of Teufelsdröckh in his high vantage point in the tower, detached yet concerned. It is another classic statement of the ironic view.

The Carlylean theory of heroes one would not expect Trollope to be much concerned with, his novels are so avowedly and determinedly antiheroic. But as late as his *North America* (1862) there is an interesting trace of Carlylean hero-thinking. He is speaking of the American propensity to overpraise almost any of their own distinguished men, and this propensity is absurd. "But," he says, "hero-worship and love of country are not absurd . . . and a capacity for such worship is something. Indeed, the capacity is everything, for the need of a hero will at last produce the hero needed."[21] It would seem that here some of the doctrine had stuck with him.

Carlylean points for Trollope, however, are generally blunted by the coming to terms with the actual. In his maturity he did his major literary-historical study in his two-volume work on Cicero. And there he is spurred by what seems like an anti-Carlylean motive: he deplores the hero-worship of Caesar, so common among historians, especially in the recent work of Froude. He declares that Caesar (presumably a Carlylean hero-as-king) was for all his brilliance an unscrupulous man, giving only second place to *humanitas*. Cicero is the real hero, for his devotion to the Republic, his incorruptibility, his high sense of public morality, for his engagement as advocate and public man, and for the very qualities that make him such a hero of letters: his sensitivity of mind, his learning, the precedence he gives to morals, practical morals as in the *De Officiis*. He takes us, Trollope says, "out of dead intellectuality into moral perceptions,"[22] out of theory into practice. And he is finally a hero for his sublime honesty, which is what makes his writings still valid for us. In an allusion to Carlyle's "Condition of England," Trollope calls one chapter "The Condition of Rome," and thereby, like both Thomas and Matthew Arnold, and Froude and Mommsen, and literate nineteenth-century people generally, indicates that ancient history has lessons for us now. He notes the prevalence of public corruption and the spread of Caesarism. He corrects what he feels to be a misinterpretation by Froude, that Cicero had condoned the assassination of Caesar, by his "Cum vivere ipsum turpe sit nobis"; Trollope insists with what seems

21. *North America*, ed. Smalley and Booth (New York, 1951), p. 507.
22. E.g., *Cicero*, I, 2–3.

good sense to me that this is best translated as "When even to draw breath of life at such a time is a disgrace to us!"[23] Cicero was aware, that is, of the Thug-ism Caesar represents. And the rest of his career, Trollope is at pains to show, is a struggle—which he probably knew was doomed—to act by legal means in the best interests of the republic. Not to opt out, but to come to terms, even to support the lesser of two evils, at every point to lend his power to bend away from the greater evil, knowing politics as "the art of the possible." And for Trollope, Cicero is the hero. I see in all this a case study which modifies the Carlylean doctrine.

In his novels, he forces principle to come to terms with circumstances, with the possible. Again and again he insists that his "heroes" are not heroic. His amiable young men can be in love with two women at once; noble deeds are done, but not without backward glances. Nora Rowley in *He Knew He Was Right* refuses the hand of an earl for her own true love, a humble journalist, but not without recurrent lively regrets for the property and the title and the grandeur. Trollope's most admirable hero is finally Plantagenet Palliser; and he is a deplorable failure at the power game. As prime minister, he discovers he is only part of a ploy to maintain a coalition in the interests of others; and he fails to accomplish anything because he is so stubbornly honest and too fastidious to make deals with the money and the power. He emerges as our "hero," the embodiment of the Trollopian moral ideal of the "gentleman." There is a parallel between Trollope's early creation of Mr. Harding and his later one of Palliser: although very different characters, both are remarkable artistic achievements in the way they exact our sympathetic admiration for their virtue, and yet are at the same time very alive and very funny. Palliser perhaps is the more remarkable, as he is a hundredfold more developed and elaborated, in a much more complicated, worldly, and sophisticated society. It is very sad such excellence does not necessarily make a good leader. But do you, for that reason, opt out? Palliser, sick at heart to find corruption in his own cabinet, says to his friend the Duke of St. Bungay:

"It makes me feel that an honest man should not place himself where he may have to deal with such persons."

"According to that," says St. Bungay, "the honest men are to desert their

23. Ibid., p. 5.

country in order that the dishonest men may have everything their own way" [*The Prime Minister*, LVI].

Palliser cannot answer.

Carlyle, though very much engaged in the literary world, seldom found himself where he had to deal with dishonest persons, or—in practice—with moral dilemmas. As sage, he could stay relatively aloof and pure, and he prophesied, and taught the right principles of action. Trollope, however, was a public servant, and as Post Office clerk and then official, he was confronted repeatedly with *les hommes moyens sensuels*. One of his first duties as Post Office Surveyor in Ireland had been

to balance a defaulting postmaster's accounts, find out how much he owed, and report on his capacity to pay. . . . At that time, though the sums dealt with were small, the forms of dealing with them were very intricate. I went to work, however, and made that defaulting postmaster teach me the use of those forms. I then succeeded in balancing the account, and had no difficulty whatever in reporting that he was altogether unable to pay his debt. Of course he was dismissed;—but he had been a very useful man to me.[24]

It could be called a "deal." The man is culpable, and Trollope uses him, and is able to do him some service in turn (one supposes if not reported as "unable to pay" he might have been imprisoned). The man is sufficiently punished by dismissal. And so here is a *case*, where the precisionist (or sage) might object, but the casuist (or novelist) sees nothing dishonorable or illegal or immoral, and there is a usefulness to be reaped.

The confrontation with cases kept the novelist's wisdom practical and supple. There is a similarity with Henry Fielding, who as magistrate may be supposed to have kept keen his sense of practical ethics, and whose novels profit by that keenness. Trollope even ran for parliament, and found that in hopes of serving his country he had to dirty himself with campaign practices. The story is told in all its rich irony and pathos in the election chapters of *Ralph the Heir*. In life he ran for office, and acted. In his novels he faces up to office, and practice. He complains of Carlyle that "his theories were all beautiful, and the code of morals he taught us certainly an improvement in the practices of the age. . . . But when he became practical,

24. *Autobiography*, p. 55.

the charm was gone" (*The Warden*, XV). When he gets to cases, that is, it doesn't work. Adjustments, modifications must be made. One comes to terms even with evil in order to be able to do anything. He quotes Cicero: "The very possession of power is an evil in itself. But without that evil you cannot have the good which the institution contains."[25]

It was the *Latter-Day Pamphlets* that caused Trollope to formulate his differences with Carlyle. I cannot but think the pamphlet "Jesuitism" would have put him off particularly. Trollope, through his parents and his Irish, French, and Italian friends, had much respect for the Roman Catholic Church. Carlyle's attack is, of course, on the vices of casuistry, notoriously associated with Jesuitism. But there is a benign kind of casuistry, and I have argued elsewhere that Trollope's art itself consists in casuistry, in taking up those cases in all their well-developed circumstantialities, where the right course is not clear, and where what one might have thought unalterable principle must, in charity, bend to circumstances, just such cases as Cicero takes up in summary form in the *De Officiis*. And yet, I would say, Trollope's moral passion, like Cicero's, is none the less for all this adjusting. It seems to me that it is the very passion of Carlyle that activates Trollope to work out his cases. His novels bring the intense moral concern of Carlyle to terms with what is actual.

Those recurrent attacks of Carlyle's on the novelists, on "the long ear of Fiction" and the moral obliquity of its practitioners, must have stung Trollope especially because of his reverence for the man. He quotes one painful one: "Fiction,—my friend, says the master, you will be surprised at last what a cousinship it has to lying."[26] Such jibes I think instigated the formulation of Trollope's own theory of fiction as moral. "The preaching of the day is done by the novelist, and the lessons which he teaches are those to which men and women will listen."[27] Everyone reads novels, and so it is through them that you can reach people. Thackeray, whom he admired so, was, he says, "ever crying his sermon, hoping ... to do something towards lessening the evils round him."[28] Trollope borrows even from Carlyle himself, from a scornful passage in "The Hero as Man of Letters" where Carlyle

25. *Cicero*, II, 311; *De Legibus*, lib. III, ca. x.
26. "Essay on Carlylism," p. 304.
27. "Editor's note" in the first issue of Trollope's own magazine, *St. Paul's*, 1 (Oct. 1867), 5.
28. *Thackeray*, English Men of Letters Series (London, 1867), p. 205.

declares books do affect behavior: "They persuade men. Not the wretchedest circulating-library novel, which foolish girls thumb and con in remote villages, but will help to regulate the actual practical weddings and households of those foolish girls."[29] "The actual practical weddings and households" are no small matter to Trollope. With Arnold, he would undoubtedly believe that conduct is the greater part of religion. And just because novelists do have an influence on conduct, he would encourage "a just appreciation of the excellence of their calling, and a general understanding of the high nature of the work which they perform." Poetry does rank higher than fiction; the poet, with his "all but divine grace of words . . . can teach his lessons somewhat as a god might teach." (We have a parallel here to Carlyle on artist-prophet and Arnold on poetry-religion.) But the novelist's lessons "tend to the same end" as the poet's. "By each, equally, may true honour, true love, true worship, and true humanity be inculcated; and that will be the greatest teacher who will spread such truth the widest." Trollope has much to say on how the novelist's method is to present behavior options, or roles. The young woman who has followed Beatrice Esmond's story may well say "Oh! not like that;—let me not be like that!" And Trollope says, "If I can teach politicians that they can do their business better by truth than by falsehood, I do a great service."

All these passages are from the *Autobiography*,[30] that work which Trollope wrote to be published posthumously, where he outdoes even himself in honesty. Especially here he has no occasion for false modesty. What shocked the age of Henry James when the *Autobiography* was published was—first—the interest Trollope took in making money (his "trade"), and—second—his simplistic theory of fiction. But when one knows the subtlety of his novels, it may appear at last that the simple principle does function, and functions well, just because the practice is so subtle. In *The Way We Live Now* we see a set of people whose derelictions are very slight, for the most part. There is some literary reviewing that is not quite disinterested, some politicking that is not quite clean, the acceptance of hospitality from a known swindler. It is not so awfully sinful and is maybe even somewhat familiar. There is no shadow of preaching to put us off, and it is all laid out in such engaging detail, and so dead clear, we just might feel inclined to say, "Oh! not like that!" If the novelist can "preach"

29. *Works*, V, 160.   30. *Autobiography*, pp. 181–187.

in this way, says Trollope, "then I think Mr. Carlyle need not call him distressed, nor talk of that long ear of fiction, nor question whether he be or not the most foolish of existing mortals."

In his defense of the genre, Trollope insists again and again, with some ironic pleasure undoubtedly, that he is a *mere* novelist; he loves to compare his work to a trade, shoemaking especially, and teases his more high-flown friends by making much of the regularity of his working hours. But he really claims for novels the greatest moral value. He does it by minimal definitions and ironic understatements. His projected History of English Fiction, he tells us in the *Autobiography*, was intended as a vindication:

Thinking much of my own daily labour and its nature, I felt myself first to be much afflicted and then deeply grieved by the opinion expressed by wise and thinking men as to the work done by novelists. But when, by degrees, I dared to examine and sift the sayings of such men, I found them to be sometimes silly and often arrogant. . . . The novelist, if he have a conscience, must preach his sermons with the same purpose as the clergyman, and must have his own system of ethics.[31]

It was not Trollope's way to preach as Dickens does with a caricatured morality, nor as Carlyle does, with a Juvenalian acid. His way was more the way of Horace, as he indicates in a very interesting letter: "Horace, who is playful and even good-natured in his very satyres did probably teach men to be less absurd."[32] The claims are modest in their terms, as in the very title of his lecture on "English Prose Fiction as a Rational Amusement,"[33] but in truth Trollope places the novel very high indeed, as we might now. Professor Lionel Stevenson had a vision of the University of Utopia where the reading of Victorian novels plays a very large part, and I think the graduates of that academy would really learn to be less absurd.[34]

Trollope's own program for the novel, then, is formulated in reaction to Carlyle. Carlyle is the idealist-theorist, but Trollope is ever the existentialist: I mean that for him existence always does take precedence over essence. Carlyle really knows the relationship well enough: "Alas," he declares, "we know very well that Ideals can never

---

31. P. 182.   32. *Letters*, p. 266.

33. Published in *Four Lectures*, ed. Morris L. Parrish (London, Constable, 1938).

34. "The Rationale of Victorian Fiction," an address delivered on the occasion of the dedication of the Bradford A. Booth Memorial Room in the UCLA Library, published in *Nineteenth-Century Fiction*, 27 (March 1973), 391–404.

be completely embodied in practice."[35] Trollope's study is that *degree*
to which practice can be adjusted to the Ideal, the ideal of Carlyle's
Anti-cant, of Cicero's *humanitas* and *honestum*, of Christian charity.
And so he studies those cases which are interesting for the way in
which the adjustment must be made. The metric system is a wonderful intellectual idea, but Palliser and his colleagues had a devil of a
time making it work out in the reform of English currency. We see
their struggles in *The Eustace Diamonds*, in the chapter "Quints or
Semitenths." It *has* taken a long time to work out. Palliser himself,
who in office had failed because of his own high ideals, adjures his
colleague: "These moral speculations, Mr. Finn, will hardly bear the
wear and tear of real life" (*The Prime Minister*, LXXII).

So Trollope's work is, throughout, to bring the Carlylean ideal face
to face with real life, and his work retains its validity just because the
moral ideal is so strong with him, at the same time that he is the
most developed of all Victorian novelists in psychological realism.
The Carlylean passion extends even to this very matter of "realism"
itself. Carlyle's story of *The Diamond Necklace* (1837) is one of the
things Trollope singles out for praise, for "artistic workmanship," in
his "Essay on Carlylism"; and I think Carlyle's admonishments in
Chapter I, "The Age of Romance," stayed with Trollope throughout.
"The Age of Romance has not ceased," says Carlyle; "it never ceases."
"The Nineteenth [Century] is hardly a whit less romantic than the
Ninth, or any other." "Romance exists," he declares; and it exists "in
reality alone":

> The thing that *is*, what can be *so* wonderful; what especially to us that *are*,
> can have such significance? Study Reality ... search out deeper and deeper
> its quite endless mystery: see it, know it; then, whether thou would learn
> from it, and again teach; or weep over it, or laugh over it, or love it, or
> despise it, or in any way relate thyself to it, thou hast the firmest enduring
> basis: *that* hieroglyphic page is one thou canst read on forever, find new
> meaning in forever.[36]

I think Trollope relates himself to reality in all these ways, and relates us to reality thereby. His loving, careful, and extensive repre-
sentations of reality are as they are because he has this Carlylean
sense of wonder at the astonishing fact of being and becoming. This

35. "The Hero as King," *Works*, V, 197.
36. "The Diamond Necklace," *Works*, XXVIII, 324, 327, 329, 330.

is the religion of Natural Supernaturalism, and the essential fact about Trollope is that it is his religion as well as Carlyle's.

With *La Vendée* Trollope renounced the "romantic" kind of Romance for that of Reality. It was necessary to him to try it, of course; how determinedly experimental he is! But it was not his métier. In 1857 he took his manuscript *The Three Clerks* to market, and a publisher's man advised: "I hope it's not historical, Mr. Trollope? Whatever you do, don't be historical; your historical novel is not worth a damn."[37] So the market was against the historical, but I don't think that disappointed Trollope much. In the background of his mind were Carlyle's words:

Such being the intrinsic quality of this Time, and of all Time whatsoever, might not the Poet who chanced to walk through it find objects enough to paint? What object soever he fixed on, were it the meanest of the mean, let him but paint it in its actual truth, as it swims there, in such environment . . . an indestructible portion of the miraculous All,—his picture of it were a Poem. . . . the mystic 'actual truth' . . . [inviting] even Prosaists to search for it![38]

Carlyle himself in *The Diamond Necklace* was enthralled with the search for the "actual truth" of a case through a multifaceted record, somewhat like Browning in *The Ring and the Book*. For his "Old Yellow Book" he has the *Affaire du collier*, Paris, 1785. The first volume, he says, has some twenty-one memoirs, "not, of course, Historical statements of truth; but Culprits' and Lawyers' statements of what they wished to be believed; each party *lying* according to his ability to lie. To reach the truth, or even any honest guess at the truth, the immensities of rubbish must be sifted, contrasted, rejected."[39] Carlyle proceeds then to work through to the sensational romance of this true story. His sense of the marvelous yet never quite resolvable ambiguity of things is something like Browning's, and is, in spite of his theory, a step toward the Victorian demonstration of relativism. Trollope makes his fictions "true" by presenting in them the many facets of actuality. *Orley Farm* is a fine example of this multiplicity of views, even to the many lawyers, and also participants and bystanders, not only lying, but also telling the truth according to their varying abilities to tell the truth.

37. *Autobiography*, pp. 189–191, passim.
38. *Works*, XXVIII, 329.   39. *Works*, XXVIII, 334 n.

As to realism itself, Trollope explains in his *Autobiography* that a false dichotomy in novel criticism has sprung up, a dichotomy of sensational-realistic:

The novelists who are considered to be anti-sensational are generally called realistic. I am realistic. My friend Wilkie Collins is generally supposed to be sensational. . . . All this is, I think, a mistake,—which mistake arises from the inability of the imperfect artist to be at the same time realistic and sensational. A good novel should be both, and both in the highest degree. If a novel fail in either, there is a failure in art. . . . Truth let there be,— truth of description, truth of character, human truth as to men and women. If there be such truth, I do not know that a novel can be too sensational.[40]

If you count it all up, Trollope's novels do have plenty of the sensational: murders, suicides, adulteries, bastards, neurotics, psychotics, suppressed or tampered wills, trials-at-law—God's plenty, in fact. And all with a "truth" so overwhelmingly successful that it got around for years that he is the great master of the ordinary, the commonplace. Even Henry James was bamboozled. How strikingly close to Carlylean theory, however, is his insistence on the sensationalism of reality!

Even the *locus* of the Carlylean theory had a special importance for him, I think. He admired *The Diamond Necklace*, and it may be that his own story of a diamond necklace took its conception from Carlyle's. *The Eustace Diamonds* concerns a necklace of fabulous value, being played—for all it's worth—by a heroine who is like Carlyle's: clever, unprincipled, with a fine flair for the dramatic. Carlyle's Comtesse de Lamotte he calls an "artist," a "dramatist." And such too is Trollope's Lizzie Eustace, with her dramatic manipulations, her play-acting, and finally her psychosis. She is a pathological liar. There is an abundance of sensations and mysteries in the work, and I do not believe any critic has ever objected that it is improbable or "unrealistic." And so it makes a nice exhibition for the sensational-realistic theory. One delightful side-effect of its "realism" is in its legal aspect. Trollope applied to a lawyer friend, Charles Merewether, for a legal opinion, so complete and lifelike are the details and complexities, and Merewether's legal opinion on heirlooms was incorporated into Chapter XXV. Trollope notes, with what satisfaction we can imagine, "I am told that it has become the ruling authority on the subject."[41] Carlyle had investigated the ramifications of a real

40. *Autobiography*, pp. 189–191, passim.
41. Ibid., p. 98.

diamond necklace case; Trollope invents a case so well that it has an Organic Filament reaching back into actuality.

The essence of the novel, however, is in the ironies of a hundred different and shifting aspects of the events, each party lying according to his ability, or telling the truth if it is to his interest, or—most heroic—occasionally telling the truth even if his own sense of right and justice is outraged thereby. That was the circumstance with the lawyer Camperdown when he was faced with the Dove (Merewether) opinion. Organic Filaments connect Lizzie's motives and lies with an immensely complicated network of her friends and acquaintances, enemies, suitors, and their families; the fate even of the poor American girl forced into marriage for her friends' financial benefit which depends on Lizzie's credit as she supplies the wedding presents, in return of course for certain advantages to herself. We see the complications from the points of view of all these people, and the police, the detectives, the lawyers. And then further, we see more remotely the gossip, the rumors, and the press; how it looks in London, how it looks in Scotland. Most remotely, how it looks to the grand society at Matching Priory: the worldly old duke dying, but delaying his death to see how it all turns out, having to be reminded of the details but nevertheless enlivened by there being a "pretty" woman, and so devilish clever; and how the reports and gossip are relayed to him by the attractive widow Madame Goesler; and therefore Lady Glencora must be ever more closely on the watch for fear he should take it into his head to marry Madame Goesler and thereby disadvantage her own husband his heir, and their offspring. There are even political ramifications: it was "a matter of faith with all the liberal party that Lady Eustace had had something to do with stealing her own diamonds. . . . the old duke was anxious that one of his own order should be proved to have been the thief, as the plunder taken was so lordly" (LIV).

This leaves us very far out, on a Filament of a Filament, like the remotest nerve-end; but while we still have hold of it, we can follow it back to Carlyle's All. We could be reminded, too, that criticism too often *dis*-connects—disconnects novels, for instance, from the other Letters, verbal Messages, paper and other Packages. It is Carlyle himself who would teach us that they do indeed connect. "The Wise Man stands ever encompassed, and spiritually embraced, by a cloud of witnesses and brothers." To know this, to trace even some connections between two great Victorian writers, is to come into better communion with them both, and maybe into that "living, literal *Communion of Saints*" that Carlyle speaks of.[42] It is not really a literal one, but a metaphorical one—and we, having learned from Carlyle, might value it all the more for that.

42. Harrold, *Sartor*, p. 247.

Ruskin's Discipleship to Carlyle: A Revaluation

GEORGE ALLAN CATE, *University of Maryland*

Victorian critics began to regard Ruskin as a disciple of Carlyle in the early 1850's, and the Victorian reading public became convinced of that discipleship when Ruskin surprised them with *Unto This Last* in 1860. Since then, readers and students of Ruskin have continued to assume that Ruskin was a complete disciple of Carlyle. Their assumptions have been justified not only by the many obvious borrowings from Carlyle found in Ruskin's works but also by Ruskin's public references to Carlyle as his master throughout the last thirty years of his writings.[1] As early as 1854 he claimed in a public lecture that he "owed more to Carlyle than to any other man,"[2] and by 1856 his allegiance was so obvious that he felt it necessary to confess it in the third volume of *Modern Painters*. He looked, he said, "most of all to Carlyle, whom I read so constantly that, without willfully setting myself to imitate him, I find myself perpetually falling into his modes of expression. . . . I find Carlyle's stronger thinking colouring mine continually."[3] Nearly twenty five years later, in a letter of August 1880, Ruskin could still say of Carlyle, "We feel so much alike, that you may often mistake one for the other now."[4]

Ironically, however, the very conspicuousness of Ruskin's discipleship has preserved it from careful scrutiny. Until the late 1950's, only F. W. Roe's *The Social Philosophy of Carlyle and Ruskin* (1921) made any extended attempt to deal with the Carlyle-Ruskin relationship. The pivotal chapter in this book, entitled "Master and Disciple," did little more than cull material from several published sources in order to demonstrate briefly Ruskin's "almost uninterrupted relationship of mutual affection and admiration"[5] with Carlyle. This treatment was so limited that Francis G. Townsend, in his

---

1. I.e., the years from the late 1850's to the late 1880's.
2. In a lecture on "Decorative Colour" reported in *The Works of John Ruskin*, ed. E. T. Cook and Alexander Wedderburn (London, 1903–1912), XII, 507. Cited below as Ruskin, *Works*.
3. Appendix III of *Modern Painters*, III, in Ruskin, *Works*, V, 427.
4. Letter to Susan Beever, Ruskin, *Works*, XXXVII, 320.
5. New York, 1921, p. 143.

excellent study of Ruskin, could say in 1951 that "the careful tracing of Carlyle's influence on Ruskin remains to be done. It is a remarkable omission of scholarship."[6] Townsend's challenge has not yet been fully answered, but recent steps have been taken in the right direction. Within the last ten years, scattered comparisons of some of the ideas of Carlyle and Ruskin have been made in an article by William R. Thurman and in excellent books on Ruskin by George Landow and James Sherburne;[7] and new efforts have been made to examine previously unpublished or unnoticed materials concerning the relationship between the two great Victorians. The chief contribution in this area is C. R. Sanders' invaluable article of 1958,[8] in which Professor Sanders adeptly examines the thirty-six then known letters from Carlyle to Ruskin (nineteen of which were published for the first time) "to look at Ruskin through Carlyle's eyes."[9] A few years later Charles Kegel combined the new material from Sanders with published material drawn from previous Ruskin scholarship and wrote a ten-page article which surveyed the general course of Ruskin's close personal affection for Carlyle;[10] but it was far too brief, and it remained in the tradition of uncritical reassertion of Ruskin's strong dependence upon Carlyle.[11]

Following this work and with the help of Dr. Sanders, the present writer has been collecting and editing the complete correspondence between Carlyle and Ruskin for several years now, as well as con-

6. F. G. Townsend, *Ruskin and the Landscape Feeling* (Urbana, Ill., 1951), p. 64 n.

7. See William R. Thurman, "Carlyle, Browning, and Ruskin on One Purpose of Art," *South Atlantic Bulletin*, 37 (May 1972), 52–57; George P. Landow, *The Aesthetic and Critical Theories of John Ruskin* (Princeton, 1971); and James Clark Sherburne, *John Ruskin, or the Ambiguities of Abundance: A Study in Social and Economic Criticism* (Cambridge, Mass., 1972).

8. "Carlyle's Letters to Ruskin: A Finding List with Some Unpublished Letters and Comments," *Bulletin of the John Rylands Library* (Sept. 1958), 208–238. Cited below as Sanders, *CLR*.

9. Sanders, *CLR*, p. 208.

10. C. Kegel, "Carlyle and Ruskin: An Influential Friendship," *Brigham Young University Studies*, 5 (Spring-Summer 1964), 219–229.

11. Other brief articles should also be mentioned here: Donald R. Swanson's "Ruskin and His 'Master,'" *Victorian Newsletter*, 31 (Spring 1967), 56–59, and Roger Fulford's "Ruskin's Notes on Carlyle," *Times Literary Supplement*, 16 April 1971, p. 453, which discusses for the first time the markings and marginal comments Ruskin made in 1889 in his personal copy of C. E. Norton's edition of *The Early Letters of Carlyle*. Fulford's article brings to light the mixture of irascible and astute comments that are, as he says, "among the very last things written by Ruskin" before his final insanity. Eloise K. Goreau's "Carlyle and Ruskin: The Private Side of the Public Coin," *Victorian Newsletter*, 46 (Fall 1974), 15–19, overcorrects the imbalance of previous scholarship by too strongly emphasizing Ruskin's independence of Carlyle.

sulting the various repositories of Carlyle and Ruskin material in both America and Great Britain.[12] While nothing startling or dramatic has been unearthed, there has been more than enough to provide many new details about the nature and duration of the Carlyle-Ruskin relationship, and there is much fresh suggestion for further inquiry. Accordingly, the present writer would like to take still another step towards Townsend's unreached horizon by offering the reader a more complete history of Ruskin's discipleship to Carlyle— a broader and more detailed picture, as it were, made possible for the first time because the letters and related material let us see the continuum of the Carlyle-Ruskin relationship, with its emergent patterns, shifting emphases, and varying points of intensity. There is not room here for much more than a brief, highlighted history, of course, but it is hoped that the combination of broad perspective and new detail will at least allow the reader to see the subject steadily and whole, and that one may thus be able to form some general and tentative revaluation of Ruskin's discipleship.

That discipleship is more complex than previous scholarship would have us believe. The chief complication arises from the fact that Ruskin's relationship to Carlyle was not merely intellectual, but deeply personal and emotional; and no surveyor of the subject can afford to ignore either aspect in concentrating upon the other. Ruskin knew Carlyle's works throughout the last sixty years of his life; but he was also a close friend of Carlyle's for at least thirty-one of those years, from the time he was thirty-one until he was sixty-two. Anyone familiar with Ruskin's life knows that while these were the years when his literary powers were at their height and his social philosophy was developed fully, they were also the years in which he suffered from a gradual progression of physical and psychic problems which was to end in the pathetic mental derangement of the final eleven years of his life (he died in 1900). Carlyle thus became linked to both the intellect and the heart of Ruskin, and any attempt to estimate Ruskin as his disciple must cope with the trying fact that Ruskin's dual dependence upon Carlyle is often difficult to

12. A ten-year search has so far located approximately one hundred and fifty letters between Carlyle and Ruskin, covering a twenty-eight-year period from 1851 to 1879. Seventy-five of these have not yet been published. In addition, there are approximately fifty letters (thirty unpublished) between Ruskin and Jane Carlyle, Ruskin and Carlyle's niece Mary Aitken, Thomas Carlyle and Ruskin's father, and (one letter) between Carlyle's brother John and Ruskin.

separate from an independence of which Ruskin was not always aware. When one surveys the whole course of that discipleship, it would seem that, paradoxically, Ruskin's allegiance to Carlyle was always strong enough to be the chief influence upon the major changes in his career, but never really strong enough to erase Ruskin's own identity as a literary and prophetical influence upon his age. The pattern which emerges is in fact similar to the pattern of relationship between Ruskin and his father—one of independence in the midst of dependence, conducted under Ruskin's changing concepts of himself.

A favorite piece of evidence for demonstrating Ruskin's discipleship to Carlyle has always been the seemingly sudden transformation of Ruskin from Art Critic to Social Critic at the time of the publication of *Unto This Last* in 1860. There can be do doubt that Carlyle did much to inspire this transformation, but when one examines this supposed dividing line in Ruskin's career, deep and immediate questions arise. First, Ruskin's transformation was not really so sudden as it seemed, for much of his social criticism can be found emerging throughout his works for at least a full decade before 1860. Secondly, while it is known, and Ruskin himself admitted, that Carlyle's thought influenced these works, Ruskin at the time was careful to define the limits of Carlyle's influence and insist that he had come upon his thoughts independently. When Ruskin stated in volume III of *Modern Painters* that Carlyle's thought colored his own continually,[13] he added the proviso, "but what I have of my own is still there,"[14] and in a letter to Carlyle on 23 January 1855 he discussed his debt to Carlyle in the following terms:

it is very difficult always to know how much one is indebted to other people. . . . The fact is, it is very possible for two people to hit *sometimes* on the same thought—and I have over and over again been somewhat vexed as well as surprised at finding what I *had* and *knew* I had, worked out for myself, corresponded very closely to things that you had said much better. . . . How much your general influence has told upon me, I know not— but I always confess it—or rather boast of it, in conversation about you.[15]

While it is tempting to see this statement as a necessary assertion of originality for the sake of Ruskin's self-respect, it is probably wiser to accept it as literally true. Ruskin's life and works for more than a

13. Quoted above, in the text at n. 3.
14. Ruskin, *Works*, V, 428.   15. Ibid., XXXVI, 183–184.

decade prior to 1855 show a gradual awakening of attention to social problems which seems to have been independently precipitated; and the development of his social conscience in the 1840's seems to have been a natural one which was really hastened and fortified, rather than instigated, by his concurrent exposure first to Carlyle's works and then to Carlyle himself. During those years, Ruskin seems to have brought himself into a condition of instinctive sympathy towards Carlyle's thought, and he was ripe for the strong influence of Carlyle's personality when he finally met Carlyle at the end of that decade.

Ruskin's first reading of Carlyle seems to have occurred in 1841. In a letter to W. H. Harrison, dated 6 June 1841, he inquired: "What are these Carlyle lectures [i.e., *Heroes and Hero-Worship*]? People are making a fuss about them, and from what I see in the reviews, they seem absolute bombast—taking bombast, I suppose, making everybody think himself a hero." [16] The first mention of Carlyle in his diary, entered on the same day but obviously after the letter to Harrison, shows that he had just read Carlyle's *Heroes*, and his reaction was negative. [17] Despite this, W. G. Collingwood, a friend and biographer of Ruskin, has speculated that Ruskin "might . . . have been spurred the more into energy by that enthusiastic doctrine of action," [18] for Ruskin had just had an intense period of depression and (in a decision which is the first in a series which runs as a motif through his life) had resolved to "*do* something, to *be* something useful," [19] and to begin *Modern Painters* with the knowledge that he was now employed on a definite mission. Both E. T. Cook and Joan Evans have also endorsed this belief that Carlyle may have inspired Ruskin towards the writing of *Modern Painters*,[20] but there is little evidence to prove it.

Mrs. Anne Thackeray Ritchie has remarked that Ruskin "came under Carlyle's influence" somewhere "between the publication of the first and second volumes of *Modern Painters*," [21] (i.e., between

16. Ibid., p. 25.
17. See *The Diaries of John Ruskin*, ed. Joan Evans and J. H. Whitehouse (Oxford, 1956), I, 199. Ruskin says, "Read some of Carlyle's lectures. Bombast, I think; altogether approves of Mahomet, and talks like a girl of his 'black eyes.' "
18. Collingwood, *The Life and Work of John Ruskin* (London, 1893), I, 94.
19. Ibid.
20. See Cook's article in the *DNB*, and Joan Evans in *John Ruskin* (London, 1954), p. 83.
21. *Records of Tennyson, Ruskin, and Browning* (London, 1892), p. 103.

1843 and 1846), and we do know that Ruskin first read Carlyle's *Past and Present* in 1843, shortly after the book was published.[22] This may have been a more momentous event, for *Past and Present* was one of the three books by Carlyle which most influenced Ruskin throughout his career; but there were too many other influences, and too many independently achieved parallels to Carlyle's thought in Ruskin's life at the time, to let us make a clear judgment about the immediate effect of *Past and Present*. The two men, after all, shared a common Romantic heritage in their belief that nature is in essence spiritual, vital, and organic, and as such could only be truly seen by non-empirical and intuitive modes of apprehension. They also shared the Romantic belief that the spiritual state of the perceiver is of utmost importance in the effort to see truth and beauty. It is not surprising, therefore, to find Ruskin insisting as early as 1845 that it was not so much the "love of frescoes" that man needed; it was the "love of God and his creatures; . . . a total change of character [in the] disgusting nineteenth century."[23]

The year 1845, in fact, has now come to be seen as a signal one in the history of Ruskin's thought. In that year, at the age of twenty-six, Ruskin felt guilty because of the easy luxury of his life. He described to his parents his feeling: "As I came back to my soufflée and Sillery, I felt sad at thinking how few were capable of having such enjoyment, and very doubtful whether it were at all proper for me to have it all to myself."[24] He was also beginning to feel alienated from his parents, and in a small but significant gesture of defiance he went to Italy by himself for the first time to prepare for his second volume of *Modern Painters*. There he opened his eyes to many new things. Not only did he first see the beauty of the early Italian painters, and so begin to question the Evangelical faith which could not account for his strong response to this "superstitious" art; but he also began to think more about social problems. Francis Townsend, for instance, feels that the tendency towards social criticism may actually have begun in 1845 because of Ruskin's recognition in Italy that the laws of man correspond to the laws of nature.[25] In a recent edition of Ruskin's letters to his parents in 1845, Harold I. Shapiro has con-

22. See Derrick Leon, *Ruskin: The Great Victorian* (London, 1949), p. 239; and Ruskin's letter to George Richmond in his *Works*, XXXVII, 361.
23. Quoted in J. A. Hobson, *John Ruskin: Social Reformer* (London, 1898), p. 34.
24. Quoted in E. T. Cook, *The Life of John Ruskin* (London, 1911), I, 175.
25. Townsend, p. 32.

cluded that "one can see in the [Italian] tour, in the historical interest
which these new concerns inevitably aroused, in his reading of Sis-
mondi, in his observations of men and manners, and in his increasing
self-examination, the beginnings of his later social criticism. If, before
the tour began, [Ruskin] had serious doubts about what he was to do
with his life—and he seems to have had them—by the end of it he
had confirmed his vocation."[26] Finally, John D. Rosenberg has pointed
out that, by the end of 1846, Ruskin's new concern for society had
begun to show in his works to such an extent that it brought about a
change in the tenor of all subsequent writings, in which "Ruskin became less moved by the beauty of art and nature than by the waste,
mystery, and terror of life."[27] Clearly this *was* an important year for
Ruskin, and it produced many changes which were to lead to his
friendship with Carlyle.

After 1845, there began to appear some cracks in Ruskin's religious
devotion and in his faithfulness to his parents—cracks which continued to widen for the rest of his life. In 1846 he became depressed,
and early in 1847 his recovery from that depression produced, according to E. T. Cook, "inner questionings on the foundations of a
religious faith now first being shaken." This was followed by a visit
to a friend at Crossmount, where he had his first clear thoughts on
social questions—thoughts which Ruskin later remembered as being
"scattered afterwards up and down in *Fors* and *Munera Pulveris*."[28]

Through 1848 the uneasiness between him and his parents, his religion, and even his love of nature continued. The great revolutionary
events of 1848 increased his confusion. He was deeply affected, his
sympathies were aroused, and his sense of guilt grew: "I begin to feel
that all the work I have been doing . . . [is] ineffective and frivolous—
that these are not times for watching clouds or dreaming over quiet
waters, that more serious work is to be done." To another correspondent he wrote: "Tell me whether it is of any use to write or think
about painting any more, now . . . . I feel very doubtful whether I
am not wasting my life."[29] Quite clearly, Ruskin was experiencing a

26. H. I. Shapiro, *Ruskin in Italy: Letters to His Parents, 1845* (Oxford, 1972),
pp. xviii–xix.

27. J. D. Rosenberg, *The Darkening Glass: A Portrait of Ruskin's Genius* (New
York and London, 1961), p. 22.

28. Cook, *Life*, I, 212 and 215.

29. Cook, *Life*, I, 221–222. Ruskin to Mary Russell Mitford, 21 April 1848; and
Ruskin to George Richmond, 1 May 1848.

deep change of attitude and a crisis in self-definition which were to make him especially susceptible to Carlyle's urgent messages and personal power over others. Like Carlyle, he had come to distrust the judgment of the multitude by 1849, and he suspected any system which made that judgment the supreme tribunal of justice. In his *Seven Lamps of Architecture* of that year, he denounced the idea of liberty as the "most treacherous, indeed, of all phantoms," and in a true Carlylean manner he asserted that obedience to universal and social law is the foundation of real freedom.[30] The *Seven Lamps* contain many more hints of Ruskin's growing social concern—especially his interest in the question of the relationship between work and the inner condition of the worker. "I do not mean work in the sense of bread," he said, "I mean work in the sense of mental interest."[31] One sentence in particular shows the influence of Carlyle's *Past and Present*: "It is not enough to find men absolute subsistence; we should think of the manner of life which our demands necessitate; and endeavour . . . to make all our needs such as may, in the supply of them, raise, as well as feed, the poor."[32] These were indeed new notes for the great Art Critic to sing to his unwary public.

This point marks the first appearance of a consistent pattern that runs throughout Ruskin's life and has much to do with his nearness to Carlyle. Born in 1819, Ruskin had the habit of pausing at the end of every decade after 1839 to see how far he had come in life. This fascinating habit of self-review was prompted by his restless sense of mission and it was usually accompanied by a desire to do something useful with his life. In his 1868 lecture on "The Mystery of Life and Its Arts" Ruskin identified the decade of the 1840's as "the ten strongest years of my life (from twenty to thirty)"—and said that he spent them vainly in showing England the true worth of the painter Turner.[33] He then implied that his next decade was spent in putting futile effort into the work of architecture, which would bring him up to the year 1859, the time of his full commitment to social criticism. By the end of his talk he indicates that he is about to begin another, still different, decade in his life. As we shall see, what is especially significant about this pattern is that Carlyle was in some way involved

30. Ruskin, *Works*, VIII, 248 and 250.
31. Ibid., p. 261.
32. Ibid., p. 264.   33. Ibid., XVIII, 148.

in every one of Ruskin's ten-year intervals of self-review and prep-aration for change after 1839, at increasing degrees of intensity.

When one reviews the growth of Ruskin's social conscience, fa-milial difficulties, and religious doubts throughout the 1840's, and then considers his need to do "more serious work" in 1849, it becomes obvious that Thomas Carlyle was probably the one man in England who could meet Ruskin's personal needs at that time. For by 1849 the condition of Ruskin coincided well with the condition of Carlyle himself. The idea of a vital, dynamically whole society which could foster the growth of each individual in it to the highest level of his inner capacities became the chief preoccupation of Carlyle in the 1840's and was the source of his subsequently intense denunciation of his own society. Carlyle saw that idea threatened and trampled on by the "juggernaut" of "mechanism" in his own day, and as the 1840's ended he tried ever more desperately to make his fellow men open their spiritual eyes and look at the true "facts" of reality. He felt strongly that England especially would suffer death and decay un-less each Englishman learned to distinguish sham from the reality of Nature's true laws. When Ruskin finally met Carlyle personally some-time in 1850,[34] he met a man who, in Emerson's words, had come to "think it the only question for wise men, instead of art and fine fan-cies and poetry and such things, to address themselves to the prob-lems of society."[35] For a man in Ruskin's state the call from the recent author of the *Latter-Day Pamphlets* to work strenuously upon the "condition-of-England question" could not have been more time-ly. It was sent out to a brilliant young man with a recently galvanized sense of mission, extended sympathies for the working classes, and broadened views on many matters—especially religion.

The earliest record of Ruskin's meeting with Carlyle shows Ruskin seeking Carlyle's advice on religion. John Welsh, in his journal of 6

34. The date of Ruskin's first meeting with Carlyle has never been exactly de-termined, but the best available evidence points to 1850 as the most likely year. A letter published in Sanders, *CLR*, p. 208, from Carlyle to his brother John on 18 December 1850, speaks of a recent visit by "Ruskin and Wife" in terms which suggest that Carlyle had not known Ruskin very long. The earliest known witnessing of a meeting between Carlyle and Ruskin is an entry in the journal of Mrs. Carlyle's cousin John Welsh, which records a visit by Ruskin to Carlyle's house just before 6 July 1850. See Leonard Huxley, "A Sheaf of Letters from Jane Welsh Carlyle," *Cornhill Magazine*, NS 41 (Nov. 1926), 629.

35. *The Complete Works of Ralph Waldo Emerson*, ed. E. E. Emerson (Boston and New York, 1904), X, 497.

July 1850, speaks of a visit made to Carlyle in which "Mr. Ruskin drew out Mr. Carlyle's religious opinions and by judicious questioning hemmed him into expressing his whole *confession*. He denies the personal existence of a devil—he says that he feels a devil within him but denies that any power can clip the wings of that devil but his own. Christianity seems to be with him out of date and something else must supply its place although what it is he gives no utterance."[36] Welsh's summary may perhaps be mildly uncomprehending, but it shows nicely the kind of religious temperament Ruskin was consulting. Long before 1850 Carlyle had left his "Hebrew old clothes" behind him, and urged a return to the basic truths of humanity found in all religions. Ruskin, whose weakening faith had been further diminished by his studies of geology, now found a man who could understand his feelings and help him to broaden his views. As Van A. Burd has recently said of Ruskin at this time, "Geology having breached his orthodoxy, as it did Tennyson's, Ruskin's mind was now open to other forces. In Thomas Carlyle . . . he found another Evangelist brought up in the Calvinism of the same lowland Scotland from which he himself was descended, and one who had known the 'fever-paroxysms of Doubt.' . . . Inspired by German idealism he brought Ruskin in touch with a new tolerance based on a universal religion which knew no denominational creeds. . . . This tolerance, having been rooted in Ruskin, grew steadily after 1850."[37] Not long after his conversation with Carlyle, Ruskin published in March 1851 the first volume of his *Stones of Venice*, in which his contrast between a nation's *vital* religion and its superficial *formal* religion much resembles Carlyle's broad view of religion as simply the primary vital fact in men's life. *The Stones of Venice*, in fact, shows Ruskin arriving at Carlylean perceptions in many different ways. Its famous chapter "The Nature of Gothic," with its assault upon the degrading nature of contemporary industrial work and its Carlylean contrast of the modern with the medieval workman, is of course the most obvious example. But Francis Townsend has also noted that Ruskin's concept of Nature came to resemble Carlyle's even more closely by the time of the second volume of *The Stones of Venice*. Ruskin, Townsend remarked, now insisted that the true artist

36. Quoted in Huxley, cited in n. 34 above.
37. Van Akin Burd, *The Winnington Letters: John Ruskin's Correspondence with Margaret Alexis Bell and the Children of Winnington Hall* (Cambridge, Mass., and London, 1969), pp. 67–68.

must "face the facts" of Nature, portraying all without knowing what the good of it is, and yet confident that the good will emerge[38]—a concept very similar to that expressed by Carlyle in *Past and Present* and in some sections of his *Latter-Day Pamphlets*. We may also note that in the first volume of *Stones*, Ruskin drew a parallel between the vitally religious national character of Venice and the rise of Venice's best *political* leaders as well as its artists—a parallel which was part of Ruskin's more general warning that his history of the rise and fall of Venice might have exact relevance to the state of contemporary England.[39]

On 6 March 1851 Ruskin also published a pamphlet entitled "Notes on the Construction of Sheepfolds." This work was a somewhat harsh attempt to separate the Gothic Revival from its association with the revival of Roman Catholicism in England. However, it also appealed for unity within the Protestant church by insisting that a general allegiance to the Scriptures themselves would eliminate all schisms, and by further insisting that man's Christianity is determined not by what he professes but how he conducts his life. These views, of course, are still further evidence of Ruskin's wider search for religious truth under Carlyle's influence. They also present evidence that Ruskin's thought was now beginning to flow into the larger stream of the Broad Church Movement—a stream which sprang from the inexhaustible mind of S. T. Coleridge and which had by 1850 caught up Carlyle and many others in its strong currents. The "Sheepfolds" pamphlet, in fact, prompted the Reverend F. D. Maurice, who by that time had become the chief guide and inspiration of the movement, to write to Ruskin. As a result, Ruskin was brought into close contact with Maurice and his friends throughout the 1850's. The more liberal tendencies in Ruskin's religious thought were thus intensified; and the influence of Carlyle's doctrines of work and social involvement was reinforced by Ruskin's eventual friendship with the men who had founded the Christian Socialist movement under Maurice's direction. The Christian Socialists were especially devoted to improving the lot of the working classes through practical action and education; and when they founded their Working Men's College in October of 1854, Ruskin agreed to teach a drawing class and remained active in the College until 1860. Although he never became a member of the Christian Socialists, it is clear that he sympathized with their

38. Townsend, pp. 59–64. 39. See Ruskin, *Works*, IX, 17 ff.

aims. His sympathy is even more easily explained by the fact that
the Christian Socialists had also been influenced by Carlyle's writings. However tenuous the question of Ruskin's involvement with the
Christian Socialists may be, there is thus at least a visible consistency
behind his attractions to the movement in the early 1850's.[40]

Carlyle himself saw this and all the other signs of Ruskin's development towards his own views. His initial response to Ruskin was
ambiguous, for he spoke of him as a "dainty dilettante soul,"[41] had
an innate aversion to Ruskin's preoccupation with the Fine Arts, and
had difficulty tolerating Ruskin's voluble and effervescent personality,
which he compared to "a bottle of beautiful *soda-water*."[42] And yet
he saw much in Ruskin that he admired. He sensed Ruskin's essential
similarity of attitude and encouraged the growth of Ruskin's social
conscience at a time in the 1850's when Ruskin's own father was wor-
riedly trying to suppress such tendencies.[43] His letter to Ruskin of

40. The question of Ruskin's specific indebtedness to the Broad Church movement
—and especially to that movement's offspring, the Christian Socialists—is still unan-
swered. C. R. Sanders, in his *Coleridge and the Broad Church Movement* (Durham,
N.C., 1942), p. 264, first drew attention to the apparent connection, but it has not
been explored. Charles E. Raven, in his *Christian Socialism: 1848–1854* (London,
1920), pp. 352–353, says that Ruskin was one of the teachers of the Working Men's
College who were "strangers to the Christian Socialists" in 1854, and then says that
"the experience of working men which he [Ruskin] obtained during the years of
his connection" with the College "gave him his first impulse" to write "his sociological
books." He then claims that the influence of these books was immense, "and here
again the ultimate origin of that influence is the Christian Socialist Movement."
When one asks why Carlyle might not be included as an earlier origin of that influence, one is confronted with Raven's assertion that, while Carlyle contributed to
the inspiration behind the Christian Socialist Movement, "it is not to Carlyle that
it owes any original inspiration," for the real founder of the movement was John
Malcolm Ludlow (pp. 54–56). Van Akin Burd, in his introduction to the *Winnington
Letters*, pp. 68–70, provides a more balanced, though less assertive, view. He explains
that Ruskin had never met Coleridge or any of the "first generation of Coleridge's
disciples"—John Sterling, Connop Thirlwall, Julius C. Hare, and Thomas Arnold. By
1850, however, Ruskin had known some of the "second generation" Coleridgeans,
such as Arthur P. Stanley and F. W. Robertson. He met Maurice in 1851, and
probably met Benjamin Jowett before 1855. As for the Christian Socialists, Burd
indicates that "Ruskin was wary of organized movements such as Christian Socialism,
but still he read Kingsley's novels, defended him in 1853 against the 'practical people,'
and spoke well of *Alton Locke*" in 1856. Burd adds the fascinating detail that Ruskin's
friend Miss Bell—herself a believer in Broad Church views—had a portrait of Ruskin
placed alongside those of F. D. Maurice and Julius C. Hare in a room in her school,
which "suggests that she must have sensed that Ruskin had some affinity with these
spiritual godsons of Coleridge."
41. In his letter to his brother John, 18 Dec. 1850, quoted in Sanders, *CLR*, p. 209.
42. From his letter to his brother John, 27 Nov. 1855, quoted in Sanders, *CLR*, p. 213.
43. When Ruskin, in 1851, wrote three letters to the *Times* on the subjects of
taxation, voting, and education, his shocked father forbade their being printed, calling

9 March 1851 praised *The Stones of Venice* for its social message especially, and seemed aware that Ruskin was about to embark on a new voyage towards social criticism. "The spirit and purport of these Critical Studies of yours are a singular sign of the times to me, and a very gratifying one," he wrote; "Right good speed to you, and victorious arrival on the farther shore!" Noting the element of historical comparison and warning to England in Ruskin's work, he then added his own opinion on the future and made gracious reference to Ruskin's "Notes on the Construction of Sheepfolds":

It is a quite new "renaissance" I believe, we are getting into just now; either towards new, *wider* manhood, *high* again as the eternal stars, or else into final death, and the murk of Gehenna for evermore! A dreadful process, but a needful and inevitable one; nor do I doubt at all which way the issue will be, though which of the extant nations are to get included in it, and which to be trampled out and abolished in the process, may be very doubtful. God is great:—and sure enough, the changes in the construction of Sheepfolds, as well as in other things, will require to be very considerable! [44]

There is no doubt that Ruskin was encouraged by this praise at this crucial time in his life. He could now be assured that his great new acquaintance was not only in favor of his efforts, but had perceived that he had in Ruskin an independent ally in the war against the shams and amorality of mid-Victorian industrial society. Although Ruskin continued to be a prophet of Art during the early 1850's, he had also joined Carlyle in preaching the salvation of humanity. Since Ruskin and Carlyle both emphasized the relationship between true sight and the moral condition of the perceiver, they now sorrowfully agreed that the question of vision was deeply fused with the "condition-of-England" question. From 1850 onward they were together in demanding the "change of heart" that was necessary for the change of sight that could produce a national eye for worth.

But once again, we must beware of asserting that Ruskin had now become an actual disciple of Carlyle. Their letters show that the two men developed closer personal bonds after the annulment of Ruskin's marriage in 1854, and that Ruskin relied all the more on Carlyle's encouragement as he proceeded through his transitional decade of the

---

Ruskin's writings on politics "Slum Buildings which are liable to be knocked down." See Ruskin, *Works*, XII, lxxxiv.

44. In Collingwood, I, 151–152.

1850's. But they also show that Ruskin did not yet think of himself as a follower of any "master." While he began to lose interest in criticism of Art as early as 1856 and concurrently began to study other social and philosophical problems, he still thought of himself as an independent student trying to work out problems on his own. An extremely interesting letter to Carlyle in October of 1855 shows not only his scattered and divided interests at the time but also his early, independent preparation for his future metamorphosis into a full-fledged social critic in 1860.

In speaking of his busy preparations for third and fourth volumes of *Modern Painters*, Ruskin says significantly: "I have had to make various remarks on German Metaphysics, on Poetry, on Political Economy . . . all of which subjects I have had to 'read up' accordingly. . . . My studies of political economy have induced me to think also that nobody knows anything about that; and I am at present engaged in an investigation, on independent principles, of the nature of money, rent, and taxes, in an abstract form, which sometimes keeps me awake all night."[45] Here and elsewhere Ruskin seems in fact to be thinking of himself as a student who has finished his apprenticeship work in Art by 1856 and is slowly preparing for the new task that lies ahead, although with great uncertainty and with eventual despair. In a preliminary sally into social criticism he delivered his lecture on "The Political Economy of Art" in December of 1857, maintaining his stance of independence (while at the same time adopting a deft argumentative strategy) by declaring that he had "never read any author on political economy, except Adam Smith, twenty years ago."[46] The strain of developing such an independent transformation, however, proved to be a telling one after 1857. With Carlyle's encouragement, Ruskin was now entering the crucial period in which he would finally reject both his mother's Evangelical beliefs and his father's mercantile principles. It would not be long before he would again sink into depressive feelings and inevitably repeat the familiar

45. Published in Collingwood's one-volume revised edition of his *Life and Work of Ruskin* (London, 1900), pp. 158–159. Cited below as Collingwood (rev.).

46. Ruskin, *Works*, XVI, 9–10. Ruskin, in this lecture, also moves independently into a concept that Carlyle held. He asserts that a nation is a family joined together in fraternity, and adds that where there is brotherhood, there must be a "head, or father, as well" (Ruskin, *Works*, XVI, 24). For further discussion see Gaylord C. LeRoy, *Perplexed Prophets* (Philadelphia, 1953), p. 92.

pattern of soul-searching that emerged at the end of every decade of his life.

In the meantime, Carlyle had been watching Ruskin's progress since 1855 with great hopes, but also with considerable reservations. He much admired Ruskin's sincerity and style, and told him so many times. "The feeling you have about matters is altogether my own," he wrote in December of 1855.[47] In March of 1856 he assured Ruskin, "Your book is scattering the astonished cohorts of chaos into strange agitated groups, I perceive . . . a salutary [effect] by way of preliminary. Go on and prosper."[48] In May of 1856, after reading the fourth volume of *Modern Painters*, he told Ruskin: "You have an enviable and admirable power of clearing off, in articulate swift piercing utterance, the divine indignation that may be lying in you against the genus charlatan; . . . and proceed[ing] to new enterprises: . . . be thankful to Heaven."[49] But Carlyle was equally concerned about Ruskin's mercurial mind, his instability, and his impatient idealism. "My impression generally is that you go too fast," he wrote to Ruskin on 23 May 1855; "in many senses this;—and that you will have to learn . . . what infinite profit there occasionally is in sitting absolutely down . . . and *doing nothing*."[50] Each one of the letters quoted above also contains some form of criticism or cautionary advice for Ruskin. The letter of 6 December 1855 warns Ruskin: "you have not yet hacked your sword blunt in striking at the stony head of Human Stupidity, but rush in upon it as if it were *cleavable* or conquerable,— more power to your elbow." And Carlyle's letter of 2 May 1856 urges Ruskin to "be gentle withal" with the "comfortable R.A." who reads Ruskin's books but cannot change. "Consider," Carlyle warns, "that it is a stupid bedrid old world, *torpid* except at meal-time this long while; and never would, in Art or elsewhere, correspond anyway handsomely to the Ideal of its duties." Despite these criticisms, Carlyle urged Ruskin to visit him more often, and he began to read Ruskin's works with waxing interest as Ruskin approached the fitful end of the decade.

In 1858 Ruskin's long debate with his Evangelical religion finally ended in a Waldensian chapel in Turin, where, as is well known, he

47. 6 Dec. 1855, published in Sanders, *CLR*, p. 214.
48. 5 March 1856, hitherto unpublished, MS: NLS, Acc. 3187.
49. 2 May 1856, hitherto unpublished, MS: NLS, Acc. 3187.
50. Sanders, *CLR*, pp. 211–212.

heard a "little squeaking idiot" preach Calvinistic damnation and left "a conclusively unconverted man."[51] His growing alienation from his parents, and his increased dedication to the relief of human misery and folly, rendered him depressed and paralyzed in will. He felt himself alienated from everything and once again, as in 1849, was overcome with a sense of uselessness. In March of 1859 he wrote to the Carlyles about his "entirely dim notions of what ought to be done,"[52] and on the twenty-third of November in the same year he told Mrs. Carlyle: "I think I shall have to give up painting—writing—talking—everything but reading—and I read little now but Mr. Carlyle. Fiction sickens me because it is fiction. . . . Truth depresses me because it is true."[53] In the midst of this dark period, Carlyle again encouraged Ruskin. "That heaving about," he said in a letter of 19 April 1859, "and circling among the eddies, is not a pleasant process; but you will . . . have various bouts of this kind in your wide voyage; and they are not unsalutory, still less can be dispensed with, tho' so disagreeable to the natural man."[54] His efforts were apparently effective. In gratitude, Ruskin told Carlyle in late December of 1859, "I'm going to make Christmas and New Year's presents of 'Past and Present' chiefly. I find everything that has to be said on any matter is all in that, and other people may for ever hold their peace."[55] He then went off to Chamonix in May of 1860, and in July the first of his essays that were collectively called *Unto This Last* appeared in the *Cornhill Magazine*.

However much it may have been inspired by Ruskin's long association with Carlyle, *Unto This Last* was strictly Ruskin's own book. In its subtle style, sharp analysis, and specific identification of issues, it represents the fructification of the social conscience that had been growing in Ruskin since the mid-1840's. Although Ruskin told a friend that Carlyle had "led the way" for the insights in the book,[56] it is obvious that the work is the development of the studies that Ruskin had been pursuing "on independent principles" since 1855. It is significant that Carlyle is nowhere mentioned in the work. Ruskin, it would seem, still did not think of himself as a dependent thinker or a spokesman for any master's key thoughts. Rather, he seems to have thought of himself as the spokesman for that common experience of

51. Ruskin, *Works*, XXIX, 89.   52. Ruskin, *Works*, XXXV, 304.
53. MS: NLS, 555.4.   54. Sanders, *CLR*, p. 215.
55. MS: NLS, 555.7.
56. See his letter to Dr. John Brown, 11 Nov. 1860, in Ruskin, *Works*, XXXVI, 349.

everyman which exposed the false view of man propounded by the political economists of the day, and it is on this ground—his own—that he chose to stand or fall in public view.

Unfortunately, he fell. The essays were denounced and ridiculed so violently that Thackeray, the editor of the *Cornhill*, had to stop publishing them after the October number. Ruskin was more dismayed than he had ever been before. "I cannot write when I have no audience," he wrote to his father on 15 November 1861. "Those papers on political economy fairly tried 80,000 British public with my best work; they couldn't taste it; and I can give them no more."[57] His parents had also been alarmed over his supposedly new ideas, and this further estranged him from them. Feeling rejected by both his British audience and his parents, Ruskin went in self-imposed exile to Switzerland in the years 1861–1863. Again his feeling of uselessness and of religious doubt returned, and his health declined. On 28 August 1861 he wrote to Carlyle that he could "do nothing this year," and was "expecting only death" (that is, he no longer believed in the soul's immortality). "The great questions about Nature and God" had so overwhelmed him that both his thoughts and his health were "overturned."[58]

But Ruskin *did* have an audience, and a powerful one—Thomas Carlyle. *Unto This Last* seemed to him to be the fulfillment of all his hopes for Ruskin, and he responded with enthusiasm. On 29 October 1860 he sent Ruskin a magnificent letter of praise for the book, and more or less officially confirmed the younger man as his acknowledged aide in the lonely battle against the host of "Dismal-Science people": "If you chose to stand to that kind of work for the next seven years, and work out there a result like what you have done in Painting: yes, there were a 'something to do,'—not easily measurable in importance to these sunk ages. Meantime my joy is great to find myself henceforth in a minority of *two* at any rate!"[59] To bolster Ruskin's spirits further, he made many visits to Ruskin and his parents in 1860 and 1861, trying hard to mend the rift between parents and son. And he also tried hard to keep Ruskin writing. In the summer of 1861 he wrote a letter to James Anthony Froude, editor of *Fraser's Magazine*, upon which Froude wrote to Ruskin, offering to publish any new

57. Cook, *Life*, II, 42.   58. Ruskin, *Works*, XXXVI, 382.
59. In Van Akin Burd, "Ruskin's Antidote to Carlyle's Purges," *Boston University Studies in English*, 3 (1957), 51–57.

comments Ruskin cared to make about political economy. It was enough to wake Ruskin into further effort. The result was a series of "Essays on Political Economy" which appeared in *Fraser's* during 1862, and which were published in book form ten years later as *Munera Pulveris*, with a dedication by Ruskin to "the man who has urged me to all chief labour—Thomas Carlyle."

When public outrage caused Froude to stop publishing Ruskin's "Essays on Political Economy," however, Ruskin again despaired of continuing. Even before the essays had begun to be published, Ruskin had written to C. E. Norton: "But all things seem to go wrong at present. . . . I have earache, indigestion, and appear on the whole to be only beginning my walk through the 'Rue St. Thomas de l'Enfer' on my way to 'das Ewige Nein.' "[60] The public's hostile reaction to the "Essays," coming when Ruskin was in such a condition, seemed to confirm his worst thoughts about the world and himself; and for a time he resolved to dwell in permanent exile in Mornex.

But by this time Carlyle was too much in favor of Ruskin's writings to allow them to stop. He praised Ruskin's efforts before many of his friends, wrote to Ruskin's father to assure him of his son's real greatness, and wrote letters to Ruskin himself in which he described the "Essays" as "rising into the sphere of Plato."[61] By the middle of 1864 Ruskin felt better and plunged into new work.

When we look at the works that Ruskin wrote from 1862 onward, an interesting fact appears: these works are frequently filled with direct quotations from Carlyle, and in them Ruskin proclaims his intellectual obligations to Carlyle in many ways. In a footnote to the thirty-seventh paragraph of the second "Essay on Political Economy" (September 1862), for instance, Ruskin says that he has not cited authorities to support his statements because, in scattered passages in Carlyle's *Sartor Resartus, Past and Present*, and *Latter-Day Pamphlets*, "all has been said that needs to be said, and far better than I shall ever say it again." Similar self-effacing references to Carlyle's precedence and superiority appear often in Ruskin's works thereafter, ostensibly signifying his strong declaration of discipleship to Carlyle. When we remember Ruskin's earlier assertions of independence, it would seem that Ruskin had now come to think of himself as an actual

60. 19 Jan. 1862, in Ruskin, *Works*, XXXVI, 405.
61. E.g., 30 June 1862, in Collingwood (rev.), p. 202.

follower of Carlyle's doctrines and therefore felt that he should give
public reverence to his "master"; but it also seems that this was a very
deliberate decision. Ruskin's motivations remain difficult to simplify
at this point. In 1862, for instance, he told his father that he thought
himself "far the inferior of men like . . . Carlyle,"[62] and so his publicly
avowed allegiance to Carlyle may simply have been genuine admiration for a better man. Then, too, Carlyle had "confirmed" him as a
disciple in his letter of 29 October 1860. Following a suggestion from
H. V. Routh, we must also remember that Ruskin had to face the
hostility of the public by himself after the publication of *Unto This
Last*,[63] and that frightful experience may have convinced him that
it would henceforth be wise to be more visibly associated with a man
who was respected by that same public as one of its two greatest
sages (Tennyson being the other). Faced with further tasks of social
criticism, and having grown much closer to Carlyle in the early 1860's,
Ruskin found it intellectually necessary to be influenced by Carlyle,
psychologically comforting to be intimate with him, and professional-
ly necessary to be deferential to him.

Whatever the motivations on Ruskin's part, the years from 1860
to 1867 were the best and strongest period of both friendship and
discipleship for Ruskin and Carlyle. During these years, the two men
were brought closer together by the deaths of Ruskin's father in 1864
and Mrs. Carlyle in 1866. They exchanged many letters and pleasant
visits, with Carlyle continually praising Ruskin's writings and Ruskin
constantly trying to cheer Carlyle out of the sense of being written
out, old, and ultimately ineffective.

If any time were to be cited as that in which Carlyle and Ruskin
reached their highest point of mutual affection and action, perhaps
the months between the spring of 1866 and the spring of 1867 should
be it. After this time, Ruskin's growing mental troubles and Carlyle's
advanced old age produced a gradual lessening of sympathies; but
during this time both men were genuinely close to one another.
After his wife's death in April 1866, Carlyle needed Ruskin as much as
Ruskin needed Carlyle, and he asked Ruskin to "come *oftener* to see

62. 29 June 1862. MS: Yale.
63. *Money, Morals, and Manners* (London, 1935), pp. 78–79. Routh claims that
only Ruskin earned the "implacable hostility" of educated conservatives. "Carlyle and
Froude might denounce . . . the economic thinkers. Ruskin dares to meet them
on their own ground and to demonstrate the errors of their ways."

me, and speak *more* frankly to me (for I am very true to your highest interests and you) while I still remain here."[64] And Ruskin, in helping Carlyle on the defense committee for the unlucky Governor Eyre of Jamaica in 1866, could be rewarded by the feeling of actually standing side by side with Carlyle, working, if only for a month, in a truly active partnership or "minority of *two*." In his *Time and Tide* letters of the spring of 1867 Ruskin in fact said of Carlyle, "I only speak of myself together with him as a son might speak of his father and himself, not on any term of other equality."[65] The two men had reached a plane of friendship that rose above their consciousness of each other's weaknesses and was soon to become a quasi-filial relationship. Out of such strength, it seemed, Ruskin could "go on and prosper" in his social mission for many years to come.

But there were soon ominous signs that this was not to be. In 1867 Ruskin began to have the mental symptoms which he later called "the first warning mischief to my health."[66] They were the sufferings prelusive to Ruskin's eventual mental breakdown over twenty years later—morbid fits of despondency, sleeplessness, nervous prostration, floating sparks imagined before his eyes, and many dreams and nightmares—and they were to increase in frequency as the years wore on. By 1867 also, Ruskin was in the midst of an agitated three-year waiting period imposed upon him when he proposed marriage to a young Irish girl, Rose LaTouche, in 1866. The story of Ruskin's love for the lovely but pathetic Rose is too long and well-known to retell here. One can only say that by May of 1867 she was in his mind constantly, and his obsession over her kept him in frequent inner turmoil until her death in 1875, with severe effect upon his personality. It even caused a short-lived quarrel between Carlyle and Ruskin during the summer of 1867. In late May of that year, when Carlyle publicly denied the report of a conversation of his that had been published in one of Ruskin's *Time and Tide* letters, Ruskin felt that Carlyle had injured his chances to gain the hand of Rose LaTouche. He assailed Carlyle intemperately for two months. Some indication of the depth of his irrationality can be seen in this passage from his letter to Carlyle on 12 June 1867:

One of the things that has struck deepest in me, in this, is the heartlessness with which, when I had told you that I was fighting a battle of bitterest

64. 10 May 1866, in Ruskin, *Works*, XVIII, xlvii.
65. Ruskin, *Works*, XVII 476.   66. Quoted in Cook, *Life*, II, 114.

pain, now at the very crisis when of all things . . . honour should be done for me by all who loved me for my love's sake—that you should have forgotten . . . and written the most dishonouring words that could be set down in public sight. . . . Your books have, from this one thing, become at once as a tinkling cymbal to me—and whatever the commonest wretches now assert against them—I am powerless *now* to deny![67]

Eventually Ruskin recovered his perspective, and his resumed friendship with Carlyle in fact became a filial bond between a lonely, sad old man and a tortured and unstable younger one between the years 1868 and 1878. But that friendship never again approached the state of mutual warmth and action that it had attained before June of 1867.

By 1868 Ruskin also began to realize that Carlyle, now seventy-three years old and suffering from increasing tremors in his right hand, was "old and weary, and feels that he has done his work."[68] This knowledge that he was the only active member of the "minority of *two*" had a deep effect, for there is much evidence that Ruskin now became conscious of the need to begin still another new period in his life, similar in pattern and importance to the decisions we have seen him make at the end of the two previous decades in his career. In possible allegiance to the doctrine of practical action that had been so strongly announced in "The Everlasting Yea" chapter of *Sartor Resartus*, he wanted to turn from theory to practice, from thought to work.

Just as he had been in the years at the end of the 1840's and the 1850's, Ruskin became inert and retrospective. In his lecture "The Mystery of Life and Its Arts," delivered in Dublin on 13 May 1868, he reviewed the previous decades of his life, judging them failures and claiming that the real answer to life can be found only by joining with men who have determined to "do something useful"—men who "dig and weave," who "plant and build," and whose "deeds are good, though their words may be few." "Whatsoever thy hand findeth to do—do it with thy might," he concluded, citing the same verses of Ecclesiastes that Carlyle had cited in "The Everlasting Yea."

In the spring of 1869 Ruskin had still another fit of despondency, his worst since 1861. Overwhelmed by a sense of futility and his obsession with both social evils and private anguish, he turned more and more to Carlyle and the concept of action that he had advocated

67. MS: Ruskin Galleries of Bembridge School, Isle of Wight.
68. Ruskin *Works*, XVII, 478.

in his Dublin lecture of a few months before. On 1 May 1869 he told Carlyle in a letter, "I have the Sartor with me also—it belongs to me now—more than any other of your books. I have nearly all my clothes to make, fresh—but more shroud shape than any other."[69] As usual, Carlyle responded to Ruskin's condition by praising his younger ally's works, and urging him on towards confidence. "Pluck up a heart," he told Ruskin on 17 August 1869. "And don't say 'most great thoughts are dressed in *shrouds*': many, many are the Phoebus Apollo celestial arrows you still have to shoot into the foul Pythons and poisonous abominable Megatheriums and Plesiosaurians that go staggering about, large as cathedrals, in our sunk epoch again."[70] Strengthened by this advice as well as his own desperate need for action, Ruskin in the summer of 1869 formed a strange scheme to curb the torrents of the Alps with dams. When he came to London in September of the same year, he brought fresh plans to found his experimental agricultural community called St. George's Guild—an idealistic enterprise which he thought of (to Carlyle's surprise) as merely his attempt to actualize Carlyle's "grander exhortations . . . in *Past and Present*."[71] He also made plans to publish a series of letters to his St. George workmen in a continuing work called *Fors Clavigera*; and he accepted a new position as Slade Professor of Art at Oxford, hoping that he could attain wider usefulness by influencing the young men there in the direction of social action.

He discussed his projects with Carlyle, and while Carlyle had private doubts about them, he did not discourage Ruskin. Since he now saw himself as the only active member of the "minority of *two*," Ruskin felt even more that he was a disciple carrying on the work of his enfeebled master. After he had begun his new work, in fact, he referred to it in a letter to Carlyle as "the fulfillment, so far as is in me, of what you have taught me."[72] Throughout the 1870's he relied heavily upon Carlyle for comfort even more than for advice. He even sent Carlyle the proofs of his various works before letting them go to press, just as he had done with his own father. It would appear, then, that the fulfillment of his Carlylean mission was thus one of the chief reasons for his new decision to launch into this final, most active phase of his career.

69. Ibid., XXXVI, 565.
71. Ibid., XXX, 95.
72. 1 May 1871, ibid., XXXVII, 30–31.

70. Ibid., XIX, lxx–lxxi.

Ruskin's letters and works of the 1870's unfortunately demonstrate the excruciating irony of this decision; for they chiefly constitute an immediate record of the psychic problems which caused Ruskin to fail in his new mission, and they show us Ruskin moving farther away from Carlyle at the very time he believed he was closest to him. In his resolution to begin a new period of action under Carlyle, and in his realization that the prophet's mantle of Carlyle had now been placed on his solitary shoulders, Ruskin had to face the challenge of this transferred prophethood with the added burden of a divided mind and a weakened body. At a time when he most needed self-harmony he had it least. Illness, the indecision of Rose LaTouche, renewed religious questions and awareness of the problem of evil in Nature, loneliness and failure, and the strain of adopted prophethood all combined to undermine his efforts in the early 1870's; and to all this was added a renewed interest in art which caused ambivalence towards his chosen role of social savior. In the letters of *Fors Clavigera* (numbers 1 and 61) he confessed that all of his new projects were "a byework to quiet my conscience, that I might be happy in what I supposed to be my own proper life of art teaching," and that problem plagued him ever afterwards. He had to give *himself*—not just what he had—and the gift could not be made: "I want to lead strongly now, in this *Fors* movement, for I know it must be done, not said, and I am so luxurious and dependent on all that I say people should be independent of. . . . One can't preach simplicity of life with one's room-furniture worth [£]30,000; and I've got to preach simplicity of life, if *anything*."[73] A final, pathetic irony in it all is the fact that Ruskin often could not get guidance and answers from Carlyle at the very time when he was busily supplying Carlylean answers to his own disciples.

Carlyle continued to praise each of Ruskin's works as the decade of the 1870's began, but privately he was as alarmed as he was hopeful about Ruskin's efforts. *Fors Clavigera* and its associated idealistic projects seemed at the least "chimerical" to him, and he told his brother John in late 1870 that he hoped that "Ruskin will bethink him and drop the matter in time . . . though alas, I fear he will plunge into it all the same."[74] In April of 1872 he wrote mixed words in a letter to Emerson:

73. Ruskin to Carlyle, 17 July 1874, MS: NLS, 556.87.
74. 27 Dec. 1870, MS: NLS, 527.37.

There is nothing going on among us as notable to me as those fierce light-ning-bolts Ruskin is copiously and desperately pouring into the black world of anarchy all around him. No other man in England that I meet has in him the divine rage against baseness that Ruskin has. . . . Unhappily he is not a strong man; one might say a weak man rather; . . . though if he can hold out for another 15 years he may produce, even in his way, a great effect.[75]

But, as we know, Ruskin was not able to "hold out" for fifteen more years. Even by 1872, events had driven him to new depths of anguish. The death of his mother and his old nurse left Ruskin with a sense of homeless orphanhood; he was nearly killed by a severe illness at Matlock in the summer of 1871; and then, early in 1872, Rose La-Touche at last decided to refuse him. As a consequence, Ruskin ex-perienced frequently alternating periods of confidence and depressed anxiety, and he made a desperate effort to fight even harder against what he felt to be overwhelming personal and public forces. In a letter to John Forster on 20 December 1872 Carlyle noted that Ruskin was "fallen into thick quiet despair again on the personal question; and meant all the more to go ahead with fire and sword upon the universal one."[76]

But Ruskin now felt himself to be alone in a futile fight against evil and ignorance. In a touching letter of October 1873 Ruskin told Carlyle of his "sorrow at the silence to the public which mere bodily weakness now imposes" on Carlyle, and then spoke of his own sad feelings: "I have not the least pleasure in my work anymore, except because you and Froude and one or two friends still care for it. One might as well talk to the March dust as to the English of today. . . . Besides this, the loss of my mother and my old nurse leaves me without any root, or, in the depth of the word, any home, and what pleasant things I have, seem to me only a kind of museum of which I have now merely to arrange the bequest."[77] Sympathetic to the fact that Ruskin was "treading the winepress alone; and sometimes feels his labours very heavy,"[78] Carlyle continued to encourage him, praising *Val D'Arno* especially for its "new ideas" and its evidence

75. 2 April 1872, in *The Correspondence of Emerson and Carlyle*, ed. Joseph Slater (New York and London, 1964), p. 589.
76. MS: Victoria and Albert Museum.
77. Ruskin, *Works*, XXXVII, 72–73.
78. Carlyle to C. E. Norton, 3 Nov. 1873, MS: Houghton Library, Harvard.

of his "old nobleness and fire."[79] Ruskin responded warmly to this
kindness, and by December of 1873 he began his letters to Carlyle
wtih the salutation "Dearest Papa," signing himself at one point,
"Ever your loving disciple—son—I have almost now a right to say."[80]

This significant shift in self-concept from disciple to "son" continued for several years afterwards. Paradoxically, it became strongest
by the time Ruskin's growing instability of character was actually
loosening the bonds between himself and Carlyle, and at a time when
Ruskin felt most adrift from his surrogate father in his search for
ideas to strengthen him. Ruskin decided to write to Carlyle almost
every day in the summer of 1874, just as he used to write to his own
father, and in these letters one can see the dark forces within him
begin to redirect his Carlylean journey of action towards the black
waters of passive despair. They are rife with revelations of Ruskin's
growing delusions and obsessions and his keen concern for common
man; but most importantly they reveal his sense of religious emptiness and a deep attraction to the simple forms of faith he now saw
in the Italian peasants and priests.

From Rome on 19 May 1874 Ruskin wrote to Carlyle: "I am almost
paralyzed in my own work, now by . . . chiefly the aspect taken by
religion,—staggering me in what I most want to be strong in faith
of. . . . If only I could enter into the hearts of . . . these friars!"[81]
On 1 June 1874 he wrote that nothing was "impressive to him now
—all things have become to me so ghastly a confusion and grotesque
mistake and misery, that I *feel* nothing . . . and enjoy nothing."[82]
Later in June, he pathetically asks Carlyle to give him some kind of
helpful insight into Carlyle's own faith, and even pleads with Carlyle
to tell him what to believe:

None of your readers, I believe . . . know precisely . . . what sympathy you
have with the faith of Abbot Samson, or St. Adalbert—I don't know myself.
To me the question of their faith is a fearful mystery. . . . But I don't know
what your own inner thoughts are of the faith.[83] . . . You have also shown
the power of living without any faith—in charity and utility—as Frederick.
. . . But you don't say what you would have Frederick be? You don't say
what a Master ought now to teach his pupils to believe.[84]

79. Carlyle to Ruskin, 31 Oct. 1873, in Ruskin, *Works*, XXIII, lv.
80. Ruskin, *Works*, XXXVII, 74–75.
81. MS: NLS, 556.72.   82. MS: NLS, 556.77.
83. 24 June 1874, in Ruskin, *Works*, XXXVII, 115–116.
84. 27 June 1874, ibid., pp. 118–119.

Not unnaturally for one who was writing to a man who claimed to have mastered *Sartor Resartus*, Carlyle responded to these letters with gentle wonder, and referred Ruskin to a passage in *Past and Present* which praises man's conscience and "the infinite nature of Duty" that is central in all of us, and then asserts that "Justice and Reverence are the everlasting Law of this Universe."[85] But this reference had no effect, for Ruskin insisted a month later, "I can't get my foundation on *any* faith."[86]

By this time, in fact, Ruskin's search for faith turned him from the kind of non-sectarian religion that Carlyle had helped him adopt as far back as the 1850's, and as a result of his stay at Assisi he began to sympathize with the beauty of the Catholic faith—at one point even imagining himself as a member of the third order of St. Francis. When he returned from Italy he was temporarily in better spirits, but the cheerfulness was deceptive, for Ruskin never really solved his spiritual problems, and they were to intensify past endurance.

Furthermore, he now began to feel the pangs of age and declining powers. In one of the most moving of all his letters, Ruskin spoke of both his spiritual confusion and his sense of decrepitude. On 21 July 1875 he told his "Papa" of his

being so depressed and so overworked . . . by the . . . thoughts of the passing spring days . . . so full of cloud and flower sight or question, now—as it seems to me—only to be rightly or at all dealt with by the knowledge and feelings which I have only gained in declining life, by warnings too clear, know cannot last but a few years, if that, in available strength. . . . I mean, that every cloud on the hills is a problem to me, every weed on the banks . . . and I want to begin all over again, with a boy's strength.[87]

"I must find some way out of this turmoil," he said to Carlyle in September of 1875,[88] and while he tried to hide his unrest under feigned cheerfulness, his behavior belied his efforts. When Carlyle, trying as always to encourage Ruskin, dedicated his *Early Kings of Norway* in 1875 to "dear aethereal Ruskin, whom God preserve," Ruskin could only write back gratefully: "I am so very lonely now, missing father and mother more and more every day, and having no more anything to look forward to here, but the gradual closing in of

85. 15 July 1874, in Sanders, *CLR*, p. 233. The passage from *Past and Present* is in *Works*, X, 108–109.
86. To Carlyle's niece Mary Aitken, 18 Aug. 1874, MS: NLS, 556.94.
87. MS: NLS, 556.108.   88. 1 Sept. 1875, MS: NLS, 556.109.

all, and feeling, for you, with continually increasing respect and love, more and more sorrow as I felt myself also entering with you the time of waiting."[89] After 1875, Ruskin's personality slipped beyond the healing grasp of Carlyle's fatherly friendship, while Carlyle watched helplessly. Finally, in February of 1878, Ruskin had his first attack of delirium. It lasted for months, and he was yet to have more frequent attacks, though he still had before him another ten years of scattered and distracted activity before he completely succumbed.

After his recovery in 1878, however, he still remained faithful to Carlyle, and the two men kept their friendship until Carlyle's death finally dissolved the "minority of *two*" on 5 February 1881. Then there emerged the last and saddest chapter in the history of Ruskin's discipleship to Carlyle. Two weeks after Carlyle died, Ruskin had his second attack of madness—a terrific delirium which lasted a month and was, according to Ruskin, "partly brought on by the sense of loneliness—and greater responsibility brought on me by Carlyle's death."[90] When he recovered he vowed again to throw himself "into the mere fulfillment of Carlyle's work," and, in what was almost an exact repetition of his decisions made in 1870, he began once again to send out his monthly *Fors Clavigera* letters. The idea of continuing Carlyle's work may also have contributed to his unfortunate decision to resume his Oxford lectures despite his weakened mental condition. In the days left to him before his permanent insanity in 1889, his devotion to Carlyle never wavered, and the social conscience that his "master" and "Papa" had helped to nurture remained with him until that sad final time.

In looking back over this survey of the major aspects of the history of Ruskin's discipleship, we may venture to make a few limited conclusions—limited, of course, because a really complete estimate of Ruskin's debt to Carlyle cannot be made without adding the abundant biographical details and the complete comparison of both men's thought that have remained outside the scope of this narrative.

One main point has been so often cited that it can simply be summarized now. Ruskin's social conscience began to emerge in the middle of the 1840's, and as it came to occupy more of his attention it caused him to seek a useful mission in life through repeated at-

89. 15 Nov. 1876, MS: NLS, 556.116.
90. Ruskin, *Works*, XXXVII, 361.

tempts to change his goals and himself at the end of every decade after 1839. Carlyle's influence upon these attempts seems to have grown with each successive decade, but only in Ruskin's 1869 decision to enter a phase of sheer action can we safely say that Ruskin submerged his own independent identity under that influence—and by then the growing fragmentation of his interests and personality made that submergence only temporary. This brief history has shown the progressive weakening of Ruskin's psychological condition, and it is obvious that this weakness grew in him while his feelings of discipleship to Carlyle grew as well. Ironically, the two forces culminated conjointly by the late 1860's, and effectively canceled out Ruskin's intentions to carry out Carlyle's work in the 1870's.

The few years from the time just after the publication of *Unto This Last* until 1867 or so seem to be the really vital and effective period of Ruskin's relationship to Carlyle. By 1861 Carlyle, perhaps even more than Ruskin, decided that Ruskin was his disciple. Throughout the 1860's this mutual decision helped Ruskin to adopt the public role of disciple in order to put both his own and Carlyle's ideas before the public in Ruskin's own manner. The result was that the mutual attitudes and thoughts of *both* men were actualized through the medium of Ruskin's books.

But Ruskin, after all, knew only the older, "latter-day" Carlyle; and while he was chiefly influenced by the works he mentions frequently —*Sartor Resartus, Past and Present,* and the *Latter-Day Pamphlets* —he was really influenced by their social pronouncements, which were the result of the experiences of an earlier Carlyle whom Ruskin never knew. And while this new acquaintance with those special aspects of Carlyle's personality and works helped to bring forth Ruskin's social writings and strengthen his own voice for the delivery of his humane, analytic gospel of anti-Mammonism, it placed him at a great disadvantage when he decided to devote himself to a Carlylean decade of action in 1869. For Ruskin, while sharing many of Carlyle's social thoughts, had never shared the earlier Carlyle's *experiences* which produced those thoughts, and therefore never attained Carlyle's sustained vision and self-unity necessary to carry him through the supposed "mere fulfillment" of his Carlylean discipleship in the 1870's.

Lacking Carlyle's self-harmonizing experiences, Ruskin thus also lacked the philosophical insight which allowed Carlyle to see immediate evils while at the same time envisioning change in terms of centuries. He therefore saw the decayed "condition-of-England" as a much more urgent and alarming phenomenon than even Carlyle did, and became far more impatient. As Carlyle constantly suggested to him, he went too fast, trying to instigate the mechanisms for immediate change at a rate which left Carlyle shaking his head in disbelief. The result, as Carlyle well knew, was frustration and the inevitable ineffectiveness that comes from trying to realize the ideal in the actual too quickly in this torpid world.

Most revealing of all is Ruskin's persistent request to Carlyle for religious guidance. Religion occupied Ruskin's thoughts even more than it did Carlyle's, and the fact that he had to ask Carlyle what to believe in the mid-1870's, after having told Carlyle in 1869 that *Sartor Resartus* "belonged to him," reinforces the idea that Ruskin never really absorbed Carlyle's complete concepts because he never experienced them fully. Remembering Ruskin's view of himself as having begun his walk down the Rue St. Thomas de l'Enfer in 1862, we might further borrow terms from *Sartor* and suggest that Ruskin's walk never reached the place where he stopped to have his "whole ME" stand up to proclaim the Everlasting Nay or the Everlasting Yea which gave Diogenes Teufelsdröckh the self-knowledge, sympathy, and "new eyes" that converted him to positive action. When Teufelsdröckh abandoned his self-concern and went off to dedicate his life to action, he did so because he had attained an inner harmony which made his deeds the extension of his faith and being. But when Ruskin, in the 1870's, vowed to begin his multifarious projects, he did so because he hoped that action would produce faith and inner harmony. The natural result was the numerous but incomplete deeds attempted in the 1870's as well as a lack of coherent direction, accompanied by a tense search for faith and a final need to accept the universe on some spiritual principle. Thus we can see him searching desperately for meaning in his later years, while the possibility of the religious experience of *Sartor* fades further away from him than ever. And all that while, Carlyle the man remained present to Ruskin as a friend and even a substitute father in Ruskin's mind, but (like Ruskin's own father) was really powerless to help or change Ruskin's independent course.

But with all of this, it would be wrong to think of Ruskin as a man who tried and failed to be a mere disciple of Carlyle. He was a man in constant debate with himself, always intellectually honest, and aware of his changing courses of life. Much of his power comes from this; for it gave him close rapport with his own readers and a following of his own. In this way, Ruskin helped to reinvigorate the influence of Carlyle's work through the agency of his own style and its more winning tone and temper, in the years when the aging Carlyle felt himself too weary and seldom spoke for himself. He thus carried Carlyle's banner above his own into the intellectual battle-ground of the later nineteenth century, and even carried it to places where Carlyle could never have gone. He may have absorbed Carlyle incompletely and become less of a disciple of Carlyle than he believed he was, but in a larger sense he may have achieved a better disciple-ship to Carlyle than many people have since recognized. Attaching himself to Carlyle, he furthered Carlyle's cause by remaining himself through it all and retaining the unique qualities which, while they brought him to self-destruction, brought him also to greatness.

Carlyle and Meredith

LIONEL STEVENSON, *Duke University*

I

The most explosive impact in English literature during the nineteenth century is unquestionably Thomas Carlyle's. From about 1840 onward, no author of prose or poetry was immune from his influence. In discussing this topic, it is not necessary to observe the customary precautions as to opportunities of contact. Any writer who was not aware of Carlyle and his opinions would have been totally isolated from the contemporary world. After the middle of the century he became a personal monument as well as a producer of books: like Coleridge in the preceding generation, he resided in an esoteric sanctuary, admission to which was one of the rites of passage whereby an ambitious young author sought initiation.

Carlyle's influence was not only potent but also exceptionally complex. Even among his ardent disciples there were few who did not protest at some time or another against his excesses of assertion. Conversely, his most pertinacious adversaries were seldom immune from his power. Some of them went through a period of acceptance and later rebelled; others shaped their independent views under the compulsion of challenging his. Carlyle cannot be ignored in any consideration of Mill or Arnold any more than in a consideration of Ruskin or Kingsley.

An excellent case history of the Carlyle pervasion is provided by George Meredith. Here all the elements are represented: the personal acquaintance at a formative moment, the enthusiastic response to stimulating ideas, the experimentation with florid rhetoric and poetic imagery in prose style, and the exasperated perception of the master's defects.

Meredith had been a neighbor of the Carlyles in Chelsea during two years starting in 1857, while he occupied lodgings in Hobury Street, King's Road; but his first personal encounter with them occurred after he published *The Ordeal of Richard Feverel* in the summer of 1859, at which time he moved to the country. In his various subsequent references to their meeting, he was not more explicit than this in dating the event, and so his biographers—myself included—inferred that the lapse of time was relatively brief. A letter to Mrs. Carlyle, however, which I am permitted to cite through the kindness of Professor C. L. Cline, suggests that the acquaintance may not have begun until three years later. Writing from Esher on 2 July 1862, Meredith acknowledges receipt of two letters from Mrs. Carlyle. "I dare say," he replies, "you did not intend the first of them to flatter me but it's as well to confess that it had that effect." Her second letter was an invitation to visit the Carlyles in Cheyne Row, and in accepting it he adds, "I am very desirous of paying my respects to Mr Carlyle."[1] While this letter is not positive proof that there had been no previous meeting, the whole tone of it suggests that this was a first occasion, and the assumption harmonizes well enough with Meredith's later statements.

His only written references to their relationship are of the briefest. In a letter to André Raffalovich about Carlyle's *Reminiscences* (23 May 1882) he says: "I knew them both. She did me the honour to read my books, and make him listen to extracts, and he was good enough to repeat that 'the writer thereof was no fool'—high praise from him."[2] Writing to Louisa Lawrence (25 September 1883) Meredith remarks: "I . . . acknowledge, as Carlyle said to me, that Göthe is the pattern for all who would have a directing hold on themselves."[3] Twenty years later, more frequent conversations with Carlyle are implied in a letter to Lady Ulrica Duncombe (19 January 1902): "He commended the study of Goethe to me constantly."[4]

Meredith's oral reports of the acquaintance went into more detail, and several of his friends recorded these reminiscences, though with considerable differences. Meredith was a notorious *raconteur*, who dramatized an anecdote every time he repeated it. Besides, the hearers probably did not take down verbatim transcripts, but wrote their impressions from memory, perhaps after an interval. Under

1. C. L. Cline, "Meredith's Meeting with the Carlyles," *Times Literary Supplement*, 9 Nov. 1973, p. 1380. See also Pierre Coustillas' letter to the same journal, 23 Nov. 1973, p. 1449.
2. C. L. Cline, ed., *The Letters of George Meredith*, 3 vols. (Oxford, 1970), II, 661. Meredith had this episode in mind when he wrote in 1896, in a review of Alice Meynell's essays: "It does not seem to me too bold to imagine Carlyle listening, without the weared gesture, to his wife's reading of [these essays], hearing them to the end, and giving his comment: 'That woman thinks!' " "Mrs. Meynell's Two Books of Essays," *National Review*, 27 (Aug. 1896), 769.
3. *Letters*, II, 715.   4. *Letters*, III, 1417.

these conditions, the remarkable fact is not the variations in detail but the basic similarity that enables us to arrive at a sort of consensus impression of what occurred.

The story of the original encounter first appeared in print in 1888, in an article by J. M. Barrie:

Carlyle, I happen to know, was acquainted with "Richard Feverel"; his wife read it aloud to him, and he was so pleased that he said, "This man's no fule." This is not the whole story. First Mrs. Carlyle read the book herself, and many times she flung it aside in irritation before becoming reconciled to Mr. Meredith's yoke.[5]

Barrie's positive tone, along with the fact that he had recently become one of Meredith's devoted young friends, indicates that he had learned the anecdote from Meredith's own lips.

The most familiar version is probably that of Edward Clodd, since it was reproduced in David Alec Wilson's detailed biography of Carlyle. Meredith described the episode to Clodd in the early nineties, but Clodd's *Memories* were not published until 1916, and so an opportunity for distortion is not precluded. Clodd claims to report Meredith's words:

Feverel was written at Chelsea. . . . In my walks I often came across Carlyle, and longed to speak to him. One day my publishers received a letter from Mr. Carlyle asking about me. Then I called on them. Carlyle told me that his wife disliked *Feverel* at first, and had flung it on the floor, but that on her reading some of it to him he said,—"The man's no fool"; so they persevered to the end. He said that I had the making of a historian in me; but I answered that so much fiction must always enter into history that I must stick to novel-writing.[6]

Other records of Meredith's recollection of the event are more circumstantial. A journalist named Arthur J. Ashton interviewed Meredith in August 1879 but did not print his report until 1924:

He said in effect, "Carlyle was always trying to get me to write history. Novels were no good. 'Ye must write heestory.' So one day I said, 'Carlyle, do you know what historians remind me of?' 'No.' 'They are like a row of men working in a potato field, with their eyes and noses down in the fur-

5. J. M. Barrie, "Mr. George Meredith's Novels," *Contemporary Review*, 54 (Oct. 1888), 575.

6. Edward Clodd, *Memories* (London, 1916), p. 148. In his letter to the *Times Literary Supplement*, cited in n. 1, Pierre Coustillas points out that this account in Clodd's *Memories* is based on his diary entry for 23 Feb. 1893.

row, and their other end turned toward Heaven.' I thought he would be very angry; but he only listened, and sighed, and then said, 'Well, perhaps that's varra true.' He never asked me to write history again."[7]

In 1896 Frederick York Powell, in a letter to Oliver Elton, reported Carlyle's advice and Meredith's objection, but not the lively simile of the potato-diggers:

The story is that Mrs. Carlyle begged Carlyle to read *Richard Feverel*. He did so, and said, "Ma dear, that young man's nae fule. Ask him here." When he came, as Meredith himself told me, he talked long with him on deep things, and begged him to come often. He said, "Man, ye suld write heestory! Ye have a heestorian in ye!" Meredith answered that novel writing was his way of writing history, but Carlyle did not quite accept that, though he did not argue against it, but rather doubted over it, as if there were more in it than he had thought at first.[8]

Perhaps the most dependable report is provided by J. P. Collins, who interviewed Meredith in 1905 and 1906 and claims to have made full notes after each visit. He quotes Meredith thus:

I was bold enough to show some of my early work to Carlyle, and he advised me to turn to history as the repository of facts. I said to him, with all deference, I thought there were greater things in the world than facts. He turned on me and said, "But facts are truth, and truth is facts." I said, "No, pardon me; if I may say so, truth I take to be the broad heaven above the petty doings of mankind which we call facts." He gave me a smile of pity for my youth, as I suppose, and then said, "Ah weel, if ye like to talk in that poetic way, ye may; but ye'll find it in your best interest, young man, to stick to Fahcts."[9]

Elsewhere in the article, Collins adds another scrap of the Carlyle-Meredith conversations: "I remember saying to Carlyle once, 'Sir, there is one man made for your pen, and that is Bismarck,' but he shook his head and answered me sadly enough, 'Too late.'"

Meredith may have felt more warmly drawn to Jane Welsh Carlyle than to her husband, partly perhaps because of her early recog-

7. Arthur J. Ashton, *As I Went on My Way* (London, 1924), p. 82.
8. Oliver Elton, *Frederick York Powell*, 2 vols. (Oxford, 1906), I, 227–228.
9. J. P. Collins, "Conversations with George Meredith," *Pall Mall Magazine*, 50 (Nov. 1912), 671–680. Without citing a source, one of Meredith's biographers strips the visit of any dialogue whatsoever: "The sage, smoking his pipe, listened in stony silence during the whole visit. As young Meredith rose to go, Carlyle broke in with the words, 'This has been a very pleasant evening. Come again.'" R. E. Sencourt, *The Life of George Meredith* (London, 1929), p. 22.

nition of his talent, partly because she was a sort of archetype of the witty Meredithian heroine. In his letter to Raffalovich he gives his impression of the Carlyles' domestic atmosphere:

Between him and his wife the case is quite simple. She was a woman of peculiar conversational sprightliness, and such a woman longs for society. To him, bearing that fire of sincereness, as I have said, society was unendurable. All coming near him, except those who could bear the trial, were scorched, and he was as much hurt as they by the action rousing the flames in him. Moreover, like all truthful souls, he was an artist in his work. The efforts after verification of matters of fact, and to present things distinctly in language, were incessant; they cost him his health, swallowed up his leisure. Such a man could hardly be an agreeable husband for a woman of the liveliest vivacity. They snapped at one another, and yet the basis of affection was mutually firm. She admired, he respected, and each knew the other to be honest. Only she needed for her mate one who was more a citizen of the world, and a woman of the placid disposition of Milton's Eve, framed by her maker to be an honest labourer's cook and housekeeper, with a nervous system resembling a dumpling, would have been enough for him.[10]

The foregoing opinion is reinforced by one of Meredith's remarks to Collins:

They say he was unapproachable; I never found him so. Mrs. Carlyle once said to me: "Thomas is hard to bear with now he has finished the first volume; what he will be like when he gets into the third I can hardly bring myself to think." But he was soon restored, and after an hour's talk with him, he would recall something or other he had said, and end it all with a great peal of laughter.[11]

The friendship with Mrs. Carlyle continued until literally the end of her life. While her husband was absent in Edinburgh, Meredith spent an afternoon with her on 20 April 1866, the day before her sudden death.[12]

II

Throughout his letters and conversations, Meredith consistently ranked Carlyle as the foremost of his contemporaries, though usually

10. *Letters*, II, 661.
11. See Collins, cited in n. 9 above. Mrs. Carlyle refers to her husband's work on *Frederick the Great*, the first two volumes of which were published in 1858.
12. S. M. Ellis, ed., *The Hardman Papers* (London, 1930), p. 127.

with distinct qualification. While sitting to G. F. Watts for a portrait in 1893, he remarked:

"I believe that this age will be ranked as the most heroically striving of any time," and he attributed much of this earnestness to the work of Carlyle. Of this he said, "It will last, but how it is impossible to say; whether as classical work or as absorbed by his generation and transmitted, none can say as yet. He has taught all earnest people today that they have to take life seriously and do some work for the world—that there is a yea and a nay, and they must make choice of one or other." . . . They then spoke of Tennyson, Mr. Meredith saying that he was the most natural, the most spontaneously natural, of human beings. "So was Carlyle," he added, "though perhaps less direct. He had the look of Lear encountering the storm on the Cornish [sic] coast," Mr. Meredith continued. "You have given him that look in your portrait."[13]

In the interview with Collins, Meredith talked about how so many writers, such as Dickens and George Eliot, were seduced by public adulation:

"Carlyle, now," Meredith went on, "was preserved from all this folly by his great and saving grace of humour. It sweetened the great humanity in him, and revived him after his enormous labours. No one knows the extraordinary pains he took, or how he toiled so that every word of a sentence should fall on the ear with the emphasis it carried in his mind." . . .

I ventured to say: "Most of us have a grudge against Carlyle, and that is for the savage way in which he dealt with Charles Lamb."

"Well," was the retort, "there were reasons there, or excuses at any rate. Carlyle was a man to whom the realities of life were solemn things, and he did not know, he could not see, that the flippancy and banter he detested were Lamb's way of making those realities endurable. It is more than probable that Carlyle never knew the tragic undercurrents of Lamb's life; although if one had enlightened him, he would have pondered them over for a moment, I dare say, and then dismissed the matter with a 'Puir creature, puir creature!' . . .

"It was very grievous to think of his coming to the end of his stupendous labours, and so much of them expended on historical research. History is a thankless field for a man of such gifts as his. What could he have said if he could have known that a single generation would overlay his work with new investigations and discoveries? So far as the evidence was available in his day, his 'French Revolution' was perfect, yet already we know that his view of the flight to Varennes was wrong. In the matter of 'Frederick'

13. M. S. Watts, *George Frederick Watts*, 2 vols. (London, 1912), II, 231.

he fared rather better, for he had the advantage of new material, and he went over much of the ground himself. That is what helped him for the battles, and his battle scenes are magnificently, Homerically done. I had the chance of judging them in 1866, for I was war correspondent to the *Morning Post* in Vienna. . . . And I remember realising on the actual field how Carlyle, with the few materials at his command, must have striven and worked to obtain such a grasp as he did of the conditions of the struggles in 'Frederick.' " [14]

Meredith summed up this opinion in a comment to Elizabeth Haldane, who reports: "In 1895 I remember lunching with his daughter and having some serious talk with him. He spoke of Carlyle as a great romancer, but not as an historian." [15]

Such conversational remarks as the foregoing are strongly reinforced by passages about Carlyle in Meredith's correspondence. The earliest ones occur in letters to his idealistic and impetuous friend Frederick Maxse. On 15 January 1866 he wrote:

In reading Carlyle, bear in mind that he is a humourist. The insolence offensive to you, is part of his humour. He means what he says, but only as far as a humourist can mean what he says. See the difference between him and Emerson, who on the contrary is a philosopher. The humourist, notwithstanding, has much truth to back him. Swim on his pages, take his poetry and fine grisly laughter, his manliness, together with some splendid teaching. It is a good set-off to the doctrines of what is called the "Empirical school." I don't agree with Carlyle a bit, but I do enjoy him. [16]

Four years later (27 December 1869) Meredith resumed his remarks, this time with reference to a letter that Maxse had received from Ruskin:

It is the spirituality of Carlyle that charms him. . . . Mill is essentially a critic: it is his heart, not his mind, which sends him feeling ahead. But he really does not touch the soul and springs of the Universe as Carlyle does. Only, when the latter attempts practical dealings he is irritable as a woman, impetuous as a tyrant. He seeks the short road to his ends: and the short road is, we know, a bloody one. He is not wise; Mill is; but Carlyle has most light when he burns calmly. [17]

A week afterwards (2 January 1870) Meredith returned to the discussion of Ruskin's views:

14. See Collins, cited in n. 9 above.
15. Elizabeth S. Haldane, *From One Century to Another* (London, 1937), p. 165.
16. *Letters*, I, 327.   17. *Letters*, I, 410.

It's difficult to speak mildly of a man who calls John Mill blockhead, and dares to assume Carlyle's mantle of Infallibility on the plea that it is his "master's." Still I agree with much that he says of Carlyle. I hold that he is the nearest to being an inspired writer of any man in our times; he does proclaim inviolable law: he speaks from the deep springs of life. All this. But when he descends to our common pavement, when he would apply his eminent spiritual wisdom to the course of legislation, he is no more sagacious nor useful nor temperate than a flash of lightning in a grocer's shop. "I purify the atmosphere," says this agent. "You knock me down, spoil my goods and frighten my family," says the grocer.—Philosophy, while rendering his dues to a man like Carlyle and acknowledging itself inferior in activity, despises his hideous blustering impatience in the presence of progressive facts.

Read the *French Revolution* and you listen to a seer: the recent pamphlets, and he is a drunken country squire of superordinary ability.

Carlyle preaches work for all. Good. But his method of applying his sermon to his "nigger" is intolerable.— Spiritual light he has to illuminate a nation. Of practical little or none, and he beats his own brains out with emphasis.[18]

As shown by the foregoing letter, Meredith seems to have admired Carlyle most either as the adversary of Utilitarianism or as the picturesque historian of the French Revolution. On 1 January 1873, writing to the editor of the *Pall Mall Gazette* about a series of articles against Mill by Fitzjames Stephen, he called them "the prose of Carlyle's doctrines, valuable, profitable."[19] Commenting to John Morley about his "Robespierre" (15 August 1876), he wrote, "It sent me to Carlyle. He bears the re-reading. Still that kind of thing will not do. It is our only history of the French Revolution, and is in as much disorder as the Paris of Danton."[20]

Meredith's general appraisal of Carlyle is best summarized in the 1882 letter to Raffalovich, already quoted in part above. He accuses Raffalovich of lacking "an accurate knowledge of his works, nature, and teaching," and goes on:

Our people over here have been equally unjust, with less excuse. You speak of vanity, as a charge against him. He has little, though he certainly does not err on the side of modesty:—he knew his powers. The harsh judg-

18. *Letters*, I, 411–412. "Recent pamphlets" may refer as well to "Shooting Niagara; and After?" (1867) as to the *Latter-Day Pamphlets* (1850).
19. *Letters*, I, 474.   20. *Letters*, I, 521–522.

ment he passed on the greater number of his contemporaries came from a very accurate perception of them, as they were perused by the intense light of the man's personal sincereness. He was one who stood constantly in the presence of those "Eternal verities" of which he speaks. For the shallow men of mere literary aptitude he had perforce contempt. . . . He was the greatest of the Britons of his time—and after the British fashion of not coming near perfection; Titanic, not Olympian: a heaver of rocks, not a shaper. But if he did no perfect work, he had lightning's power to strike out marvellous pictures and reach to the inmost of men with a phrase.[21]

After Carlyle's death, Meredith's regretful diminution of respect was expressed in two letters (8 and 12 September 1887) to Richard Garnett about his short biography of Carlyle:

You have sounded him accurately. It is not needed to analyze the nature and office of the "prophet," as I am tempted to do, when I see a dry pump where the spring once jetted. The task of great men is to silence them all after a space, when it is found that their heads do not grow to philosophy.

. . .

It is good to hear that Emerson follows your Carlyle. But of Emerson, though he was not the greater man, I would never say that he pumped harsh wind for water and creaked in the process. He stood lean by comparison, but he struck the taproot of a forest-tree into our Mother Earth, and had consequently the unfailing flow of our sap through him to the end. His prescript for men, was the crystal spring of her depths. Carlyle forced at their mouths his fiery old Hebrew drug. The truth that he had in him was for our immediate adoption—or we perish. Temperament betrayed his piercing insight. So it is with the prophet. And by the way, the preacher likewise played him false at times. I found in my last reading of the Abbot Samson, that the text was beaten out drawlingly thin. Posterity will bark at him for his iteration; will, accepting him, insist that he live in extracts, while it clasps full volumes of his inferior in power, the rational philosopher, who draws from Earth, yields refreshingly, loses nought of hope.[22]

From all the evidence it is clear that in spite of reservations and disappointments, Meredith continued to regard Carlyle as undeniably the most dynamic force and the most eminent figure among the authors of the Victorian era. His principal cause for dismay was Carlyle's reactionary political stand in *Shooting Niagara; and After?* In a poem written in 1867, "Lines to a Friend Visiting America,"

---

21. *Letters*, II, 661.　　　　　　22. *Letters*, II, 884–886.

Meredith presented a lugubrious survey of the Mammonism and timidity dominating the English intellectual climate, and deplored Carlyle's failure to indict the prevailing moral inertia:

> A poet, half a prophet, rose
> In recent days, and called for power.
> I love him; but his mountain prose—
> His Alp and valley and wild flower—
>
> Proclaimed our weakness, not its source.
> What medicine for disease had he?
> Whom summoned for a show of force?
> Our titular aristocracy!

Meredith's emotional attachment to Carlyle survived, but his reason rebelled against his increasing dogmatism.

III

From an early date the reviewers of Meredith recognized his affinity with Carlyle. In the first extended critical essay on his work, printed only five years after *Richard Feverel*, Justin M'Carthy said:

Mr. Meredith is often strikingly like [Jean Paul] Richter in style, with, almost as a matter of necessity, a considerable dash of the Carlyle phraseology. Here and there, indeed, something of unmistakable and pure Carlyle flashes in. Life, as seen in certain worldly and cynical eyes, is for instance described as "a Supreme Ironic procession with Laughter of Gods in the background," and many such sentences occur here and there which read as if they were fairly plucked out of *Sartor Resartus* or *The French Revolution*.[23]

Fifteen years later, reviewing *The Egoist*, Richard Holt Hutton remarked:

The writer has an individuality; he is a humourist. He makes us think of him a great deal, not by directly introducing himself to us, as Thackeray does, but after the same fashion that we are led to think of Carlyle while reading his *French Revolution*. In fact, Mr. Meredith often calls up an image of a handsome, witty, polished juvenile cousin of Carlyle, in eighteenth-century costume, with neat, powdered wig, lace ruffles, and silk

23. Justin M'Carthy, "Novels with a Purpose," *Westminster Review*, 26 (July 1864), 25.

stockings, of keen and curious vision, but too courteous to be profound or stirring.[24]

Another reviewer of *The Egoist* added a third specimen of geniuses burdened with obscurity of style: "Mr. Meredith's style is a cross between Mr. Carlyle's and Mr. Browning's, if such a compound be imaginable. It is a nut confessedly hard to crack."[25] This triad soon became a critical cliché. George Moore made the same comparison in 1888: "Carlyle, Mr. Robert Browning, and George Meredith are the three essentially northern writers; in them there is nothing of Latin sensuality and subtlety."[26] The triad turned up a decade later in the *Yellow Book*, where J. M. Robertson declared of Meredith: "he entrenched himself in the Carlylean and Browningesque manner, personifying the multitude as one lumpish hostile entity, or organized body of similar entities."[27] After another decade the triad had crossed the Atlantic and was elaborated by Stuart Pratt Sherman: "In the plastic time of his youth, he, like Browning and Carlyle, was his own master of rhetoric. Like Carlyle, he wrote prose as if Dryden had never shown the superiority of Charles the Second's English to the flowered and conceited exuberance of the Elizabethans. Like Browning, he wrote verse as if Pope had not died to save us from the sins of the metaphysical school."[28] It remained for Percy Lubbock, the next year, to undertake a differentiation within the triad: Meredith "was only incidentally a painter of nature and society; essentially he was an interpreter of one and a critic of the other. The distinction places him nearer Carlyle than Browning."[29]

Meanwhile other critics had been defining specific Carlylean elements in Meredith's work—poetry as well as prose. A reviewer of his *Poems and Lyrics of the Joy of Earth* commented:

Carlyle himself was not more impressed by the conception that man forms part of a system which is controlled by unalterable laws; but Mr. Meredith differs from Carlyle in thinking less of the conditions in which the order of the universe works disaster than of those which bring good to men. And men interest him even more than nature; he has a profound and curious

24. *Spectator*, 52 (1 Nov. 1879), 1383.
25. *New Quarterly Magazine*, NS 3 (Jan. 1880), 230.
26. George Moore, *Confessions of a Young Man* (London, 1888), p. 257.
27. J. M. Robertson, "Concerning Preciosity," *Yellow Book*, 13 (April 1897), 104.
28. Stuart P. Sherman, "George Meredith," *Nation*, 88 (3 June 1909), 554.
29. Percy Lubbock, "George Meredith," *Quarterly Review*, 212 (April 1910), 210.

knowledge of the forms of evil which spring from "egoism"; but his perception of these things does not lead him to indulge in Carlyle's scorn.[30]

In reviewing *Diana of the Crossways* (1885), the *Times* observed: "Mr. Meredith might pose for the Carlyle of fiction, so rugged is his style, so uncouth his ellipses, so powerful the collocation of his words."[31] Not long afterwards, these ideas were expanded in the enthusiastic article that the youthful George Pierce Baker wrote for the *Harvard Monthly*:

even as Carlyle rushed out his ideas in a style often uncouth, but always emphatic and forcible, so this author in striving to express his exact meaning, sometimes makes a sacrifice of elegance and force. Indeed, I cannot but believe that Mr. Meredith has felt strongly in style and thought the influence of Thomas Carlyle. At times he writes in the half-allegorical, abrupt, metaphorical phrases of the author of *Sartor Resartus*. . . . Nor do the two men seem to me very unlike as thinkers. Both recognize the omnipresent struggle in the universe; with both the cry is for more light, for more free intellectual play. Both hate sham and sentimentality. Both paint without idealization, yet both look for ultimate growth and success, in spite of the faults and failings of mankind. May not Mr. Meredith be called the Carlyle of fiction?[32]

In the first book-length study of Meredith's work, Richard LeGallienne termed a passage in *Beauchamp's Career* (1875) about Carlyle, "a masterly description of a style with which Mr. Meredith's own has much of essential relationship"; and later he remarked: "he is more than usually dowered with the prophetic 'scorn of scorn' for the paltry imitations that usurp the worship of the world. Not Carlyle himself had a more white-hot hatred of 'simulacra.' "[33]

In 1897 Arthur Symons unexpectedly applied a currently fashionable critical term to the two authors: "Like Carlyle, but even more than Carlyle, Mr. Meredith is in the true, wide sense, as no other English writer of the present time can be said to be, a Decadent. . . . What Decadence, in literature, really means is that learned corruption of language by which style ceases to be organic, and becomes, in the pursuit of some new expressiveness or beauty, deliberately abnor-

---

30. *St. James's Gazette*, 6 (25 June 1883), 7.
31. *Times*, 1 June 1885.
32. George P. Baker, "George Meredith," *Harvard Monthly*, 2 (June 1887), 145.
33. Richard LeGallienne, *George Meredith: Some Characteristics* (London, 1890), pp. 10, 73.

mal."[34] Meredith was understandably annoyed by the epithet, and he wrote scornfully to his French friend and translator, Henri Davray, that the article was "entirely misleading, and to entitle me a 'Decadent' is ludicrously childish."[35] It may be noted, however, that he does not disavow Symons' linking of him with Carlyle, an opinion which he must have become well accustomed to after seeing it voiced at intervals over thirty years.

At the very outset of his literary career, Meredith was already saturated wth Carlyle's influence. His first work of prose fiction, *The Shaving of Shagpat* (1856), reflects Carlyle in style, in method, and in ideas. The kinship is well summarized by René Galland:

Carlyle l'avait aidé à formuler ses ambitions, à préciser les vertus viriles que doit acquérir le Héros: l'endurance, le courage, la sincérité, "l'effort incessant pour discerner les vraies règles de l'Univers, en connexion avec lui-même et son but, et pour les suivre." Après "les Héros," il avait lu *Sartor Resartus*, et la fantaisie de Carlyle habillant à l'Allemande son héros de la pensée . . . avait trouvé en Meredith un disciple préparé. . . . Il avait apprécié le vigoureux humour avec lequel une feinte gravité philosophique déshabille tous les mensonges sociaux, cette puissante imagination créatrice de symboles, évocatrice de vie, et ces contrastes soudains de grotesque et de sérieux, de fini et d'infini qui font de *Sartor* un chef-d'œuvre unique et profond. . . . Il retrouvait d'ailleurs, dans la philosophie des habits, l'exaltation de l'âme vivante, seule réalité, de l'individu supérieur, en lequel et par lequel Dieu travaille pour l'humanité, héros de l'Intellect qui détruit les symboles morts vides de sens, et, crée des symboles véritables, vraies œuvres d'art, au moyen du Rire libérateur.

Galland believes that the *Latter-Day Pamphlets* also exerted a powerful influence on Meredith's thinking. He points to passages which dwell upon two of Meredith's persistent themes: "All so-called 'reforms' hitherto are grounded either on openly-admitted egoism . . . or else upon this of remedying social injustices by indiscriminate contributions of philanthropy." Present-day Christianity is "fashioned . . . out of extinct cants and modern sentimentalities." Galland calls special attention to a passage which expresses a crucial idea in *Shagpat* and all Meredith's work: "the Destinies are opulent; and send here and there a man into the world to do work, for which they

34. Arthur Symons, "A Note on George Meredith," *Fortnightly Review*, 62 (Nov. 1897), 676.
35. *Letters*, III, 1295.

do not mean to pay him in money. And they smite him beneficently with sore afflictions, and blight his world all into grim frozen ruins round him, . . . they scourge him manifoldly to the due pitch, sometimes nearly of despair, that he may search desperately for his work, and find it; they urge him on still with beneficent stripes when needful, as is constantly the case between whiles."

Galland comments on the passage thus:

Relisons le premier chapitre de *Shagpat*, qui a pour titre *les Rossées*: nous y trouvons l'homme prédestiné qui pour devenir le maître d'un Evénement, doit dépouiller sa vanité, accepter la leçon des faits, endurer la faim, la soif, être patient, faire servir l'épreuve à tremper sa volonté. . . .

Et de même, les vers souvent cités de la conclusion conseillent "l'humble acceptation des lanières cinglantes," des coups qui changent en lions les hommes et leur donnent du cœur pour faire triompher l'esprit sur la chair. Là Carlyle, et peut-être Browning, semblent marier leurs expressions favorites, autant que leurs idées, à celles de Meredith. . . . La conception fondamentale—du héros libéralement fustigé par le sort—est tout Carlyléenne et l'humour qui le déguise en sac-à-chiffons (Bag-a-rag) et qui prend pour type de la Bêtise une tête embroussaillée (Shaggy pate) ne l'est pas moins. On pense malgré soi aux sacs de notes en désordre qui contenaient la philosophie de Teufelsdröckh. Ce que ce dernier est à Carlyle, Shibli Bagarag l'est à Meredith. Cette œuvre de jeunesse est le Pourana . . . où il a versé pêle-mêle toutes ses idées (qui sont pour une bonne part celles de Carlyle) en laissant à la fantaisie le soin de les produire. Et de même que *Sartor Resartus* est autobiographique, *Shagpat* l'est aussi dans une certaine mesure. . . . Son imitation de Carlyle est moins une parodie qu'un délicat hommage, une forme subtile de flatterie pour "le foyer ardent auquel il a allumé ce qui brûle de plus clair en son âme."[36]

The fullest treatment of Carlyle as a seminal presence in Meredith's fiction is provided by Jack Lindsay. In the course of his book on Meredith he devotes no less than twelve pages at various points to aspects of this matter, particularly in chapters 7a and 10a. With his Marxist predilection, Lindsay declares:

We must grasp the positive elements which Meredith, like Dickens, drew from Carlyle's thought if we are to understand his consciousness of the political struggle and the way in which he expressed that struggle in artistic terms. . . . He continued to admire Carlyle for his power to break

36. René Galland, *George Meredith: les cinquante premières années* (Paris, 1923), pp. 108–111.

through the thick falsities of their world with a sharp phrase, a momentary depth of realization; but he more and more despised his reactionary rage, his inability to relate his deep insights to the forward movement of society through democratic struggle.[37]

Lindsay cites apposite passages from *Past and Present*, the *Latter-Day Pamphlets*, and the essay on Goethe which foreshadow Meredith's views on Sham, Egoism, and Sentimentality.[38] Elsewhere Lindsay undertakes to define the resemblances in their style. Of *The French Revolution* he remarks:

The imagery and rhythm which embodied a powerful sense of the period's revolutionary upheavals could not be ignored. The young were conquered. . . . It is a style of *action* and *impact*. The clipping of definite or indefinite articles gives a breathless directness; the personifications generalize the particular and thus underline the historical moment, its deep significance; the pictorial sharpness adds to the sense of participation in the event. . . . It is this kind of effect at which Carlyle is an adept, and in which he so proliferates that he may be said to have brought a new quality into prose, a quality based in action and participation. What Meredith responds to and develops in his own way is that new element.[39]

It is worth noting, however, that Meredith warned a young enthusiast against the seduction of imitating Carlyle. When J. Cotter Morison had finished the first draft of his *Life of St. Bernard* in 1861, he

took his MS to George Meredith, who having found his style too Carlylese, proceeded to impress the fact upon the writer by reading out portions and exaggerating the traces of Carlyle's influence. Morison bore the ordeal for a time, then got up, and in tones of despair announced his resolve not to publish his work, whereupon Meredith reassured him by telling him that the matter was good, and that all that was needed was an improvement in the manner.[40]

It is fifty years since Galland wrote, and almost twenty since Lindsay, but one finds that Meredith's most recent critics are still asserting Carlyle's essential role in his early fiction. Of *Shagpat*, Ian Fletcher says:

37. Jack Lindsay, *George Meredith: His Life and Work* (London, 1956), pp. 73–75; see also pp. 66–67, 71–72, 89.
38. Ibid., pp. 97–98.
39. Ibid., pp. 346–347.
40. James Sully, *My Life and Friends* (London, 1918), p. 269.

It was from Carlyle that Meredith caught the model of a prose lyrical, capricious, proffered from an elaborately mystifying stance. In *Sartor*, Carlyle uses distancing as a double-edged weapon. . . . Style as buffer can encompass style as mimetic fullness, can include the possibility of its own failure, absorbing doubt just as the device of distancing absorbs the commitment problem. This is of the first importance in approaching the problem of tenor and vehicle in *Shagpat*. The two works are so closely related on every level that one can only select what seems important to Meredith's reading of *Sartor*. . . . Carlyle's Teufelsdröckh, . . . like Meredith's Shibli, passes through phases of negation, indifference, and rebirth. Like Sartor [i.e., Teufelsdröckh] Shibli asserts self as the first source of value; like Sartor, Shibli discovers that analogical thinking is inadequate; nothing is symmetrically as it seems or should be: there is no mirroring relationship between man and Nature. Symbols, the geography of signs, are worshipped when their value has become extrinsic merely. . . .

The action of *Shagpat* obviously parallels that of *Sartor* through Shibli's attempt to remove an extrinsic symbol. . . . Meredith's fantasy acts out Carlyle's insight that each man creates his own universe of signs, but that signs condition roles (the automatically locking throne and the grafted crown in Aklis).

Fletcher continues at considerable length to develop the resemblances between the two books not only in ideas but also in phraseology.[41]

In the same collection of critical essays, Arnold Kettle emphasizes the Carlylean elements in *The Ordeal of Richard Feverel*:

The key-figure behind Meredith, for better and for worse, is undoubtedly Carlyle. It was from Carlyle, more than from anyone, that he gained his insight into the British world of his time—his sense of the corrupting power of the cash-nexus, of the social movement from the world of Sir Austin Feverel and Everard Romfrey to that of Manchester and of the consequences of this in human alienation and impoverished relationships. . . .

The Ordeal of Richard Feverel is even more closely connected with Carlyle than *Beauchamp's Career*. And whereas in the later novel, through its strong framework of political actuality, the problems Carlyle raises are elucidated, rendered more concrete, carried forward even, . . . in *Feverel* the Carlylean cloudiness is mirrored rather than dispersed. Because in *Feverel* politics appears only on the sidelines (like the information that Austin Wentworth is a republican) the Romantic elements in both Carlyle

41. Ian Fletcher, ed., *Meredith Now: Some Critical Essays* (London, 1971), pp. 53–57.

and Meredith are given freer play. . . . If Meredith—or Carlyle—had drunk less deep of the Romantic draught they would certainly not be the writers they are; but it is also doubtful whether they would have been writers at all.[42]

In her essay on *Evan Harrington*, Margaret Tarrant shows that this novel too is impregnated with Carlyle, particularly in the significance of Evan's father's vocation as a tailor:

At one point in *Evan Harrington*, Drummond Forth, referring to the history of the Great Mel, comments that there is "material enough for a Sartoriad" (279). This reference to Carlyle is not fortuitous. Many of the concerns of *Sartor Resartus* have been incorporated into *Evan Harrington*. Meredith's suggestions of possible titles alone would indicate this: "What say you to these titles? 'The Substantial and the Essential' (Bad, but better than 'Shams and Realities.')" In Book II of *Sartor Resartus*, Teufelsdröckh, considering the calculation of a "Statistics of Imposture" asks: ". . . what almost prodigious saving may there not be anticipated, as the *Statistics of Imposture* advances, and so the manufacturing of Shams (that of Realities rising into clearer and clearer distinction therefrom) gradually declines, and at length becomes all but wholly unnecessary!" In *Evan Harrington*, Meredith concerns himself with just these "Statistics of Imposture" and with his own concern to separate and analyse the "Shams" and the "Realities."

Carlyle's short section on the tailor in *Sartor Resartus* throws considerable light on the tailoring motif in *Evan Harrington*. . . . Clothes may lend the wearer a symbolic aura of authority or reverence, yet beneath them he remains Falstaff's "forked Radish with a head fantastically carved." In *Evan Harrington* Jack Raikes is the most extreme example of this, since he holds a regular income at the whim of the eccentric Tom Cogglesby only if he wears a tin plate inside his trousers. Miss Louisa Carrington uses dress as a concealment of a disfiguring skin disease which she hopes will pass unnoticed by her fiancé until after they are married, while Caroline Strike hides the marks of her husband's brutality by a careful arrangement of her draperies. . . .

The tailor . . . is the creator of the basic symbols used by Society to indicate and support the hierarchical structure. As such, his knowledge and skill place him in the position of Shelley's poet, and the analogy . . . is also reversed when poets and moral teachers become a "Species of Metaphorical Tailors." An awareness of this transference of role is, I believe, crucial to the understanding of Evan's (and indeed Meredith's) position. . . .

42. Ibid., pp. 202–204.

Retaining his identity as tailor, [the Great Mel] is simultaneously actor and potent hero of myth. . . . Here is the embodiment of Carlyle's tailor / poet whose poetic creation is his own style of life and enduring reputation. . . . In her own way [the Countess de Saldar] too is the tailor / poet of *Sartor Resartus.* . . .

Evan Harrington appears to be an exploration of contradictory reactions toward a similar social conflict taking place in Meredith the tailor / poet. He himself is Carlyle's metaphorical tailor who sees through the pretences and protective garb of the upper classes, but he is also the tailor who cannot gain acceptance into the environment which, for all its flaws, is still so desirable.[43]

IV

Though all Meredith's novels reveal signs of the Carlyle influence, the one that is overtly impregnated with it is *Beauchamp's Career.* It is Meredith's only political novel, in which he sets out to depict the current condition of England by portraying the conflicts of parties and ideologies. Apparently he had been brooding over Carlyle's invidious contrasting of fiction with history. In the opening chapter he affirms explicitly that he is undertaking to offer an impartial survey of contemporary history, such as his mentor would approve:

. . . following the counsel of a sage and seer, I must try to paint for you what is, not that which I imagine. This day, this hour, this life, and even politics, the centre and throbbing heart of it (enough, when unburlesqued, to blow the down off the gossamer-stump of fiction at a single breath, I have heard tell), must be treated of: men, and the ideas of men, which are—it is policy to be emphatic upon truisms—are actually the motives of men in a greater degree than their appetites: these are my theme; and may it be my fortune to keep them at blood-heat, and myself calm as a statue of Memnon in prostrate Egypt! [chap. 1].

John W. Morris has examined the Carlylean echoes in this paragraph, not only in ideas but in phrases and images.[44]

The hero of the novel is modeled closely on Meredith's headstrong,

43. Ibid., pp. 98–101, 108, 110, 112.

44. John W. Morris, "Beauchamp's Career: Meredith's Acknowledgment of his Debt to Carlyle," in *Studies in Honor of John C. Hodges and Alwin Thaler*, ed. R. B. Davis and J. L. Lievsay (Knoxville, Tenn., 1961), pp. 102–103. Norman Kelvin questions whether the "sage and seer" is Carlyle (*A Troubled Eden*, Stanford, 1961, pp. 89–90), but the evidence for the attribution is strong.

doctrinaire friend Frederick Maxse, with whom he had been discussing Carlyle for at least six years by the time he began writing the book in 1872. Maxse's early interest in Carlyle had been destroyed by Carlyle's apostasy from democratic ideals. In a lecture on "The Causes of Social Revolt" in that year, Maxse vilified Carlyle as "the most powerful calumniator of democracy," the "apostle of king-ship, force, oppression, and servility," who praises the "heaven-born docility of man."[45] There is some irony, then, in Meredith's demonstration of how much of Nevil Beauchamp's radicalism derives from the Sage of Chelsea.

Beauchamp is depicted as falling under Carlyle's spell at an early age. He became a midshipman at fourteen and during his first voyage developed a taste for adult books which horrified his surrogate mother, Rosamund Culling, his guardian's housekeeper:

His favourite author was one writing of Heroes, in (so she esteemed it) a style resembling either early architecture or utter dilapidation, so loose and rough it seemed; a wind-in-the-orchard style, that tumbled down here and there an appreciable fruit with uncouth bluster; sentences without commencements running to abrupt endings and smoke, like waves against a sea-wall, learned dictionary words giving a hand to street-slang, and accents falling on them haphazard, like slant rays from driving clouds; all the pages in a breeze, the whole book producing a kind of electrical agitation in the mind and the joints. . . . To her the incomprehensible was the abominable, for she had our country's high critical feeling; but he, while admitting that he could not quite master it, liked it. He had dug the book out of a bookseller's shop in Malta, captivated by its title, and had, since the day of his purchase, gone at it again and again, getting nibbles of golden meaning by instalments, as with a solitary pick in a very dark mine, until the illumination of an idea struck him that there was a great deal more in the book than there was in himself. . . . Rosamund sighed with apprehension to think of his unlikeness to boys and men among his countrymen in some things. Why should he hug a book he owned he could not quite comprehend? He said he liked a bone in his mouth; and it was natural wisdom, though unappreciated by women. . . .

Nevil proposed to her that her next present should be the entire list of his beloved Incomprehensible's published works, and she promised, and was not sorry to keep her promise dangling at the skirts of memory, to drop away in time. For that fire-and-smoke writer dedicated volumes to the praise of a regicide. Nice reading for her dear boy! [chap. 2].

45. Lindsay, p. 193.

Carlyle provides the inspiration of Beauchamp's determination to devote himself to a quixotic campaign of national leadership intended to rescue his country from faction and materialism. Throughout the later part of the book, the Carlylean force is embodied in Nevil's political mentor, the radical Dr. Shrapnel. Though several other people (including perhaps Meredith himself) contributed traits to the portrait of this assertive idealogue, he recognizably resembles Carlyle not only in physical appearance but also in his opinions, his dogmatism, and his metaphoric prose. All this is well illustrated during the Doctor's first conversation with Rosamund Culling. In a tirade against family tradition, he asserts:

"No man ever did brave work who held council with his family. . . . The family view is everlastingly the shopkeeper's. Purse, pence, ease, increase of worldly goods, personal importance—the pound, the English pound! Dare do *that*, and you forfeit your share of Port wine in this world; you won't be dubbed with a title; you'll be fingered at! Lord, Lord! is it the region inside a man, or out, that gives him peace? *Out*, they say; for they have lost faith in the existence of an inner. They haven't it. Air-sucker, blood-pump, cooking machinery, and a battery of trained instincts, aptitudes, fill up their vacuum" [chap. 2].

As the interview proceeds, Rosamund begins to recognize why the Doctor's style is so baffling to her:

It was perceptible to her that a species of mad metaphor had been wriggling and tearing its passage through a thorn-bush in his discourse, with the furious urgency of a sheep in a panic; but where the ostensible subject ended and the metaphor commenced, and which was which at the conclusion, she found it difficult to discern—much as the sheep would be when he had left his fleece behind him.

Later in the book, Shrapnel's Carlylean rhetoric is well exemplified in a long letter to Beauchamp:

"Work at the people! . . . Moveless do they seem to you? Why, so is the earth to the sowing husbandman, and though we cannot forecast a reaping season, we have in history durable testification that our seasons come in the souls of men, yea, as a planet that we have set in motion, and faster and faster are we spinning it, and firmer and firmer shall we set it to regularity of revolution. *That means life.* . . . Recognize that now we have bare life; at best for the bulk of men the Saurian lizard's broad back soaking and roasting in primeval slime; or say, in the so-called teachers of men, as much of life as pricks the frog in March to stir and yawn, and up on a flaccid leap that rolls him over some three inches nearer to the ditchwater besought by his instinct. . . .

"Professors, prophets, masters, each hitherto has had his creed and system to offer, good mayhap for the term; and each has put it forth for the truth everlasting, to drive the dagger to the heart of time, and put the axe to human growth!—that one circle of wisdom issuing of the experience and needs of their day, should act the despot over all other circles forever!— so where at first light shone to light the yawning frog to his wet ditch, there, with the necessitated revolution of men's minds in the course of ages, *darkness radiates*" [chap. 29].

When the central portion of Shrapnel's epistle is reduced by Beauchamp's cousin to a few key phrases, it reads like a summary of Carlyle's doctrines: "History—Bible of Humanity; . . . Permanency— enthusiast's dream—despot's aim—clutch of dead men's fingers in live flesh. . . . Man animal; man angel, man rooted; man winged."

Professor Morris has thoroughly analyzed the Carlylean elements in *Beauchamp's Career*, not only in opinions and in general style but also in many specific phrases. He concludes that the book "is clearly an astonishing double tribute to Carlyle. Meredith pays Carlyle the writer the tribute of appropriating his theory of biography-history for the novel; he pays Carlyle the seer the tribute of picturing his ideas as the principal creative forces of his age."[46]

Shortly after writing *Beauchamp's Career*, Meredith composed his *Essay on the Idea of Comedy* (1877; published 1897); and it, too, contained a passage of praise for Carlyle, qualified with serious doubt as to his soundness of judgment:

Taking a living great, though not creative, humourist to guide our description: the skull of Yorick is in his hands in our seasons of festival; he sees visions of primitive man capering preposterously under the gorgeous robes of ceremonial. Our souls must be on fire when we wear solemnity, if we would not press upon the shrewdest nerve. Finite and infinite flash from one to the other with him, lending him a two-edged thought that peeps out of his peacefullest lines by fits, like the lantern of the fire-watcher at windows, going the rounds at night. The comportment and performances of men in society are to him, by the vivid comparison with their mortality, more grotesque than respectable. But ask yourself, Is he always to be relied on for justness? He will fly straight as the emissary eagle back to Jove

46. Morris, p. 106.

at the true Hero. He will also make as determined a swift descent upon the man of his wilful choice, whom he cannot distinguish as a true one. This vast power of his, built up of the feelings and the intellect in union, is often wanting in proportion and in discretion. Humourists touching upon History or Society are given to be capricious.

In Meredith's next novel, *The Egoist* (1879), an allusion to Carlyle, again identifying him as a "humourist," occurs in the opening chapter, which sets forth Meredith's theory of comedy and of egoism in peculiarly metaphorical terms. When Henri Davray was translating *The Egoist* into French in 1898, Meredith warned him: "You will find the introductory chapter rather stiff work, and should be told that the pretended testimony to the merits of Comedy is in the vein of Carlyle."[47] While by no means ill-natured, the parody is a mischievous exaggeration of Carlyle's verbal mannerisms. The most notorious passage reads:

Who, says the notable humourist, in allusion to this Book [of Egoism], who can studiously travel through sheets of leaves now capable of a stretch from the Lizard to the last few poor pulmonary snips and shreds of leagues dancing on their toes for cold, explorers tell us, and catching breath for good luck, like dogs at bones about a table, on the edge of the Pole? Inordinate unvaried length, sheer longinquity, staggers the heart, ages the very heart of us at a view. And how if we manage finally to print one of our pages on the crow-scalp of that solitary majestic outsider? We may with effort get even him into the Book; yet the knowledge we want will not be more present with us than it was when the chapters hung their end over that cliff ye ken of at Dover, where sits our great lord and master contemplating the seas without upon the reflex of that within!

In other words, as I venture to translate him (humourists are difficult: it is a piece of their humour to puzzle our wits), the inward mirror, the embracing and condensing spirit, is required to give us those interminable milepost piles of matter (extending well-nigh to the very Pole) in essence, in chosen samples, digestibly.

With typical Meredithian irony, the author simultaneously exalts the merits of the Comic Spirit and demonstrates it in action through directing laughter toward Carlyle's inflated style.

After the foregoing review of the evidence, it is difficult to think of any other literary influence that has been so pervasive as that of

47. 22 March 1898, *Letters*, III, 1295.

Carlyle on Meredith without reducing the disciple to a mere imitator. Meredith retained full independence, not only in the development of his own ideas and techniques but also in perceiving the shortcomings of the writer to whom he owed so much.

"Analyzing humanity back into its elements": Browning's Aristophanes' Apology and Carlyle

CLYDE DE L. RYALS, *Duke University*

One of the salient characteristics of Browning's work from *Paracelsus* on is its dualistic nature. The physical world is, on the one hand, depicted as a place of diversity, grotesqueness, multitudinousness, and near-chaos in which the splendors of eternity are hidden behind a veil; on the other hand, it is shown to be the arena in which man realizes his potentialities and rises to higher things. Human character is likewise painted in dualistic terms: composed of the practical and worldly and, at the same time, of the divine and mysterious. Browning's poetry thus portrays man placed on the isthmus of a middle state, seeing that his home is earth but also perceiving that his true domicile is elsewhere, his real values different; and it delineates man held in tension by a polarity of opposing thrusts, one transcendental or upwards towards the infinite and one descendental or downwards towards the palpable.[1] In other words, Browning's thought bears an amazing similarity to Carlyle's.

One day the full story of Browning's relationship with Carlyle will be told and then will be proved the truth of Richard Garnett's observation that Browning was "the poet whose genius has more affinity to Carlyle's than that of any other contemporary."[2] My purpose here is

---

1. In surveying the world of Browning's poetry J. Hillis Miller says: "The poet faces in two directions, upward toward the transcendent God, and downward toward God as incarnated in the creation." *The Disappearance of God* (1963; rpt., New York, 1965), p. 112.

2. Richard Garnett, *Life of Thomas Carlyle* (London, 1887), p. 146. The fullest account of Browning's personal relationship to Carlyle is to be found in William Clyde DeVane, *Browning's Parleyings: The Autobiography of a Mind* (New Haven, 1927), pp. 14–36. Charles Richard Sanders notes the similarities between Browning's and Carlyle's poetic theory in two articles: "Carlyle, Browning, and the Nature of a Poet," *Emory University Quarterly*, 16 (Winter 1960), 197–209, and "Carlyle, Poetry, and the Music of Humanity," *Western Humanities Review*, 16 (Winter 1962), 53–66. Charlotte Crawford Watkins notes reflections of Carlyle in the poem published immediately prior to *Aristophanes' Apology*, in "Browning's 'Red Cotton Night-Cap Country' and Carlyle," *Victorian Studies*, 7 (June 1964), 359–374. Connections between Carlyle's doctrines and the poems "Transcendentalism" and the parleying "With Bernard De Mandeville" have been noted by Richard D. Altick in his

more modest. In this essay I should like to suggest that *Aristophanes'*
Apology (1875), a poem of Browning's later years, owes a debt to
Carlyle not only in its thought but also in its structure.

Early in her correspondence with Robert Browning, Elizabeth Barrett wrote in praise of "the great teacher of the age, Carlyle, who is
also yours & mine. He fills the office of a poet—does he not?—by
analyzing humanity back into its elements, to the destruction of the
conventions of the hour."[3] The future Mrs. Browning's words about
Carlyle are, as we shall see, similar to those applied to Euripides in
Aristophanes' Apology. For Browning, like his wife, always saw the
poet as one who had to overcome the conventions and thus the limitations of his time to present a vision of humanity in its noblest aspects and highest potentialities. In part, no doubt, the two poets
learned from Carlyle himself, especially from his lectures on *Heroes*
and Hero-Worship, that it is the function of the modern man of letters
to discern the "Divine Idea of the World" and "in a new dialect" make
his insights available to his generation so that he utters a "Prophecy
in these most unprophetic times."[4]

Throughout his life, but particularly in his later years, Browning
was diffident about discussing not only his poetic practice but also his
poetic theory. Hence his *Essay on Shelley* is of considerable interest
for the light it throws on his ideas about poetry and, additionally, for
its reflection of some of the thought of Carlyle. In the essay Browning
contrasts two different kinds of poets. The objective poet reproduces
"things external . . . with an immediate reference, in every case, to the
common eye and apprehension of his fellow men. . . . Such a poet is
properly the ποιητής, the fashioner; and the thing fashioned, his
poetry, will of necessity be substantive, projected from himself and
distinct."[5] Shakespeare is offered as an example of this kind of poet.
Like Carlyle's Shakespeare in "The Hero as Poet," Browning's ob-

---

"Browning's 'Transcendentalism,'" *Journal of English and Germanic Philology*, 58
(Feb. 1959), 24–28, and by DeVane in his book on the *Parleyings*. A long essay by
C. R. Sanders on the Carlyle-Browning relationship appears in the Autumn 1974
and Spring 1975 issues of the *Bulletin of the John Rylands Library*.

3. *The Letters of Robert Browning and Elizabeth Barrett Browning, 1845–1846*, ed.
Elvan Kintner (Cambridge, Mass., 1969), I, 29.

4. *Works*, V, 156–157.

5. *Robert Browning's Complete Works*, Florentine Edition, ed. Charlotte Porter
and Helen A. Clarke (New York, 1910), XII, 284. All quotations from Browning's
published works are from this edition and are given by line number.

jective poet works unself-consciously and leaves little autobiographical imprint on his art so that, in Carlyle's words, "we have no full
impress of him there" (V, 110). The subjective poet "of modern
classification," on the other hand, writes "not so much with reference
to the many below as to the One above him." Thus he writes about
his own soul. "Therefore, in our approach to the poetry, we necessarily approach the personality of the poet; in apprehending it we
apprehend him" (XII, 286). Shelley presumably is an example of
this kind of poet,[6] one who, as Carlyle remarked of Goethe, leaves
his "inward life . . . nobly recorded in the long series of his Writings"
("Goethe's Works," XXVII, 430).

While making no claim for the superiority of one type over the
other, Browning did foresee that in the future a greater kind of poet
might arise. "If the subjective might seem to be the ultimate requirement of every age, the objective, in the strictest state, must still retain
its original value. . . . Nor is there any reason why these two modes of
poetic faculty may not issue hereafter from the same poet in successive perfect works, examples of which . . . we have hitherto
possessed in distinct individuals only" (XII, 288).

The *Essay on Shelley* provides some of the ideas later elaborated
in *Aristophanes' Apology*. And apparently those ideas were partly
formed under Carlyle's influence. "I have put down a few thoughts
that presented themselves," the poet wrote to Carlyle just after completing his essay, "one or two, in respect of opinions of your own (I
mean, that I was thinking of those opinions while I wrote)."[7]

What is owing to Carlyle in the essay is primarily the method of
argument, what Elizabeth Barrett called "analyzing humanity back
into its elements." For like Carlyle, Browning proceeds dialectically,
balancng the "descendental" objective poet against the "transcendental" subjective poet, and ends by suggesting a possible synthesis,
the "whole" poet who sees both high and low, perceiving not only
men and women but also the divine in them. The poetics of the
Essay on Shelley, then, resembles Carlyle's, which Charles Richard
Sanders has characterized as follows: "Just as in *Sartor Resartus* the
opposite ideas in *descendentalism* and *transcendentalism* comple-

6. Philip Drew reads the essay in a different fashion: he does not believe that
Browning classified Shelley as a subjective poet. See his book *The Poetry of Browning:
A Critical Introduction* (London, 1970), pp. 6–8.

7. *Letters of Robert Browning Collected by Thomas J. Wise*, ed. Thurman L.
Hood (London, 1933), p. 36.

ment and interplay with one another, in Carlyle's thinking about the music of poetry 'the eternal melodies,' 'sphere music,' must somehow be brought down to earth, without any diminution of its heavenly quality, and find for itself utterance in a voice which is, in the strictest sense of the word, *human*."[8] In their poetics as in their philosophy at large both Carlyle and Browning are apparent dualists who constitutionally see the world in terms of opposites. Ultimately, however, they are monists. G. B. Tennyson says of Carlyle: "His monism is an ineffable concept, not a system; and the habitual dualism of his writings is designed to demonstrate an underlying inexpressible unity in all phenomena. . . ."[9] The same observation could, I believe, be applied to Browning.[10] It is not surprising that Carlyle was much impressed with the *Essay on Shelley*, though disparaging the ostensible subject of the essay: "Poor Shelley, there is something void, and Hades-like in the whole inner world of him; his universe is all vacant azure . . . ; the very voice of him . . . has too much of the *ghost!*—In a word, it is not with Shelley, but with Shelley's Commentator, that I take up my quarters at all: and to this latter I will say with emphasis, Give us some more of *your* writing, my friend; we decidedly need a man or two like you, if we could get them!"[11]

In spite of his admonition to Browning to write more, Carlyle by and large never cared very much for the poet's work after *Men and Women* (1855).[12] The chief exceptions to his dispraise were the two Greek poems, *Balaustion's Adventure* and *Aristophanes' Apology*, especially the latter.[13] Perhaps Carlyle liked the second Greek poem because he saw so much of himself reflected in it. For it contains not only the repeated use of the Carlylean metaphor of divestiture— "Masks were down/And robes doffed now" (581–582)—and certain

8. Sanders, "Carlyle, Poetry, and the Music of Humanity," p. 62.

9. G. B. Tennyson, *Sartor Called Resartus* (Princeton, 1965), p. 151. See also Charles Frederick Harrold, *Carlyle and German Thought: 1819–1834* (New Haven, 1934), p. 119.

10. For a different view see Henry Jones, *Browning as a Philosophical and Religious Teacher* (Glasgow, 1891). In arguing for a split in Browning between the head and the heart Jones says: "The evidence of the heart, to which he appealed, was the evidence of an emotion severed from intelligence, and, therefore, without any content whatsoever" (pp. 340–341).

11. A. Carlyle, *CMSB*, pp. 292–293.

12. See Charles Richard Sanders, "Some Lost and Unpublished Carlyle-Browning Correspondence," *Journal of English and Germanic Philology*, 52 (April 1963), 323–335.

13. *The Diary of Alfred Domett, 1872–1885*, ed. E. A. Horsman (London, New York, and Toronto, 1953), pp. 161, 181.

Carlylean locutions such as the description of Aristophanes as being like "his own Amphitheos, deity/And dung" (227–228)—it employs not only these but also (and more importantly) the Carlylean contrast and interplay between transcendentalism and descendentalism to make a statement about poetry and the nature of man.

The third longest of Browning's works (after *The Ring and the Book* and *Sordello*) and certainly the most erudite,[14] *Aristophanes' Apology* in both length and learning is a formidable poem, almost universally misprized and neglected.[15] I propose here to regard it as, formally, a further attempt on Browning's part to experiment with and overcome the limitations of the dramatic monologue and, thematically, an expression of his Carlylean philosophy that human beings must accept the antinomies of existence without strict adherence to one pole of a dialectic. The form of the poem is extremely complex, but the work is so designed that the form, organic as Carlyle would require, is reflective of the theme. To quote Roma King on Browning's earlier monologues, "the unity is a tension produced by the interplay of opposing intellectual and moral forces"; the *Apology* is a dramatization of what David Shaw calls the poet's "dialectical temper."[16] Early in the poem Balaustion says, without necessarily accepting her own statement, that "progress means contention" (141). Accordingly the poem progresses by statement and counterstatement,

14. In his attempt to recreate life in Athens at the time of the death of Euripides, Browning ransacked the scholarship on fifth-century Greece so that, as he was to say some years later, "the allusions require a knowledge of the Scholia, besides acquaintance with the 'Comicorum Graecorum Fragmenta,' Athenaeus, Alciphron, and so forth" (Hood, *Letters*, p. 208).

15. The critical literature on the poem is slight. Most of the scholarship has been concerned with classical sources: Carl N. Jackson, "Classical Elements in Browning's 'Aristophanes' Apology,'" *Harvard Studies in Classical Philology*, 20 (1909), 15–73; T. L. Hood, "Browning's Ancient Classical Sources," *Harvard Studies in Classical Philology*, 33 (1922), 79–180; Frederick Tisdel, "Browning's *Aristophanes' Apology*," *University of Missouri Studies*, 2, No. 4 (1927). While a study of the sources of *Aristophanes' Apology* is interesting and informative, I cannot agree with the scholars who claim that "the best approach to genuine understanding of the poem is through a study of the sources of Browning's information" (Tisdel, p. 1). Instead I believe, to quote the anonymous review of *Balaustion's Adventure* in the *Examiner* for 12 August 1871, that "the story has so filtered through Mr. Browning's mind that it is a thoroughly original poem, and as such it claims to be read and mastered before classical criticism is allowed to play." Donald Smalley provides an interesting account of the poem as an early parleying (with Browning's critics) in "A Parleying with Aristophanes," *PMLA*, 55 (Dec. 1940), 823–838.

16. Roma A. King, Jr., *The Bow and the Lyre: The Art of Robert Browning* (Ann Arbor, 1957), p. 140; David Shaw, *The Dialectical Temper: The Rhetorical Art of Robert Browning* (Ithaca, 1968).

being divided into three main parts—Aristophanes' apology, Balaustion's admonishment of him, and a translation of Euripides' *Herakles* —with a prologue and a conclusion. As I see it, the translation is not a mere flexion of Browning's classical muscles but an organic part of the work whose full title is *Aristophanes' Apology; Including a Transcript from Euripides: Being the Last Adventure of Balaustion.*

At first glance the form is reminiscent of that of *Balaustion's Adventure*: a combination of three dramatic modes—monologue, dialogue, and fully realized drama—resulting in a multilevel technique first essayed in *The Ring and the Book.* Browning learned earlier in his career that both monologue and dialogue suffer the limitation of the speakers' personalities. Seeking to overcome this limitation and to arrive at a more nearly objective mode, he included a play in *Balaustion's Adventure.*[17] But even there the hoped-for objectivity of the *Alkestis* was diminished by Balaustion's commentary on and her version of the play. Browning must have reasoned that one way to circumvent the subjectivity of his monologist was to provide within the monologue a full-fledged drama, the most objective of literary forms, unedited and without commentary. The special pleading of the two characters in the dialogue, the "contention" of which Balaustion speaks, could thus perhaps be resolved by a play which is not bounded by an immediate audience—in this case, Balaustion and Aristophanes and, maybe, Euthukles—and which presumably did not owe its origin to any strategic purpose. To include a complete play might then be the real "progress," the objectification and resolution of diverse points of view.

If I am correct in my guess at Browning's intention, we can then understand the reason for the nature of the translation of the *Herakles.* It is extremely literal, what Browning called in his Preface to his translation of the *Agamemnon* of Aeschylus "a mere strict bald version of thing by thing" giving only "the action of the piece"; and to most lovers of poetry it is barely readable. It is not that Browning was incapable of making beautiful translations—*teste* the *Alkestis* in *Balaustion's Adventure*—but that with the *Herakles* he wished to be as neutral and objective in style as possible. Within the design of the poem the *Herakles* would be the "pure" statement distinct from the biased utterances of Aristophanes and Balaustion.

17. See my essay *"Balaustion's Adventure*: Browning's Greek Parable," *PMLA*, 88 (Oct. 1973), 1040–1048.

What we have then in *Aristophanes' Apology* is a complicated work in three different parts and three different modes. It is important to say, however, that the subsuming formal locus of the poem is Balaustion's monologue, in spite of the fact that she is by no means the main character. It is she who tells us all, and consequently the poem is ultimately hers. The poem exists because she decided to talk. And why does she speak? To distance and objectify a personal dilemma; that is, to alleviate present suffering—the collapse of Athens before Spartan invaders and her own retreat to Rhodes—by talking about it:

> That fate and fall, once bedded in our brain,
> Roots itself past upwrenching; but coaxed forth,
> Encouraged out to practise fork and fang,—
> Perhaps, when satiate with prompt sustenance,
> It may pine, likelier die than if left swell
> In peace by our pretension to ignore,
> Or pricked to threefold fury, should our stamp
> Bruise and not brain the pest.
>
> (151–158)

So "wanting strength," she will "use craft, / Advance upon the foe I cannot fly, / Nor feign a snake is dormant though it gnaw" (148–150). Yet simply to relate what happened and to dwell on her own involvement in it will offer no relief. What is needed is a "middle course." Out of the experience she will devise a play: "What hinders that we treat this tragic theme / As the Three taught when either woke some woe" (158–160). The fall of Athens will be the tragedy which will "re-enact itself, this voyage through" (168). She and her husband will be the chorus.

Balaustion is thus the poet-maker and the commentator-chorus. Her narrative is necessarily to be her story, with her as an actor in the piece. She will not only mold the narrative but also project her own character into the drama, with a prologue which she will "style" from her own adventure (184–185). Immediately we realize that little objectivity can be gained this way. For she can only delude herself that she will be able to transcend the limitations of her own personality. In effect the Balaustion of the poem is really two characters —her present self and her re-creation of her past self. As her present self she is subject to the same vacillation between hope and despair as other people and shares with them all the earthly desires which characterize the human condition (1–3, 39–46). In her re-created self, on the other hand, she is depicted only as one who constantly stands as the representative of hope and idealistic thought, the advocate of soul who recoils from "fleshly durance dim and low" (42). It is this imagined self that can declare upon first hearing of Euripides' death: "Thank Zeus for the great news and good!" It is the present real self however that suffers intensely the loss of a beloved poet who had become her friend: "no Euripides / Will teach the chorus, nor shall we be tinged / By any such grand sunset of his soul" (214–216). What we have in her monologue, therefore, is two narrative perspectives: the Balaustion who talks to her husband and the Balaustion who tells Euthukles, in an unfinished sentence: "I somehow speak to unseen auditors. / Not *you*, but—" (242–243). Or to put it another way, what we find in her narrative is a disjunction between her present and past voices.

Like nearly all of Browning's monologists, Balaustion speaks out of a compelling need of personality. She says plainly that she speaks only to escape "not sorrow but despair, / Not memory but the present and its pang" (2–3). Yet we wonder whether there might not be still another reason: a need, so often felt by other characters in Browning, to justify herself. As earlier remarked, she presents herself in her story as wholly the advocate of idealistic thought, ever shunning "body" in favor of "soul." And in her representation of herself she strikes us as more than a little too soulful and, possibly, self-righteous. We detect at least a hint of truth in Aristophanes' characterization of those like Balaustion who dream of themselves as the "sole selected few / Fume-fed with self-superiority" (2681–2682). In fact, we are led to wonder just how much of "body" she suppresses.

Balaustion's prudery is readily discernible. What distresses her as much as the fall of Athens is the licentiousness which she believes caused and accompanied it (95–102), and what troubles her most about Aristophanes is not his satire but his frank celebration of man's animal nature. Perceiving her extreme repugnance to talk of sexual matters, the comic poet gently mocks at this element in her character (2020–2024) and suggests that she is but the "merest female child" whom he will try not to offend (773–777). The Athenians chide her for her refusal to attend Aristophanes' comedies and wonder that she is "wife and ignorant so long" (415). She prizes Euripides' *Hippolytus* mostly because of its presentation of Phaidra as "the chaste" who died distraught rather than "loose one limb / Lovewards, at lambency of honeyed tongue, / Or torture of the scales which scraped her snow" (420–426). In brief, there is in her nature more than a little of deep loathing of the physical.

Browning allows us to catch sight of this aspect of her in order to suggest a certain deficiency in her make-up. He would have us see that his monologist seeks to obviate a very basic part of human nature and, further, that she herself half understands that her denial of the body is not totally to be applauded. Her monologue is therefore in part an effort to convince herself of the rightness of her ideals and of the idealism which she believed Euripides taught and which she fain would live by. While Euripides was alive and Athens stood, she needed not to be reassured. But now unable to support her belief in the reality of the ideal because of the present loss of the great ideals in her life—namely, Euripides and Athens, whose demise she equates and collapses into one moment in time—she is "wanting strength," for in her present position she feels the need for her customary props. Originally, as we learn in *Balaustion's Adventure*, her attachment to Euripides was wholly altruistic. But in *Aristophanes' Apology* it is more personal, more necessary for self-sustainment. Through Euripides she won her husband, her home, her friends; through him she achieved all that Athens symbolized for her. Thus a loss of her beloved dramatist is a deeply personal loss, and any threat to Euripides and his ideals as she understood them is a threat to herself. So she speaks not to Euthukles but to "unseen auditors," and so she seeks to combat Aristophanes, whose diatribes against Euripides she conceives as assaults upon herself and her ideals. In the Conclusion to the poem she makes explicit her identification of herself, her husband, her home, and Euripides: "Saved was Athenai through Euripides, / Through Euthukles, through—more than ever—me, / Balaustion, me who, Wild-pomegranate-flower, / Felt my fruit triumph, and fade proudly so" (522–525). Her utterance is, then, limited by her strategic purpose, which is a justification of her own philosophy and ultimately of herself.

If Balaustion's constant plea is for "disembodied soul" flying "distinct above / Man's wickedness and folly" (39–46), it is because she espouses only one aspect of man's nature, the transcendental, and denigrates the other. She stands, that is to say, for one pole of a dialectic and as such represents but a limited truth. The other pole, the descendental, is figured in Aristophanes, who defends "body" as vehemently as Balaustion advocates "soul."

Aristophanes, though more interesting a character than Balaustion, is just as doctrinaire as she. Like her he insists that there is but one way of understanding life, although, as we shall later see, his "apology" is more limited in its vision than the man himself is. To Aristophanes, Euripides is to be regarded as an opponent, not because he dislikes the tragic dramatist but because Euripides taught that there is no single way in which truth is to be apprehended. Euripides questioned everything, to the point where he left "no longer one plain positive / Enunciation incontestable / Of what is good, right, decent here on earth" (2221–2223). He would not accept any aspect of life as a fixed truth; instead he would "refine, refine, / Divide, distinguish, subtilize away / Whatever seemed a solid planting-place / For footfall" (2215–2218).

As in Balaustion's viewpoint there is a disjunction between past and present, so in Aristophanes' there is a fear that the values of the past cannot be crystallized; somewhat like Balaustion he despairs that change means the end of his most cherished values. No Rhodian but a native Athenian, he loved a small, self-contained Athens whose citizens believed themselves "undoubted lords of earth." Here indeed was civilization, and beyond was only "barbarism." Athens was enough; the present was all-sufficient. Why then should a man wish to consider anything above or beyond this happy moment in time where all was easy and beautiful? Euripides and his friends, however, have quite perversely changed all this (1971–2019), introducing "restless change, / Deterioration" (2024–2025). Socrates urged understanding at the expense of mystery, Aristotle demanded questioning and argument, Euripides debased both kings and gods (2472–2479). Why, if as Euripides claimed, "There are no gods," then "Man has no master, owns, by consequence, / No right, no wrong, except to please or plague / His nature" (2140–2143). That is why in his plays Aristophanes' whole aim has been to flog with the club of comedy those fellows who would change the customs of Athens (1850–1854), drawing his "Comic steel" to cut this "poison-tree" (2269–2273). As for his own teaching, he has insisted upon respect for kings and gods (2480–2485) and has urged the populace to "accept the old, / Contest the strange" (2649–2650). His plays have been "acted in the interest of truth, / Religion, and those manners old and dear / Which made our city great . . ." (447–449).

Aristophanes claims that his object has been "sustainment of humanity" (1887). To be sure, he admits, the doctrines of Euripides and his coterie are not totally without validity. But they are not such as will nourish the populace. They preach "purity" (1882), asking men to "Unworld the world" (1952). Indeed, the whole thrust of "modernism" has been to exalt spirit at the expense of sense. And what can a common lout know of spirit? No, Euripides has offered ethereal vapors to men who want and need rich red wine. The tragic dramatist has presented an unreal picture of life, showing men not as they are but as they perhaps could be. Hence his plays are factitious because they render a vision of a world "where what's false is fact," where ugliness is transformed into beauty, where life itself is disguised as immortality. "No, this were unreality" (2157–2160, 2166). Such teaching is pernicious and must not be tolerated.

Aristophanes, on the other hand, knows that "men are, were, ever will be fools" (1649). He does not show them as half-angels: "I paint men as they are" (2129). "Strong understander of our common life" (1886), he does not renounce life, degrade the hero, deny the gods, make men and women and slaves all equal as does Euripides (2176–2179). On the contrary, "I stand up for the common coarse-as-clay / Existence,—stamp and ramp with heel and hoof / On solid vulgar life . . ." (2683–2685). His plays consequently have been an antidote to the "poison-drama of Euripides" because they recall "our commonalty" to "primæval virtue, antique faith" which flourished ere these so-called days of enlightenment (1061–1066). And "once true man in right place, / Our commonalty soon content themselves / With doing just what they are born to do, / Eat, drink, make merry, mind their own affairs / And leave state-business to the larger brain" (2449–2453).

Throughout his conversation with Balaustion we see that he is not so much berating Euripides as attempting to justify himself. If his plays have been vulgar, it is because men are vulgar and incapable of understanding refinement. If they expound the virtues of the status quo, it is because the populace is resistant to change. Man, as Aristophanes sees him, is basically an animal, a creature of sense: "Eat and drink, / And drink and eat, what else is good in life?" (1089–1090). To try to show him as something else is to elevate him to a station which he cannot comprehend and certainly cannot sustain.

Aristophanes personally can conceive of a new kind of comedy, but in one lifetime there is not sufficient time to "penetrate encrusted prejudice, / Pierce ignorance three generations thick" (843–844). In fact, he did once attempt a comedy in good taste containing absolutely nothing base, but it did not win acceptance. So, using a Carlylean metaphor, he says that he has kept to the old ways: "Purity? / No more of that next month, Athenai mine! / Contrive new cut of robe who will,—I patch. . ." (1140–1142). There will doubtless come a time when a new kind of comedy is possible—"When laws allow" and "Had I but two lives"—but as things stand he must simply carry on in a vein started by other men, which means that he will spend his life planing the knobs and adding shining studs to the club of comedy (837–850). Besides, a new art demands of the artist seclusion and loneliness: "No such thin fare feeds flesh and blood like mine" (934). In the end, therefore, Aristophanes places himself squarely at the pole of sense opposite the pole of spirit occupied by Balaustion.

Neither Balaustion nor Aristophanes is fully at ease with the extreme position each takes. Browning would have us see that, in the words of his Rabbi Ben Ezra, "All good things / Are ours, nor soul helps flesh more, now, than flesh helps soul!" As Carlyle taught, perhaps more insistently than any other nineteenth-century English thinker, body and soul stand in need of each other. That is why Aristophanes seeks out Balaustion (see lines 763–772, 1521–1529) and why she recalls, a year later, his visit to her. In the midst of despair body and soul meet to find comfort. The whole discussion of the differences between comedy and tragedy evidences their awareness of incompleteness. Aristophanes says that comedy, dwelling on all the ugliness and absurdity of life, suggests by contrast the perfection which man might attain (1762 ff.); and he also admits, though fleetingly, that tragedy presents a vision of truth which might be grasped. Both comedy and tragedy have the same end in view, even if they go about it by different means. Therefore, "Both be praised" (1465). He and Euripides do not differ in their aims, only in their methods (2550–2567). The comic poet and the tragic poet each serve "complex Poetry," which operates "for body as for soul." The man who dares disjoin these, by ignoring either body or soul, "Maims the else perfect manhood" (1471–1480). As for Aristophanes himself, he will defend, at least at this moment, "Man's double nature" (1494).

Prior to his nocturnal visit Balaustion had deemed Aristophanes among the basest of humanity, the great enemy and defamer of her "soulful" Euripides. She is surprised to find him both "impudent and majestic" (617), "like some meteor-brilliance, fire and filth, / Or say, his own Amphitheos, deity / And dung" (226–228):

> What I had disbelieved most proved most true.
> There was a mind here, mind a-wantoning
> At ease of undisputed mastery
> Over the body's brood, those appetites.
>
> (620–623)

At this moment of confrontation each stands (in the Carlylean sense) naked, stripped of disguises and attitudes. "You see myself?" asks Aristophanes:

> Balaustion's fixed regard
> Can strip the proper Aristophanes
> Of what our sophists, in their jargon, style
> His accidents? My soul sped forth but now
> To meet your hostile survey,—soul unseen,
> Yet veritably cinct for soul-defence
> With satyr sportive quips, cranks, boss and spike,
> Just as my visible body paced the street,
> Environed by a boon companionship
> Your apparition also puts to flight.
> Well, what care I if, unaccoutred twice,
> I front my foe—no comicality
> Round soul, and body-guard in banishment?
> Thank your eyes' searching, undisguised I stand.
>
> (763–776)

As for Balaustion she appears as but the "merest female child" (804): "I who, a woman, claim no quality" (2739). And bare of externals, each can recognize the worth of the other. Yet the longer they talk, the more they resume their customary attitudes. Aware of the need that body has for soul and flesh for spirit, they nevertheless retreat to their opposite poles, since apparently they can orient themselves only by one position. Their dialogue ends up as two monologues, an expostulation and a reply. What is needed is some way to join the two in more nearly perfect counterpoint. And this is precisely the purpose served by the *Herakles*. For Euripides himself is not the antagonist which Aristophanes fancied him nor is he quite the disembodied spirit whom Balaustion pictured. He is, in this poem at any rate, one who, speaking to both soul and sense, creates the kind of drama reflective of a true understanding of human nature.

Like Carlyle's Heroic Men of Letters, Euripides recognized that his world was in a period of transition—from a mythifying past to a more secular future—and it was his task to help ease the pangs of this change. From the beginning he "shrank not to teach, / If gods be strong and wicked, man, though weak, / May prove their match by willing to be good" (428–430). Then in his *Elektra* he first "dared bring the grandeur of the Tragic Two / Down to the level of our common life, / Close to the beating of our common heart" (Conclusion, 481–483). He showed that the old gods are dead but that a new kind of responsibility had been placed on men: mankind has to rely upon itself. Instead of the old gods there is "Necessity," which signifies "Duty enjoined you, fact in figment's place, / Throned on no mountain, native to the mind" (2147–2149).

During this trying period in history, art too must undergo change. The old categories of tragedy and comedy no longer are adequate to the new age. Euripides envisioned a new type of drama in which comedy and tragedy meet, one which "Fain would paint, manlike, actual animal life, / Make veritable men think, say and do" (1312–1313). He himself had attempted such a new mode but had not perfected it, this task awaiting "the novel man / Born to that next success myself foresee" (1321–1322). "Never needs the Art stand still," he told Aristophanes (1304). An artist must always be remolding the old; otherwise art becomes stale and retrogressive (1321 ff).

The *Herakles*, the last work of Euripides presented to Athens, embodies all these ideas. In the *Alkestis*, which played such a vital role in Balaustion's first adventure, Herakles was represented as an heroic redeemer. Now in this play, which forms part of Balaustion's last adventure, Herakles is stripped of his heroic and godlike nature to stand revealed as a fully human being. The whole point of the drama is to humanize Herakles so that he shares common ground with all other men, who are subject to necessity and have not the heroic stature which hitherto has exempted Herakles from subjugation to it. For the first time he comes to know that compensatory virtue—love, *philia*—

which makes necessity bearable and life endurable. The play shows that man, finding himself in tragic circumstances, can redeem himself by love. Indeed the drama demonstrates that modern man is beyond tragedy and even provides him with a new mythology: a change from outmoded heroic strength to very human fortitude, courage, and endurance. This is the point which Herakles iterates in his final lines: "whoso rather would have wealth and strength / Than good friends, reasons foolishly therein."

The drama stands in striking contrast to the views of both Aristophanes and Balaustion. The gods are dethroned, a hero is stripped of his power, the gentle virtue of love is triumphant—everything that Aristophanes professes to despise is there to be found. As for Balaustion, this is not the "cheerful weary Herakles / Striding away from the huge gratitude, . . . / Bound on the next new labor 'height o'er height / Ever surmounting,—destiny's decree' " (511–515), the Herakles whom she would follow. The play shows that Balaustion's belief in the essential spiritual nature of man is a distortion of man's true nature. For the *Herakles* demonstrates that in the best of men there are seeds of animalistic behavior, that to be human is also to be weak. Euripides here insists, as did Teufelsdröckh in *Sartor Resartus*, that the human condition is a dialectic between strength and weakness, hope and despair, good and evil. As Theseus says, "none of mortals boasts a fate unmixed" (1414).

At the end of the reading of the play Aristophanes penetrates to the perception that he and his plays have been defective to the extent that they have misrepresented the human condition. "Much may be said for stripping wisdom bare" (Conclusion, 16), he says, referring doubtlessly to his encounter with Balaustion as well as to the reading of the play. "The ripe old man ought to be as old as young— / As young as old. I too have youth at need" (Conclusion, 14–15). He should have been less resistant to change, more willing to experiment with his art. Yet the insight is fleeting, for almost immediately he claims, illustrating by the game of kottabos, that Euripides was fixed so that he could see only the lofty and good, while he, Aristophanes, glimpses successively the low and wrong as well as the high and right. "Man's made of both," he says (Conclusion, 54), forgetting of course that the second part of the dialectic he has almost completely suppressed. Nevertheless, he is now willing to admit the dual nature of man, which previously he had tended to deny, and within his heart he knows that he has failed where Euripides has more nearly succeeded:

> There's no failure breaks the heart,
> Whate'er be man's endeavor in this world,
> Like the rash poet's when he—nowise fails
> By poetizing badly,—Zeus or makes
> Or mars a man, so—at it, merrily!
> But when,—made man,—much like myself,—equipt
> For such and such achievement,—rash he turns
> Out of the straight path, bent on snatch of feat
> From—who's the appointed fellow born thereto,—
> Crows take him!—in your Kassiterides?
> Half-doing his work, leaving mine untouched,
> That were the failure.
>
> (Conclusion, 67–78)

In the figure of Aristophanes Browning once again turns to one of his favorite speculations, namely, why men fail to live up to their best capacities and potentialities. The answer here adumbrated is similar to that formerly offered: men fail when they do not admit the dual thrusts of their natures and recognize only one pole of the dialectic tension.

With Balaustion it is not so much a case of success or failure. For as she herself says, she can "claim no quality" (2739), lacking the creative quality of the artist. From the *Herakles* however she learns that the body has as much claim to consideration as the soul. Aristophanes has his genius and deserves recognition. No longer is it a question of "the antagonist Euripides" who contended with the comic dramatist (3464), but rather of "Euripides and Aristophanes," who each sow a seed and "Seed bears crop, scarce within our little lives" (Conclusion, 280–282). Her reconciliation with Aristophanes is, nevertheless, but momentary. She ends her story by condemning the licentiousness of Aristophanes' next play, *The Frogs*, and ascribing the fall of Athens to the deleterious effects of comedy. At the end Euripides and Aristophanes remain for her poles apart. As she nears Rhodes, her vision remains a transcendental one: the wind and waves sing out that Euripides lives. Yet the poem does not end as it began, for language has relieved the despair which she had experienced at the beginning. The "middle course" of which she spoke in the beginning has had the desired effect, having allowed her to rise above despair to greet the morn of her new life in Rhodes with hope: "Life detests black cold" (Conclusion, 601).

It should be readily apparent that in writing about fifth-century Athens Browning was also dealing with the analogous cultural situation of the nineteenth century. At a time when an established civilization was waning the poet offered, to those who would make the application, a message of hope, a message strongly echoing that of his mentor, Carlyle.[18] Though the old gods might be dead or dying, there was no reason to despair. Though customs may change, chaos is not the only alternative. Though the conventional literary categories might no longer prove adequate, new ones would arise. All this is summed up in the final lines when Balaustion joyfully sings: "There are no gods, no gods! / Glory to God—who saves Euripides!"

With *Aristophanes' Apology* Browning stretched the dramatic monologue almost to its breaking point. The poem makes a tremendous demand on the reader, requiring him to bear in mind two long monologues and a complete play—5,711 lines in all—and to remember that they are set within the confines of one dramatic monologue. It is no wonder that most contemporary reviewers could make neither heads nor tails out of it or that to most readers even today it remains hopelessly confusing.

What Browning was attempting was exactly what Balaustion (3435–3445), Euripides (1302–1305), and Aristophanes (1468–1494) speculate on in their discussions of a new type of drama and what the poet had suggested as a possibility in the *Essay on Shelley*. More especially it was what Aristophanes speaks of in the Conclusion when he alludes to the future poet who, "by mechanics past my guess," will take in both high and low, right and wrong, "every side at once, / And not successively" (57–59). Here Browning has essayed to give an overview of man and life in general, not sequentially but simultaneously. It was a bold experiment, the most daring that he ever made with the dramatic monologue. That he could go no further is indicated by the fact that he never returned to it again as the mode for a long poem.

18. See "The Hero as Man of Letters," V, 170–177. See also the chapter "Organic Filaments" in Book III of *Sartor Resartus*. In the "Phoenix Death-Birth" of society Carlyle sees that new powers will arise in response to the death of the old. The essential hopefulness of the young Carlyle is perhaps best indicated by the title which he gave to his most famous book—*Sartor Resartus*.

There are no direct references to Carlyle in *Aristophanes' Apology*, as there are in other works of Browning's later career. Yet no one who reads the poem carefully can come away unconvinced that the thought and even the form bear at least some imprints of Carlyle's influence. Carlyle was very much on Browning's mind at this period of his life. This is signified not only by the fact that Browning alluded to him by name in the poems published immediately before and after *Aristophanes' Apology*—namely, *Red Cotton Night-Cap Country* (1873) and *The Inn Album* (1875)—but also by the fact that Browning dedicated his third Greek poem, a translation of the *Agamemnon* (1877), to "my venerated friend Thomas Carlyle," a "dear and noble name." This was the very friend whom he describes in his penultimate volume, the *Parleyings with Certain People of Importance in Their Day* (1887), as "magisterial in antithesis" ("With Bernard De Mandeville," 41). Browning may not have learned directly from Carlyle the dialectical method which characterizes *Aristophanes' Apology*—admittedly, the method is common in the nineteenth century—but in all likelihood it was Carlyle who more than anyone else taught him that the strange and discordant dualisms of which the Editor speaks in *Sartor*[19] may be reconciled, by love, into a higher, dynamic harmony, represented in this poem by Euripides and his *Herakles*.

19. Harrold, *Sartor*, pp. 186–187, 192–193.

Parody as Style: Carlyle and His Parodists

G. B. TENNYSON, *University of California, Los Angeles*

> *If one likes a thing very much,*
> *parodies don't hurt one's love.*
> —Charlotte Mary Yonge

It is greatly to be regretted that Max Beerbohm has left us no parody of Carlyle.[1] Had he done so it would surely have been the best we have. Moreover, it would probably have cast more light on the character of Carlyle's style than many a treatment of the matter as such. For to make parody effective the parodist must have penetrated to the essence of an author's style. Something of this sort is intimated by the most satisfactory of dictionary definitions, that in the *OED*: "A composition in prose or verse in which the characteristic turns of thought in an author or class of authors are imitated in such a way as to make them appear ridiculous, especially by applying them to ludicrously inappropriate subjects; an imitation of a work more or less closely modelled on the original, but so turned as to produce a ridiculous effect." The operative phrase from a critical point of view is "the characteristic turns of thought in an author." Unless the parodist has penetrated to what those are, he may produce an apparent parody, but one that in the long run does not satisfy and has no staying power.

Most students of parody have recognized the implicit critical nature of the enterprise. Louis Untermeyer quotes Isaac D'Israeli to the effect that parody is a piece of "critical exposition."[2] Other commentators have said much the same, using such expressions as "a department of pure criticism," and a "form of criticism" to define parody.[3] They have also often noted that behind the parody there must be admiration and even love.

---

1. But see Beerbohm's vignette on Victorian memorists, "A Point to be Remembered by Very Eminent Men," in *And Even Now and a Christmas Garland* (New York, 1960 [1920]), pp. 86–92. In this essay I have omitted consideration of Meredith's parodies of Carlyle, which are discussed in Professor Stevenson's study.

2. Louis Untermeyer, *Collected Parodies* (New York, 1926), p. 1.

3. Christopher Stone, *Parody* (London, n.d.), p. 18; Sir Arthur Quiller-Couch,

But despite the general agreement that a parodist must penetrate to the essence of an author's thought and manner and hence must engage in an act of criticism in creating his parody, there has been little or no effort to see what such an undertaking might reveal about the author parodied. The case of Carlyle is typical. Although Carlyle would seem to be eminently suited for parody, having given his name to a style—Carlylese—that in itself suggests parody, he has been in fact relatively little parodied and those parodies that do exist have never been widely known or systematically examined to see what they reveal about Carlyle's style. Some things, however, they certainly do reveal, and this is why they repay study.

The first known parody of Carlyle is surprisingly early. It appeared in June 1833 in *Fraser's Magazine*, which later that year was to begin the serialization of *Sartor Resartus*. But since *Sartor* had not yet appeared, the chief source for the style represented by the parody is Carlyle's work as a translator from German and his early essays. The passage of parody occupies the first paragraph of a three-paragraph long sketch of Carlyle, which was Number 37 in Fraser's "Gallery of Literary Characters" and was accompanied by the celebrated Maclise sketch of the young Carlyle. Though unsigned, the literary portrait is the work of William Maginn, *Fraser's* editor. The parody passage is short enough to reproduce in full:

Here hast thou, O Reader! the from stone-printed effigies of Thomas Carlyle, the thunderwordoversetter of Herr Johann Wolfgang von Goethe. These fingers, now in listless occupation supporting his head, or clutching that outward integument which with the head holds so singular a relation, that those who philosophically examine, and with a fire-glance penetrate into the contents of the great majority of the orb-shaped knobs which form the upper extremity of man, know not with assured critic-craft to decide whether the hat was made to cover the head, or the head erected as a peg to hang the hat upon;—yes, these fingers have transferred some of the most harmonious and mystic passages,—to the initiated, mild-shining, inaudible-

---

"Foreword," in *Parodies and Imitations Old and New*, ed. J. A. Stanley Adam and Bernard C. White (London, 1912), p. xi. See also A. S. Martin, *On Parody* (New York, 1896), pp. 89–116. The phrase "department of pure criticism" appears to be originally Owen Seaman's; see Walter Jerrold and R. M. Leonard, eds., *A Century of Parody and Imitation* (London, 1913), p. v. The idea that parody involves love appears frequently in studies of parody, but it is qualified by Lutz Röhrich in *Gebärde, Metapher, Parodie* (Düsseldorf, 1967), p. 215: "Die weitverbreitete Meinung, man könne nur parodieren, was man liebe, gilt doch wohl nur sehr bedingt. Viel häufiger ist Parodie das Zeichen eines Überdrusses."

light instinct—and to the uninitiated, dark and untransparent as the shad-ows of Eleusis—of those forty volumes of musical wisdom which are com-monly known by the title of *Goethe's Werke*, from the Fatherlandish dialect of High-Dutch to the Allgemeine Mid-Lothianish of Auld Reekie. Over-set Goethe hath Carlyle, not in the ordinary manner of language-turners, who content themselves with giving, according to the capacity of knowingness or honesty within them, the meaning or the idea (if any there be) of the original book-fashioner, on whom their secondhand-penmongery is employed; but with reverential thought, word-worshipping even the articulable clothing wherein the clear and ethereal harmony of Goethe is invested, Carlyle hath bestowed upon us the *Wilhelm Meister*, and other works, so Teutonical in raiment, in the structure of sentence, the modula-tion of phrase, and the round-about hubble-bubble, rumfustianish (*hüb-ble-bübblen, rümfustianischen*), roly-poly growlery of style, so Germani-cally set forth, that it is with difficulty we can recognise them to be translations at all.[4]

This hitherto neglected parody of Carlyle is worth close examina-tion because it offers so many of the features that were to characterize subsequent parodies. Some of them indeed are rather crudely han-dled, but that makes for easier analysis and more immediate recog-nition.

First, Maginn has perceived Carlyle's device of creating English compound words to render German originals, with the concomitant placement of the original immediately thereafter in parentheses. In the specific instance here—"*hübble-bübblen, rümfustianischen*"—the parodist appears to have gone about his procedure in reverse and to have first thought up an English phrase and then rendered it into German, for the umlauts are especially unconvincing and the German expression sounds very English. But Maginn may have been reaching purposely for the absurd to emphasize his point.

Perhaps more instructive is the opening in which Maginn adopts the vocative case. Most of Carlyle's parodists have seen fit to do the same somewhere in their parodies in response to Carlyle's fondness

---

4. *Fraser's Magazine*, 7 (June 1833), 706. The attribution to Maginn has long been accepted and is confirmed by Walter Houghton et al., eds., *The Wellesley Index to Victorian Periodicals* (Toronto, 1972), II, 338. The only previous mention of Maginn's parody that I have found is by George Kitchin, *A Survey of Burlesque and Parody in English* (Edinburgh, 1931), p. 266; but Carlyle himself comments on Maginn's piece in a letter to his mother, *Letters of Thomas Carlyle, 1826–1836*, ed. Charles Eliot Norton (London, 1889), pp. 367–368. He says, it is "hardly intelligible (not at all so except to persons of the craft), but complimentary enough, and for so foolish a business may be considered as better than a wiser thing."

for direct address and apostrophe. It is one of the means Carlyle developed for attracting his reader's attention and for involving the reader in his discourse; and it is one of the devices by which Carlyle's prose gains so much vitality. It is also the natural mode of the speaker and sermonizer. Thus Maginn begins his parody with a direct address to the reader, and he also casts his address, as Carlyle so often does, in the archaic and Biblical second person familiar, a device that became a Carlyle trademark. He also makes use of inversions, as do subsequent parodists. Later in the passage Maginn uses the archaic third-person singular, though perhaps with less telling effect than his use of the second person. Likewise, some of Maginn's coinages—"thunder-wordoversetter," for example—capture indeed a principle of Carlyle's style, but fail somehow to convey the proper flavor. More Carlylean is Maginn's coinage "fire-glance" and especially the felicitous "secondhand-penmongery," a word that captures not only Carlyle's habit of coinage for his own purposes where the language needed to be expanded to incorporate his ideas, but also his habit of finding such coinages necessary when he chose to disparage a subject. Many of Carlyle's most characteristic noun coinages are words ending in -dom, -ness, -ery, -hood, and -ism. Often by the very conjunction of parts, they convey contempt, but they can also be highminded, as in "capacity of knowingness" in the *Fraser's* parody. Maginn is the first to perceive this characteristic.

Where Maginn's parody fails to reach the highest level is in its total impact, a matter as difficult to assess as the total impact of a passage of the genuine article from Carlyle's own writings. It would seem, however, that the failure resides in Maginn's inability to sustain the tone of some of his successful passages, not only the fine opening phrase, but such a passage as "with reverential thought" through "invested," which touches upon the tone of the authentic Carlyle, but which remains somewhat isolated in the passage as a whole. Still, Maginn's parody deserves considerable credit as the first of its kind, especially when we reflect on the fact that it is based on the Carlyle of *German Romance*, *Wilhelm Meister*, and the *Edinburgh Review* essays, not on the Carlyle of *Sartor Resartus*, *The French Revolution*, or *Past and Present*, and even less on the Carlyle of *Latter-Day Pamphlets*, which was to provoke the greatest number of Victorian parodies of Carlyle and to fix, as it were, the tone of most of the parodies.

But before the *Latter-Day Pamphlets* (1850) provoked their flood of Carlyle parodies there were two others, one British, one American. The British parody is perhaps best described as only a potential parody, for it is not clear that there is a full parodic intent behind it. It is John Sterling's portrait of the recluse Collins in his 1838 novel *The Onyx Ring*. The possible parody resides chiefly in Collins' manner of speaking, which is described by others in the story as "quaint" and "vigorous" and "wild." One character says Collins' speech haunts one long afterward, and another says that Collins' "vehement lava-lumps and burning coals . . . may be no mere showy firework, and do shoot out from a hot central furnace." The narrator relates that a Collins utterance is often "violent and picturesque, but luminous as a burning arrow." When Collins himself appears he lives up to these advance notices by speaking very like Thomas Carlyle:

Well, no one can deny that the whole of man is included between his hat and shoes. In these mysterious integuments are concealed the extreme boundaries of his Being, which, though certainly finite, philosophers aver to be all but infinite.[5]

Other Carlylelike utterances, especially turning on clothing, can also be found:

When I am not in a very ferocious humour, I do not mind seeing a soldier; for I know that what he and his dress are, and mean. But some lord or linen-draper coxcomb in the masquerade dress of a soldier is a thing to be drifted, as soon as possible, down the great sewer of perdition. The uniform on such shoulders is a red rag thrown into the kennel; and the biped is but the fleshly effigy of a man, a good deal more offensive than a wax one at a puppet-show.[6]

Collins goes on to denounce lies in poetry and to extol the virtue of pure fact. Later he denounces the pursuit of happiness, and yet later he lauds work: "We must have done once for all with cobwebs and rose-vapours, election ribbons and rockets, flummery and finery of all kinds. Sentimental sighing has no business in a world where there are so many heart-broken groans."[7]

5. John Sterling, *The Onyx Ring*, in *Essays and Tales*, ed. Julius Charles Hare (London, 1848), II, 538–539. For other Collins passages see esp. chaps. 23–25, pp. 518–548, and chaps. 28–30, pp. 563–596. Sterling's novel first appeared in *Blackwood's* in 1838.

6. Ibid., p. 541.

7. Ibid., p. 546.

Given Sterling's association with Carlyle and his celebrated early critique of *Sartor Resartus* with its emphasis on Carlyle's style, it is only reasonable to suppose he had Carlyle in mind in his portrait of Collins. How much, however, is intended to be parody and how much imitation of a more neutral kind—or even simply novelistic exploitation of Carlyle's manner—is hard to determine. Parody does, after all, depend upon the reader's knowing the subject of the parody, which Sterling's *Blackwood's* readers *may* have done, although not so certainly as Trollope's readers later. In any event, Sterling's semi-parody is certainly early in the field and deserves note as the first appearance of Carlyle in a novel, an area in which he was to be parodied several times more.

The other of the pre-*Latter-Day Pamphlets* parodies is from an American source. James Russell Lowell in the first edition of his *Biglow Papers* offers a number of imaginary reviews or puffs of the work he is presenting.[8] One of these purports to be a section from the "World Harmonic-Aeolian Attachment" and it is very much in Carlyle's manner.

Lowell is the first of several parodists to incorporate his Carlyle parody into a broader strategy having to do with his own work. Lowell makes use of the device of quoting from reviews not only to parody Carlyle but to parody the practice of such citation itself, since his work had not yet appeared and therefore had not yet generated any reviews. In so doing, however, Lowell is only adapting Carlyle's own technique in *Sartor Resartus* in the quotations from such as the "Bookseller's Taster." Lowell, however, has fabricated his citations; Carlyle was actually quoting.

Lowell captures a number of Carlyle mannerisms with some success. His coinages, for example, are generally superior to those in *Fraser's* and he has a feel for Carlyle's use of apostrophe:

Under mask of quaintest irony, we detect here [in *The Biglow Papers*] the deep, storm-tost (nigh shipwracked) soul, thunder-scarred, semi-articulate

8. [James Russell Lowell], *The Biglow Papers* (Cambridge, Mass., 1848), pp. 5–7. Lowell's parody is reprinted in Walter Hamilton, *Parodies of the Works of English and American Authors* (London, 1889), VI, 214–215. Another pre-*Latter-Day Pamphlets* parody is apparently the fugitive piece by William Bell Scott mentioned in his *Autobiographical Notes* (New York, 1892), I, 159. Scott says it was published in "an obscure magazine" and titled "More Letters of Oliver Cromwell." In it "the style of Oliver was satirised, and the style of Carlyle imitated." I have not been able to trace the article.

but ever climbing hopefully toward the peaceful summits of an Infinite Sorrow. . . . Yes, thou poor forlorn Hosea, with Hebrew fire-flaming soul in thee, for thee also this life of ours has not been without its aspects of heavenliest pity and laughingest mirth.[9]

Lowell is the first to exploit Carlyle's device of regularizing all comparison of adjectives to the German manner, omitting almost entirely to use the English "most" for the superlative degree; and Lowell has also captured Carlyle's frequent reliance on litotes for effect, especially in direct address. Lowell's parody is in general a superior performance. To be sure, Lowell had the advantage over Maginn in issuing his parody in 1848 by which time Carlyle's characteristic style was widely known. It is also fortunate that Lowell wrote before the *Latter-Day Pamphlets*, by which time Carlyle's reputation, especially in the American North, had begun to fall.

Even though Carlyle's reputation suffered some decline as a result of the *Pamphlets*, that publication can be credited with provoking the greatest number of parodies of Carlyle, including one of the best. Shortly after the appearance of the *Pamphlets* there were two parodic treatments in *Punch*.[10] Neither is in the narrow sense a full parody, but both have substantial elements of parody in them. The first figures Carlyle as hailed before Mr. Punch on the charge of "being unable to take care of his own literary reputation," as a result of the intemperance of the *Pamphlets*. This treatment is more concerned to berate Carlyle for his ideas than for his style; inevitably, however, the style comes in for its lumps. *Punch* pictures Carlyle as indifferent to the charge and as given to calling Mr. Punch "a windbag," a "serf of flunkeydom,' and "an ape of the Dead Sea," these being virtually direct citations from Carlyle rather than parody. However, one of the "witnesses" in the case, one "John Nokes, a policeman with a literary turn," testifies that he has followed Carlyle's career from earliest times and "marked with considerable anxiety, an increasing wildness, a daring eccentricity of manner in the doings of the accused, frequently observing that he delighted to crack and dislocate the joints of language, and to melt down and alloy sterling-English

9. Lowell, p. 6.
10. "A Very Melancholy Case" and "Carlyle Made Easy," *Punch*, 18 (Jan.–June 1850), 107, 110. These parodies are most accessible in Jules Paul Seigel, ed., *Thomas Carlyle: The Critical Heritage* (New York, 1971), pp. 318–321.

into nothing better than German silver." Finally, Carlyle himself is called upon to testify, and he replies as follows:

'Preternatural Eternal Oceans'—'Inhuman Humanitarians'—'Eiderdown Philanthropy'—'Wide-reverberating Cant'—'Work Sans Holiday'—'Three Cheers more, and Eternal, Inimitable, and Antipodean Fraternity'—'Pump-kindom, Flunkeydom, Foolscapdom, and Pen-and-Inkidom!'[11]

Here we are in the realm of parody, and from this short passage one can discern some of the features of Carlyle's manner that most struck contemporary readers. The first is that of Carlyle's dwelling on eternal matters—"Preternatural Eternal Oceans." And this same utterance is typical of Carlyle's habit of investing some natural concrete object —here "Oceans"—with a wider significance by modifying it with abstract adjectives—"Preternatural, Eternal." Then, to gain the opposite effect, Carlyle will modify an abstraction—"Philanthropy"— with some concrete and visually suggestive adjective—"Eiderdown" —usually in order to belittle the abstraction. One might almost call these techniques basic to Carlyle's thought, and *Punch* has pinpointed them sharply. Likewise, *Punch* is on to Carlyle's coinages in *-dom* for meiotic effect, just as Maginn saw Carlyle using *-ery* for the same purpose. This too is basic to Carlyle's method. He takes an object— *flunkey*—and by nominalizing it with *-dom* makes it into a condition or activity meriting contempt. *Punch*'s parodist has neatly compressed some typical Carlylisms into a short space.

Also instructive is the second *Punch* treatment, it too provoked by the *Latter-Day Pamphlets*, for in this spoof *Punch* undertakes to render into conventional English a passage from the first of the pamphlets, *The Present Time*. Brevity again permits citation in full. *Punch* offers the original Carlyle in the left-hand column and its own rendering in the right:

THE TEXT	THE SENSE
A terrible *new* country this: no neighbours in it yet, that I can see, but irrational flabby monsters (philanthropic and other) of the giant species; hyaenas, laughing hyaenas, predatory wolves, probably *devils*,	This is a novel, alarming, state of things. There are no agents but ourselves at work in it that I can perceive, except irrational, unsound preachers of chimeras (philanthropic and other deceivers) of great note;

11. Seigel, p. 319.

blue (or perhaps blue and yellow) devils, as St. Guthlac found in Croyland long ago. A huge untrodden, haggard country, the "chaotic battlefield of Frost and Fire"; a country of savage glaciers, granite mountains, of foul jungles, unhewed forests, quaking bogs; which we shall have our own ados to make arable and habitable, I think!

abusive and satirical journalists, literary wolves that prey on the public morals; probably certain magazines of evil tendency, blue, or perhaps blue and yellow magazines [coloured like the] devils [which] St. Guthlac found in Croyland long ago. An indefinite unexplored dreary state of things, the arena of diametrically opposed principles; an age of frozen charities, stubborn prejudices, filthy mazes of immorality, unreclaimed populations, and social bases threatening to give way; a state of things which I think we shall have sufficient work of our own to render capable of improvement, and orderly enough for us to exist under it.[12]

The most striking thing about the foregoing treatment, apart from the fact that it implicitly treats Carlyle as himself the parodist who needs explication, is that it requires almost twice the space to render Carlyle into conventional English as it required Carlyle to make his utterance! Yet this is not a mistake on the part of the *Punch* author, despite the fact that economy of expression is not often associated with Carlyle. By the time of his mature style Carlyle had indeed developed a highly compressed mode of writing that at times resembles jottings or transcribed obiter dicta with the connectives left out. By its expansion of the text *Punch* has pointed up Carlyle's habit of suppressing parts of speech for the sake of impact. Carlyle frequently makes an initial statement which is modified or elaborated upon in a subsequent string of qualifying phrases and clauses: "A terrible new country this" is the kernel of a series of elaborations that *Punch* feels compelled to render with whole new sentences and lengthy clauses, but that Carlyle compacts into a single utterance. The same procedure is followed with Carlyle's second sentence. *Punch* in its treatment also makes clear that Carlyle's animal imagery and his topographical imagery carry with them symbolic meanings applicable to

12. Ibid., pp. 320–321. Note, however, that Seigel's text drops a line of Carlyle's original, although it appears correctly in *Punch*.

the realities of the present day. In all, *Punch* performs in its un-parody something of the critical function of parody proper.

Latter-Day Pamphlets also lies most directly behind what is surely the best-known parody of Carlyle, that by Trollope in *The Warden*.[13] The treatment in *The Warden* is perhaps best remembered simply for the satiric naming of Carlyle as Dr. Pessimist Anticant, but it also contains extensive passages of parody proper, namely, a very direct parody of *Latter-Day Pamphlets*. This is preceded, however, by a retrospective parody of the early Carlyle with some characteristic touches: " 'Oh, my poor brother,' said he, 'slaughtered partridges a score of brace to each gun, and poets gauging ale-barrels with sixty pounds a year, at Dumfries, are not the signs of a great era.' " Trollope proceeds in this manner, with liberal use of the vocative, for about a paragraph; then he comments for the reader on the merits of it all. He finds these considerable in the early Carlyle, but the later Carlyle is a different matter. He provokes Trollope to a parody of the *Latter-Day Pamphlets* in the form of an attack on "despatch boxes," based on the pamphlet *Downing Street*. This is rendered chiefly in the form of many exclamations and the piling up of names of political figures.

Neither of these preliminary parodies would merit much attention if they were not followed by a sustained parody of the *Pamphlets* in the form of a hypothetical pamphlet titled *Modern Charity*, one of Dr. Anticant's series of monthly pamphlets "on the decay of the world." In this quite brilliant, though not entirely charitable, parody, Trollope justifies the introduction of Dr. Anticant into his novel, for he has *Modern Charity* concern itself with the very ecclesiastical abuse that *The Warden* is built around. Trollope seizes upon the Carlylean device of contrasting past and present:

"Heavens, what a sight! Let us with eyes wide open see the godly man of four centuries since, the man of the dark ages; let us see how he does his godlike work, and again, how the godly man of these latter days does his."[14]

The remainder of the parody develops the contrast. The pious wool-carder of the fifteenth century has been succeeded by a clergyman who takes and gives not:

13. Anthony Trollope, *The Warden*, World's Classics (London, 1942), pp. 179–187. The Carlyle parody appears with a Dickens parody in chap. 15, "Tom Towers, Dr. Anticant, and Mr. Sentiment."
14. Ibid., p. 185.

" 'Twas thus that an old man in the fifteenth century did his godlike work
to the best of his power, and not ignobly, as appears to me.

"We will not take our godly man of later days. He shall no longer be a
woolcarder, for such are not now men of mark. We will suppose him to
be one of the best of the good, one who has lacked no opportunities. Our
old friend was, after all, but illiterate; our modern friend shall be a man
educated in all seemly knowledge; he shall, in short, be that blessed thing
—a clergyman of the Church of England!

"And now, in what perfectest manner does he in this lower world get
his godlike work done and put out of hand? Heavens! in the strangest of
manners. Oh, my brother! in a manner not at all to be believed but by
the most minute testimony of eyesight. He does it by the magnitude of his
appetite—by the power of his gorge; his only occupation is to swallow the
bread prepared with so much anxious care for these impoverished carders
of wool—that, and to sing indifferently through his nose once in the week
some psalm more or less long—the shorter the better, we should be inclined to say.

"Oh, my civilised friends!—great Britons that never shall be slaves, men
advanced to infinite state of freedom and knowledge of good and evil—
tell me, will you, what becoming monument you will erect to an highly-
educated clergyman of the Church of England?"[15]

Although Trollope misses some aspects of the essential Carlyle,
such as word coinages and general verbal exuberance, he has caught
some that are often slighted by other parodists. The most notable of
these is Trollope's greater sensitivity to Carlyle's rhetorical rhythms
—the building up of momentum before the deflation, for example.
Trollope also captures something close to Carlyle's punctuation, a
matter somewhat neglected by other parodists. Above all Trollope
has seen into Carlyle's mode of thinking in regard to the spiritual
basis of all actions and into Carlyle's conviction that the modern
world shows a spiritual poverty in contrast to the medieval world.
Not until Joyce will there be another parodist who more effectively
incorporates his parody of Carlyle into his own work and advances
the movement of that work through his parody.

There are several other Victorian parodies of Carlyle, mostly
anonymous, that have been collected by Walter Hamilton.[16] These
merit some brief consideration, although none adds extensively to
the features already noted in earlier parodies.

15. Ibid., pp. 186–187.   16. Hamilton, VI, 211–215.

One anonymous parody of *Latter-Day Pamphlets* applies Carlyle's acerbic manner to the question of bloomerism and concludes with some verve as follows:

But here we are we, my friends in this mad world, amid the halooings and bawlings, and guffaws, and imbecile simperings, and titterings, blinded by the November smoke fog of coxcombries and vanities, stunted by the perpetual hallelujahs of flunkeys, beset by maniacs and simpletons in the great lunes and the petty lunes; here, I say, do we with Bloomerism beneath us bubbling uppermost, stand, hopelessly upturning our eyes for the daylight of heaven, upon the brink of a vexed unfathomable gulf of apehood and asshood simmering for ever.[17]

A parody from 1872 sets Carlyle on the topic of the Tichborne Trial. It has the virtue of recognizing the extent to which Carlyle relies on dialogue in his writing and it has some other moments of felicity:

After all, is not Insanity just what is the matter with this English Bull just now? Is there Sanity for all among us butchers, bakers and candlestick-makers, red tape dummies, black crape ludicrousnesses, Puseyisms, Benthamee Radicalisms, Church and Statisms, Dilettantisms, Mammonisms, double-barrelled Aristocracies, and inane Chimaeras generally.[18]

Two parodies from 1879 were written in response to a newspaper competition in which the challenge was to write a piece on Gladstone's portrait by Millais in the manner of Carlyle.[19] The chief interest of these two lies in the *donnée* of the competition, the recognition that Carlyle is at his best in pen portraits. This device was to form the point of departure for the most satisfying of all Carlyle parodies, that by Hugh Kingsmill, which will be considered later.

Hamilton also notes four parodies from a competition by the *Weekly Dispatch* in 1882, one offering two brief portraits "omitted" from Carlyle's *Reminiscences*, again reminding us of Carlyle's special gift for literary portraiture.[20]

---

17. Ibid., p. 211.   18. Ibid., p. 212.
19. Ibid., pp. 212–213.
20. Ibid., pp. 213–214. Hamilton also notes for completeness three other parodic treatments: the first, titled "Shows and Shams," appeared in *Banter*, 11 Nov. 1867, and parodied Carlyle on the Lord Mayor's Show for that year; the second titled "Music in the Drawing Room," appeared in the Christmas number of the *World*, 1879; the third is the pamphlet by P. P. Alexander, *Carlyle Redivivus* (Glasgow, 1881). Even Hamilton considers these treatments of insufficient merit to justify reprinting.

There are no other important parodies of Carlyle within his own lifetime, but one can speak of a parodic tendency even in otherwise serious criticism, especially in the Victorian age. Passage after passage in authors from John Sterling to Walt Whitman sounds like imitation or mockery of Carlyle's style.[21] These occur most often when the critic is discussing Carlyle's style as such, as though the author sensed that the uniqueness of that style could best be conveyed by transmitting the flavor of it rather than talking about it. Moreover, these passages often exhibit the features that have been noted as the most striking in the parodies proper: use of the vocative, the stringing together of appositional constructions, and the borrowing or adapting of Carlyle's habits of word coinage. These are so constant a feature of the parodies and of the critical judgments and imitations that they suggest that no reader of Carlyle remains unaffected by them. The widespread use of such devices suggests too that they are more than mere tricks of Carlyle's style, that they are essential to it.

There are also what we may call the informal parodies and parodists, those who from time to time mocked Carlyle's style in brief patches in their conversation or writing. The earliest and probably always the best of these was Jane Welsh Carlyle, who could write simultaneously criticism and parody of Carlyle's style as early as 1822 in a letter to Carlyle himself:

Besides this there is about your letter a *mystery* which I detest—It is so full of *meaning* words underlined—meaning sentences half finished, *meaning* BLANKS with notes of admiration—and *meaning* quotations from foreign languages that really in this abundance of *meaning* it seems to indicate I am somewhat at a loss to discover what you will be at.[22]

And a month or so later Jane tweaks Carlyle parodically again:

Admire me—by all means admire me, since it be your pleasure so to do— but—for mercy's sake—let it, henceforth be in *silence*.— And tell me no more of the "*helpless* AGITATIONS" *into which my displeasure throws you* —if you would not have me to repeat the experiment, for my amusement—

---

21. A representative sample of these can be found in Seigel's collection. See especially the following authors and passages: Alexander Hill Everett, p. 37; W. M. Thackeray, p. 73; John Sterling, p. 133; William Henry Smith, p. 213; Peter LePage Renouf, p. 232; Elizabeth Barrett Browning and R. H. Horne, p. 239; H. D. Thoreau, p. 282; Edgar Allan Poe, p. 303; William Edmonstoune Aytoun, p. 325; George Eliot, p. 411; Walt Whitman, p. 457.
22. *CL*, II, 19–20.

for, really, Mr Carlyle, in a state of *"helpless* agitation," at a girl's frown, is, to me, a far more ludicrous spectacle than the Elephant dancing waltzes to the beat of a little drum. But *I must not take notice of your absurd expressions—Oh! No—that is very unkind—"It is cruel and unjust to be angry at what you say or do, for you Mean well."* [23]

All of the above is at the very beginning of their relationship, making Jane beyond question Carlyle's first parodist. And throughout her life she took delight and displayed no small parodic skill in using certain of the more portentous Carlylisms in a jocular way, especially through the device of quoting Carlyle back at himself. Jane Welsh Carlyle must have been but the most distinguished of a number of Carlyle associates who jestingly imitated the Master in letter and speech.

The decline of Carlyle's reputation after his death may account for the fact that there are only two substantial parodies of Carlyle in the twentieth century, though there are countless parodic flashes, usually of a contemptuous nature, in twentieth-century criticism on Carlyle. Still, the two twentieth-century parodies are among the best that have ever been offered, and they deserve to be better known than they are.

The earliest of the two is the Carlyle passage in James Joyce's "Oxen of the Sun" episode in *Ulysses*.[24] In that episode Joyce parodies many authors and styles, moving from early English to the present day as a parallel to the birth pangs and delivery of child by Mrs. Purefoy at Dr. Andrew J. Horne's National Maternity Hospital. By the nineteenth-century passage birth has been accomplished and congratulations are in order before the company sets off for the pub. There is no clear agreement among Joyce scholars as to the exact limits of the passage parodying Carlyle, and some even seem to doubt that Carlyle himself is directly parodied at all.[25] But any reader of

23. Ibid., p. 51. Of this letter the editors say: "Throughout this letter Jane mocks phrases in Carlyle's letter to her of 13 Feb." Instances of Jane's continuing parody of Carlyle can be found throughout the later correspondence, usually in letters to Carlyle but occasionally also in letters to others.

24. James Joyce, *Ulysses* (New York, 1961), pp. 423–424. The episode is also in Dwight Macdonald, ed., *Parodies: An Anthology from Chaucer to Beerbohm—and After* (New York, 1960), pp. 522–543. The Carlyle passage appears on pp. 540–542.

25. Macdonald cites Stuart Gilbert's *James Joyce's "Ulysses"* and consultation with Richard Ellmann as his authority for ascription of passages in the "Oxen of the Sun" episode to specific authors. He considers the Carlyle parody to include also the paragraph preceding the one given here, the paragraph beginning "Burke's!" and ending "storkbird for thee?" However, Harry Blamires, in *The Bloomsday Book: A Guide*

Carlyle will agree that the following paragraph towards the end of the episode can only be a parody of Carlyle, if indeed the parody does not begin yet a paragraph earlier:

The air without is impregnated with raindew moisture, life essence celestial, glistering on Dublin stone there under starshiny coelum. God's air the Allfather's air, scintillant circumambient cessile air. Breathe it deep into thee. By heaven, Theodore Purefoy, thou hast done a doughty deed and no botch! Thou art, I vow, the remarkablest progenitor barring none in this chaffering allincluding most farraginous chronicle. Astounding! In her lay a Godframed Godgiven preformed possibility which thou has fructified with thy modicum of man's work. Cleave to her! Serve! Toil on, labour like a very bandog and let scholarment and all Malthusiasts go hang. Thou art all their daddies, Theodore. Art drooping under thy load, bemoiled with butcher's bills at home and ingots (not thine!) in the countinghouse? Head up! For every newbegotten thou shalt gather thy homer of ripe wheat. See, thy fleece is drenched. Dost envy Darby Dullman there with his Joan? A canting jay and a rheumeyed curdog is all their progeny. Pshaw, I tell thee! He is a mule, a dead gasteropod, without vim or stamina, not worth a cracked kreutzer. Copulation without population! No, say I! Herod's slaughter of the innocents were the truer name. Vegetables, forsooth, and sterile cohabitation! Give her beefsteaks, red, raw, bleeding! She is a hoary pandemonium of ills, enlarged glands, mumps, quinsy, bunions, hayfever, bedsores, ringworm, floating kidney, Derbyshire neck, warts, bilious attacks, gallstones, cold feet, varicose veins. A truce to threnes and trentals and jeremies and all such congenital defunctive music. Twenty years of it, regret them not. With thee it was not as with many that will and would and wait and never do. Thou sawest thy America, thy lifetask and didst charge to cover like the transpontine bison. How saith Zarathustra? *Deine Kuh Truebsal melkest Du. Nun trinkst Du die suesse Milch des Euters.* See! It displodes for thee in abundance. Drink, man, an

---

through Joyce's Ulysses (London, 1966), p. 162, writes as follows about the nineteenth-century passage: "Stylistically we are now firmly established in the nineteenth century, and Stuart Gilbert cites Landor, Macauley [sic], Dickens, Newman, Pater, and Ruskin as among the models here imitated. But Joyce's experiment is not a simple chronological series of pastiches. There are sentences which recall Meredith and Carlyle, and sentences which carry the flavour of quite other ages." Later it becomes clear that Blamires considers what I and Macdonald hold to be the Carlyle parody to be twentieth-century material, for of this passage he writes: "We are in the twentieth century at last." Weldon Thornton in *Allusions in Ulysses* (Chapel Hill, N.C., 1968) finds no Carlyle allusions in this or in any other section of *Ulysses*, but his study is concerned with direct echoes and allusions to particular works, not with imitation or stylistic affinity.

udderful! Mother's milk, Purefoy, the milk of human kin, milk too of those burgeoning stars overhead, rutilant in thin rainvapour, punch milk, such as those rioters will quaff in their guzzlingden, milk of madness, the honey-milk of Canaan's land. Thy cow's dug was tough, what? Ay, but her milk is hot and sweet and fattening. No dollop this but thick rich bonnyclaber. To her, old patriarch! Pap! *Per deam Partulam et Pertundam nunc est bibendum!*

Joyce exploits most of the devices already noted as essential in Carlyle parodies: the exclamations, the apostrophes, the congeries of strung-out appositions, the direct address in the second person familiar, suppression of subject, inversions, biblical language, the liberal use of the imperative, and the inclusion of German. But Joyce does more. To an even greater degree than Trollope, Joyce captures the urgency, the excitement, the intensity of Carlyle, at his most impassioned. Indeed, it is almost a return to the early Carlyle after the excess of bilious *Latter-Day Pamphlets* imitations. For Joyce is the most verbally fecund of Carlyle's parodists and thus the most like Carlyle himself. He even captures in that verbal riot Carlyle's inclination towards alliteration: "scintillant circumambient cessile air," "rutilant in thin rainvapour." Joyce notes too Carlyle's use of the obscure word: "A truce to threnes and trentals and jeremies and all such congenital defunctive music."[26]

Joyce has also adapted his parody to his own larger strategy in *Ulysses* and to an even greater degree than Lowell or Trollope did. If anything, Joyce so fully adapts his parody into his own strategy that its parodic dimension is reduced. It is less a parody for being more a part of Joyce's novel, and less a parody for being more like Joyce's own style and thought. Still, Carlyle's "characteristic turns of thought" are unmistakably there, even if transmuted by Joyce's own Carlyle-like genius. Thus there is something more than usually perverse about Dwight Macdonald's judgment of this parody:

Immediately before this collapse into mongrelized incoherence, we have the parody of Thomas Carlyle, who racked and tortured our sweet English tongue as mercilessly as any pidgin-speaking South Sea islander; that he was considered a literary giant (instead of the inventor of *Time*style)

26. Thornton, pp. 347–348, notes that "threne" and "defunctive music" both occur in Shakespeare's "The Phoenix and the Turtle."

shows a decline in standards; using Carlyle's frenetic, bastardized style as the transition to the death of English in the gutter was one of Joyce's happiest inspirations.[27]

Carlyle's torturing of our sweet English tongue was also a form of play so very like Joyce's own that we might consider Joyce not so much the parodist of Carlyle's style as the inheritor of it.

Even in the face of the brilliance of Joyce's parody, one is still tempted to say that the most recent parody of Carlyle is the most satisfying, the most fully parodistic; it is the piece by Hugh Kingsmill titled "Some Modern Light-Bringers, As They Might have been Extinguished by Thomas Carlyle."[28] Kingsmill takes six twentieth-century authors and offers a paragraph or two on each in the manner of Carlyle. The six are: G. B. Shaw, H. G. Wells, Marcel Proust, D. H. Lawrence, Lytton Strachey, and James Joyce. Kingsmill's method is to combine the pen portrait approach that Carlyle so often used on his contemporaries with the succinct literary-philosophic disposal that Carlyle applied with such a liberal hand. Of Shaw, for example, Kingsmill has Carlyle call him a spinster whose solution to the world's ills is to issue everyone a weekly monetary scrip: "A right spinsterish nostrum, or cure-all, this; properly conceivable indeed only by a spinster—of the family-solicitor-independent-means species, I would say." H. G. Wells is disposed of in a most Carlylean fashion as "not easily accessible for deeper soundings"; and Proust evokes the kind of scorn Carlyle held in store for such as Swinburne: "A wretched, diseased, little quack, Proust, who proclaims it salutary for internal complications that men should crawl through their own entrails with a microscope." D. H. Lawrence likewise is swiftly extinguished: "Poor ghastly Lawrence! A sadder sicklier Guy Fawkes simulacrum of prophet and light-bringer I have not looked upon; fit only to be tossed above a rubbish heap of dead branches and like combustible matter, and there utterly consumed, with all his Bedlam rout of worshippers, male and female—female preponderating, I opine!"

But the jewel of the collection is Kingsmill's rendering of Carlyle's revenge on Lytton Strachey, and it deserves citation in full:

27. Macdonald, p. 524.
28. *Bookman*, 12 (1932), 766–768. These parodies were also published, but without the Joyce parody, in the *English Review*, 56 (1933), 23–27. Hugh Kingsmill was the pseudonym of Hugh Kingsmill Lunn. It is perhaps not quite accurate to call

Our wart School of Modern Portraiture I name Biographer Strachey and his apes, blasphemously scribbling for pence their *Acta Stultorum,* or Deeds of the Fools. As tho there were no other veracity about a Hero but his warts! As tho brave Oliver's Monition to Court Painter Lely had been: "Meddle not with my face! Paint my warts only!"

Terrible, almost despairful to me in its inward signification for these babbling godless times, the thought of those other *Acta,* called *Acta Sanctorum,* or Deeds of the Saints, which the old monk penned up there in Iona, a thousand years and more gone now, in that age named Dark by us (Dark! Oh Heaven! By what impenetrablest pall of blackest Erebus are *we* encompassed then?). I scarcely know a beautifuller object than that old monk, seated there in his grim wind-and-water pounded islet, a nimbus of saints' faces—to his poor dim sight quite wartless!—smiling down upon him, as most painfully with squeaking goose-quill he traces out his pious chronicles. Modern enlightened eyes blink rather rapidly at that monk, I conjecture, and modern enlightened minds reflect—how very chilly that good foolish man must certainly have been! For my part I fancy a quite other interior warmth in that monk than what our modern heating contrivances procure a man! I think he could very well dispense with our modern heating contrivances, could that monk, upon whose upturned face an unspeakable radiancy of Heaven's light shone down between the black tempest-riven clouds, to whose ears the roaring winds and waters were the very voice of God—made audible for him!

Look a little upon that picture, steam-heated Biographer Strachey and you others of the Wart-School generally! Bethink you if it were not wisely done to unwrite your Gospels according to Judas Iscariot; if it were not really the prudentest act you could perform to fling back your thirty or thirty thousand pieces of silver on account of royalties—ere it be too late![29]

With a fine sense of anticlimax Kingsmill concludes with a one-sentence treatment of James Joyce that suggests something of what Carlyle might have thought had he read the Joyce parody of himself in *Ulysses:*

Kingsmill's the most recent parody of Carlyle. That distinction should be given to G. B. Tennyson's *Carlyle and the Modern World* (Edinburgh: Carlyle Society [1972]), which contains many passages of Carlyle parody in the form of criticism of modern critics of Carlyle.

29. Kingsmill, p. 768. Kingsmill knew how to take care of Lytton Strachey in any case. He had already parodied his *Eminent Victorians* in a fine piece titled "Joseph," *English Review,* 54 (1932), 399–404.

"Jakes" Joyce I call him, and wish him what he most prizes—an easy passage. But out of my sight![30]

No analysis of Kingsmill's parody is possible. It stands as it is. He has so superbly caught the later Carlyle manner and so exquisitely joined it to appropriate subjects that the parody runs the risk of some of Beerbohm's, namely that of not seeming to be a parody at all but the genuine article. Kingsmill's treatment makes up for the lack of a Beerbohm parody and it demonstrates the truth of the sentiment that, "if one likes a thing very much, parodies don't hurt one's love."

30. Kingsmill, p. 768.

Grecian Destiny: Froude's Portraits of the Carlyles

JOHN CLUBBE, *Duke University*

Froude's statements on biography, when brought together, indicate that he believed the most important task the biographer faced was to attempt to fathom the essence of his subject. Asked in 1889 to write a biographical sketch of Disraeli, he told Lady Derby that his "difficulty [was] to find out the real man that lay behind the Sphinx-like affectations."[1] The next year (having written the study) he told Stuart J. Reid, "It is worse than useless to attempt the biography of a man unless you know, or think you know, what his inner nature was."[2] When Carlyle died in 1881, many Englishmen revered the man as much as they admired his writings, yet few suspected the complexity of the "real man," the mysteries of his "inner nature."

In his biography of the Sage of Chelsea, published in four volumes in 1882 and 1884, Froude attempted to reveal the sources of Carlyle's greatness and to give his contemporaries a true notion of Carlyle's importance for Victorian England. Yet he did not wish to efface the warts in the portrait he drew of Carlyle's character and personal life. Thus he wrote a biography designed, as he recognized, more for posterity than for his contemporaries. The light of moral strengths intermixed with the shadow of personal failings make a rich, many-hued portrait, frank yet penetrating, but one that was to draw down on Froude the wrath of those unprepared for and unused to candor in biography. Yet for all the candor and the many years he had had to puzzle over Carlyle's "inner nature," he never seems to have been quite certain that he had seized its essence. His correspondence with Ruskin, recently published, suggests that doubts remained even after he had completed his biography of Carlyle:

I preferred *not* to attempt to describe (directly) C's character. I preferred to let it appear in the story and in his own clear letters.— Indeed I do not know that I could have described it. . . . He was not selfish, not consciously

1. Waldo H. Dunn, *James Anthony Froude: A Biography*, 2 vols. (Oxford, 1961; 1963), II, 562.
2. Ibid., p. 569.

or deliberately selfish, not selfish at all in the ordinary sense but he required everything to be sacrificed to his convenience. He was intensely occupied with his work & with 'the message' which he had to deliver— He never considered those he lived with in the smaller things of every day life. Where they had worked & slaved for him he was really grateful, but he was too shy—or too *something*, to show it.[3]

In his effort to fathom the elusive *"something"* in Carlyle's being—a being which in its complexity must surely rival Johnson's or Byron's— Froude drew upon all the energy and talent he possessed to write the work which he justly regarded as his most important.

The biography aroused immense controversy when it appeared, and that controversy has continued, with some abatement in recent years, into the present. "The criticism of the book," wrote Isaac W. Dyer, Carlyle's bibliographer, in 1928, "is much more drastic than failure properly to distribute material or draw a pen portrait satisfactory to Carlyle's friends. Mr. Froude is charged with actual misrepresentation. The main issue between Froude and the Carlyleans is his treatment of the relations between Carlyle and his wife. This is the nub of the Carlyle-Froude controversy."[4] In this essay I will avoid as much as possible involvement in the recriminations and ripostes which have characterized that long-protracted controversy; since the publication in 1930 of Waldo H. Dunn's *Froude and Carlyle: A Study of the Froude-Carlyle Controversy*—a study favorable to Froude—the tide of commentary has swung increasingly in Froude's favor.[5] Rather, I will focus on the Carlyles as depicted in Froude's pages.

Surprisingly little attention has yet been paid to Froude's work as an achievement in the biographical art.[6] To say this is not to deny that various writers—including several of his detractors—have praised

3. *The Froude-Ruskin Friendship as Represented through Letters*, ed. Helen Gill Viljoen (New York, 1966), p. 46.

4. *A Bibliography of Thomas Carlyle's Writings and Ana* (Portland, Maine, 1928), p. 347.

5. See especially Hyder E. Rollins, "Charles Eliot Norton and Froude," *Journal of English and Germanic Philology*, 57 (1958), 651–664, and Edward Sharples, Jr., "Carlyle and His Readers: The Froude Controversy Once Again" (Ph.D. dissertation, University of Rochester, 1964).

6. Two exceptions are Harold Nicolson, in *The Development of English Biography* (London, 1928), and Richard D. Altick, *Lives and Letters: A History of Literary Biography in England and America* (New York, 1966). Waldo H. Dunn's *English Biography* (London and New York, 1916) treats Froude enthusiastically if somewhat uncritically.

the biography's literary artistry; but no one, to my knowledge, has gone much beyond a few generalizations in trying to demonstrate wherein it lies and to what purpose. My chief object in the present study is to indicate what that artistry reveals about Froude's biographical technique—his portrait-painting faculty, in particular—as he shaped his interpretation of the Carlyles. I also wish to suggest some of the consequences of that artistry as we attempt to assess their characters in his pages. My intention, however, is not to define once again the nature of the Carlyles' relationship with each other or to pass judgment on the validity of Froude's interpretation of that relationship, though judgments will sometimes be implied. Rather, it is to examine his presentation and to interpret the psychology behind his method of portraiture. Only when we see what Froude was doing will we be in a position to judge the degree of his success or failure in representing the Carlyles. First, it will be necessary to say something about Froude's understanding of the biographer's role and to view it within the context of his relationship with Carlyle himself.

II

Carlyle always insisted that the cardinal virtue in biography was honesty. Not to be honest in regard to Carlyle himself, Froude believed, would be false to Carlyle and to the values in which he believed. One of Froude's peculiar distinctions is that he wrote perhaps the only nineteenth-century English biography to imply—in Victorian England he could do no more than that—the importance of sex in marriage. In Froude's view, both Carlyle and Mrs. Carlyle would have been happier not married to each other. He said it boldly and he said it often. To a reader today such an assertion about a relationship between two people may seem harmless enough, but the Victorians did not condone lightly open criticism of marriage. That Froude dared to say what he did, especially in regard to such a well-known couple, scandalized many. But what the irritation of his early readers blocked them from seeing were his repeated affirmations of Carlyle's greatness: greatness as a thinker and prophet certainly, but equal greatness as a man. No subsequent biographer has presented Carlyle the man to better advantage than Froude. If approached without prior bias, his portrayal will impress by its honesty. Honesty was his goal and remains, to a remarkable degree, his achievement. And it is an astonishing achievement for a biographer who knew his subject as well as Froude knew Carlyle and who published the final volumes of his work within three years of Carlyle's death.

In 1887 Froude wrote *My Relations with Carlyle*, a defense of his actions in writing the biography which he prepared for possible use after his death. He noted in it that Carlyle "had said in his journal that there was a secret connected with him unknown to his closest friends, that no one knew and no one would know it, and that without a knowledge of it no true biography of him was possible. He never told me in words what this secret was, but I suppose he felt that I should have it from his papers."[7] The passage in Carlyle's Journal to which Froude refers can only be the entry of 29 December 1849, which Froude published at the beginning of the third volume of his biography:

Darwin said to Jane, the other day, in his quizzing-serious manner, "Who will write Carlyle's life?" The word, reported to me, set me thinking how *impossible* it was, and would for ever remain, for any creature to write my "Life"; the *chief* elements of my little destiny have all along lain deep below view or surmise, and never will or can be known to any son of Adam. I would say to my Biographer, if any fool undertook such a task, 'Forbear, poor fool'; let no Life of *me* be written; let me and my bewildered wrestlings lie buried here, and be forgotten swiftly of all the world. If thou write, it will be mere delusions and hallucinations. The confused world never understood, nor will understand, me and my poor affairs; not even the persons nearest me could guess at them. . . .[8]

Froude did not comment on this passage, but he understood it, as *My Relations with Carlyle* makes clear, in the light of his conversations with Geraldine Jewsbury, a close friend of Mrs. Carlyle's.

---

7. London, New York, and Bombay, 1903, p. 17. Froude's children did publish this document after his death; they were goaded into doing so by charges made by Sir James Crichton-Browne in his Introduction to *New Letters and Memorials of Jane Welsh Carlyle*, ed. Alexander Carlyle, 2 vols. (London and New York, 1903).

8. Froude, *Carlyle*, III, 1–2 (corrected). "Darwin" is the Carlyles' friend Erasmus Darwin (1804–1881). Earlier, in his Journal of 10 October 1843, Carlyle had written in a similar vein: "To have my Life surveyed and commented on by all men, even wisely, is no object with me, but rather the opposite; how much less to have it done *unwisely*. The world has no business with my Life; the world will never know my Life, if it should write and read a hundred 'biographies' of me: the main facts of it even are known, and are like to be known, to myself alone of created men" (III, 1 [corrected]).

"Geraldine when she heard that I was to undertake the Biography," Froude told Ruskin, "came to me & said that I ought to know that Carlyle 'was one of those persons who ought never to have married,' and that this was at the bottom of all the trouble. . . ."[9]

Nothing in the Journal passage, however, implies that Carlyle's "secret" was sexual in nature. Carlyle speaks only of "elements in my little destiny" that "have all along lain deep below view or surmise." What he says of himself there would hold true for most human beings. Froude himself came to have doubts that in supposing the Journal passage to refer to sexual impotence he had interpreted it correctly. "I am not sure that I know now what he meant," he admitted in *My Relations with Carlyle* (p. 20). His admission in no way denies the value of his hypotheses concerning the Carlyles' relationship, but suggests instead that, like a good historian, he continued to weigh the evidence and to consider the different interpretations it allowed. It also suggests that if in his biography he was to indicate something of the nature of their relationship (as he understood it), from first acquaintance through courtship and marriage and during the course of their lives together, he would have to do so indirectly.

Froude's unpublished correspondence reveals that he worried whether he had told too much. His critics from the first berated him for his lack of tact. In letters he defended himself, saying that he was following Carlyle's wishes and his oft-expressed desire for honesty in biography. Still, one can legitimately wonder if Carlyle himself would have disapproved of the "revelations" which Froude made about him in the biography. Might he not have faulted him, not for telling too much, but for telling too little? Froude had unease on this score too, as an unpublished letter to William Allingham, written within weeks of Carlyle's death and discussing the forthcoming *Reminiscences*, reveals:

I alone am responsible—on me let the responsibility rest. . . . As to mention of particular people, I have left out (as I thought) every word that could hurt. *He* however when I consulted him as to what should have been done about those of whom *she* speaks, said It can do no body any harm to know what a sensible woman as she was thought of them— I have not acted on this large permission—nor should I.[10]

9. Letter dated 29 Nov. [1886], in Viljoen, pp. 64–65.
10. Letter dated 18 Feb. [1881], MS: University of Illinois. Cf. Froude, *Carlyle*, I, xiii.

The devotion to truth which Carlyle affirmed as necessary to the writing of biography he had the strength of mind to insist be followed in regard to his own. In the remarkably creative years following the death of his wife in 1866 he had written the *Reminiscences* and annotated the *Letters and Memorials of Jane Welsh Carlyle*, yet quite understandably he shrank from publishing the result of these labors during his lifetime. And when it came to telling Froude exactly what to do with the manuscripts he entrusted to him his resolution apparently faltered. But on one point it did not falter: he *would* have his own life judged by the biographical principles he had advocated over a lifetime. This decision is a striking instance of the heroic strength of character he displayed right to the end of his life.

Froude's purpose in depicting Carlyle as he did can be seen in an unpublished letter of 3 December [1882] to Martin F. Tupper, who had written to thank him for the pleasure he had derived from the first two volumes:

In the midst of the foolish clamour which has been raised over my life of Carlyle a few persons like yourself have been able to discern his true likeness. By & bye the judgement of the few will be the judgement of the many. His life in my opinion was as noble as his writings and may well stand as an example of integrity & simplicity to all English men of letters[.] We sorely need an example of this kind for our profession tends to vanity and is not a wholesome one[.]

My own Endeavour was to paint him as I knew him. A true likeness to him but of my ability.— Like the Princess ["Persiz" and "Parisad" *crossed out*] on the mountain side I have been deafened by the voices from the enchanted stones telling me that I was a fool that I was this and that. But I write on trying to do what I know Carlyle expected of me, and I have at least contributed something towards a real understanding of his character.

The work however speaks for itself[.] I can say no more about it. I am pleased to find that I have conveyed to your mind the same image which I had upon my own.[11]

A biographer's psychological understanding of his subject can always be challenged, and when we have two beings as enigmatic and contradictory as Thomas and Jane Carlyle the possibilities for misinterpretation of evidence increase proportionately. Froude, however, seems to present not only a convincing but also a fundamentally trust-

11. The letter is dated only by the day and month. 1882 seems most likely. MS: University of Illinois. Froude alludes in his analogy with the Princess to a tale in the *Arabian Nights.*

worthy study of the Carlyles and their marriage. He remains by far the most intelligent biographer that Carlyle has had, certainly the most astute psychologically, and he had the advantage of knowing both Carlyles better than did any other biographer. No apology is now needed for his interpretation of Carlyle's life. His work, with all its flaws, not only "speaks for itself" but also contributes impressively "towards a real understanding of his character." It has set the standard against which succeeding biographies of Carlyle must be judged.

Froude began his career as a novelist, and critics have observed that his interest in the techniques of fiction and his penchant for dramatic contrasts continued in his histories and biographies. His first important work was an autobiographical novel *The Nemesis of Faith* (1849). When the young Moncure D. Conway read it in the early 1850's, he thought—as did others at the time—that Froude might be the "Coming Man" in the area of fiction. "Later and more critical readings of the *Nemesis*," Conway observed, "have convinced me that such was indeed the natural bent of Froude's genius; and notwithstanding his splendid achievements in history and criticism I have never felt quite satisfied that had he adhered to the original direction he might not have attained a more unmarred success." He concluded that "every work Froude thereafter wrote is suffused with the imaginative genius which bequeathed to us this marvellous *Nemesis of Faith*."[12] Conway's observations have especial value, coming as they do from a man who had read many of Froude's writings and who had known him well. Froude's later work, as we shall see, does indeed bear the imprint of his apprenticeship in fiction, and will show him refining the narrative techniques he was working out in the 1840's. He once declared, in an oft-cited statement, that "the most perfect English history which exists is to be found, in my opinion, in the historical plays of Shakespeare,"[13] and in his twelve-volume *History of England from the Fall of Wolsey to the Spanish Armada* (1856–1870) he sought to capture the living essence of history in dramatic confrontations among the great figures of the Renaissance.

Froude used dramatic techniques and models in his biography of Carlyle both to heighten narrative impact and, more importantly, to

12. Introduction to *The Nemesis of Faith* (London, 1903), pp. xiv and xv. Subsequent citations from this edition.

13. *Short Studies on Great Subjects*, 4 vols. (London, 1895), II, 596; cf. also I, 33–34, and Froude, *Carlyle*, IV, 201, for similar opinions.

make implications regarding the Carlyles which he could not make directly. "The facts must be delineated first with the clearness and fulness which we demand in an epic poem or a tragedy," he wrote in the biography. "We must have the real thing before we can have a science of a thing" (IV, 203). Epic and tragedy provided, in Froude's view, the best models for the literary artist seeking to represent "the real thing" in biography, and the works that proved most instructive to him in writing of the Carlyles were *The Faerie Queene* and the Greek tragedies centering on Oedipus and Iphigenia. Because he used *The Faerie Queene* in more obvious ways than he used Greek tragedy, I examine it first as the model upon which he based his representation of the Carlyles' friendship with Lord and Lady Ashburton. Then I turn to Greek tragedy and study in particular the figures of Oedipus and Iphigenia to suggest that in highly significant ways they stand behind the portraits he drew of the Carlyles.

III

Froude considers "the Lady Ashburton business" in his third volume. Carlyle had met Lord Ashburton, then Sir William Baring, in 1839, but not until about three years later did he begin to attend the grand *fêtes* held at Bath House, the Barings' London home. There Lady Harriet, his wife, reigned as one of the queens of London society. An imposing woman, she liked to have literary men adorn her gatherings and she soon evinced a preference for Carlyle. Gradually he became "enchanted"—the word is Froude's—with her and soon was a regular guest either at Bath House or at one of the Barings' country estates: Bay House, their seaside home near Alverstoke; Addiscombe Farm, their Surrey villa; or, most frequently, the Grange, their squat mansion, unlovely but grand, in Hampshire. The Carlyles, usually together but sometimes separately, paid to the Grange at least one visit of several weeks each year from 1844 until Lady Harriet's death in 1857. All who came into her presence admitted her brilliance in society and her powers of conversation. She had wit, intelligence, a marked gift for repartee. Her friends she held despite—or because of —her imperial manner. At times her tone waxed positively insolent, and there were others besides Mrs. Carlyle whom it offended. It is perhaps not surprising that Carlyle should fall under the sway of a woman unlike any other he had ever met. It is even less surprising that Mrs. Carlyle would resent in some way a woman who was her equal in intellect and wit. In time, she came to see Carlyle's homage to her as a threat to her existence with her husband. Although the Carlyle-Ashburton relationship is difficult to consider without reference to the larger context of the Froude-Carlyle controversy, I will limit myself here to an examination of the manner in which Froude used *The Faerie Queene* as a literary model on which to focus his interpretation of the personalities involved.[14]

Spenser's *Faerie Queene* had long exercised a potent hold on Froude's imagination. He has Markham Sutherland recall, in the autobiographical *Nemesis of Faith*, that in his childhood "The Faerie Queen . . . was only second to the Bible with me" (p. 75). Sutherland understood the poem with the intensity of childhood vision: "In truth the allegory was not thought much of; Una was a fair damsel in distress—the lion a real, good, grand, noble lion, such as we saw at the menagerie; how I hated that Sansfoy for killing him" (p. 76).

Froude saw Lady Harriet as "Gloriana," the idealized representation of Queen Elizabeth found in the preface to *The Faerie Queene.* He describes her effect on Carlyle:

He at first enjoyed the society of a person who never bored him, who had a straight eye, a keen tongue, a disdain of nonsense, a majestic arrogance. As they became more intimate, the great lady affected his imagination. He was gratified at finding himself appreciated by a brilliant woman, who ruled supreme over half of London society. She became Gloriana, Queen of Fairyland, and he, with a true vein of chivalry in him, became her rustic Red Cross Knight, who, if he could, would have gladly led his own *Una* into the same enchanting service. The "Una," unfortunately, had no inclination for such a distinguished bondage [III, 342–343].

The interrelationships among Lady Ashburton (Gloriana), Carlyle (the gallant but occasionally obtuse Red Cross Knight), and Mrs. Carlyle (Una, the faithful believer in him) are usually present in Froude's mind even when not pointed to directly. He focuses first on the difficulties Mrs. Carlyle had in assuming a satisfactory relationship with Lady Ashburton:

14. Iris Origo presents a balanced overview of "The Carlyles and the Ashburtons" in *A Measure of Love* (London, 1957). Her essay should be read as a complement to my discussion. "Carlyle's letters," she writes, "are those of a neurotic and demon-haunted man, who in middle age has fallen, not precisely in love, but into an *amitié amoureuse* with a great lady whose brilliance has charmed him out of his gloom" (p. 121).

No one could suspect [her] of intending to hurt Mrs. Carlyle; but either she never observed her discomfort, or she thought it too ridiculous to notice. She doubtless tried in her own lofty way to be kind to Mrs. Carlyle, and Mrs. Carlyle, for her husband's sake, tried to like Lady Harriet. But it did not answer on either side, and in such cases it is best to leave things to take their natural course. When two people do not agree, it is a mistake to force them into intimacy. They should remain on the footing of neutral acquaintance, and are more likely to grow into friends the less the direct effort to make them so.

From this general analysis of the difficulties of forced friendship, Froude moves to the level of allegory:

Gloriana may have a man for a subject without impairing his dignity—a woman in such a position becomes a dependent. Carlyle unfortunately could not see the distinction. To such a lady a certain homage seemed to be due; and if his wife resisted, he was angry. When Lady Harriet required her presence, she told John Carlyle that she was obliged to go, or the lady would quarrel with her, "and that meant a quarrel with her husband."[15] The Red Cross Knight was brought to evil thoughts of his "Una" by the enchantments of Archimage. To a proud fiery woman like Mrs. Carlyle the sense that Lady Harriet could come in any way between her husband and herself was intolerable [III, 372–373].

"Things had not come to this point during the Bay House visit [November–December 1845]," he adds, "but were tending fast in that direction, and were soon to reach it" (III, 373). A few pages later he observes: "The condition which she had wrought herself through her husband's Gloriana worship would have been ridiculous if it had not been so tragic—tragic even in its absurdity, and tragic in its consequences" (III, 385).

In considering Carlyle's friendship with Lady Ashburton in *My Relations with Carlyle*, Froude does not retreat from the position he maintained in the biography: "It was of course the purest Gloriana worship, the homage of the slave to his imperious mistress" (p. 19). He does not refer to *The Faerie Queene*, or to Lady Harriet as Gloriana, elsewhere in his analysis of the Carlyle-Ashburton relationship. Nor does he have to, for he has fixed indelibly in his readers' minds the context in which they should regard it.

The overall design of *The Faerie Queene* was to have Prince

15. See *New Letters and Memorials of Jane Welsh Carlyle*, ed. Alexander Carlyle (London and New York, 1903), II, 34.

Arthur emerge as the complement and fit mate of the "Faerie Queene,"
or "Gloriana." "In that Faery Queene," Spenser writes in the dedicatory letter to Ralegh, "I meane glory in my generall intention, but in
my particular I conceive the most excellent and glorious person of
our soveraine the Queene, and her kingdome in Faery land."[16] The
first book is "of the knight of the redcrosse, in whome I expresse
Holynes," and as a champion of Holiness he represents the Anglican
Church. In Froude's conception of Carlyle within the context of his
relationship with Lady Ashburton, Carlyle may be seen to embody
the virtues—and the faults—of the Red Cross Knight; also, he is St.
George, patron saint of England, and in a wider sense still he is Prince
Arthur seeking fulfillment in "Gloriana."

In the first book of this intensely moral poem, Una (or true religion)
comes on a white ass to the court of Gloriana to beg that one of her
knights undertake to slay the dragon which keeps her mother and
father prisoners. The Red Cross Knight, arrayed in the armor of God,
undertakes the adventure. For a while he is accompanied by Una, but
through the wiles of Archimago (hypocrisy) he is separated from her
and is led away by Duessa (the Roman Catholic religion) to the
House of Pride. After a number of adventures the Knight and Una
are finally reunited.

In his characterization of Carlyle as the Red Cross Knight, Froude
would undoubtedly have expected his readers to recall such a line in
Spenser as "He so ungently left her, who she lovéd best" (II, viii). No
explicit comment by Froude could have served him better in his
attempt to render Carlyle's slavish homage to Lady Ashburton and
his perhaps unconscious but nevertheless real rejection of Mrs.
Carlyle:

> For unto knight there is no greater shame,
> Than lightnesse and inconstancie in love;
> That doth this Redcrosse knights ensample plainly prove.
>
> (IV, i)

Such lines might well "ensample" Carlyle's behavior in deserting his
"Una."

Una, the maiden so "ungently" abandoned, spends most of the first
book of *The Faerie Queene* trying to find and preserve the Red Cross

16. *Edmund Spenser's Poetry*, sel. and ed. Hugh Maclean, Norton Critical Edition
(New York, 1968), p. 2. I give quotations from Book I of *The Faerie Queene* parenthetically in the text by canto and stanza number.

Knight from harm—surely, as Froude would have recognized, an ironic reversal of roles: "In wayes unknowne, her wandring knight to seeke, / With paines farre passing that long wandring Greeke" (III, xxi). Spenser describes her as "forsaken Truth" seeking "her love," and indeed she is almost an incarnation of love and heavenly beauty. Stressed throughout the narrative are her purity of character and motive. Especially poignant is the following description. Una,

> Though nor in word nor deede ill meriting,
> Is from her knight divorcéd in despaire
> And her due loves derived to that vile witches [Duessa's] share.
>
> Yet she most faithfull Ladie all this while
> Forsaken, wofull, solitarie mayd
> Farre from all peoples prease, as in exile,
> In wildernesse and wastful deserts strayd,
> To seeke her knight; who subtilly betrayd
> Through that late vision, which th'Enchaunter wrought,
> Had her abandond. She of nought affrayd,
> Through woods and wastnesse wide him daily sought;
> Yet wishéd tydings none of him unto her brought.
>
> (III, iii–iv)

"To sinfull house of Pride, Duessa / guides the faithfull knight"— so announces the motto to the fourth canto of the first book. The Red Cross Knight "had faire Una lorne [left], / Through light misdeeming of her loialtie" (IV, ii). The House of Pride is described as "a stately Pallace built of squaréd bricke" (IV, iv); yet it is soon seen to be insubstantial in its foundation and structure. In Froude's lively imagination the House of Pride may correspond, I suspect, to the various homes of the Ashburtons, in particular the Grange, to which the Carlyles made a series of visits. While he probably does not intend an exact correlation between the House of Pride and its hosts and the Grange and its owners, he may have expected his more discerning readers to see a complex web of indirect associations between the reality of the interlocking relationships and Spenser's poem and settings.[17]

17. Froude does not mention Duessa, the personage who brings the Red Cross Knight to the House of Pride. Although it would have been impossible for him to name her in his biography, he may well have intended her characterization in *The Faerie Queene* to be somewhere in the back of his readers' minds as they read his narrative of Carlyle's gradual entanglement with Lady Ashburton. Una speaks of Duessa as "Mine onely foe, mine onely deadly dread." Her name indicates that she is of

In the tenth canto Una brings the Red Cross Knight to the House of Holiness. There, as Maclean notes, he "is cleansed by penance and repentance, and instructed in Christian love. . . . Each significant detail of this Canto contrasts with its counterpart in Canto iv, as the House of Holiness . . . matches and counters the House of Pride" (p. 111). If it is the revelation of Una (Mrs. Carlyle) which brings the Red Cross Knight (Carlyle) to his senses, so we may assume that it was Mrs. Carlyle, more particularly his idealized memory of her after her death, that brought Carlyle to a truer perspective of the pain he had, largely unconsciously, caused her in life through his homage to Lady Ashburton. And their home at 5 Cheyne Row he indeed converted to a "House of Holiness," in which he repented his sins and religiously treasured each relic associated with her.

Before we condemn Froude for his unbridled bent for fictionalizing in regard to the Carlyles and the Ashburtons, we do well to remember that the source of much of his information was Geraldine Jewsbury and that many traits in his portrait of Mrs. Carlyle originate in her words. In a letter to Froude, dated 22 November 1876, she describes Mrs. Carlyle's character and tells him of her trauma during the Lady Ashburton years. She sent the letter to correct and supplement what she had previously told Froude, and presumably what she says in it was further supplemented in the deathbed conversations (she died in 1880) which Froude mentions. The letter thus helped determine Froude's conception of Mrs. Carlyle, for it was largely through Miss Jewsbury, an intimate friend but at times an unreliable witness, that Froude learned of her misery. Miss Jewsbury's compelling account must be read with caution:

. . . I feel how poor & *misleading* is all I have said to you about her. I have told you facts but failed to give you any clue to them. She was more abidingly & intensely miserable than words can utter—the *misery* was a *reality* no matter whether her imagination made it or not. With her habit of push-

---

double-nature, and the adjective "false" often precedes it. " 'I that do seeme not I, Duessa am' " (V, xxvi)—a line whose syntactic complexity mirrors her capacity for deceit. "In his falséd fancy" Red Cross takes her "to be the fairest wight, that livéd yet" (I, xxx), and for a while he is sorely enmeshed in her wiles. Her sway over him is, however, never uncontested and remains far from complete. It may be as much the conception of Carlyle's being captured by the false Duessa, as it is the conception of him being enslaved by the regal Gloriana, that Froude intends his readers to divine. If this hypothesis is correct, Froude is fictionalizing out of the poem rather than paralleling something in it, for in Spenser's terms Gloriana and Duessa are in no way rivals for Red Cross and indeed present totally contradictory images.

ing every thing to the extreme—& of expecting to find the most *logical* consecutiveness in what people said did & professed, I don't know wh. fared the worse the people or herself. Mr Carlyle once said to me she had the *deepest* and tenderest feelings—but narrow. Any other wife would have laughed at Mr. C's *bewitchment* with Lady A. . . .

Lady A. was admired for sayings & doings for wh. *she* was snubbed. *She* saw through Lady A's little ways & *grande dame* manners. . . .

She contrasted them with the daily, hourly endeavours she was making that his life sh*d* be as free from hindrances as possible. He put her aside for his WORK—but lingered in the "Primrose path of dalliance" for the sake of a great lady who liked to have a philosopher in the chair. . . .

Mrs. Carlyle was *proud*, & proud of her Pride—it was indeed enormous, but a quality she admired in herself & others. The only person who ever had any influence over her was her Father—he died when she was 14, & she was left to herself. Her Mother & she never agreed well when *together*, tho' she adored her at a distance & worshipped her after she was dead. Now about another point on wh. you have perhaps wrong ideas—wrong because they are the natural conclusions you w*d* be quite led to make from certain facts—some of which I told you myself—& you remarked. "But was it not behaving very ill to Carlyle?" NO—her allegiance was never broken, *that*, you *must* please believe on my word—she liked to be worshipped, to have people give their life and soul & spirit to her—I mean those whom she "allowed to love her" as she would have put it, but *all* even the only two she *really cared for* & who had the power *to make her suffer*—broke themselves against a rock, her *will* was as strong as her *Pride*, & she *never* did anything in her life wh. she w*d* have considered ignominious. . . .

The clear pitiless common sense wh. she *always* kept never failed her. She was not heartless, for her feelings were *real* & *strong* but she had a genuine *preference* for *herself*. From her earliest girlhood this was her characteristic in all matters where men were in question. She *would* be the *first* person with everybody man or woman whom she cared for enough to wish to to [sic] subjugate. . . .

The lines on which her character was laid down were *very* grand, but the result was blurred & distorted & confused. . . .

In marrying, she undertook what she felt to be a grand & noble life-task. A task which as set forth by himself touched all that was noble & heroic & inspired her imagination from its difficulty; she *believed* in him— . . . .

She was to be the companion-friend, help-mate, *her own* gifts were to be cultivated & recognised by him. She was bright & beautiful with a certain *star like* radience [sic] & grace. . . .

She had gone off into that desert [Craigenputtoch] with him, she had taken up poverty, obscurity, *hardship* even, cheerfully willingly & with an enthusiasm of self-sacrifice—only asking to be allowed to minister to him. The offering was accepted but like the precious things flung by Benvenuto into the Furnace when his statue was molten they were all consumed in the fierce flame—& *he* was so intent & occupied by what he was bringing forth that he could take no heed of the individual treasures, they were all swallowed up in the great whole—in her case it was the *living creature* in the midst of the fire which felt & suffered. She once told me what the earliest period of her married life was . . . , six years she lived there—she had undertaken a task & she *knew* that whether recognised or not, that she *did* help him. Then they came back to the World—& the strain told on her then— she did not falter from her purpose of keeping & shielding him—but she became *warped.* "We have this treasure in earthen vessels." . . .[18]

Froude, by skilfully alluding to *The Faerie Queene* at crucial moments in his account of the Carlyles and the Ashburtons, shapes his portraits to powerful, if obvious, effect. Now that we have seen him bending his interpretation of a relationship to maintain a literary analogy, we are in a better position to grasp the less obvious but equally deliberate artistry he practiced with Greek tragedy.

IV

If critics early noted the presence of *The Faerie Queene* in Froude's work, they have completely overlooked his use of Greek tragedy in depicting the drama of the Carlyles.[19] Tragedy, as practiced by the Greeks, is a relatively pure and concentrated form of art. Life's myriad complexity is distilled in it to an irreducible essence. Characters are shaped, situations are presented, to realize a dynamic interaction between character and situation upon which the dramatist focuses intensely. In Froude's case, his desire to shape his characters rendered them dramatically vivid, but his artistic technique, given that he was dealing not with legends but with real persons, inevitably led

18. MS: Harvard. Unfortunately this letter is neither in Miss Jewsbury's hand nor complete, for at the head of it the copyist has written "Extracts from a letter of Miss Jewsbury about Mrs. Carlyle to Mr. Froude." The portion we have left is, however, in her characteristic style and seems true to what we know of her opinions of Mrs. Carlyle. As there are no paragraph divisions in the manuscript, I have begun a paragraph after each set of ellipsis periods which presumably denote omissions in the original letter. Sir James Crichton-Browne discusses this letter (but only quotes a few words from it) on pp. xlix–li of vol. I of Alexander Carlyle's edition of *New Letters and Memorials of Jane Welsh Carlyle.*

19. Waldo H. Dunn in *English Biography* almost intuited this connection: "To one who reads with open, unprejudiced mind, the story of Carlyle's life unrolls itself with a power not unlike that of the greatest Greek drama" (p. 171).

to distortion. In reading his pages we have always to balance the gain in dramatic intensity against the distortion.

During his childhood Froude made an intense, if sporadic, study of the Greek tragedians. Not only were the Greeks his first love but they remained his favorite reading throughout life. He read the classics habitually, with ease and with pleasure, and he often referred to them in his writings. They served him not only as models upon which to mold his ideals of moral excellence but also, increasingly as the years went by, as relief from contemporary realities. Conway, in his Introduction to *The Nemesis of Faith*, had noted that "the depth and intensity of the Greek drama pervade his work" (p. xiii). Froude's knowledge of Greek tragedy finds expression in his biography of Carlyle, I suggest, in at least two ways: first, he introduced the device of the Greek chorus to allow him to comment obliquely on the events he described; second, he consciously drew his portraits of Thomas Carlyle and Jane Welsh after models in Greek drama, Carlyle after Oedipus, Mrs. Carlyle after Iphigenia.

Several times in his first volume Froude refers to himself as the chorus commenting on—to an extent participating in—a fateful series of events. He saw the interlocking lives of the Carlyles as a personal drama which in its intensity approached Greek tragedy. As their biographer, he took upon himself the role of the chorus observing this tragedy. In Greek drama the chorus functions as the consciousness of the people; but, more important still, it serves as interpreter to the audience of the human events being unfolded upon the stage. It was in this role of interpreter of the Carlyles to his contemporaries that Froude saw himself.

Only after quoting from Carlyle's letter to Jane Welsh of 20 January 1825 does Froude openly introduce himself as the "chorus" in the "long drama" of the courtship (I, 284, 363). This letter Froude viewed as the decisive turning point in Carlyle's largely epistolary wooing of Miss Welsh. First he gave extracts from her letter to Carlyle of 13 January 1825, where she had written "I love you . . . but I am not *in love* with you—that is to say—my love for you is not a passion which overclouds my judgement; . . . it is a simple, honest, serene affection, made up of admiration and sympathy."[20] Carlyle's reply of 20 January is a carefully reasoned refutation of all her arguments against marriage. In it he reaffirms his love and asks "a noble

20. *CL*, III, 249.

being" to consent to "unite our resources, . . . her judgement, her patience, prudence, her true affection, to mine."[21] After quoting extensively from these letters Froude wrote: "The functions of a biographer are, like the functions of a Greek chorus, occasionally at the important moments to throw in some moral remarks which seem to fit the situation" (I, 284). And the remarks which he thought appropriate to insert at this fateful moment in both their lives are these: "The chorus after such a letter [Carlyle's of 20 January] would remark, perhaps, on the subtle forms of self-deception to which the human heart is liable, of the momentous nature of marriage. . . . Self-sacrifice it might say was a noble thing. But a sacrifice which one person might properly make, the other might have no reasonable right to ask or to allow" (ibid.). In saying this he obviously has in mind Miss Welsh's answer of nine days later. It showed that Carlyle's arguments had made an impression upon her, for she wrote: "Not many months ago, I would have said it was impossible I should ever be your wife; at present I consider this the most *probable* destiny for me." A year and a half later she told Carlyle that she had considered herself his "affianced wife" from this time forward.[22]

Froude, strongly influenced by Geraldine Jewsbury, had come to the conclusion that Carlyle "was one of those persons who ought not to have married."[23] Yet he could not say this openly. A mask was needed, and the device of the Greek chorus came conveniently to mind. This device was made necessary by a change of course he determined upon in 1880. "By this time," he wrote in *My Relations*, "I had drifted towards a cowardly conclusion that I would suppress Mrs. Carlyle's letters after all, that I would write a biography such as would most surely be to my own advantage, dwelling on all that was best and brightest in Carlyle, and passing lightly over the rest. I wrote the first volume of the 'Life' as it now stands in this sense" (p. 30). This disclosure suggests why Froude felt obliged to adopt the device of the chorus in his first volume. He could not state overtly what he thought of the Carlyles' marriage, but acting as the chorus he could imply his real views to discerning readers.

We have already looked at the passage in Carlyle's Journal in which he had said that no one could write a biography of him because no

21. Ibid., p. 258.
22. Ibid., III, 266; IV, 112. The Greek chorus continues to rumble at strategic moments in the courtship—e.g., Froude, *Carlyle*, I, 347.
23. *My Relations with Carlyle*, p. 21.

one could understand the mystery which enveloped his life. But if Carlyle could never be completely understood, his life at least had analogies with figures of the past. Froude sought in these analogies clues that would help him unravel Carlyle's personality. In this search he had help from Carlyle, who often saw himself in relation to others. Carlyle's favorite image of himself was as a prophet alone in the desert, his spirit unbowed, his message of dire import unheeded or misunderstood by an indifferent world. He speaks of himself as "Ishmael . . . cast forth into the Desert, with bow and quiver in his coat of wild skins";[24] and at one point Froude dutifully speaks of Carlyle as "fated to be an Ishmaelite" (III, 11). At other times Carlyle saw himself as Isaiah, as John the Baptist, as St. Anthony, as "the poor Arab," as a "Bedouin," or even as Faust. Froude often returns in his biography to the comparison with a prophet isolated, seeing Carlyle alternatively as Isaiah or Jeremiah. At the time of his marriage, speaking of Carlyle's search for spiritual truth, he notes ironically that "apostles in St. Paul's opinion were better unwedded" (I, 285), and later compares him explicitly to the apostle to the gentiles (IV, 266). He does not restrict himself, however, to Biblical figures: he draws analogies with medieval "knight errants," Dante, Don Quixote, and figures of classical mythology and Renaissance epic. In an unpublished letter he observes of Carlyle that "Nature meant him for a Norse scald."[25] A few instances will suffice to demonstrate Froude's analogical bent. Speaking of Carlyle's failure to dispel Mrs. Carlyle's suspicions concerning his relationship with Lady Ashburton, Froude writes that "Carlyle in such matters had no more skill than the Knight of La Mancha would have had" (III, 386). In *My Relations with Carlyle*, he refers to Carlyle's correspondence with Lady Ashburton as "masses of extravagant letters . . . to the great lady as ecstatic as Don Quixote's to Dulcinea" (p. 18). To suggest Carlyle's slavish devotion to her, he draws upon Tasso's *Gerusalemme Liberata* and classical mythology: "Rinaldo in the bower of Armida or Hercules spinning silks for Omphale" (p. 19). Carlyle's character and acts, in Froude's view, might be evoked by any or all of these analogies with figures of the past. No one by itself "explained" him,

24. *Letters of Thomas Carlyle 1826–1836*, ed. Charles Eliot Norton (London, 1889), p. 464.
25. Froude to Charles Graves, Bishop of Limerick, 22 May [1884]. MS: Duke. The other analogies are drawn from the biography and from *My Relations with Carlyle*.

but all helped at one time or another to illuminate the shadowy dimensions of his character.

Yet no analogy left Froude certain that he had really seized that mystery. "There is something *demonic* both in him and her which will never be adequately understood," he says at one point.[26] Before Mrs. Carlyle's death in 1866, Carlyle had seemed to Froude a man "apart from the rest of the world, with the mask of destiny upon him, to whom one could not feel exactly as towards a brother mortal."[27] His sense of mission put inseparable barriers between himself and other men. But Mrs. Carlyle's death transformed both Carlyle and the nature of Froude's relationship to him. He came to see Carlyle not only more often but in a different perspective. Carlyle undertook a repentance for what he considered his grave failings toward her in life. It was "a repentance so deep and passionate" that it "showed that the real nature was as beautiful as his intellect had been magnificent. He was still liable to his fits of temper. He was scornful and overbearing and wilful; but it had become possible to love him— indeed, impossible not to love him." Equally dramatic and far-reaching was the change in Froude's sense of his relationship to Carlyle. From awe before a revered mentor he moved to an awareness of Carlyle as a tormented human who felt he had sinned greatly but who was now conscious of his sin and was prepared to make ample and extended atonement for it. And if "the remorse was needed," Froude added, the "expiation" was "so frank and so complete that it washed the stain away."

References to the lives of the Carlyles singly or together as participants in a tragedy occur frequently in Froude's writings about them. Not until 1871, however, when Carlyle gave Froude the material which constituted the letters and memorials of Jane Welsh Carlyle and his reminiscence of her life, did the dimensions of the mystery— the "something *demonic*" in both Carlyles—begin to come clearly into focus. He read the documents left him, he wrote in *My Relations*, "and then for the first time I realised what a tragedy the life in Cheyne Row had been—a tragedy as stern and real as the story of Oedipus" (p. 13). In the anguished weeks before he wrote *My Relations*, he had voiced

---

26. Froude to Mrs. Kingsley [Oct. 1884], in Herbert Paul, *The Life of Froude* (New York, 1905), p. 331.

27. This and subsequent quotations in this paragraph from *My Relations with Carlyle*, pp. 12, 13.

the dilemma of his recognition in the privacy of his journal. The description of Carlyle given there applies as well to Oedipus:

What, in the name of truth, ought I to have done? It was a tragedy, as truly and as terribly as Oedipus; nor was the character altogether unlike. His [Carlyle's] character, when he was himself, was noble and generous; but he had absolutely no control over himself. He was wayward and violent, and perhaps at bottom believed himself a peculiar man who had a dispensation to have things his own way.[28]

In his effort to penetrate Carlyle's inner nature Froude found at its heart a paradox, a paradox of which the only explanation lay in the mysterious figure of Oedipus. The indefinable "something *demonic*" in Carlyle led Froude to see him as a reincarnation of Sophocles' hero. Carlyle, as Oedipus before him, exemplifies the insoluble riddle of man's nature.

Oedipus the King and *Oedipus at Colonus* provided Froude with his surest clue to understanding Carlyle: he saw his character to be as complex, irrational and mysterious as that of the Theban king. This revelation did not come until Froude had known Carlyle more than two decades. Only in *My Relations with Carlyle* and in his journal (neither intended for publication) does he draw the intriguing parallel between Oedipus and Carlyle; he does not mention Oedipus in the biography. But there, ironically sometimes, more often seriously, he speaks of the Fates "doing their very worst to Carlyle" (II, 67). Carlyle became for him a man who wrestled with the Fates: only the Greek conception of the doomed tragic hero met the measure of his greatness. Before 1866, his career recently crowned by the publication of the final volumes of *Frederick the Great*, Carlyle is the mighty hero of *Oedipus the King*; after 1866, his life broken by Mrs. Carlyle's death, he becomes the tragic wanderer seeking salvation of *Oedipus at Colonus*.

Oedipus the King is usually assigned to the early 420's B.C. In it Oedipus is pictured as a bewildering combination of strengths and weaknesses: he is, in H. D. F. Kitto's words, "intelligent, determined, self-reliant, but hot-tempered and too sure of himself."[29] What happens to him we see to be largely the result of the interaction of these conflicting characteristics. He becomes the victim of his virtues. "No

28. Entry of 25 February 1887, in Dunn, II, 550.
29. *Greek Tragedy: A Literary Study* (Garden City, N. Y., 1954; Anchor Books), p. 143.

extant tragedy so bristles with tragic irony" as Oedipus circles around the truth and occasionally brushes against it.[30] We wait in expectation, watching the circles gradually contract, for the full shock of impact. The chorus of the Old Men of Thebes expresses a view of life which dilates with meaning for Oedipus and beyond him:

> What man, what man on earth wins more
> of happiness than a seeming
> and after that turning away?
> Oedipus, you are my pattern of this,
> Oedipus, you and your fate!
>
> (ll. 1190–1194)[31]

The fate of Oedipus, the chorus finds, is typical: he is a "pattern" of human life and fortune. What has happened to him is part of the drama of erring humanity. "Although Oedipus is by far the greatest sufferer in the play," Kitto observes, "he is not the only one. There are others who suffer, not by any means in the same degree, but in the same way" (p. 145).

When Oedipus learns the truth he blinds himself in a fit of passion. It is an act freighted with symbolic overtones: he lived in darkness when he had his sight, now he cannot see—but he *sees* who he is and he begins to understand what he has done. Throughout the play Oedipus comes across as an appallingly strong character, with the strength of a man in his prime. He is the fitting instrument of his own punishment. "Only such a catastrophic self-punishment can break him so that, within moments, he has turned into an old man." Having been a tragic figure driven by his destiny, he now becomes even more than that: "a unique individual, and, somehow, a great man" who has created that destiny of his own will. Oedipus is crushed, but Oedipus is great.[32]

Oedipus at Colonus (c. 405 B.C.), the product of Sophocles' extreme old age, was also presumably the culmination of his thought about a figure who had taken up much of his mind's best energies since *Antigone* (440 B.C.). It shows Oedipus, twenty years a wanderer,

30. Richmond Lattimore, *The Poetry of Greek Tragedy* (Baltimore, 1957), p. 83. My understanding of Sophocles in this and the following paragraphs owes much to the fine studies by Lattimore and Kitto.

31. Sophocles, *Oedipus the King*, trans. David Grene, in *The Complete Greek Tragedies*, ed. David Grene and Richmond Lattimore (Chicago, 1954), p. 64. Subsequent quotations are identified only by line numbers in the text.

32. Quotations from Lattimore, p. 91.

finding a home at last among the "sacred Furies" in a grove outside Athens. He enters "old, blind, bearded and ragged, but carrying himself well." To his daughters he says: "Suffering and time, / Vast time, have been instructors in contentment" (ll. 7–8).

In his essay "England's Forgotten Worthies" (1852), Froude expressed a view of old age which directly parallels his consideration of Carlyle as a modern Oedipus. He describes two kinds of old age. One he compares to "the slow-dropping mellow autumn of a rich glorious summer" and finds that "in the old man, nature has fulfilled her work." Such an old age, he concludes, "is beautiful, but not the most beautiful." Unqualified admiration he reserves for a higher kind of existence: "There is another life, hard, rough, and thorny, trodden with bleeding feet and aching brow; the life of which the cross is the symbol; a battle which no peace follows, this side the grave; . . . this is the highest life of man. Look back along the great names of history; there is none whose life has been other than this."[33] Although referring to England's "forgotten worthies" of the sixteenth century, Froude intends his words to apply to "the great names of history." Elsewhere he wrote that "the Greeks thought that the highest knowledge could be obtained only through pain and mortification."[34] Oedipus was one of those who knew both in abundance in his declining years. Carlyle was another.

Oedipus, arriving at Colonus, had come to the end of a long road. As a man he has nothing more to learn, but we soon realize that his character has undergone no essential change. "I suffered those deeds more than I acted them," he says (ll. 266–267). In many respects he is a terrible old man. But he remains part of the pattern of mortality. Antigone exclaims: "For you will never see in all the world / A man whom God has led / Escape his destiny!" (ll. 251–253). Sophocles, in a magnificent choral ode, compares him to a storm-beaten cliff raising its head defiantly above its surroundings:

> Think of some shore in the north the
> Concussive waves make stream
> This way and that in the gales of winter:
> It is like that with him:

33. *Short Studies*, I, 492.
34. "Lord Macaulay [a review of Trevelyan's *Life*]," *Fraser's Magazine*, 93 (June 1876), 693.

The wild wrack breaking over him
From head to foot, and coming on forever. . . .

(ll. 1240–1244)

"Sophocles is declaring that the sin of Oedipus is real," David Grene points out in his fine commentary on the play; "that the consequences in the form of the loneliness, neglect, and suffering of the years of wandering are inevitable; but that the will and the consciousness are also some measure of man's sin—and when the sinner sinned necessarily and unwittingly, his suffering can be compensation enough for his guilt." [35]

Froude considered Carlyle to be the greatest man of his age. No one, not even Ruskin, took up Carlyle's opinions concerning man and society with the fervor and strong conviction of Froude. He saw Carlyle as a man who by sheer force of character dominated his contemporaries, whose gospel was needed to guide a troubled England, and whose vision of society would be vindicated a hundred years hence. Then in 1866 he saw a personal tragedy of immense proportions strike his hero. Carlyle was metamorphosed. To be sure, traits of the old Carlyle remained. He was still proud, domineering, at times inconsiderate of others; but he also revealed depths of sorrow and repentance for his treatment of Mrs. Carlyle which only a person of heroic dimensions could draw upon.

In alluding to Oedipus as he grapples with the paradoxes of Carlyle's character, Froude insinuates that Oedipus' strange career can in meaningful ways illuminate Carlyle's. Nineteenth-century critics of drama, from Coleridge and Hazlitt at one end of the century to A. C. Bradley at the other, tended to focus on character and to judge it on ethical grounds. In the *Poetics* Aristotle postulated the concept of hamartia, the flaw, "great or small, moral or intellectual, without which the hero would not have fallen nor his character been a tragic one. . . . Aristotelian hamartia is not *any* shortcoming which may be found in a suffering hero; it is the defect which makes his character tragically imperfect." [36] Aristotle's concept of the tragic flaw fitted well into the Victorian tradition of ethical character analysis and guided interpretation of *Oedipus the King* into the twentieth century. Froude would have been familiar with it and, most probably, would

35. Introduction to Sophocles, *Oedipus the King*, p. 5.
36. Kitto, pp. 116–117.

have endorsed it, as he would have endorsed the tragic pattern of life upon which the play insists. He would have agreed with many readers of Aristotle that in Oedipus' case his tragic flaw is hubris, or excessive pride, and that it leads directly to his fall. Thus he was led to envisage a Carlyle possessed of hubris, sovereignly independent, at times unthinking of others, yet a great man. Interpreting for his own purposes Aristotle's observations on Oedipus, Froude saw Carlyle undergoing a fundamental experience of "recognition" and "reversal." "Recognition," wrote Aristotle, "as the name indicates, is a change from ignorance to knowledge. . . . 'Reversal of the situation' is a change by which the action veers round to its opposite. . . . The best form of recognition is coincident with a reversal of the situation, as in the *Oedipus*."[37] For Froude Carlyle, in Aristotle's terms, underwent an experience of "recognition"—a moment of intense vision coming after a lifetime of blindness; it coincided with a "reversal," after which he sought to understand his life in the light of the revelatory experience. The regeneration of the fallen hero, which took place for Oedipus in the *Colonus*, took place for Carlyle in the prolonged suffering and repentance which occurred in the years following his wife's death.

Oedipus is the key to the riddle of Carlyle's character as we see it revealed in Froude's pages. Froude shaped his portrait, after the model of Oedipus, with the traits which he thought revealed the true Carlyle. Whether or not his emphases are the right ones we may debate but may never know. Froude did not believe in unimpassioned objectivity in biography and did not claim to tell all. But he told us much and gave us clues to fathom more. Once we recognize that the lineaments of his portrait of Carlyle are grounded in the character of Oedipus we are at least in a better position to understand why he drew Carlyle as he did. This, in turn, will enable us to judge more surely the validity of that portrait.

Froude's interpretation of Carlyle may strike readers today as too simplistic, accepting as it does at literal—and probably exaggerated —value almost every statement made by Carlyle of his sorrow and repentance. But in arriving at his interpretation we must remember that Froude was closely following Carlyle's own words as he read them in the *Reminiscences*, in the annotations to the *Letters and*

37. *Aristotle on the Art of Poetry* (trans. S. H. Butcher), ed. Milton C. Nahm (New York, 1948), pp. 14, 15. I have quoted the passages slightly out of order.

Memorials of Jane Welsh Carlyle, and, perhaps most significantly, in the notebooks which form Carlyle's Journal. He had access to certain materials which no subsequent biographer of Carlyle has seen. Only as all these materials become available will scholars be able to see from what his portrait of Carlyle emerged and to evaluate it accordingly. Elsewhere I have shown that many of Froude's statements regarding Carlyle's early life can be seen in clearer perspective when set against the biography of him by Friedrich Althaus and Carlyle's running commentary to it.[38] But Carlyle's personal Journal, which we know chiefly through the extracts given in Froude's biography and which remains in private hands, would seem to be a still more important source of information. "The real Carlyle is to be especially looked for in this book," Froude wrote in his biography, "for it contains his dialogues with his own soul" (III, 420). No one, not even Carlyle's nephew Alexander, has contested this statement. The Journal was read by a few others after Froude, including Alexander Carlyle and Charles Eliot Norton. Among the Norton papers at Harvard is a letter from Alexander Carlyle to Norton, dated 20 February 1902. Norton had been asked to give his opinion about what was to be done with the Journal, in particular with the fourth (and last) notebook covering the years 1867–1873. I have not found Norton's letter, but Alexander Carlyle takes up the subject in detail. In doing so he adds considerably to our knowledge about Carlyle's Journal:

My opinion of my Uncle's "Note-book IV" coincides very closely with yours as expressed in your last Letter to me. But I think it was not so much "grief overmastering strength of Character and serenity of Soul" as severe bodily ailments influencing mind and feelings (as is often the case especially in so extraordinary sensitive a being as Carlyle was) that overclouded his judgement and all but deranged his intellect. Certainly the loss of his Wife in such exceptionally painful circumstances was a crown of sorrow; but he bore this greatest of losses in a manful and dignified way *at the time* and *for months after the event*, as his Journal & letters of the period show. It was not till later when his health of body (what little health he ever had) totally failed that he began to write down the vain lamentations and useless complaints that abound in Note-book IV.

It would be impossible to give an adequate description of his state at that time (1867–1873). My late dear Wife [Mary Aitken Carlyle] who came to live with him in 1868, often told me in what a lamentable condi-

---

38. *Two Reminiscences of Thomas Carlyle*, ed. John Clubbe (Durham, N.C., 1974).

tion of health she found him. He had difficulty in digesting anything really nourishing, especially any fatty thing. By abstinence from proper food he was practically starving himself, and the Doctors (there were several in succession) for fear of offending allowed him to have his own way. He grew more and more nervous, thin & weak, till his mind especially in the mornings was often "wandering" through sheer want of bodily nourishment, as she perceived. This went on for several years, when, a crisis arriving, she called in another Doctor—a man of sense—having first privately explained the case to him. He (Dr. Blakiston it was) at once ordered nourishing diet in plenty, rich soups and fat in various forms, giving pepsine to digest it. Almost immediately the symptoms improved, he began to grow stronger; slept much better; and when his nerves became covered with a little "adipose tissue" his spirits rose, and he became calm, cheerful and comparatively happy & contented. I lived with him for more than *two years* after this (1879–81) and never noticed any trace of querulousness, misanthropy or morbid despondency such as parts of the Note-book exhibit. He often spoke to me of his Wife, and always calmly and with dignified sorrow perfectly natural, and without the slightest sign of "remorse."

It was during that dreary time of conspicuously bad health and spirits that Note-book IV was written; and its tone is a reflex of what he was feeling,—despa[i]ring & morbid. Considering this I am not much surprised at the tone: but it seems marvellous that he should have thought it his *duty* to write at all in such a condition as he was in! And, unfortunately, to make bad worse, he nearly always chose a day to write in this Note-book when he was feeling particularly sad and ill. Mary has often remarked to me that, after he had passed a sleepless night, or after any untoward even[t] had happened to him, the Note-book was sure to be brought out and an entry made; whilst for weeks, or months, during which he was fairly well and in good spirits the unlucky Note-book was never touched! Froude is about right (for once) when he says "his Journal contains chiefly a record of his sorrows." The pity is that Froude has made public so much of the Note-book. And the portions he has printed have got many a sordid twist in passing through his mill. This makes me feel that it would perhaps scarcely be prudent to destroy the original Notebook. Had Froude not printed any of it, or even had his selections from it been accurately printed, the decision to burn the original would have been a much simpler matter. But as the case now stands by destroying the original one would destroy the only certain means of ever effectively & authoritatively correcting Froude's mistakes and misrepresentations.

There is no reason, however, why a new copy of such portions of the Book as you suggest should not be made, for ordinary use. After this were done, the typed copy you now have ought to be burnt, and the Original kept strictly safe under lock and key, to be seen by no one except trusted members of the family. No one but Froude has seen the Note-book, and no one but you and Professor Masson has yet seen my copy.

Should this letter reach you before you have despatched the typed copy, I should be deeply grateful to you if you would cross out with pencil the parts of the Note-book which you think deserving deletion. I have already done the like in my copy; but I do not like to trust my own discretion alone in so important a matter.[39]

Alexander Carlyle's letter would seem to confirm that the portrait which Froude drew of Carlyle in his later years is in essence true to what he read in Carlyle's fourth notebook. It also suggests that some of the controversial stances in Froude's depiction of "the real Carlyle" during his earlier years may find support in Carlyle's notebooks covering those years. In any event, until their full publication, we remain with imperfect knowledge of Carlyle's "dialogues with his own soul."

Another dimension of the Oedipus legend concerns what we now call the Oedipus complex. To what degree, we may reasonably ask, does that particular nexus of relationships affect Carlyle? Thus far I have not discussed the better-known aspect of the Oedipus complex, that involving love for his mother and hostility toward his father. It must at least be touched upon in any discussion of Froude's presentation of Carlyle as a modern Oedipus. Although Freud adumbrated the Oedipus complex in letters before he published *The Interpretation of Dreams* in 1901, his first extended discussion of it occurs in that book. He returns to it in *Totem and Taboo* (1913) and elsewhere. In his *General Introduction to Psychoanalysis* (1920) he speaks thus of the relationship between mother and son:

From the time of puberty onward the human individual must devote himself to the great task of *freeing himself from the parents*; and only after this detachment is accomplished can he cease to be a child and so become a member of the social community. For a son, the task consists in releasing his libidinal desires from his mother, in order to employ them in the quest of an external love-object in reality. . . . In neurotics, however, this detachment from the parents is not accomplished at all; the son remains all his life in subjection to his father, and incapable of transferring his libido to a new sexual object.[40]

39. I have omitted the introductory page and a half of this letter but have quoted everything that Alexander Carlyle says concerning the Journal.
40. Trans. Joan Riviere, Permabooks (New York, 1953), pp. 345–346.

Many psychological concepts of today derive from the Greek myths; these myths, in turn, modern psychologists have found illuminating in interpreting states of mind or relationships between individuals. In this century Freud has written with great insight on *Oedipus the King*. In *The Interpretation of Dreams* he speaks of its "profound and universal power to move." "There must be something," he says, "which makes a voice within us ready to recognize the compelling force of destiny in the *Oedipus*.... His destiny moves us only because it might have been ours."[41] In writing these words Freud may have in mind the passage in which Jocasta, mother and wife to Oedipus, expresses her disbelief in the significance of dreams:

> Best to live lightly, as one can, unthinkingly.
> As to your mother's marriage bed,—don't fear it.
> Before this, in dreams too, as well as oracles,
> many a man has lain with his own mother.
> But he to whom such things are nothing bears
> his life most easily.
>
> (ll. 979–984)

As the play unfolds, these words become one of its more terrible ironies.

Froude in his understanding of human relationships showed himself to be uncannily prophetic of several of the insights which Freud was to have twenty years later. I do not wish to imply that Froude anticipated Freud in a full and conscious understanding of the nature of the Oedipus complex, but I do think that, with his unusual psychological gift, he saw some of the complex ironies of Carlyle's tragic fate in a perspective similar to that which led Freud to formulate his famous theory. Froude often stresses the closeness of Carlyle's tie to his mother, and no one who has read his correspondence with her can fail to be impressed by the strength and intimacy of that tie. The best-known "Freudian" biography of him—W. E. Halliday's *Mr. Carlyle, My Patient* (1948)—makes much of this relationship, as one might expect; yet compared to Froude's commentary, Halliday's is superficial, jargon-ridden, untrustworthy in the extreme.[42] Carlyle himself played into the hands of his modern analysts by the honesty with

---

41. Trans. James Strachey, Science Editions (New York, 1961), pp. 261, 262.
42. See also Jackson E. Towne, "Carlyle and Oedipus," *Psychoanalytic Review*, 22 (1935), 297–305. Although hardly an improvement over Halliday, this article does juxtapose in an interesting manner quotations from Carlyle and from Froude's biography.

which he depicted family relationships in his *Reminiscences*. There he says, for instance, that "it was the earliest terror of my childhood 'that I might lose my Mother'; and it had gone with me all my days."[43] Reading such a statement and others like it in Carlyle's personal writings, Froude reflects them in a quite natural—if persistent—way in his account of Carlyle's relationship with his mother. The wonder is perhaps not that he does so but that he does not make more of them. We need not agree with his reading of the evidence, but we should recognize that cumulatively he presents a persuasive, if over-drawn, interpretation of a relationship.

Of the young Carlyle, teaching at Annan Academy from 1814 to 1816, Froude observes: "Annan, associated as it was with the odious memories of his schooldays, had indeed but one merit—that he was within reach of his family, especially of his mother, to whom he was attached with a real passion" (I, 35). Not many pages later he speaks of the bond between them as "a special and passionate attachment of a quite peculiar kind" (I, 47). In chapter 10 we learn that "Carlyle . . . thought always first of his mother" (I, 178). As the courtship of Jane Baillie Welsh progressed, Froude notes: "The strongest personal passion which he experienced through all his life was his affection for his mother" (I, 232). After the marriage in 1826, he says: "Miss Welsh, it is probable, would have passed through life more pleasantly had she married someone in her own rank of life; Carlyle might have gone through it successfully with his mother or a sister to look after him" (I, 367). Near the end of the Craigenputtoch years he observes that "after his mother, he loved his wife better than anyone in the world" (II, 421). After he moved to London in 1834, Carlyle usually paid each summer a long visit to Scotland, part of which would be spent with his mother at the family farm, Scotsbrig. Of the visit in 1839, Froude wrote: "He and his old mother drove about in [the] gig together, or wandered in the shrubberies, smoking their pipes together, like a pair of lovers—as indeed they were" (III, 166). The following comment prefaces Froude's account of the death of Carlyle's mother in 1853: "His mother, whom he had

---

43. *Reminiscences*, I, 196. On the same page Carlyle writes: "This very morning [in 1866], I got into dreaming confused *nightmare* stuff about some funeral and her; not hers, nor obviously my Jane's, seemingly my Father's rather, and she *sending* me on it,—the saddest bewildered stuff." Towne comments: "A man who dreams that his mother sends him to his father's funeral is assuredly a sufferer from an Oedipus complex" (p. 305).

regarded with an affection 'passing the love of sons,' with whom, in spite of, or perhaps in consequence of, her profound Christian piety, he had found more in common, as he often said, than with any other mortal—was now evidently to be taken away from him. A feeling peculiarly tender had united these two. . . . Carlyle, as his letters show, had been haunted from his earliest days by the terror that he must one day lose her. . . . No one else, perhaps, ever completely understood his character" (IV, 137–138).

It is difficult to say conclusively what Froude intends to imply by these observations, and by others like them. He may mean them as no more than innocent asides. But seen in the light of his understanding of Oedipus, they suggest the possibility that he believed the tie between Carlyle and his mother was not only abnormally strong—he would have been repelled by both the concept and the term "oedipal" —but also that its existence was a major reason why he should never have married Jane Welsh. That Carlyle has suffered subsequently in hands less delicate than Froude's should warn anyone away from insensitive amateur psychologizing. Still, attempts will continue to be made to understand Carlyle's genius. Froude's is only the most sustained and, in my view, one of the more persuasive of past attempts. Perhaps his position here, suggestive but not affirmative, is the fairest one for him to adopt. He pushes his intuitive understanding of Carlyle's relationship with his mother as far as he dares, yet stops short of a comprehensive statement. Certainly nothing in the *Collected Letters* of Carlyle, now in progress, will warrant a future biographer's inferring more than Froude inferred. But it is likely that he distorted his portrayal by inferring too much.

v

Jane Baillie Welsh also plays a major role in Froude's biography. Of her he wrote to a correspondent: "*She* is my special legacy from Carlyle. His chief desire was that her portrait should be accurately drawn."[44] In the long eighth chapter of his first volume he goes thoroughly into her antecedents and her life at Haddington, and in his narration of Carlyle's courtship of her she holds the stage nearly as often as he does. Carlyle's reminiscence of his wife was, in Froude's

44. Froude to G. J. Holyoake [1882], in Joseph McCabe, *Life and Letters of George Jacob Holyoake* (London, 1908), II, 126.

view, "as sternly tragic, as profoundly pathetic as the great Theban drama,"[45] but in viewing her life Froude usually subsumes the Oedipus myth in favor of another myth with a still broader tragic significance. In *My Relations with Carlyle* we see him referring to the married life of the Carlyles as a "singular and tragical story" (p. 17); and to Ruskin he said: "*Her* life was a tragedy."[46] The representation of Jane Welsh Carlyle as a tragic heroine, established in the first volume, is maintained over the next three. While Froude never specifically mentions that he had a model in mind for Mrs. Carlyle, one heroine of Greek tragedy often hovered in his imagination as he wrote of her. She is Iphigenia, daughter of Agamemnon.

Iphigenia is referred to only once in Froude's biography, and then not by name. In his first authorial (or choric) comment after describing Miss Welsh's marriage to Carlyle on 17 October 1826, Froude writes: "the victory was won, but, as of old in Aulis, not without a victim" (I, 365). It *was* a victory, for the life of the Carlyles together was a triumphant achievement of the human spirit. This Froude never denied. But the price of victory for Mrs. Carlyle was, in his view, undeservedly high. From his essay "Sea Studies," written in 1874, we learn that he had pondered the meaning of Iphigenia for his own time. The conception of her character which he found in Euripides and which he analyzes in the essay fascinated him. Despite its title, the essay is largely a study of Iphigenia as a figure who incarnates the virtue of duty. Froude prized this virtue above all others and saw it as the guiding principle behind Mrs. Carlyle's existence—speaking, on one occasion, of "the sense of duty acting as perpetual curb to her impatience" (III, 393). Iphigenia's behavior under duress he found exemplary of humanity's need of duty and self-sacrifice, and he drew upon it in dramatizing Mrs. Carlyle's character and ordeal.

Euripides, of the Greek tragedians, long had appealed to Froude least. "At school I had read the statutory four plays and forgotten them, and had never looked into Euripides since."[47] But in 1874, preparing to embark on a long sea voyage to South Africa, he took with him an edition of Euripides. "In the general conception of human life," he found, "in the nature of the problems with which men of intellect were occupied, Euripides is a curious interpreter of the

45. *My Relations with Carlyle*, pp. 33–34.
46. Letter of 1 May [1886], in Viljoen, p. 46.
47. "Sea Studies," in *Short Studies*, III, 212.

elements which are now surrounding ourselves. We are travelling fast on lines parallel to those on which he travelled, and he is probably nearer to us to-day than he was to our fathers forty years ago" (p. 214). Euripides' vision of life was close to Froude's own, or so Froude thought. The crisis of later Victorian England—moral, political, religious, social—reflected a loss of belief in values, a loss which Euripides had experienced in Athens during the extended trauma of the Peloponnesian War and its sordid aftermath. Froude, by nature a pessimist, regarded himself as a latter-day Euripides, interpreting his age and upholding ideals of duty and self-sacrifice in times when, he felt, many valued them little or not at all.

During this sea voyage to South Africa he grew to understand Euripides as never before. "For six weeks," he wrote, "Euripides became an enchanter for me, and the Grecian world was raised from the dead into a moonlight visibility, with softest lights, and shadows black as Erebus" (p. 213). He responded to Euripides' sense of the eternal flux in human affairs. In his plays Fortune hurls those seemingly most favored into sudden, irrevocable eclipse, for reasons not apparent to mortals. Since man can never understand the situation in which he finds himself, he can never make purposeful or consistent choices. Thus defeat always looms before him. Of all the defeated and helpless victims in Euripides, it is Iphigenia whom Froude saw as the key to understanding the human dilemma.

"Every act of man which can be called good is an act of sacrifice," Froude prefaced his discussion of Iphigenia in "Sea Studies," "an act which the doer of it would have left undone had he not preferred some other person's benefit to his own." Fundamental to human life, in his view, was "the obligation to sacrifice self" (p. 238). "Sacrifice is the first element of religion" (p. 240), and "religion meant essentially 'doing our duty,'" Froude had written in his unfinished autobiography. "It was not to be itself an object of thought but a guide to action."[48] This position he held to all his life. "The essence of true nobility," he wrote in "The Science of History" (1864), "is neglect of self. Let the thought of self pass in, and the beauty of a great action is gone—like the bloom from a soiled flower."[49] The special distinction of the Greeks was that they understood "that all that was most

48. Dunn, I, 20. Cf. *The Nemesis of Faith*, p. 72.
49. *Short Studies*, I, 23. Cf. also the middle paragraph on the previous page.

excellent in human society was bought by the sacrifice of the few good to the many worthless."[50]

This belief in self-sacrifice remains constant in Froude's thought, and only if we recognize its pervasiveness will we understand why he saw Jane Welsh Carlyle's life in the way that he did: as a self-willed tragedy of devotion, a sacrifice not for the "many worthless" but for a man in whose greatness her belief never wavered. Froude understood Mrs. Carlyle's position vis-à-vis Carlyle so well because, in many ways, it mirrored his own. "*Mit deinem Meister zu irren ist dein Gewinn,*" he wrote in his biography of Carlyle, adapting a line from Goethe's "Sprichwörtlich": "To err with your master is your reward." And such unquestioning devotion he justifies in these astounding words: "The practice of submission to the authority of one whom one recognises as greater than one's self outweighs the chance of occasional mistake" (IV, 179–180).

Given the importance of self-sacrifice in Froude's scale of values, it can hardly surprise us that he considered the sacrifice of Iphigenia to be a central event in human history. It and the Old Testament story of Jephthah's daughter, he believed, "prepared the way in the end for the reception of the doctrine of the Christian atonement" (p. 241), for each prefigured the ultimate victim—Christ. Iphigenia's path of devotion to an ideal beyond herself was one which others had to follow if they were to develop the noble qualities in their own natures. We need not consider Froude's discussion of the plays of Euripides which take up Iphigenia, but simply note the chief result of his study: that her selfless sacrifice came to hold immense symbolic import in his thought.

When we have grasped Froude's conception of Iphigenia, we are in a position to recognize its implications for his portrait of Jane Welsh. Until 1880 he felt he could not be truthful about the Carlyles' marriage,[51] but by 27 June of that year he had already written the entire first volume and three-fourths of the second (II, 356). Thus he wrote nearly the first half of his biography under a quite different conception of biographical responsibility than he did the second. As Froude specifically states that he did not go back to the first volume to revise his narrative of the Carlyles' courtship and marriage, it

50. Ibid., III, 241.
51. *My Relations with Carlyle,* p. 30.

seems reasonable to assume that in the final two volumes his portrayal of their relationship would be more direct and frank—and indeed it is. The only way he could present in the earlier volumes what he considered to be the "tragedy" of Miss Welsh's marriage to Carlyle was by means of suggestion and allusion, and in doing so he used the legend of Iphigenia's sacrifice as a model upon which to mold his interpretation of Miss Welsh's own sacrifice.

Froude, as we have seen, understood the passage in Carlyle's Journal, in which he exclaims that no one will ever fathom his life, in the light of conversations and correspondence with Geraldine Jewsbury alleging Carlyle's sexual impotence. She told him Carlyle was incapacitated for marriage. "I was not unprepared to hear this," Froude wrote Ruskin in 1886,

for I had gathered as much from one of his letters. He says also in his Journal that there was a secret about his life unknown to his dearest friends.— Afterwards when Geraldine was in her last illness when she knew that she was dying, and had no more to do with idle gossip, she repeated this and gave me long & really terrible accounts of the life in Cheyne Row. . . . Here was the especial sting of the Lady Ashburton business for companionship was all that he had to give & this was transferred—.[52]

Believing this and yet not able to say so directly, Froude sought to present his case partly through adopting the device of the Greek chorus, partly through presenting his hero as a figure of Oedipean dimensions deeply attached to his mother, and partly through use of the Iphigenia myth. Once Mrs. Carlyle had made her "sacrifice," nothing more could avail. Froude closes his account of her courtship and marriage thus: "I well remember the bright assenting laugh with which she once responded to some words of mine when the propriety was being discussed of relaxing the marriage laws. I had said that the true way to look at marriage was as a discipline of character" (I, 367).

VI

"For history to be written with the complete form of a drama," Froude wrote in "The Science of History,"

52. Letter dated 29 November [1886], in Viljoen, pp. 65–66.

doubtless is impossible; but there are periods, and those the periods, for the most part, of greatest interest to mankind, the history of which may be so written that the actors shall reveal their characters in their own words; where mind can be seen matched against mind, and the great passions of the epoch not simply be described as existing, but be exhibited at their white heat in the souls and hearts possessed by them. There are all the elements of drama—drama of the highest order—where the huge forces of the times are as the Grecian destiny. . . .[53]

He believed that "the inner nature of the persons of whom [history] speaks is the essential thing about them" (IV, 201). To reveal this inner nature he chose to present his characters as participants in a drama. This method of portraiture he had seen used by Carlyle to great effect. "Dramatists, novelists have drawn characters with similar vividness, but it is the inimitable distinction of Carlyle to have painted actual persons with as much life in them as novelists have given to their own inventions, to which they might ascribe what traits they pleased" (IV, 204). The writing of dramatic history that was also true history posed a great challenge to the literary artist.

In judging Froude's life of Carlyle one cannot emphasize sufficiently its literary and quasi-mythic sources of inspiration. They are the work's strength and its weakness at the same time. Precisely because Froude was a literary artist he could, like his Master, take the raw material that was the lives of the Carlyles and shape it into a literary work. For the same reason he could leave out the countervailing testimony (as he did in writing his histories) in order to throw his thesis into bolder relief. "My own difficulties have arisen rather from the excess of material than the absence of it," he wrote a correspondent about the biography.[54] To reduce chaos to cosmos he chose, in Greek tragedy, a dramatic model that took away as much freedom as it allowed. It is perhaps unfortunate that to depict the lives of the Carlyles Froude did not choose Shakespearean drama as his model. Its multifaceted understanding of humanity in the form of numerous, highly individualized characters would have better captured the heterogeneity of the Carlyles and their circle. And yet adopting Shakespearean drama

53. *Short Studies*, I, 35–36.
54. Froude–G. J. Holyoake [1882], in Joseph McCabe, *Life and Letters of George Jacob Holyoake* (London, 1908), II, 126. I acknowledge a particular debt to G. B. Tennyson in formulating some of the ideas in this paragraph, and to Charles Richard Sanders in the paragraph following.

as a model might have resulted in the biography never being written, in that it would have required an extraordinary effort of mind to have recreated the Carlyles, their friends, and their age within manageable proportions and endowed with the life of Shakespearean drama. The purer form of Greek tragedy with its sternness and inexorability, its few strong characters locked together under the aegis of a "Grecian destiny," did restrict Froude in limning his portraits, but it also allowed him to shape those portraits out of the overwhelming mass of materials he was confronted with. If the result is a somber work, one which usually fails to recognize the moments of sunshine in the lives of the Carlyles, it is also a work of stark dramatic power.

Many charges have been leveled against Froude's achievement. Besides accusing him of misinterpreting the relationship between the Carlyles, critics have asserted that he lacked a sense of humor (thus making insufficient allowance for Carlyle's own), that he misunderstood Carlyle's religious position, that he misjudged Carlyle because he was an Englishman and Carlyle a Scot, that he suffered from "constitutional inaccuracy," and that he even went so far as to distort evidence consciously. Although these charges are by and large unfair to Froude, this is not the place for a detailed consideration of them, especially as they have been dealt with, for the most part adequately, in Waldo H. Dunn's *Froude and Carlyle* and more recently in the dissertation by Edward Sharples, Jr. Both Dunn and Sharples, however, omit from consideration one area in which Froude falls down badly and which is directly relevant to his treatment of the Carlyles—namely, Carlyle's capacity for friendship. He enjoyed a number of close friendships and a wide circle of acquaintances all his life, yet one would hardly guess from Froude's pages that Carlyle was a social and, at times, convivial being. In defense of Froude's slighting this aspect of Carlyle's character, we must remember that he did not meet Carlyle until 1849, when Carlyle was fifty-three, and that he did not get to know him well until 1861, when Carlyle was sixty-five. He thus knew personally and intimately only the older Carlyle, the Sage of Chelsea. For the earlier Carlyle he relied on the mass of correspondence left to him for his use and above all, it would seem, on the Journal. Doing so kept his narrative close to primary sources but also led to distortions in emphasis. Carlyle had a gift for exaggeration, a capacity in discussing ordinary matters to plumb the depths of pathos, and he frequently indulged himself. Instead of discounting this tendency in Carlyle, Froude interpreted what he read in the correspondence and elsewhere too literally. He also failed to take into consideration that after Carlyle married Jane Welsh they corresponded only when apart. Their letters indeed show that they could quarrel, but they also show that each had an extraordinarily deep trust and belief in the other. Because the day-to-day harmony which must have been theirs during much of their lives is rarely described in the correspondence, it consequently does not often find its way into Froude's account. We rarely sense in his pages that Carlyle had a great love for his wife and that it was fully reciprocated.

Froude's portraits of the Carlyles came into being not because he was inaccurate, or misrepresented the evidence, or had a jaundiced mind, or bore them deliberate malice, but because he had strong artistic as well as dramatic instincts. What Harold Nicolson has called the "momentary ardour of his imagination" occasionally overburdened his emphases and distorted his sense of proportion.[55] Froude the artist betrayed Froude the biographer. He became trapped by the portrait he was painting. The artistic technique he had determined upon led him unconsciously to falsify the life of his characters. His portraits are true as far as they go, but the models which inspired them—Oedipus and Iphigenia as well as Una, Gloriana, the Red Cross Knight, and the others—in part predetermine their contours. Yet these same models give his portraits tremendous psychological life and a tragic reverberation of their own. The intensity of their life nearly a hundred years after the publication of the biography is fair indication that they will continue to influence our conception of the Carlyles.

---

55. *The Development of English Biography*, p. 129. A. C. Benson in *Rambles and Reflections* (New York, 1926) makes the same point in a different way: "Froude had a strong romantic element in him, and when he had made up his mind about a subject, he saw facts not as they were, but by the light of his own imagination. Froude was wholly incapable of deliberate distortion, but his subconscious mind was too strong for him" (p. 122).

Index